D0857035

IMPASSE AND INNOVATION IN PSYCHOANALYSIS

Clinical Case Seminars

edited by

John E. Gedo and Mark J. Gehrie

THE ANALYTIC PRESS

1993   Hillsdale, NJ   London

Copyright © 1993 by The Analytic Press, Inc.
  All rights reserved. No part of this book may be reproduced in any
  form: by photostat, microform, retrieval system, or any other
  means, without the prior written permission of the publisher.

Published by The Analytic Press, Inc.
365 Broadway, Hillsdale, NJ 07642

Set in Zapf Book by Lind Graphics, Inc., Upper Saddle River, NJ

Library of Congress Cataloging in Publication Data

Impasse and innovation in psychoanalysis : clinical case seminars /
  edited by John E. Gedo and Mark J. Gehrie.
     p.   cm.
  Includes bibliographical references and index.
  ISBN 0-88163-142-6
  1. Psychoanalysis—Case studies. 2. Psychoanalysis—Methodology.
3. Impasse (Psychotherapy) I. Gedo, John E.   II. Gehrie, Mark
Joshua
  [DNLM: 1. Psychoanalytic Therapy—methods.   WM 460.6 0587]
  RC509.8.05   1993
  616.89′17—dc20
  DNLM/DLC
  for Library of Congress   92-49405
                                                   CIP

Printed in the United States of America
10 9 8 7 6 5 4 3 2 1

Table of Contents

Introduction

In 1988–89, the editors of this volume offered an elective seminar at the Chicago Institute for Psychoanalysis entitled, "The Integration of Theory and Technique." The course was open to candidates who had completed the required four-year curriculum and to interested members of the faculty. Offered for five quarters over the course of consecutive academic years, the seminar was attended by a changing group of 10 to 12 participants—aside from the instructors, only one or two members took part throughout the effort. The class met for two hours every other week for a total of 30 sessions.

Participants were provided with a reading list of some highlights of the literature on the theory of psychoanalytic technique, starting with Freud's *Papers on Technique* and concluding with representative examples from the recent past.[1] The first sessions of quarters #1 and #3 were devoted to the presentation of maximally complex and difficult analytic cases from the current practice of the senior instructor, John E. Gedo. In the middle of these exercises, participants were invited to volunteer to present current analytic cases of their own in which technical problems posed an interesting challenge.

By the end of the first quarter, encouraged by the liveliness and novelty of the seminar discussions, Mark J. Gehrie decided to record subsequent

---

[1]These included Ferenczi and Rank, 1924; Fenichel, 1941; Stone, 1965; Kohut, 1984; and Gedo, 1979 (chaps. 1, 2, 16), 1981a (chap. 4), 1984 (chap. 1), 1986 (chaps. 11, 12), and 1988 (Epilogue).

sessions on tape. Because this procedure was originally instituted without any definite agenda in mind, no provision was made to make recordings in Gehrie's absence. Somewhat later, Gedo and Gehrie independently concluded that the seminar proceedings might form the backbone of a useful book about the most controversial aspects of contemporary analytic technique, and they decided to explore the feasibility of transcribing the taped recordings.

Because of incomplete recording, technical failures, and problems of confidentiality, only four case presentations turned out to be publishable. All of these, however, involved more than one session of the seminar, so that these cases actually represent nine meetings of the class. Fortunately, the usable transcripts included one of Gedo's presentations, one by another faculty member, and two by articulate candidates. (We regret that both faculty members were men and both candidates women, but we do not feel that this bias in sampling is unacceptable.)

We have decided to organize this material in a sequence different from that of the dates of presentation. After a chapter devoted to a discussion of the difficulties we detected in the use of the standard technique of psychoanalysis, we follow with a case of Gedo's that exemplifies great alterations in technique, consciously undertaken for reasons spelled out in the discussion. The second case was presented by a faculty member, who also adjusted his technique to meet the emergent requirements of a series of therapeutic crises but felt very apologetic about these decisions to depart from analytic traditions. Next, we offer the presentation of a candidate who vainly tried to stick to a technique as close as possible to classical analysis; the work was prematurely interrupted, but the patient later returned for further (nonanalytic) assistance. The last case illustrates a candidate's decision to be flexible in her technical approach in circumstances that did not permit her choices to be made on grounds referable to reliable information about the analysand, so that the analyst's personality was the decisive factor in the course she selected.

The raw transcripts have been carefully edited in the following ways: information that might reveal the identity of patients and analysts (where applicable) has been deleted or disguised. ("Chicago" may have been altered to "Boston" or, to make matters truly unpredictable, it may have been left as "Chicago.") Repetitions, apparently meaningless utterances, undecipherable passages where several people are talking at once, and other "noises" have simply been eliminated. Gross errors in syntax have been corrected. Where the choice of words was confusing or offensively infelicitous, our corrections have been placed within brackets. As a result, everyone has been made to sound a great deal more articulate than he or she was *in vivo*.

Each case presentation is preceded by a brief Introduction and is followed by a lengthier Commentary, both by Mark Gehrie. These commentaries highlight the main issues in each case and the principal problems addressed by the discussion in the seminar or, in some instances, matters that should have been confronted but were not given sufficient attention. Every chapter culminates in a sequence of notes by Gedo (keyed to specific points in the seminar transcript or in Gehrie's commentary) that provide matters for consideration that could not be raised in the seminar (either for lack of time or in the interests of preserving the peace) and attempt to clarify some of the issues left in doubt by the original discussion. These notes may be read either to supplement the seminar discussion or commentary at appropriate junctures or as coherent essays representing Gedo's second thoughts about the clinical material and its technical handling. The chapters devoted to these four specific cases are followed by a concluding Overview on which the editors worked in collaboration.

Questions of Basic Psychoanalytic Technique

Among the cases presented in our seminar, few lent themselves to the application of the basic technique of psychoanalysis as has been described in the standard references of the past generation (for instance, in Stone, 1965). Because every presentation involved some impasse or crisis in treatment, the analyses that did not call for any departure from basic technique were necessarily instances of mismanagement, which have not been included here.

From this series of presentations, it has been possible to single out a number of technical issues that contributed to the unsatisfactory course of many analyses. In this chapter, we review these questions in what we hope is a logical sequence; insofar as possible, we use excerpts from the relevant seminars as part of this discussion.

Diagnosis, Nosology, and the Strategy of Treatment

Inexperienced analytic candidates tend to fall back on their prior experiences as psychotherapists to master the uncertainties of embarking on their initial efforts to perform psychoanalysis. This unacknowledged resort to nonanalytic ideas about psychopathology and its treatment often determines in advance the outcome of the analytic attempt—particularly if the supervisor colludes in focusing on questions of psychiatric nosology (often dressed in the language of psychoanalysis, for instance, "Is this an oedipal neurosis or a narcissistic personality disturbance?") instead of calling attention to issues of transference and the defenses against its emergence. About one instance of this kind, the seminar proceeded as follows:

"GEDO: This case is an important prototypical example. . . . What I am about to say applies to many, many cases. The understanding of the material that you convey—apparently with your supervisor's approval—assumes too much. You are both too fast [in reaching closure]. You thought you knew what things meant just because similar things mean that to the majority of people. You assume that [your patient] is like everybody else. You offer this interpretation to the patient, and the patient says there's something to it. The patient doesn't reject it, won't reject it, can't reject it, because in fact it's more or less true, except—it's utterly unimportant. The trouble is, this is not where this woman lives.

"The [screen memory you recounted] can have umpteen meanings, and the oedipal meaning is probably there. The fact that she had the fantasy that her parents never had intercourse after—whenever—may not be used to substantiate the contention that either positive or negative oedipal configurations are the crux of the matter. Unusual people have unusual reasons for everything they do, and think, and feel."

"QUESTION: Do you have a sense of what may be more central?"

"GEDO: There is no knowing. Once again: one must proceed from the surface downward. That's the surface. You pushed through! You reached into the pie and you pulled out a plum—the oedipal plum. You worked with it; it was there. She improved. And you have the fruits of the work you have done. But you have done the work in an unsystematic, disorderly way, by going too deep too soon. The character defenses are still there. One doesn't know what's underneath.

"When I have done second, third, and fourth analyses with people who look like this to begin with, what has generally come out is that some plum was pulled out and though [the interpretation] wasn't untrue, the issue was not central. It wasn't as important as many other matters—of some importance, but the importance has to be contextualized. [There] is a system of many problems that are tied together. You pull out one and you create internal chaos. You have to work from the surface down!

"The nature of this defensive organization—it would be better to think of it as an adaptive organization—[was determined sometime during] adolescence. That is what you have to investigate very carefully at the beginning of the analysis, and underneath you may find anything. How about a sadistic perversion, for instance? Why not? Or a masochistic one. Or a fetish. If this [unusual] adaptation is really a defense against some pathology, it's scarcely going to be a defense against [what you diagnosed as] an oedipal victory. [That is] inherently not likely."

"PRESENTER: There *is* a sadistic perversion."

"GEDO: *Now* you're talking. You should have told us that in the first place. So how much does that have to do with the Oedipus complex? Of course, anything is possible, but that's not the horse I would bet on in this race! Has the perversion entered the transference? No wonder [this analysis cannot be finished]. These are very, very difficult cases, and they take a terribly long time. But one can't be too careful; slow, easy, don't shoot till you see the whites of their eyes! Don't say anything until you are 200% sure."

Because a diagnosis based on behavioral phenomena gives the therapist an illusion of understanding the patient's personality structure and inner life, it will generally predetermine the nature of the analytic interventions. The outcome might be called a manualized, template-oriented approach to analysis, lacking the inductive flexibility required (in our view) to deal with this highly complex undertaking. This technical error leads to an overcommitment to specific formulations—what one might also call a technique of omniscience. Hence this procedure amounts to "wild analysis" (Freud, 1910), the use of a technique based on the assumption that the analyst's formulations of the meanings of the patient's behavior are unfailingly accurate. The resulting confusion creates iatrogenic problems subsequently easily misdiagnosed as part of the psychopathology.

In several instances presented at the seminar, a putative diagnosis was actually made on the basis of historical data alone. In these cases, the Clinic Committee of the Institute, the candidate, and the supervisor concurred in using the evaluation process to arrive at a tentative formulation of a psychiatric diagnosis. Such practices are extremely widespread, in spite of innumerable *caveats* in the literature (e.g., Kohut, 1971) about the impossibility of making valid distinctions of this kind on the basis of historical data alone. Kantrowitz (1987) has documented the lack of reliability of initial assessments even about the question of analyzability—a matter of less complexity than that of deciding which developmental phase contributed most to pathogenesis.

Commitment to a Favored Clinical Theory

In many cases that reached an impasse, this stalemate was a result of unchecked reliance on a favored clinical theory. Although such theories are relevant in a broad spectrum of circumstances, they are not actually intended to illuminate any particular analysand's inner life. By reducing human complexity to relatively simple schemata, the use of theories to

make deductive inferences about patients misses the overriding importance of the individual's own hierarchy of meanings, his or her core
experience of life.

One example of this kind of neglect occurred in a stalemated analysis
presented in the course of its tenth year. The candidate reported that
early in the treatment her patient (an intellectual blue-stocking and a
spinster) had attempted to present her with a gift of personal historical
significance. When asked what this enactment had meant to the analysand, the candidate could only say that she did not accept the patient's
offer when it was first made. She later relented, although not because she
had learned the significance of the proposed gift. (In all probability, the
change in tack had to do with the adoption of some ideas about self
psychology as the candidate's orienting clinical theory.) At the time of her
presentation, she still had no idea about the meaning of this transaction.

Another way to put this matter is to say that some of the candidates
who presented in the seminar were unable to grasp the meaning of the
patient's communications precisely because they were thinking solely
about theory-laden categories of meaning, and not about the experience
of the patient. They had a need to remain anchored within a focused
template of "psychoanalytic" reasoning about the patient's experience.
Such schemata lead to certain assumptions about the meaning for the
patient of various events, but without adequate data to substantiate these
claims thoroughly.

Complexity is added to the muddle by the fact that the interpretations
are often partially correct, leading to the inability of the patient to refute
them convincingly and, worse, to the analyst's reinforced conviction that
the "plum" that was "pulled out of the pie" contains all the significant
meanings that exist. To state this in still another way, the psychoanalytic
view requires that the uniqueness of every analysand be regarded as
fundamental from the very beginning; it is ignored in favor of nosological
"plums" only at great peril.

Failure to Agree on Rational Goals for the Treatment

In their eagerness to fulfull training requirements, candidates all too often
failed to look into the prospective analysand's reasons for seeking treatment. Consequently, there was seldom an explicit agreement about rational goals to be pursued through the analytic effort, and in several cases
the participants agreed to collaborate although they had radically different notions about the aims of the procedure. In one seminar, Gedo
commented, "And so the great analytic machine swallowed her up, processed her, and she came out at the other end as an analysand."

If one is not overly concerned about ultimate prognosis, it may be feasible to overlook these issues of motivation for treatment, at least at the beginning of the analysis. Candidates are, however, usually desperately eager to score a success with their supervised cases, so that they cannot really afford to take them into analysis on the basis of some mutual misunderstanding. Impasses that develop as a result of such a disparity of goals among the participants amount to a clash of *Weltanschauungen*. (For a report of several analytic failures caused by false consensus about treatment goals, see Gedo, 1981a, chap. 3.)

Although it has been customary to disavow that analysis has therapeutic aims beyond the fulfillment of process criteria for reaching a natural termination, Lawrence Friedman (1988) has convincingly shown that the analyst "as operator" cannot avoid commitment to the improvement of the analysand's adaptation. At the same time, the particulars of that adaptive change must be acceptable to the patient if treatment is to avoid becoming a power struggle.

The subculture of the psychoanalytic community, extraordinarily resistant to change over the past century, has clung to prejudices about the pathological import of religious faith, the overriding importance of sexual activity for adaptive equilibrium, and some of Freud's other personal hobby-horses of the 1890s. In this sense, psychoanalysis misused becomes an ideology, promulgated under the guise of a quasi-medical procedure; in this debased version, our work parallels that of C.G. Jung, who finally revealed his psychology as the carrier of a message of that kind in the autobiography he wrote in old age (Jung, 1963). A generation ago, Philip Rieff (1966) predicted the coming triumph of such therapeutic cults (see also Gedo, 1986, chap. 14).

In performing so-called analyses in the service of proselytizing for a new, secular creed, it is unnecessary to pay heed to the patient's goals and values; to the contrary, it is incumbent on the analyst-shaman to ritualize the analytic procedure, to convey a catechism limited to certain familiar verities—in other words, to conform to a template.

In the foregoing sense, the psychoanalytic community constitutes a unique subculture within society as a whole, and every encounter between an analyst and a patient from "the outside" has to overcome the problem of a severe cultural gap.

The Problem of a Cultural Gap

The deck is stacked against an analyst's treating someone from an entirely different cultural background with no knowledge of that background. An analyst relies heavily on shared cultural meanings in any analysis, as in any sort of intimate communication. Possibilities for misunderstanding are so broad as to be endless and are not correctable solely by reliance on empathy; an empathic position requires some context for shared experiences in the absence of which others will of necessity be substituted, experiences that may or may not have anything to do with the experience of the patient.

Beyond such a "confusion of tongues" in the analytic situation, the analyst's failure to appreciate the extent of mutual misunderstanding transforms the transaction into a tug-of-war about the "correct" perception of reality. As Modell (1990) has discussed in detail, such an impasse is likely to be experienced in the transference as an attempt at brainwashing, which, on the deepest level, is bound to be resisted. When such situations go unrecognized, many patients are likely to lapse into hopelessness and silences, or compliance with the "program."

The cultural differences between most prospective patients and their analysts-to-be are not so great as to predetermine the failure of any therapeutic couple to attain a "shared language" (see Gedo, 1984, chap. 8)—or, as Modell (1990) put it, a "shared reality." To put the matter somewhat differently, a doctrinaire analyst's inattention to a patient's individuality, an unrelenting focus on the patient's putative illness (to the exclusion of healthy aspects of the personality), merely repeats the errors Freud (1905) made with one of his earliest analytic cases, the celebrated Dora—yet, in the literal sense, Freud and his patient shared a common cultural background.

Cultural differences, particularly the difference between the analytic subculture and its surround, become a major obstacle to therapeutic progress if they cause analysts to fail to allow patients to be truly *different* from themselves. This is particularly likely to occur when the analyst projects his or her own psychology onto a more complex personality—a situation that is a mirror image of the ones Kleinians call "projective identification." Freud's assumption that an adolescent girl should be willing to welcome sexual advances from a man whose wife is her father's mistress constitutes a similar misattribution of behavioral imperatives in his treatment of Dora.

To illustrate the ubiquity of psychoanalytic prejudices of this kind, Gedo relates the following anecdote:

"Once I presented a case to Margaret Mahler, 20-odd years ago, what I considered to be a very successful analysis of a woman who came to me after a psychotherapy in which she had been sexually abused, with the connivance of her husband, who had referred her to this therapist. Not to make this story too long, she got out of this marriage and became a college teacher, an independent person. She was a woman of 45 when we finished. Margaret Mahler said, 'And did she get remarried?' I was stunned! And I said, 'No. She lived in a very conservative suburb, she didn't have much opportunity for that sort of thing.' Mahler said, 'Well, does she have affairs?' I said, 'This is an upper-class lady, that's not the way it's done.' And Mahler said, 'Let's hear another case.' Literally. Such are the prejudices within psychoanalysis."

Countertransference Issues

It may surprise some readers that, as far as the presenters were concerned, countertransference issues did not appear to play any major role in producing the difficulties described in the seminar presentations. In only one case did a presenter indicate that the therapeutic impasse was, in large measure, created by her inability to master her countertransference. According to her, this was the sense of being excessively burdened by her intractable analysand—as the latter's mother had presumably been burdened in the past. Operating at this time within a self-psychological framework, the analyst implied that her aversive reaction was grossly unempathic and created a traumatic situation (presumably within a "mirror transference," although the presenter was consistently unable to state generalizations of this kind in any of the alternative technical vocabularies available). She labeled the behavioral consequences of this trauma "tension states," probably in deference to Gedo's terminology in *Models of the Mind* (Gedo and Goldberg, 1973).

It has become acceptable to refer to the analyst's emotional responsiveness to the transference as "countertransference," thereby eliminating the vital distinction between appropriate reactions (which the analyst should be able to contain and turn to account in discerning the nature of the transference constellation) and those leading to dyadic enactments (see Gedo, 1988, chap. 9) of the kind reported in the case under discussion.

Since it is by no means clear that the real obstacle to progress was the analyst's inability to avoid repeating the mother's failures with her formidable child (as the patient herself is reported to have stated, she was ready to forgive those who were merely defeated by her intransigence!), the analyst may have been off the mark in blaming herself for creating difficulties through countertransference reactions. It is equally likely that her affective reaction should merely have alerted her to the operation of a hostile mother transference.

Transference in the Here and Now Versus Reconstruction of the Past

In response to inquiry about the manner in which phase-specific material appeared in the transference, candidates often displayed considerable confusion about the way in which vital unresolved issues are relived within the psychoanalytic situation. Instead of relating the relevant vicissitudes of the patient–analyst relationship, they tended to summarize a series of reconstructions about the childhood past. What is worse, often they did not specify whether those conclusions were reached on the basis of the unrolling of a sequence of transference reactions or whether they were the kinds of "dynamic formulations" demanded of participants in psychoanalytic training programs, that is, essentially speculative. (The clinical details sometimes provided, such as transactions between patients and their parents in the recent past, suggested that the issues did not enter the transference.)

The presenters' inability to answer this question in a coherent manner convinced us that, if any organized process supervened in the treatment, the analyst remained ignorant of it. For all intents and purposes, such therapies had been chaotic because neither participant was able to attribute a meaningful gestalt to its manifold vicissitudes. As the case mentioned in the discussion of countertransference issues illustrates, candidates were often unable to distinguish their affective compliance in reliving a childhood transaction as transference from inappropriate counterresponses. Whatever the cause of their confusion, some of these beginners tried to resolve it by assigning their analysand to membership in one or another nosological category, as if a "diagnosis" would resolve their uncertainties and relieve them of the task of monitoring transference developments.

The Problem of Superego Analysis

We found it particularly striking that many candidates in the seminar appeared not to grasp the concept that superego contents require careful scrutiny, as does any other compromise formation. Occasionally one or another student gave voice to the notion that these internal guidelines constituted psychopathology whenever they differed from the candidate's own standard of conduct. In one presentation, the analyst revealed an overt attempt to tilt the patient's behavior in favor of appetite satisfaction, in open disregard of the patient's ascetic morality. (This candidate insisted that he had remained "neutral," although he also reported that the analysand often experienced his activity as a pull in the direction of sexuality.)

In line with the general neglect of superego analysis, candidates seldom inquired about the sources of their patients' ideals or about the specifics of their patients' conceptions of virtue. It rarely occurred to any of them that a good analytic result might entail a new-found capacity to live up to one's highest ideals; sometimes the very presence of such ideals was mistaken for pathological grandiosity. We never encountered any awareness of the correlation of the contents of the superego with the particulars of the repudiated wishes of early childhood—neither those of the oedipal period, nor the more shameful ones of earlier developmental phases. These omissions may account, in part, for the scarcity of convincing reconstructive work in the analyses we reviewed.

The seven categories of pitfall in the use of the standard technique of psychoanalysis we have discussed in this chapter do not constitute an exhaustive list, not even of the major technical errors betrayed by the gamut of presenters in our seminar. These pitfalls did constitute problems that cropped up repeatedly. We do not intend to list the endless variety of technical errors one might encounter in a larger sample of cases. In the seminar, we heard one presentation describing an analytic impasse that seemed to be caused, at least in part, by a candidate's insistence on performing the treatment in an unsuitable setting. The resulting contingencies bordered on the bizarre, and the analyst's undeviating course could only reflect a lack of self-critical capacities that rendered him unsuitable for the profession.

In another instance, it was the analysand who seemed to be a very unusual person: intelligent, highly creative, and committed to enterprises of great ambition. The candidate, by contrast, was a person of modest talents, so much so that he seemed largely oblivious of his patient's assets. The disparity between them never could become explicit; rather, the analysand lapsed into longer and longer silences and began to feel like a "monster." Situations of this kind do not lend themselves to being neatly classified. Moreover, they are very difficult to differentiate from clinical contingencies for which the standard technique of psychoanalysis requires some form of modification.

In the four chapters that follow, we present transcripts from the seminar dealing with cases where the analyst–patient match was satisfactory, but technical innovation was required.

2

Disillusionment, Neutrality, and Instruction in Psychoanalysis

Introduction (Gehrie)

This is the case Gedo presented to start the third quarter of the seminar. It deals with the treatment of a seriously disturbed young man with an unusual combination of enormous psychological assets together with debilitating deficits. Among the challenges in this case are: a) grasping the nature and extent of the pathology; b) understanding the implications of the analyst's experience of an attitude toward this patient; and c) understanding the course and nature of the analysis itself from the analyst's point of view.

The patient was a 29-year-old law student. This was the third time that he had attempted an analysis. It began with an effort by the referring source to match the patient with this specific analyst because of qualities perceived by the source in both patient and analyst. A match was attempted on the basis of the patient's "sophistication, intelligence, and cultivation." The analyst agreed that the patient was "enormously intelligent and very intimidating." From the way this referral was made, it seems apparent that the analyst felt highly esteemed by the referring source, that the analyst was recognized by the referrer as "uniquely qualified" to help this patient, and that there was at least tacit agreement on this point. The analyst's view of the patient also contained some of these features, notably that who the patient was and where he went to school was important: "the patient was attending an elite institution, and you have to be formidably talented to be admitted." This shared sense of possessing unusual talents provided an essential, authentic underpinning for the unfolding analytic process. This authenticity of response made it possible for the patient to accept a unique (to him) form of interaction within the context of the analytic setting.[a]*

The patient sought analysis because of feeling desperate about not being able to do the work at law school, while simultaneously feeling that he should be on the Law Review. This kind of discontinuity between his performance and his ambition was also reflected in painful obsessional struggles about making choices or decisions: he seemed to have little real sense of who he was and had only grandiose fantasies about who he should be or the kind of appearance he should make. Each time some attempt to become something failed, he would embark on a new career—attempts that spanned graduate studies in English literature, becoming an avant-garde novelist and "littérateur," and finally law. In each instance, the patient obviously was not genuinely involved in the substance of the activity itself, although he was very successful in giving the appearance of commitment. A similar discontinuity was evident in his relationships with women; he claimed to be "phenomenally successful" despite his impotence. In each instance, the patient's ability to present himself as the person he wished to be seemed quite effective—up to a point—whether in graduate studies or with women, despite the underlying deficit. In all these cases, however, after a time, the façade would always collapse, and the patient would move on. Because of his family's financial assets, he was able to avoid having to support himself during this time.

The patient was the eldest of four children, all born in the space of five years, beginning when the mother was in her mid-30s. The mother spent little time at home, and the patient experienced her as unreliable and uninterested. The father, a very powerful, controlling, and successful businessman, made and lost a fortune during the time the patient was growing up and then rebuilt his business empire in recent years. The analysand went to college at a major university to which the father had donated the funds for a building. Upon his arrival, the student learned that the office of the president was open to him, "should he ever need anything."

The two previous attempts at analysis each lasted roughly one to one and a half years and ended when the patient quit. He first sought analysis after graduation from college and then dropped everything: "the city, the university, the analysis." Going to New York, he then "had a consultation with the most prestigious analyst in New York," and was referred to another "very reputable analyst." That analysis ended when, according to the patient, his parents refused to continue paying for it.

---

*Superscript letters are annotated in Clarifications and Addenda.

We are happy to be able to include this case for discussion because the structure of the analysis raises fundamental technical questions about the management of reality, the analyst's use of instruction, and the question of "analytic neutrality."

First Session

GEDO: Well, let me tell you about this clinical experience of mine which has been fascinating, relatively painless for me, but has felt like it would last forever.[b] It has, in fact, already gone on for close to seven years. I got this referral during the fall quarter sometime in 1981 from a then relatively young faculty member of the Institute with whom this person had had about a year of psychotherapy. Ostensibly this person made the referral to me (he never [sent me a patient] before or since) because he felt that I would [be] uniquely qualified to be of assistance to this person. [This] was the first hint I got that I was in for real trouble. In essence, he was saying that he felt unqualified to analyze this person; the psychotherapy wasn't going anywhere, and he correctly concluded that the only chance was to recommend an analysis, and he didn't feel up to it himself.

Now, the manifest content of what he said when he made the referral was that this man was so sophisticated, so intelligent, so cultivated, that this analyst thought that only somebody who wasn't frightened by those [qualities] could manage. And there's a bit of truth to that. Not that this man is so cultivated or so sophisticated, but he is indeed enormously intelligent, [and] he's very intimidating. He was a law student at the time, in the second year at [a preeminent] Law School. I mention the school because, as you probably know, it's really an elite institution and you have to be formidably talented to be admitted, and this man is formidably talented. He scored something fantastic on the LSATs, and when he finished high school he had scores well over 700 on the SAT in both verbal and quantitative areas.

When he came, he complained that he was very desperate; he couldn't do the work, and yet he felt he ought to be on the Law Review. He had never been quite able to do what he wanted to do. He was caught in a web of obsessional thinking. It was a problem for him to go shopping for clothes because he got so obsessive about what to choose. To buy the simplest item of clothing, he would spend two days obsessing about one [purchase] and then would end up getting nothing.

He had had two previous analytic experiences, and this was the second clue that something was very difficult and very wrong. He was 29 when I first saw him. Shortly after graduation from college he had enrolled at [an Eastern university] as a graduate student in English literature. It's an exceedingly intellectual department, very "mod," structuralism and beyond. When he [started] there, he went into analysis with a colleague in that city—somebody I know very slightly, an extremely reputable person, a sophisticated, cultivated, multilingual man, and intelligent in our business. [That treatment] lasted a little over a year, and then the patient dropped [the city, the university, and the analysis] simultaneously. As he told the story originally, he was unable to cope with the curriculum, not intellectually, but because it bored him to death. Something to think about, that he [thereupon] left town and left the analysis. He went to New York to become a novelist.

He comes from a very well-to-do family, and so he settled on the upper east side, trying to be a littérateur, and he had a consultation with [the most prestigious analyst in New York]. You know, he had good contacts and heard where the action is, and the consultant referred him to a very reputable middle-aged analyst. That analysis lasted approximately a year, a year and a half, and then, to hear the patient tell it, it stopped because his parents refused to subsidize it any further. This is a very complex story: I didn't know how complex when I first heard it, although I did have my suspicions. The reason given for the parents reneging on their promise to support all this was that they were so shocked that he was doing nothing. Indeed, during this year and a half he did *nothing*, apart from planning to write a novel. He didn't even furnish his apartment. So he was decompensated, essentially—not because he didn't have a job—because, obviously, he doesn't need to work—but because he did nothing but attend his analytic sessions.

He did have a very active life—then, before, and after—as a Don Juan. He told me that he was largely impotent but phenomenally successful with women, and considered to be an excellent lover because he was willing to engage in any sort of sexual activity the ladies required. When he came to me, he was still involved with one of the women [from] the New York period. I no longer remember whether he met her there or had known her slightly before. She was very sophisticated, very intelligent, a very aggressive architect, and was exceedingly promiscuous. She was a nymphomaniac, actually, and in no way, in *no* way could he keep up with her, and she savagely depreciated him for this. The relationship was essentially the mirror image of his relationships to [most] other women, where he had the upper hand and was very sadistic with them, [letting] them know that he didn't appreciate them in any way, [that he] wasn't faithful to them, and thus reducing them to mush. With this architect lady, the shoe was largely on the other foot.[c] So after a year and a half all that collapsed, allegedly because the parents threw up their hands and said, "This can't go on this way. This is crazy. This analysis is not helping you. We won't pay." And then he decided to get a degree in comparative literature, and he came [to Chicago] and spent about a year and a half or two [on that project].

He did write a master's thesis comparing Flaubert's *Sentimental Education* with Dostoevski's *The Devils*—not a fortuitous choice of topics, I might add. He didn't quite finish the books; he only finished the thesis, [a pattern] quite characteristic of his education. Sometimes he didn't even finish the required papers; he just persuaded the instructors that he was very capable of writing a very good paper, [so] why go through all this trouble. You know, *both* sides could skip the trouble. [This is how] he got the degree, but he understood that he couldn't go beyond the master's and get away with that. Somewhat later, after [the analysis] started, he told me that he had reread *Sentimental Education* and realized that when he wrote the thesis he didn't have the vaguest notion of what it was about. And that's correct, because he told me what he wrote in the thesis. *Sentimental Education* is one of my favorite books, so I can confirm that he [didn't have] the vaguest notion of what it is about.

So he decided to go to law school. While taking his master's he had chosen [to write about] Flaubert because Flaubert had [been forced] to attend law school by his parents. [Flaubert] got out of law school by having a hysterical seizure, [whereupon] his parents realized that there was no point in forcing the issue any further, and that's when he became free to be the great novelist. I leave it to your imagination why [the patient] chose *The Devils*. But he chose law school because it seemingly [prepared him to] satisfy his father's lifelong wish [that he] join the family business, [yet] it didn't mean [*literally*] joining the family business.

I should tell you a little bit about the family. This is a Jewish family, originally from the east [coast]. They came from a relatively humble background and gradually worked up to more and more impressive businesses, and then moved to California about the time my patient was a toddler. [On the west coast] the father got into bigger and bigger deals and made a fortune. It was quite a considerable fortune, and he sold his business to a megaconglomerate and became the chief executive officer of one division of the larger company; at that point the family fortune was over a hundred million dollars. But he rode this business into the ground and was fired and ruined. After that, he started over again, and at the time the patient started this analysis was again in command of a large business empire and was worth God knows what. The patient thought it was close to a hundred million dollars. So father is enormously capable, very bold and adventurous; something of a gambler.

The parents didn't have any children for a very long time, and my patient was the first of their four children. The mother was in her mid-30s when they started this family after many years of marriage. (I no longer remember when I learned each individual fact: I'm just trying to tell you those facts which could very well have come out in the initial history if I had asked, but I'm not absolutely sure I asked for all this.) At any rate, it sounded like the parents just suddenly decided that when they started they would have a family of four children, and they had four children in five years; boy-girl-boy-girl was the sequence. But by the time this decision was made, the family was prosperous enough [to hire] help, and there was always help. The mother was a musician, not professionally, but a serious musician. There was no professional orchestra [in their community; it had] a semipro community orchestra, and she participated in that and spent very little time at home [taking care of] the child.

In terms of how [the patient] described the parents, he wasn't all that accurate. [My account] is contaminated by what I have learned since, but [as I recall] he described the father as extremely controlling, extremely angry, formidable, inaccessible, and very insistent that he knew everything and that everything had to be his way. But not good with people, rather bewildered in human relations. I got a very hazy picture of the mother, except that she was quite unreliable. At the time the children started school, the area where they lived was still relatively sparsely settled and the school was far away, [so] they were driven back and forth, and he was always the last one to be picked up. Sometimes he would have to wait for very long periods before his mother came. He talked about the fact that he was expected to ride herd on the younger siblings and got into difficulty because he would do so in a manner that was unacceptable to the parents. He would get very irritated, and he would get rough and hurt the littler ones, and then [he] would get beaten up [as punishment].

About the time he was four or five they hired an excellent nurse-caretaker to help his mother; somebody from England. [In retrospect], the patient couldn't understand what [then] happened, but [he knew that] at one point he [was] beside himself, locked her out of the house, and insisted that she be fired. She was, or, rather, she left: she just couldn't put up with [him] any more. The problem was not only my patient's misbehavior, but largely so.

I should say a few words about his education. He and the two girls attended the same Ivy League university [to which] the father [had donated] a building. When my patient got there, the assistant to the president asked him to [his] office; they had an interview, where he was told that if he ever needed anything, he shouldn't hesitate to call. He never needed anything, because, [as a student] he never did anything. I'm being too hostile, huh? What I'm saying is not entirely accurate—what he did was become interested in Jewish theology, and he read some serious stuff [about that], but not in an organized way, and he took some courses in theology. One of the people who taught [him] was also a well-known novelist. It was this man who was my patient's New York contact. This man was homosexual, and [he] was interested in the patient as a potential homosexual partner. The patient knew that but had enough [skill] to navigate those shoals without ever being explicitly approached. The payoff was that the man was supposed to open all doors for him in New York with publishers and so on.

I haven't said anything about the brother.[d] The brother was the ally of the mother, and he's just as mysterious a figure as the mother. He's the only one who didn't get to this Ivy League university and during his adolescent years and for a little bit beyond was a rebel, very odd, very out of it, probably on drugs, going down the tubes. And then in his early 20s he underwent a radical change, went into the father's business, and became the favorite. He's allegedly doing well in middle-level executive jobs in the family empire.

Shortly after we started the analysis, the brother married a somewhat older divorced woman with a child, and since then they have had a child between them too. And the cover story is that the brother is doing well. I can't assess that; [the brothers are] not close. They've always been fierce enemies, and the patient has always felt that it was terribly unfair that the brother and the mother were so close. Apparently the brother and the mother were close because of their shared love of dogs. The brother never talked; he related to the mother's dog and the mother related to the dog, and that was the bridge between the mother and the brother. On one occasion, when my patient was home alone for the weekend, he managed through negligence to murder the mother's dog.

I'm tired of talking. What are your impressions? Would you like to analyze this man?

COMMENT: To master the art of doing nothing (though he's made some steps and done some interesting things, clearly he is very bright), that would be terrifying, that aspect would scare me. And [his] convincing people that he's doing something when he isn't doing anything—or isn't doing anything as substantive as is expected in the situation he's in . . .

GEDO: And you would be afraid that he would do nothing in the analysis, as he did nothing in the first two?

COMMENT: [That] raises a question we [discussed previously]: When the symptomatology and the personality structure is such that it potentially interferes with the patient performing analytic work, does that scare you away? How do you view that?

GEDO: Well, you are raising the question of what is the analysand's job [within] the analytic work? What would you expect of this person if you did undertake to analyze him? Let me say that both the referring physician and the patient made it very clear that by now the issue was a matter of life and death: that the patient knew that he was very near the end of any road he could travel and that suicide was not out of the question.

COMMENT: You know, what strikes me is the sense of meaningless- ness in the patient's life. That no matter what he seems to try to undertake, it's [only] because he can get some kind of feedback from somebody else or encouragement, or response. I mean, even being the oldest sibling, he couldn't do *that* right. It's like he can't do anything that makes him feel good, and I would think he would carry that over . . .

GEDO: [interrupting] Well, let me respond to that [impression], because that reflects the lacunae in the story that I have [presented]. There are things that make this man feel good, and there were seven years ago. He loved to play tennis, although he's stopped doing it because an aspiring novelist can't play tennis. It's too humiliating. I mean, Flaubert, Dostoevski, hmmm? Inconceivable! Thomas Hardy, maybe. When [the patient] was younger, he loved to throw a football around and had some success in the context of [intramural] high school competition. He could have been a quarterback, he really understood the game, and he gets a great deal of pleasure from watching football games and knowing what is going on.

COMMENT: I guess I'm a little less concerned about his doing nothing (in terms of there being some profound kind of black hole in the sky and just inertia in there) because I relate to the theme of the promise of greatness that goes unfulfilled. There seems to be a lot of power behind that promise of greatness; I think he might be able to recapture that within the analytic process. So I see that as giving promise. . . .

COMMENT: Well, you know, I'm an optimist, so I would try it.

COMMENT: What was it like relating to him? [That] would be crucial for me in terms of thinking about this, since the history leaves that very open?

COMMENT: With no [emotional] involvement with anybody at all in his life, as you have told us—*was* there anyone that he actually was involved with?

GEDO: Well, I didn't tell you about his current involvements when I first saw him. Of course, he was still the Don Juan . . .

COMMENT: But that's not a real . . .

GEDO: Golly! How do you know?

COMMENT: They were?

GEDO: Well, I didn't know. I didn't know. At the time I started with him [he had] two principal liaisons in this town. I mean, there is a girl in every port, but here he was [more or less] living with a fellow law student. She was very diligent, and, as I heard more and more about her, she sounded like quite a good person; he could appeal to such a person. Of course, he never came close to committing himself to her. She graduated and went to another city, and then they lost contact, except he knows that she got married. And then he was involved with a graduate student in another field. [She] was in analysis and was a character much like himself (like the architect had been a character much like himself). They were very mean to each other, very, *very* mean to each other. But of course [for him] people are a bit interchangeable. It's like chess pieces—eeny, meeny, miney, mo—pawn, bishop, and so on. [Yet], you know, he was still involved with the architect ten years later. How many of you would try analysis? Of course, I know it's unfair [to ask], because you know I tried it.

COMMENT: Was the implication of your comment that "it was life and death at this point" . . . was that another way of saying [that] regardless of your hesitation, [there] was in a sense no choice?

GEDO: Well, there's always the choice of saying maybe someone else [can do it], I personally can't. I have had a lifelong policy of first come, first served, and unless there was some risk of the person having to go to a hospital, I'll try it. That's been my policy; but [in addition] I was very intrigued with this man, he's very interesting. I didn't finish describing him. He considers himself good looking, although in my eyes he's not, exactly. He's apple cheeked, fair haired, but a bit too apple cheeked, it creates a kind of adolescent impression. Medium build, slender. As you can imagine, dressed with exquisite care, seven years ago in the campus mode, typically some informal shirt and cotton pants, sneakers. But you *can't* imagine how much obsessional thought went into selecting all that, and a feeling of dreadful self-consciousness that "it's not right." Not right, not right. Nothing has ever been quite right.

COMMENT: But it looks all right to other people. I mean you cannot shop and then end up looking like a slob.

GEDO: It's a matter of taste. I mean, he looks all right to me—it's all right with me. But to people in the know it might look too studied.

COMMENT: But it all matches, and it's all ironed, and he was very tidy and well put together?

GEDO: Oh, it's a bit more sophisticated than that! It looks carefully *untidy*! I mean, whatever you [might] think about, he's a little bit beyond that in having worried about these things for 30 years.

COMMENT: Was he obsessional about almost everything? I mean, how much [obsessing] was [there]?

GEDO: He's obsessional about everything, but in a particular way: with his fantastic obsessionality there's not a trace of magical thinking. He is even more matter-of-fact than his father, because he's no gambler.

COMMENT: Well, you mean he would always be stuck at deciding things: [what] is optimal? or what would come out looking right?, rather than [having] obsessions like, "If I do this particular act it will have fantastic consequences."

GEDO: That is correct. The infinite obsessionality had the quality of its being a matter of life and death to get it just right, *just* right! About a year or two later, he was involved with a very sensible young woman. At that point he had finished school, thereby ending a long history of not finishing anything. But he was looking for an apartment away from the university area and he got into an endless obsession about where to look, *where* to look. She tried to help him a little bit because she was a Chicago native, and when he revealed to her what considerations he had in mind, she said with total exasperation and shock, "My God, all you worry about is connotations!" I mean, it wasn't a question of price, or function, or anything in the real world, but [only] what a New York sophisticate would think of a person who lives on Elm Street versus a person who lives on LaSalle Street.

COMMENT: It seems to me your comment that he did no gambling really epitomizes this man. You know, he is attempting to orchestrate a life rather than live it.

GEDO: Well, your conclusion is 100% correct. But, I must say, many of the things said thus far underestimate this man. The fact is that nothing [about him] is the way it appears to be. People are exceedingly complicated. I mean, this man is a four-flusher, except in a few areas and at a few times. When he got interested in Jewish theology, he was having a real crisis of faith. He was really preoccupied, in the way some adolescents on their way to schizophrenia are preoccupied, with the existence of God. And that was genuine. But everything else is orchestrated or stage managed, and there's just no knowing what it means.

But I wasn't quite as wise as all that when I started. I now have the results of seven years of work to inform my presentation. You could say, in a sense, that he is an "as if character," except for the fact that some [of his behavior is] not "as if." Like the sadism and the masochism, like the attacks on the siblings and the murder of the dog, and the memory of the inexplicable tantrum about the governess, and the limitless ambition. If this didn't come out during the time I took the history, it came out very soon afterwards. Yes, he was in law school, but he still wanted to write the first American novel worth reading. I thought he might be somebody who has actual talent and wants to be a great artist, and the very magnitude of the ambition stops him. Flaubert, law school, epilepsy . . .

Dostoevski, hm? You know the story about Dostoevski? Dostoevski in his early 20s wrote a novel, took it to [a competent critic] who read the manuscript and said, "My God, we have another Pushkin!" This is what my patient had to match. Except he knew nothing; he knew nothing about nothing! All he knew is what the *New York Review of Books* said about things, and a few other [publications] of that kind. He hadn't read very many books, certainly not from cover to cover, but he knew what the reviews were, maybe even in 1850, huh? I mean, there was no way of his getting started, although, in fact (this comes from later seeing snippets of his writing—he occasionally would bring me a paragraph or two), he has a beautiful style, a superb command of language. He has the talent.

COMMENT: Is it *his* style? In other words, I mean, are there elements of patterning after other styles?

GEDO: I can only talk [with confidence] about his associations, because he has never written more than two consecutive paragraphs. I mean, he did write a thesis that passed muster, but during the past seven years he hasn't written two consecutive paragraphs. But he speaks very impressively, and I don't impress easily.

You haven't asked about the money. How was he going to pay for the analysis [in view of the fact that] his parents are so opposed? Well, it turns out the parents are not 100% opposed, because he's in law school— and that's already better than doing nothing in New York. And as long as he's in law school they're willing to pay his [bills], and the money he gets is enough to pay a reasonable fee. Because of the threat that the financial support would be withdrawn, I charged him my minimum fee, so that he could continue even if the parents said no once again, although I made it clear to him that if his finances were stabilized I would raise his fee to my maximum, which was certainly appropriate in terms of the family resources.

I got a very obscure story about his actual finances. I mean, either he couldn't tell me or he didn't know, or I didn't get it, or there were several versions that he told me, or all of the above. When the children were babies, the father established an arrangement whereby he held money for them in trust, substantial money, and that money was to be distributed when my patient was 25 and the youngest 21. That time happened to coincide with the father's financial collapse. So the money was distributed. I'm now telling the story as it is; I no longer remember what the obscurities were. These are the facts. He had the money for one half hour, on paper, and half an hour later, sight unseen, he signed certain documents establishing a family partnership. The father is the general partner, the children are the limited partners. And this is the money the father used to reestablish himself financially.

For years after we started, the money was said to be the father's money, and [the patient] was getting the money from home as though the parents were generously giving him an allowance. In fact, this is what we spent the first year and a half of treatment on. I mean, he talked about all sorts of things, he associated to all sorts of matters, but this was the crux of the matter; to clear up the confusion, "What are the facts about the money?" And what are the facts about the dealings between him and his family? To hear him tell it, the father was a mean man who would only give him money if he did exactly as the father wanted.

At first it sounded to me like the father was a pretty ruthless man who was trying to defraud the IRS. We finally concluded that the father, in fact, had recaptured the money not only to have capital to get started again, but because he understood very clearly that none of his four children was remotely capable of handling this money and that the money would be pissed away by one or more of them, particularly, I think, the younger son. He was [thought to be] a drug addict at the time. And the father has a kind of simplistic set of principles that he substitutes for an understanding of human relations, and one of his principles is that he's going to treat all four of his children exactly alike. So if he wasn't going to let this 21-year-old addict have the money, he wouldn't let anyone have the money. And he was safeguarding the money for them, but he liked to talk as though he were being the generous father supporting his children by doing well with the family partnership. He talked about it as "my money." But, in point of fact, when confronted by the patient—[to reach that point] took about two years to accomplish—he was perfectly realistic about whose money it was and perfectly realistic about the fact that he wasn't keeping his children on an allowance, that he was distributing to them the proceeds of the partnership as they became available. [He was] keeping very accurate, meticulous records about all this. So that it turned out that the patient had been severely paranoid about his father, really quite delusional.

How can I be so sure of all this? Well, I challenged the patient to check it out with his father. Is this an analysis, since we are preoccupied with the validity of a set of convictions, or delusions, or whatever, and whether there's any substance to them? That's the way the ball bounced, you know; whether you care to call it an analysis is something else again. No way could the patient even entertain the possibility that he had it wrong. Finally he insisted that I see his father. He challenged *me*: How did I know that his reports were reliable enough for me to come to any conclusion whatever about his father? So I did agree to do that.

COMMENT: He wanted you to meet the father?

GEDO: Yes, [ostensibly] to settle the reality testing issue.

COMMENT: So he wasn't convinced that his descriptions to you were accurate?

GEDO: Oh, come on, don't be a sucker, Doctor! This man is a psychopath, huh? He will be engaging in ad hoc argumentation, huh? If my conclusions differed from his, then he was going to argue that since I based my conclusions on his report, they had no basis to stand on.

COMMENT: That was what I was thinking about, this feeling that comes through that his first-hand experience of the world is limited. I mean, does he have some sense of that? Because he hasn't really experienced genuine affects.

GEDO: Well, he's experienced rage, at least on occasion, and he experiences despair. He experiences pleasure, particularly narcissistic gratification. You know, if he's going with a particularly beautiful and desirable woman, if he is living it up at *Le Français*! I mean, he knows a good wine from a bad one, better than you and I. Yet, what you say has a large measure of truth in it, because he reaches these moments of reality very rarely, and the rest of the time he's lost in this swirling cloud of his words, of confusion about connotations, about what does the *New York Times Book Review* say versus what does the *New York Review of Books* say versus . . .

COMMENT: Instead of reading the book for himself . . .

GEDO: Of course, he *can't* read the book for himself. He can't sit still. He has difficulty sticking to anything for as long as ten minutes. If the material is difficult, he'll fall asleep after five minutes, particularly if the material has emotional content.[e] So the Shakespearean tragedies he cannot read. *Sentimental Education* he was able to read by missing its irony and taking it at the most literal level, which deprives it of emotional content. So in terms of 95% of his life, or 98% of his life, you're perfectly right, but it's not an *incapacity*. I mean the potential for functioning is there; he avoids it.

COMMENT: Is it that he avoids it or that he's overstimulated by it?

GEDO: Well, because he knows he's so overstimulated by it, he avoids it insofar as he can. He gets into analysis, and he just floods you with confusion. If you just listen [passively], you're driven to the wall. At least I was driven to the wall. I can't listen for 45 minutes without intervening [in response] to this, "What does it mean to A and what does it mean to B, and which is better? How should one go?" He [might not] even address the principal issue of what one should do. What guidebook should one buy in order to find out what one should be? And where should one buy such a guidebook? And by that time I'm ready to scream. You know that's an individual matter, but I don't have much patience for that. So I responded by saying, "Hey, let's figure out how we can cut this short. Let's figure out a way, so you will never have to discuss this again. Never one word any more. Like the question of brown shoes and black shoes. Let's dispose of that now. Let's make an agreement. What will be simpler for you in terms of building up a wardrobe, brown or black, and stick to one, okay?" Not that it was easy for him to agree to such a deprivation in view of the adaptation of many years.

But if it strikes you as a heresy in psychoanalytic technique, or if you want to call this a nonanalysis at this point, let me just say that in order to continue to work with him, to save my sanity, I needed that. Like a fee or like an agreement not to track mud onto my carpet, or something else [essential for oneself]. Of course, it was his way of tracking mud onto people's carpets. And gradually, by agreeing on certain provisional, reasonable procedures in order to eliminate certain obsessions, the material got focused on the money and the view of the father as so threatening, so frightening, that he couldn't talk to him about anything. By the time he came into his father's presence, he was screaming, and the father [would say], "Listen, if you're going to be like that, I can't talk to you." And so, after two years . . .

COMMENT: Can I ask a question? Are you saying that certain symptoms of patients stop the analytic process in its tracks, either because you can't tolerate them or because that is their purpose, or whatever. And you would engineer a way to interfere with that?

GEDO: His characterological performance enters the analysis and wrecks [it], as it wrecks everything. So in order to have an analysis, in order [for me] not to suffer the fate the first two analysts suffered, it has to be undercut.

COMMENT: So interference may be your preliminary maneuver toward [establishing a treatment alliance]?

GEDO: Well, but I didn't do it in the spirit of *interfering*. I did it in the spirit of offering him a prosthesis, [helping him] to get along in the world in a simpler way. If one accepts that his declared intentions, to be supplied with an acceptable set of shoes, are his real intentions . . . ?[f]

COMMENT: But he had a number of other intentions that you believed were [implicated] in that behavior, such as tracking mud onto your carpet?

COMMENT: What I'm wondering is, at what point does one decide not to move in an interpretive direction, to move instead in this other direction?

GEDO: Well, there was nothing to interpret. I can assure you there was nothing to interpret, there was nothing but an empty cloud of doubt.

COMMENT: And it was literally about clothing? You were listening to [obsessions about] clothing?

GEDO: Often literally about clothing, but *never* about anything that any of you in this room would give two moments' thought to, unless you became ill.

COMMENT: Did you then become the guidebook? In other words, were you making prescriptions like—I guess the overall one is, "Let's make it simpler as a way of moving along in life?"

GEDO: "Let's make it simpler so that we can get on to an analysis." I never pretended that telling him to buy only one color of shoes is the way to live. That's just so we won't hear about the [choice of] shoes [in the sessions].

COMMENT: That's my question too. It means interfering to allow the process to happen, when the symptom shuts it down.

GEDO: But let me say that I came to the conclusion very early that the only way to insure that this person would stick with [analysis] was to be very helpful. *Really* helpful. Because behind this facade of being so sophisticated and adequate, and spouting a paragraph or two from some prestigious source, he really knew nothing about [life]. He lived in a hole in the wall and spent his life obsessing in bookstores or libraries. When he graduated from college, his father gave him $50,000. This dreadful tyrant gave him $50,000, with a "have a good time." So what does he do? I mean, what's the proper thing to do? In such circumstances one goes to Paris, right? So, how does he spend his time in Paris? He found a bookstore on the Boulevard St. Michel, and he spent all of his time there obsessing, making lists of which books he ought to have read. Well, finally, after several weeks, he couldn't stand it any more and arranged to meet one of the ladies, [perhaps] it was the architect. [I think] the architect was in London at the time, so he went to London and they engaged in their sadomasochistic dance—and then he came home.[6]

Of course, after a few episodes like that, the parents became a little reluctant to let him have his own money. But he couldn't even negotiate with them about money for the analysis. It took approximately two years to persuade him that if he became so distraught in his father's presence that he couldn't speak in a manner the father could tolerate, maybe they could discuss these things by correspondence. And then he would bring me countless drafts of letters to his father. In that sense, it's not entirely right [to say that he never produced] two consecutive paragraphs, because each letter had two or three paragraphs, but they were about a single topic. They were all superb letters, beautifully written letters, but indeed we had to go over them countless times because they were all utterly unacceptable, because the paranoid business came through loud and clear. And he was unable to put it in a neutral manner, to ask, "What's the situation?"

The situation turned out to be that the business was to be dissolved in the year 2009 and until then he wasn't entitled to a dime as a matter of right. If the general partner, his father, in the kindness of his heart decided to make a disbursement, he could make a disbursement. But if he decided to say, "In the year 2007 you will sue me if I disburse this money now, because you will say that I didn't exercise the kind of investor prudence that a general partner ought to exercise, because you wanted this built up to fifty million dollars or a hundred million dollars," then he could make no disbursement, except for charitable purposes. It was written into the general partnership that each of the limited partners would make huge charitable donations every year; they couldn't touch the money.

It's almost [time to stop for today]. Let me just tell you where we stand now, to whet your appetite and to give you courage about undertaking difficult enterprises. We're working, and there's no end in sight, no end in sight. He finished law school, and I'll tell you later how I helped him to [manage that]. He got a job in a good enough law firm. I [*should* say] an excellent law firm, but for him to accept a job in any law firm it had to be "just right". It was right enough, but he couldn't do the work, and they fired him. He was enormously relieved when they fired him, and he has not worked since, and he was able to let his parents know that he had no intention of ever working again for money, because his share of the limited partnership is now worth over five million dollars, not to speak of what he expects to inherit from the father, who is once again worth many millions. So it's absurd for him to do anything except to emulate Flaubert, if that's what he's interested in.

He's still not able to read very much; he gets too overwhelmed with envy and he gets overwhelmed by the content, the emotional content of the only kind of literature that a man like he can read without humiliation. But he has his own money now, lots of it. He persuaded his father that instead of the year 2009, the year 1989 is the proper time to dissolve the family partnership, persuaded himself and his father that his profession is "investor." That's not a joke; he means it seriously, that his principal responsibility in life is not to farm out the task of taking care of his own investments to his father, but to do it for himself. He has already received a substantial portion of his [money], which he has invested conservatively. He has moved out of the hole in the wall; he has an apartment fit for *House Beautiful*, and he has begun to collect old master drawings, largely under the impact of my evident interest in art.[h] He has become a volunteer in one of the major cultural organizations in the city. Much to his sorrow, there is no way of doing that in a literary organization; that [opportunity] does not exist. But he's active in musical and museum organizations in the city, and not only in stuffing envelopes. In one of these places he's actually being used as a research assistant. He does that on a part-time basis, and those are the red letter days of his week. He has cut out much of the skirt-chasing, [although] it's hard to know where [to place] the limits of Don Juanism: he's not exactly living a celibate life, but he has even tried to find someone he might like.

Second Session

GEDO: The clinical dilemma that I tried to describe to you was that of a third analysis, the first two done in a conventional way by very excellent people—neither of these efforts took. They failed to last beyond about a year, a year and a half. The patient was a very desperate person who was at the same time fraudulent and delinquent. A very odd family situation—you recall the monetary arrangements. He had a lot of money, but he signed over the money to his father and everyone [treated] the money as the father's money. He was getting the income from his own money, [but it] was treated as if he were receiving a generous allowance, and the last analysis was destroyed because they wouldn't give him the allowance for [such an] irrational purpose.

So, what does one do? How does one begin such an analysis? Well, of course, one begins the analysis by instructing the person about free association, but, as I told you, his associations mostly concerned empty obsessions about unbearably trivial matters. He was in law school at the time and talking about the absolute necessity of making Law Review because nothing less than that would satisfy his father.

How would you try to keep such a person in treatment? I assume that you'd *want* to keep the person in treatment in the hope that you'd be able to accomplish something eventually. You know, what might be necessary, beyond just listening?

COMMENT: Well, two things came up in the discussion last time: One was the issue that he needed to clarify [the status of the] money, because money had helped abort one of the prior treatments. And second, the issue was that you found him unbearable in terms of the obsessionality.

GEDO: Right. Those were indeed the two principal issues that we dealt with in the first couple of years of the treatment.

GEHRIE: It seems to me [one must have] some theory about the meaning of these trivial obsessions, and [some notion of] technique about what you do with that [resistance]. It seems to me that this kind of obsessionality was treated as a resistance in the previous analyses; that would be the typical, classical way of looking at this. [It follows from that view that] one would try to interpret or understand the function of the resistance. And it seems to me that that's not the way that you approached him. You described the use of a different technique: basically to say, this is intolerable, that is, to make an intervention rather than an interpretation.

GEDO: Well, that's close to correct. [Only] I don't know whether the previous analysts heard the obsessions. I have no information about how this man behaved at that time. I certainly did *not* treat this phenomenon as a resistance. I treated it as the ultimate consequence of a collapse. It's not self-regulated, autonomous behavior, but total bewilderment. Indeed, the patient was much more pained by the symptom than I was. He found this state intolerable, and he couldn't get out of it.

COMMENT: Would he report that to you, or would he go on and just present . . .

GEDO: If I gave you a direct answer I would be making it up as I go along. I don't remember how exactly this came up. It came up early enough, but I'm not sure that I knew about that for some time. But I took it as my first task to tell him how to get past that suffering. As an example of one of the less trivial obsessions: whether to try for the Law Review or not to try for the Law Review. This I do remember, and I took the attitude that this was not to be dealt with on the basis of an emotional preference, that this was *the* crucial question on which the future of the analysis depended. [At the time]

I was not absolutely clear about the family situation yet. I mean, all I heard was that he was on this allowance and that he had to fly right or the family might sever the allowance. So I told him that I felt how he would handle this Law Review business would determine the future of the analysis, and that I thought his life depended on his having a successful analysis; that I took his mutterings about suicide very seriously indeed, and that we had to collaborate, he and I; we had to preserve this analysis against all attacks. Therefore we had to work out a strategy that would satisfy his father, specifically a strategy about law school. I thought that in his present state of mental disorder there was absolutely no chance of his making the Law Review, and therefore it was essentially a medical prescription that he shouldn't try. You know, that [to try] was useless and the slippery slope to disaster, that he should figure out what would be the absolute minimum acceptable to his father and do that because he was very ill. I'm summarizing; this [thinking evolved] over several months, but this was the thrust of how I began to treat him.

COMMENT: Within those several months, were you explicit with him about this, in terms of his disability?

GEDO: Oh, yes, I'm [usually] very explicit.

COMMENT: What turned out to be minimally acceptable to his father?

GEDO: As I told you, after about a couple of years I agreed to an interview with the father, as the therapists of young children agree to interviews with parents. By that time I had decided that the diagnosis was an early arrest of development, that [my patient] functioned like a small child. And the father came in and he was a man with an offensive personality, but a perfectly [well-intentioned] man who wanted to save this offspring of his, a man who had no extraordinary demands, who was very concerned about his son's psychopathy and very concerned that I would be fooled by it. When he saw that I was well aware of his son's psychopathy, although he had no [real] hope that I could be helpful, he was certainly not opposed to treatment. And he said to me, "I used to have high expectations, but I'll be satisfied with very little now."

COMMENT: If you had concerns that he could not know what his father's actual expectations might be, would you actually encourage him to have the discussion about that with his father, rather than just [interpret the meaning of his uncertainty]?

GEDO: I took the attitude that [it would help if he had] discussions with his father about everything. Perhaps he didn't have everything right; he had never discussed these matters. I encouraged discussions, but he was unwilling to have discussions, afraid to have discussions. Whenever he had tried to have discussions in the past, he degenerated. He found himself beside himself with rage, unable to control himself, saying outrageous things until his father terminated [the confrontation]. The worst of these incidents was a discussion in which his father said, "You act like all you want from me is my money," and he screamed, "That's exactly right! That's *all* I want from you!" So he didn't want to repeat that, and I cannot tell you with what panic he reacted to all my challenges. [That outburst] wasn't a provocation at all; it was a loss of control, with *tremendous* anxiety. It wasn't exactly at the level of castration anxiety; it was more of a total panic that he would be blasted off the face of the earth, that he would cut himself off from his only source of supplies.[i]

COMMENT: Is it a situation in which you are not yet in a position to know what the patient's own sense of reality is? Or are you saying that you would instruct him to talk to his father because in reality the future of the analysis, the success of the analysis, depends on his ability to have an accurate reading on his father?

GEDO: I would [merely] instruct him on how to talk to his father without making one of these scenes. And it took two years to get to that point. And of course most of the two years were filled with the obsessions.

GEHRIE: Would you say that there was an additional purpose in doing that? That it's not just getting him to have a proper reality assessment of his father, but getting him involved in this particular procedure, the process of relying on the analyst for this kind of . . . experiment with himself? That is, that he would now become part of this [activity]. Whether or not the patient ever got a reality view of the father would be up in the air, it seems to me.

GEDO: Well, of course! I didn't at that point know that the view of his father was as unrealistic as it turned out to be.

GEHRIE: You know, I keep wondering what it was about your communication to him that allowed the analysis to proceed, because it seems to me you even gave him a goal, an instruction, that there was no way that he could at that time [carry out]. You said, "Well, you're not going to go for Law Review, and what you're going to do is find out [your father's] minimal requirements." Well, when you made that instruction to him, this man couldn't do that. [But] there's something about the communication that allowed things to proceed in some manner, so that eventually he gained the ability to find out what his father required.

GEDO: Yes, I'm very glad you put it that way. An additional motive for telling him he shouldn't go for the Law Review was that that [plan] was part of the fraudulence. He was at the beginning of the second year of law school when he started with me, and he was already feeling that he couldn't stand it, that he'd have to drop out, and that the only reason he was not dropping out was that, if he dropped, then it [would be] all over with his father. [Law school was] just the last chance, but he wasn't interested [in law] at all. He couldn't read the materials. Yet he is so bright that he could get by on the basis of going to the lectures. He didn't do any work; he was filling his days with obsessions, reading the newspaper, getting a drink, trying to make a hit on a girl, in a kind of planless, chaotic way. From the beginning I said, "Your salvation depends on giving up the fraudulence. Your motto must be truth, honor, and justice." Later on I had to add "freedom and dignity." He didn't quite grasp how fraudulent he was being, but [realizing] that [he was] didn't take too long. After some weeks—I don't know, four, eight, twelve weeks—he grasped the fact that there was no reason to pretend he was interested, and he started to take the maximum number of courses that the law school permitted to be taken in other divisions of the university, and that was quite a few.

GEHRIE: But he did that in part because of an aspect of what was contained in your communication to him and your holding out your hand to him and saying, come on, let's go, let's take a look at all this stuff.

GEDO: Well, it was *more* than holding out my hand to him, because the other part we discussed was that, of course, he had a tremendous contempt for the mental health professions, [a contempt] borrowed from his parents in part, but, even more important, borrowed from his glamorous New York contacts. Thus, before he could hear me at all I had to prove that I was at least the equal of Susan Sontag and certainly the superior of the professor and novelist who had been his mentor. He had dropped the other two analyses because those analysts were [seemingly] overshadowed by this glamorous world. He had tried to [protect] himself against that disaster by going to the famous consultant in New York, but that person was not accepting patients any more and had referred him to a younger person, so that [precaution] didn't work out.

I don't know when I realized explicitly that this was an absolute necessity, but from the first, on an unconscious level, I responded in a way that accomplished the task [of neutralizing his depreciation]: I had a spontaneous affective response that everything I heard [about this glamorous world] was ridiculous, that there was something about it—I don't know whether the reference means terribly much to you people—like the Molière play *Les Précieuses Ridicules*. (It was a great antifeminist comedy of the 17th century in which he was mocking the intellectual pretensions of women.) This young man's intellectual pretensions, this business about New York, struck me as exactly that: something truly ridiculous. So when he quoted these people, I took the attitude of saying, "Well, that's what they think on the Ship of Fools," except I didn't say it as kindly as I'm saying it now.

GEHRIE: You saw through his pretensions and communicated to him [that they were empty]. You acknowledged either with him or for him that he was in a struggle to save his life, and I don't know that that had been an experience he'd had before. Was that part of the circumstances that allowed him to be instructed? [j]

COMMENT: I wonder, was it offering instruction or was it really the communication that the analysis was everything and you would do *anything* to save the analysis, anything?

GEDO: Anything that conformed to the [principles] of "Truth, honor, justice, freedom, and dignity."

COMMENT: Right, I understand that, but I mean that you overcame his internal [imagoes]—you were going to be *bigger* than all those other people, and you were going to be the reality tester, you were going to instruct him, and you would do, [respecting] your own limits, anything to [accomplish] that.

COMMENT: It seems to me that you [are appealing] to his true self, to use that terminology, that you are involved in a fairly massive [effort to] disillusion him, in the sense that he lives in this world in which he [pretends] he is able to do all these things, and you say to him, "You're not able to do anything. You can't get anything done. You know, you're sick." But it's not only that. You also offer up the possibility that you were there to do something for him. In terms of the scheme that you and Goldberg elaborated in *Models of the Mind*, it seems to me that there's an overall business of disillusionment going on, but there's also an approach on another level, which is the level on which he doesn't have sufficient self-cohesion to make decisions in any kind of reasonable way. And at that point you come in and direct him in a way that's very parental.

Gedo: Well, [yes], parental at [the patient's] very early age. I think that's quite right. You could draw the [hierarchical] scheme on the board. His obsessions are about various illusions, but when he's obsessing like that between alternative sets of illusions then he has regressed from the realm of illusions to something even more primitive [where he loses] the very ability to determine what is real. So the content was in terms of an entire set of ideas in mode III, but the actual behavior was in mode II.[k]

Gehrie: It's interesting that you offer us at least a hope that there was something about this man that [enabled him] to accept what you offered in place of his delusional system, that he was able to accept your offer of help. At the same time, what you were helping to do was make an assessment of his delusional organization. There are [patients] who can't do that, obviously; that seems to me the point at which such a technique would cease to [be effective].

Gedo: Well, at that point one would have to try something else, but, you know all along that *this* young man [does not have] psychotic episodes. His "delusion" about his father is based on a transference. If he had said "mother" instead of "father," it would have been absolutely on the mark. Let me tell you how this shows up now, six years later. His parents were in town last weekend, so he took them to see the Gauguin show at the Art Institute and he was showing them through. He had already seen the show, and as I mentioned to you he's begun collecting really expensive stuff himself, so he's beginning to learn about these matters. And his father was quite interested, although mostly at the level of the commercial value of these things. As they went through the show my patient said, "You know, it's very interesting that toward the end of his life Gauguin hardly ever painted men." And his father said, "Oh, the reason for that is that there is a much better commercial market for paintings of pretty ladies." In the treatment [the patient] reported his great triumph [of self-restraint], "I was able to keep quiet."

But his father's predominant character pathology is that he feels like a shoe salesman. He acted like a shoe salesman when he came to see me—intimidated. And he protects himself from the feeling of helplessness and humiliation through an attitude of total cynicism.

So [according to him] Gauguin is a shoe salesman too. So much for the father.

The mother came to town a day before the father, and the patient took her out to dinner. They had a very nice time, and then he said, "Well, when you get up tomorrow, whenever you're ready, call me, and I will come to the hotel and we'll do something." And she said, "Fine." But she knew he had an appointment with me in the afternoon, and he arrived at his appointment and said, "As was to be expected, she never called." So that's the mother. He said something about the sort of excuses she would offer, and I said [correctly, as it turned out], "I *bet* you she will say nothing," [because] she is maximally hostile [to him]. When he got fired from the legal job after he finished school, he decided never to take a job again. You know, by that time it was perfectly clear that the money was his, that there was more than enough for all of his needs, in perpetuity. And she suggested that he take a newspaper route. I mean, she was *serious* [about wanting him to become a delivery boy].

COMMENT: He's treated like a mentally retarded little boy?

GEDO: No, definitely *not*! This is not to be taken as a suggestion on her part that he's mentally retarded. She knows that he's a brilliant person. It's punitive, *punitive*. What was very interesting is that in a sense she's attacking her own bad part, because she never does anything and is disorganized and helpless, and his acting that way turned out to be an identification with her.[1] The identification with his father consists of his corrosive "superiority," cynicism if you will, putting everything and everybody down; and the identification with the mother is to do nothing but be very hostile. So this is the characterological rind one has to get through in order to get a glimpse of his [private] motives. This is simply the rottenness of the state of Denmark.

You [all] look depressed. The interesting thing is that it hasn't been depressing at all. It's been fascinating. Fascinating, fun. It's been a fun treatment. It helped [that] he's so bright; I mean, even his nastiness is full of interesting information.

Well, there must be many other things that you might want to hear about.

COMMENT: I'm thinking about [your report] that early in the treatment you met his father.

GEDO: After about two years.

COMMENT: After two years. Because I was wondering whether your meeting his father helped him with reality testing, because then you had a better view of his father, rather than [one] based on [the patient's] fantasy and delusion about what his father was demanding of him. Do you think that that was very important in the treatment when you did meet his father, as when you are treating a child?

GEDO: [I believe] it was very important to meet the father, but I must say it did not help me to learn anything about the father. I learned nothing that I hadn't inferred before. I changed none of my views, right or wrong, on the basis of the meeting. I was convinced way back that the father was a perfectly decent man [who had] severe limitations. And that's what he turned out to be, a shoe salesman [with a big bank account]. What was terribly important was for [the patient] to see what his father's reaction to me would be. I had told him, "You will see that your father is not going to be hostile, [that] he's not going to be disrespectful, that he's going to come away from this meeting saying that he doesn't believe in this sort of thing, but that *I* am okay." That's exactly how it turned out. So it was an antidote to the patient's contempt [toward] psychoanalysis.

COMMENT: It seems [as if] it goes beyond the contempt about psychoanalysis. It goes to a statement about how we can acquire knowledge, and the fact that you could not acquire this knowledge [in] the way that [analysts] normally acquire knowledge.

GEDO: On the basis of the statements of the patient.

COMMENT: He was making this statement through his refusal to believe that what you were saying [was based on rational considerations]—I mean, you must have gone over this, why you thought what you did. And he's saying, no, no, you're wrong, you can't get it that way, which seems like some sort of a disorder in thinking.

GEDO: Well, right, a disorder in thinking because he too has sort of an alexithymia, though not as [severely] as his father. You know, he can't read his own feelings. He *won't* read his own feelings, is what it turned out to be. In identification with the father, he doesn't pay attention to any of that. He also doesn't pay any attention to that because the feelings that *are* there are so "bad." We're talking about an inner hell. I mean, there's *something* inside this man. He's not empty, although he sometimes wants to pretend he's empty. He's full of pus, and the pus is that he has been engaged in a 30 years' war

against his parents. I tell him that I expect it to last a hundred years
more. You know, in my ironic way I imply, "You're a ridiculous
person. Thirty, huh! A *hundred*!"

COMMENT: So in fact you demonstrated to him that you can survive
the contact with the toxic exposure and still maintain your position
about how things are going to go. You're not going to be taken over
or overwhelmed or forced to retreat into your own fraudulent
position in order to accede to whatever it was the father might
demand of you, that you're going to maintain yourself in the face of
this.

GEDO: Well, I hope so. I mean I hope it conveyed that. You know,
I'm afraid I hadn't [consciously] thought through why I was doing
these things. I just *felt* it [was right].

COMMENT: The question I still have is how and why this patient was
willing to accept what you had to say, given his position of contempt,
at least consciously.

GEDO: What I had to say about his parents?

COMMENT: Well, I think just generally, even in the quality "You
think it's 30 years? It's a hundred years!" I'm sure it's partly how it's
delivered, but why a man who at one level is so contemptuous of
mental health professionals and the intellectual climate in Chicago,
whatever, would be willing to [lie] there and listen and, more than
that accept it, work with you, appreciate it. . . .

GEDO: It's because whatever he had pretensions about, I *knew*
something about. He had written a thesis about *Sentimental Education*; I know *Sentimental Education* quite well. He had a list of x
number of great books that some day he would read but hadn't read.
I'd read most of them.

COMMENT: Does this, then, say something for the idea that there is
something in "a good match?" In other words, I would guess he
knew about you at this point.

GEDO: He didn't *know* about me, but, as I mentioned, it was a fellow
faculty member who referred him, assuming it would be a good
match.

COMMENT: You know, it seems to me that what you're saying
through all the examples is that what you did with this man was to
make yourself bigger and better than anything he could throw at
you.

Gedo: Right. I mean it's not that I *said*, "I'm a better man than your college mentor," although I said, "A college professor who makes homosexual advances to one of his students and gives an "A" when [the student] didn't write his paper, because he wants to make a hit on the student, is almost as fraudulent as your father—if what you say about his financial dealings is correct. Because, you know, you can get all your money back by denouncing him to the IRS. You do know that, if what you say is true, he committed tax fraud, and it's very serious." So I know about tax fraud too.

Comment: There's another component of this—I don't know how they go together. On one side, you make yourself bigger or stronger than anything. But you know the other thing is that there's an insistence on your part about affective honesty, no matter what, in every communication.

Gedo: Well, affective honesty in a certain sense, but just as important, [you have to be able to show *real* competence].

Comment: Yeah, but you're speaking to his affective self every time you speak to him. And one of the truths which seems to have reached him is [that] you confronted him with the superficiality of his values, his world of obsessions in which he is getting lost. I think you struck a nerve of his self-preservation.

Gedo: Well, I hope so. Although I must say [that] when he really sat up and took notice was that incident I mentioned last time, when he was looking for an apartment and one of his innumerable girl-friends lost her temper and said, essentially, "You're *crazy*! You don't look at what's a good apartment, you only worry about connotations."

Comment: It seems to me that what we're talking about is how you created an environment in which this guy could let down the pretentiousness—whatever distancing function the obsessions per se served—and come to rely on another person who would actually be helpful to him [about essentials, because] he just basically didn't know how to get along in the world at all. And so there's the question of how you build up the image in his mind of you as a reliable person—that there really is potential for finding a reliable person in this world who can help him with this stuff.

Gedo: Well, okay, that's what I was aiming for, and I demonstrated to him that I knew not only a few literary references and about tax fraud, but how to get along with people in the world, which is what he was ignorant of; [principally] I did it by helping him to manage this business about the money with his father.

COMMENT: I seem to remember a theory somewhere in which the analyst was to take a position of technical neutrality equidistant from several points in the universe?

GEDO: Didn't I do that?

COMMENT: Well, you can't say you're equidistant when you're also saying you're the affective [translator]. It seems to me that, if I've got the theory down right, technical neutrality and all that equidistance has something to do with allowing the analyst to become an object of transference. And so how do you think about the way in which you're [positioning] yourself with the patient and the kind of impact that's going to have [on the possibility of developing a] transference?

GEDO: This is the interpretation I made for the patient: I said to him—I don't know when [or how] I said it—"[I had the impression] from the beginning that what has been happening here is a repetition of your tantrum when you locked out the English nurse. That's what you did with the first two analysts; you locked them out. I'm not going to be locked out. What do you take me for, a fool? She got fed up with you and then she quit, and that's all right. I'm not criticizing *her* decision, but mental health professionals have to be a little bit more knowing than that."

GEHRIE: So your reply is that this position allowed the transference to be worked with instead of just reenacted over [and over]; that it permitted the evolution of the transference in an analytic environment as opposed to having it just be repeated and have the whole thing fall apart.

GEDO: The evolution of the nursemaid transference. The only reliable person in the childhood circle.[m]

COMMENT: The genuinely involved caretaker.

COMMENT: Well, you work on the premise, obviously, that technical neutrality [does] not necessarily involve passivity.

GEDO: Well, I have premised that of course. It doesn't. Freud did not mean that. You read the original record of the Rat Man, a five-ring circus. This laconic style that has been developed as the practical translation of the precept of neutrality is a joke. That's not neutral; that's dumb.

COMMENT: So how do you understand neutrality?

GEDO: Neutrality is equidistance from the three agencies of the mind in the tripartite model. That's what Freud meant.

COMMENT: It was only applied to a person operating in [your] mode IV?

GEDO: Well, it best applies to a person operating in mode IV, but we can apply it to *this* person by saying that since this person is paperthin with regard to ego functioning, we have to supply ego functioning. There should be three agencies, and [if] one is weak, or missing, or distorted, or however you want to put it, it's inoperative. So you have to supply ego functioning, otherwise everything is id. There is no evidence of superego functioning in the material that I have mentioned to you thus far. He murdered the mother's dog; he scorched the earth for 30 years. I mean, he's just *full* of malice, against his parents and siblings, mostly. He doesn't care about [fighting with] other people; he doesn't have enough resources to let any of his hostilities spill over to outsiders. Everything has to be saved for the war, for the great war.

COMMENT: The patient's lying on the couch, and he's saying, "I don't know what to do about this Law Review thing. Should I go for it? Should I not go for it? What does my father think?" Do you throw yourself into that discussion and have a very [definite] opinion? And his reactions to that and what that means to him, or your attempts to understand what that means to him, are how you define the transference at that time, right?

GEDO: Right.

COMMENT: There are those analysts who would respond to the patient in that situation by saying, "Let's look at what it is you want from me within this quandary of yours."

GEDO: Well, I thought I knew that he wanted reality testing from me and that it was out of the question that he would make the Law Review, totally out of the question.

COMMENT: Couldn't we try and play out the theoretical underpinnings of each of those approaches to the patient about the Law Review?

GEDO: I don't know that we can go into psychoanalytic theory about that. The theory of technique, yes. I was in Boston this week and presented some of my work, and the discussion was all about this point. "You're hectoring. This is authoritarian. What about the hidden negative transference?" Well, it's possible. If one makes a mistake; if all of this is not needed and one does it, then all those criticisms are certainly in order. In point of fact, this man's response when I said, "It's preposterous. What's the matter with you? You know that that's out of the question" was to be enormously relieved.

COMMENT: He discovered the transference by virtue of the intervention.

GEDO: Yes, yes. He started taking courses in literature, and he came to an understanding with the authorities of the law school that they would give him the lowest passing grades. I mean, they tacitly agreed that they [didn't] bother him if he wouldn't bother them. And he got by, and law school ceased to be a subject that we discussed, not because I told him I didn't want to hear about it, but because it became a nonissue. You know, then the issue became, "What am I going to do with this job in the law firm?" And the law firm made the decision on that. He couldn't do it, just as he couldn't make the Law Review. So, if you really believe in the neutrality school of thought, I don't think I was all that nonneutral. I performed certain functions on his behalf that were impaired for him. Child analysts do that all the time.

COMMENT: To put it very schematically, the patient is a man for whom you're providing ego support, and [thereby] he established some sort of balance, structurally, that allowed him to use you as a neutral object in the sense of the nursemaid transference that emerged.

GEDO: Yes, in fact, what has emerged as transference is pretty wispy. I called it the nursemaid transference. You might say it's a transference of wishes he might have had in childhood for some sort of sane caretaking. When I called his mother "dotty" I was simply using the word that he and I agreed [to use about] her. She's some kind of bizarre character. She's best characterized by an incident when she and her son were in a taxicab in New York going to the Sherry Netherland Hotel, one of the fanciest there. They got out of the taxicab and she didn't give the cabbie a tip, and he was terribly embarrassed, because of the doorman, you know. I mean that's the worst connotation, to be a skinflint, and he said, "Mother, you're forgetting the tip." And she said, "Oh, I tipped the last cabbie."

COMMENT: It would be—it's a bewildering thing! No wonder he's bewildered.

GEDO: So he has not had a transference that could be called a mother transference. I have foreclosed that possibility by acting so different from her. I mean, perhaps another analysis would have led to an [early] mother transference; this one cannot.

GEHRIE: But, you know, there's another theory that what you did was to actively offer yourself up as a selfobject in speaking to his bewildered, disorganized state.

GEDO: Well, some people talk in that vocabulary, but if we take their definitions seriously, that's not what I did. This is not what Kohut meant by a selfobject. It's because most people in that circle were utterly shocked by my technique that I left Kohut's group. They said, "That's not psychoanalysis." Whether it's psychoanalysis or not I don't know. It's just whatever you want to call it. Mark Gehrie says I should't talk like that, that I should [claim] that this is the appropriate psychoanalysis [for such a problem].

COMMENT: Could you be precise about why it's not being a selfobject?

GEDO: Because it doesn't have to do with mirroring, and it doesn't have to do with maintaining me in his eyes as some sort of idealized figure—yet that's what Kohut meant by "selfobject transference." Quite the reverse [has been the case]; there's been a terrific struggle, to overcome *defenses* against idealization.[n]

COMMENT: Is what you're doing, functioning as a selfobject but in different arenas and along different functional axes than those that Kohut described?

GEDO: Well, if you're willing to change his definition in that way, yes, of course. You know, his definition was a relatively precise one. His definition was exclusively in the realm of self-esteem regulation, and that's not what I [dealt with] here. What I did do has an effect in that realm too, of course; you do anything, and the effect spreads through every realm of function. But we're not focused on self-esteem issues. We are focused on the most practical matters imaginable. "How does one use an interior decorator?"[o]

GEHRIE: It seems to me the issue is not so much that some [self psychologists] wouldn't agree that the definition of selfobject and the [types] of selfobject transference can't be expanded; some of them believe it really ought to be expanded. It's more what you said earlier, that is, [differences about] the technique of empathic immersion. Although from where I sit, I must say that what you do does not sound unempathic. It sounds very empathic insofar as it permits this patient to grasp onto something genuine about you and use you in this fundamental way. Many self psychologists strongly object to this because it doesn't prevent the patient from becoming involved in the negative affect, getting angry, or hurt, or something like that. But that's not standard self psychology any more. That's my own view of it.

GEDO: Well, I have trouble comparing [my work] with self psychology. I mean, what I did was certainly the opposite of what Evelyne Schwaber would do, in terms of taking the subjective point of view of the analysand. I said, "Your subjective point of view is preposterous. You've got it all wrong, and this is terribly dangerous. And if you don't listen to your elders and betters, you're going to be up shit's creek without a paddle."

COMMENT: And Kohut wouldn't go for that?

GEDO: I think many self psychologists wouldn't go for that, but others would.

COMMENT: Yeah, some would.

GEDO: So, it doesn't cut across ideological lines apparently.

COMMENT: I don't know enough about where self psychology is today, but if self psychology involves the provision of parental functions that involve meeting [the analysand] at the level where he seems to be, then why is your technique something that would not be approved of by self psychologists?

GEDO: Well, if self psychology is now at that juncture, then [it has] progressed enormously from the positions that I'm familiar with. I don't think self psychology is at that juncture, but I may be wrong. There are always leaders in any particular movement who are considerably ahead of the publications in that movement. So I don't know how every self psychologist operates clinically today; I only know what has been printed. I don't think that the self psychologists have discussed doing this kind of ego-[building] work. I think that in much of their literature the position still is that they only interpret. They interpret the selfobject transferences, which is a new content to interpret, but it is plain that the technical intervention that characterizes self psychology is interpretation. In that sense the technique is as pristine as is that of ego psychology.

GEHRIE: As I understand it, another very important technical difference is that the motor of the treatment in self psychology is [provided by] the disruptions in the selfobject transference (the lack of the analyst's provision, if you will). You're saying the motor of the treatment is your recognizing that the patient either has a deficient or a distorted area of psychic functioning and your intruding into that. You're saying, "Wait a minute. Look what you're doing." So it seems that technically you're coming from very different spots.

GEDO: I wouldn't say that this man doesn't have a narcissistic character in the sense that Kohut used that word in the late 60s, but that's not the central psychopathology. The central psychopathology is an infinite rage against which there aren't even the kinds of defenses we usually encounter. He's able to tell his father, "Yes, all I want from you is your money!" And he means it at the moment, you know. He was able to murder his mother's dog. He has lurid dreams of murdering his siblings. It's true that once he had a wonderful dream of being in a procession wearing a cape the size of a football field, and we ended up referring to that as "the born to the purple" dream. You know, the princes of Byzantium were said to be born to the purple, because only the emperors could wear the color. So, sure, there's plenty of grandiosity there. Overt. When he was eight and nine years old he looked up the stock exchange reports every day in the newspaper, to check on what he was worth as a capitalist, with the fantasy, "I'm better than anyone, I have more money than anyone."

COMMENT: I'm just wondering if one way to explain the differences we're trying to pin down is that we're actually dealing with two different developmental phases. When you interpret his illusions about life, he reacts with relief, for the most part, rather than irritation, "How dare you?"

GEDO: I'm beginning to feel argumentative. I don't accept any of the premises that [you are putting] on the table. It's not exactly like that. I'm not disagreeing with illusions, because they're not *his* illusions. He knows he's a fraud and that there's very little he can do. He knows he can't sit still long enough to do anything that people would honor him for. [What seems like illusion results from the fact] that he swallows what other people say about him. First he fraudulently gets them to believe that he's something he's not, then he hears their opinions, and then his reality testing isn't good enough to resist those suggestions.

COMMENT: Well, I was sort of getting the image of a younger child being relieved by some kind of parental reality testing, as opposed to a slightly older child who, when you tell him he can't fly, looks at you with some sense of chagrin, or a "Don't tell me, I don't want to hear it" reaction. So I was wondering whether your patient was operating on an earlier developmental level than what the selfobject psychologists talk about.

GEDO: Yes, yes, that's what Dr. Gehrie alluded to half an hour ago when we were talking about the levels. This is not in mode III, which is the mode that Kohut's contribution allowed to be analyzed systematically for the first time. This is even earlier, this is the mode that you read about in Harold Searles. Searles would call this a borderline psychotic transference. I don't like that vocabulary; I'm just providing you with a translation; those are his terms.

COMMENT: I keep having this image about kids getting dressed, as if really what you're doing for this guy—I keep seeing you laying out his socks, and his t-shirt, his little Oshkosh B'Gosh overalls, and you're going to get him dressed in the morning. You know, as opposed to what happens if they really don't know quite how to dress themselves and you leave them by themselves. You can go up there an hour later and they're still playing with something else. They've sort of pushed the clothes around.

GEDO: Well, it's partly like that. It's not that for six years we've done everything the same way. He doesn't have to be told that he cannot fly, but he has to be told that he cannot read just anything and get much out of it. He had to be told that one reason he couldn't do any reading and couldn't sit still is that he started with materials much too advanced for his level of sophistication.

GEHRIE: You know, part of what I think is at issue here is that when you gave the case report [you did not make] clear that you have come to a conclusion about the [developmental] level which you consider to be really significant to address at the outset. That is, you are immersed in a level of understanding about the primitiveness and the archaic [nature] of the required level of interaction that doesn't come across from just the report about his life because of the more sophisticated aspects that are also present, so that your choice to work at this level is not immediately understood as being relevant to this profound primitivity.

GEDO: Well, it's true, but, in a certain sense, in presenting it that way I am also presenting to you the fact that I didn't know all this six years ago. It's easy to talk now, and I probably made interventions at every level in the usual way [born] of our bewilderment when we first meet a person. [Later, I] settled on the things that work. What worked was pretty primitive indeed. I don't have to lay out socks, but I have to lay out his reading. It's not that I say, "Don't read *King Lear*," as I said ["Don't try for the Law Review]." But when he shamefacedly confesses, with a master's degree in comparative literature, that he's never read any of Shakespeare's plays, I say, "So why don't you make an honest man of yourself?" So he starts with *King Lear*, and he can't hack it. And then I tell him, "Well, maybe this will be too hard [for now]. Maybe you ought to try Bernard Shaw, as a for instance."

COMMENT: And it seems to me also unfair to yourself to characterize the transference as the kind of thing that Searles talks about, because when he talks about it, he talks about a much more broadly based phenomenon in a personality in which there's very little else to grab onto for the management of it. You're talking about a person who possesses a lot of other capacities and can use this approach, whereas a lot of borderline and psychotic types could not.

GEDO: I just read Searles' latest book, and in the introduction to that book he says that he has analyzed 36 [therapists]—[cases] included in the book. And this is exactly what he found in all those analyses: [borderline *transferences* in people who are not "borderline personalities"].

When you say [my analysand] has many capacities, you raise a very interesting question. How many of these capacities does he have when left to his own devices? Not so many, not so many. I'm not the first person who has been available to him to compensate for these handicaps. I'm only the first *analyst* who has allowed himself to be used in this manner [with a view to helping him eventually to overcome them].

COMMENT: He's had the wherewithal, whatever it takes, to fabricate this life and to live on the level that he has lived, which is not nothing. I mean he's created these roles for himself and done well enough to carry it off for the most part.

GEDO: He's never had a job.

COMMENT: He hasn't had to have a job.

GEDO: Except the one at the law firm from which he got fired.

COMMENT: But he hasn't had to have a job.

GEDO: Well, true, true. But that's not how *he* felt. By the time he was at the law firm, this transaction about recapturing his money was well on the way, so he understood by then that he didn't need a job, but before that he had not understood that. You know, he was hearing from his mother that, by God, they weren't going to give him any money unless he took a newspaper route. And he was very, very embarrassed. He was relatively skilled in exploiting people to make up for his deficits and in "finding selfobjects," as some of you put it, mostly young women. When he was in New York, for instance, during the second analysis, he rented an apartment in a fashionable east-side [building], and the apartment remained empty, like the apartment of the man who commits suicide in *La Dolce Vita*. Essentially he lived off a neighbor, a young woman who was very upset and was willing to put up with him because he is—this is one of his capacities—he is very good at comforting very distressed people.

I still don't know where that comes from. I assume that that's a scenario of his emotions of earliest childhood, probably having to do with his mother.[P] But this girl was having some family tragedy; so as long as he comforted her about that, she did everything for him. When she recovered a little, she dismissed him with the final diagnosis of "Friend, you're full of shit!" So, this is how he survived, feeding off one person or another under the guise of helping that person, and full of loathing for the person in the process. He would say to me, "I wish that I could have sexual relations with somebody sometime where, when I'd wake up in the morning, I wouldn't feel nauseated about being with that person." That's a pretty low functional level. If you say that the capacities to be a Don Juan are valuable capacities, he managed.

COMMENT: If the capacity is to relate to people in fairly effective ways, one way or the other, in one arena or the other, he's effective in that.

GEDO: That's not the way he felt. He's had a relatively small number of male friends, selected on the basis of their glamor, like the novelist/mentor, although fortunately none of the others happened to be homosexual. Mostly literary types, and the relationship was around being a literary type and exchanging clevernesses, snippets from the *New York Review of Books*, or one of the fashionable critics, whom he hadn't read.

COMMENT: Well, then how could he keep it up?

GEDO: Well, silence is golden, and he read about them in the *New York Review of Books*. You know, [the way] he got through law school by attending the lectures. The relationships with the women were always based on the sadomasochistic stuff. They were ill. He felt that he was superior, and he came and they thought he was helping them in their distress, but in fact what he felt was that he was putting them down. In a certain sense, it's a sadistic perversion because he would be sexually excited by the experience of putting them down, pretending to be comforting. He felt he was utterly alone in the world.

COMMENT: Just to change the subject, I want to go back to the selfobject transference. When you intervene in the area of a psychic function (and we've all agreed that it [can be called] a "selfobject function"), it's not necessarily a *transference*, although the patient may respond to that intervention within a transference.

GEDO: Right.

COMMENT: There is a transference, though. I mean this man had some—there's a transference involved, I think, in his being able to relate to the analyst in such a way, to make use of what the analyst has to offer at that particular point. That must reflect something positive in the early mother–child relationship. He ain't that receptive, but ultimately he's receptive *enough*, and that's based on transference.

GEDO: Well, yes. That is why I have called what transpired the "nursemaid transference." [The designation] fits because, even though he knows I am of value to him, he hasn't been able to idealize [the relationship]. But my doing those things for him is unprecedented in his experience. He wouldn't even let the English nursemaid do it. Now, the reconstruction is reasonably clear—I can't give you all the evidence on which I based it, but it's reasonably clear that he wouldn't let the nursemaid do it because he thought that that let his mother off the hook, and he insisted it had to be the mother [who made reparations]. That's been the transference. It mostly involves his relationship with his parents. That's still where the affect is, like with a little child. This is the kind of situation about which Anna Freud said, "But there can't be a transference neurosis. Why? Because the children are still too involved with their parents." Now, you know, of course, on another level that's incorrect. Melanie Klein was right and Anna Freud was wrong. But this is the kind of situation which gave Anna Freud that impression. He appreciates the help that he's getting. I've had an agreement with him that he sets his own fee and he set his fee as high as is feasible for him. So he thinks well of me, but not as well as I think of myself.

COMMENT: The patient only bought one copy of each of your books. He doesn't have an idealized transference.

GEDO: He bought one copy of *one* of my books.

COMMENT: When he gets all of them, the analysis will be done.

GEDO: Have I given you that impression? Jokes aside, you know that's not what I mean. When he can share my enthusiasm about truth, honor, justice, freedom, and dignity, the analysis will become workable. But he shares his father's cynicism and his mother's commitment to injustice.

Commentary (Gehrie):

This discussion is based solely on the foregoing seminar material. To take the initial referral to Gedo and its implications first, it seemed requisite that Gedo accept the referring source's implication that he (Gedo) would not be intimidated by this patient; that things intellectual were not foreign to him, especially the worlds of art and literature to which this patient aspired; that the analyst could understand the nature of the patient's ambition, and that, while the analyst was able to understand the patient's interests, it was also possible for him to remain open to the question of what the problem with the patient's ability to perform was. Was it an issue of conflicting aims, resulting in a paralyzing inhibition? Or perhaps the symptom of an underlying deficit thinly disguised by the appearance of the ability to perform? These questions follow the description of the story of the patient's "misbehavior" regarding his nursemaid at age four or five: the patient "insisted that she be fired, and she was." This view of the patient is distinctly different from that which would result from a focus on his anxiety about the loss of his mother's attention (or abandonment by her), for example, and that the demand for the baby-sitter to be fired might have been an attempt to retrieve the mother.[q] That the patient was seen as having "misbehaved" suggests a failure of both internal and external limits, and calls for an explanation of that phenomenon that includes an assessment of the early environment and the nature of the patient's adaptation to it. Many years later, at the university, the patient was similarly unable (unwilling) to need anything—or, perhaps, to permit the need to be recognized by seeking help. His self-expression again took the form of a kind of "misbehavior": although he would study some subjects, he would do so without any depth and without any real connectedness to them. Interestingly, the brother (and parental favorite, according to the patient) was the only one of the four sibs who did not attend this university. The patient's feelings on this issue found ample expression in his "murder" of the mother's dog, to which the brother was also very close.

The seminar discussion opens with Gedo's challenge about the goals of an analysis with this patient and the nature of the inherent dangers. The central question is about what constitutes real experience for this man:

Was the experience of Don Juanism "real"?[1] What about his involvement with tennis? Gedo explains that this patient gave up tennis because his heroes "wouldn't have done that," despite his own apparently quite real enjoyment of it. The patient could not experience himself as approaching the kind of existence that he idealized so long as he engaged in such activity—and a great deal fell into this category of being "not right." Extraordinary attentiveness is paid to details, but the experience of "not being right" persists. The issue, then, is not so much his capacity for real involvements as much as his sense of failure to achieve a level of performance with which he is satisfied. He is a "four-flusher" because he tries to pass as being nearly as good as the real thing, all the while he is acutely aware of his failure. Gedo selects out particularly intense points of the patient's experience to distinguish him from an "as if" character: "You could say, in a sense, that he is an 'as if' character, except for the fact that some things are not as if. Like the sadism and the masochism, like the attacks on the siblings and the murder of the dog, and the memory of the inexplicable tantrum about the governess, and the limitless ambition."

Considering that the immensity of this man's ambition was a major factor in his repetitive failures, it is noteworthy that the patient would bring in to Gedo the occasional paragraph he had written. In the absence of process data, it can only be presumed that Gedo's response to the patient on such occasions was similar to what he revealed to the seminar—that the patient "had the talent." The combination of Gedo's confidence about his own judgments—"I don't impress easily"—and his apparent willingness to convey to the patient his sense of the patient's latent capacity must have contributed to the powerful bond that was the only hope for the analysis: that the analyst was available to be used in the service of determining what was real.

The intervening discussion about the patient's finances also addresses the issue of his unused capacities. His parents are not opposed to analysis so long as he is—in their terms—productive while he is in it. The story of the family financial history is complex and dominated by the patient's apparent confusion about how much or what monies were in fact his own. The patient's initial view was that the father was entirely in control, and "would only give him [the patient] money if he did exactly as the father wanted." Gedo reports that after two years the patient had changed his "paranoid" view of his father and was able to recognize the reality of the father's intention. This was accomplished by Gedo's insisting that the patient actually check out the situation with his father in a realistic way, to confront his "paranoid" and "delusional" notions. Obviously, this is out-of-the-ordinary technique, used here by Gedo in view of the patient's inability to utilize interpretations about his feelings toward the father. The danger of such an approach could be twofold: first, analytic neutrality was seriously jeopardized, (in the sense that the analyst overtly placed himself on one side of the issue), and, second, such an intervention might force an enactment in the transference. It is always intriguing at these junctures to speculate on alternative approaches. What if, instead of insisting on this "reality testing," Gedo had focused solely on the patient's experience of the father as a transference issue? Gedo suggests strongly that this tack would not have been productive inasmuch as the patient seemed unable to "entertain the possibility" that there was a transference involved. If the purpose of maintaining analytic neutrality is to attempt to preserve the opportunity for some subsequent interpretation of the transference, then Gedo's technique relies heavily on the analyst's judgment that in all likelihood there is no such transference or that the possibility for its interpretation is unlikely ever to emerge.

This is a profound clinical judgment that has the effect of committing the analysis to a certain course, in this instance that the nature of the underlying pathology is such that ordinary techniques will be of no avail.[s] Gedo's technique, then, presumes that, although the patient possesses the capacity to understand, he was so traumatically and repetitively overstimulated that he must avoid contact with underlying experience. Gedo, therefore, interferes actively with this [mal]adaptive remedy to overstimulation (especially since Gedo himself is becoming affected by it: "And by that time I'm ready to scream") by intruding into the obsessional attempts to self-soothe. He tells the patient that they must have "an agreement" about, say, which color of shoes to purchase because "in order to continue to work with him, to save my sanity, I needed that." This was Gedo's attempt to save an analysis that, he felt, otherwise would have foundered on the same rocks that had damaged the patient's life in so many ways; the underlying trauma made it impossible for him to go beyond this particular form of self-regulation.

Gedo imposed a solution to maintain the possibility of a relationship. They agreed "on certain provisional, reasonable procedures" in order that the analysis could proceed. It was, Gedo noted, "in the spirit of offering him a prosthesis." It could be argued that Gedo's judgment was impaired by his countertransference, that the patient's obsessions entangled the analyst in a web of his own ambivalences, making it impossible to cut through the resistance without an enactment. Two previous attempts at analysis had failed, and clearly this third attempt was already endangered. Gedo's presumption was that these symptoms were not defensive against an underlying conflict, but rather that they constituted a (faulty) restorative effort to maintain some self-integration despite "empty clouds of doubt."

What are the consequences of such an intervention? Does the analyst risk becoming the "guidebook" for the patient's life? If it is true that "behind his façade . . . he really knew nothing," then to continue to interpret symbolic conflict would be useless. Worse, it would demand a compliant response or precipitate flight from the analysis. Gedo's choices were either to continue indefinitely participating with the patient's symptoms, hoping that the relationship would offer some (other) opportunity for intervention, or to attempt to cut through the flawed bandage, in the hope of dramatically establishing a new opportunity. As he states, "I did not treat this phenomenon as a resistance [to be interpreted]."

Gedo's intervention might also be considered as a form of empathic mirroring to enable the patient to begin to take steps on his own behalf on the basis of the groundwork provided in a selfobject transference (Kohut, 1971, 1977). Gedo's ability and willingness to provide direct assistance to this patient with a developmental aim in mind appears to meet this definition, but Gedo's view is that this "assistance" was not in the service of providing a nurturant environment per se but, rather, amounted to the direct supplying of a missing piece of structure. This kind of action has a different implication functionally: it presumes the absence of capacity in this area of the personality, rather than an immaturity or incomplete development which could conceivably be stimulated into spontaneous growth via a selfobject transference. It is not possible, of course, to be certain about the actuality of this patient's structural capacities in retrospect, but only to attempt to assess the consequences of having handled the situation the way that it was done. In tandem with his approach, Gedo's diagnosis was of "an early arrest of development . . . he functioned like a small child."

Gedo's approach to the meeting with the patient's father, as well as his direct instruction about the Law Review, may also be seen in the light of his conviction that this patient functioned with an adaptation to his early deficit that at this time is characterized as "fraudulent." Gedo confronted the patient's own continuing entanglement with this adaptation, which constituted a core aspect of his survival strategy, but also of his symptomatology. Gedo contends that this man needed to know that his analyst knew that he was a "fraud"; that his analyst realized that all his posturing and grandiose plans were smoke and mirrors, a scaffolding designed to support a grossly flawed underlying structure. The result was the patient's increasing genuineness with himself.

"He didn't quite grasp how fraudulent he was being, but that didn't take too long. After some weeks . . . he grasped the fact that there was no reason to pretend he was interested, and he started to take the maximum number of courses out of the law school that they permitted, and that's quite a few."

A question from the seminar here raises a fundamental issue: was this approach in essence a "holding out your hand," in which the arrested child was walked with, and provided a developmental opportunity in the context of what had (presumably) been missed in the past? Gedo replies that "it was more than that," insofar as more than a developmental opportunity must be provided in such instances. The approach must include a way of dealing with the distortions that had resulted from the developmental failures. These are not fantasy distortions in the usual sense, but rather adaptive distortions which interfere with the attempt to provide ordinary developmental assistance. Gedo addresses these adaptive distortions in a manner calculated to engage with the nature of their specific expressions: for example, this patient's need for the "glamour world":

"From the first, on an unconscious level, I responded in a way that accomplished the task [of neutralizing his depreciation]: I had a spontaneous affective response that everything I heard [about this glamorous world] was ridiculous. . . . This young man's intellectual pretensions, this business about New York, struck me as exactly that: something truly ridiculous."

It could be argued that Gedo was relying on the impact of a kind of encouraged idealization to penetrate his patient's defensive grandiosity, and that such an approach would provide an "antidote to the patient's contempt." However, another view is that such adaptive distortions ("pus from the thirty years' war against his parents") require a refusal to participate in the "fraudulence" by demonstrating "real competence" as a "reliable person" who could not be seduced into the fraudulence. Gedo argues that reality testing was crucial for this patient's ability to believe that the analysis was worth anything, and that such interventions are not authoritarian demands requiring compliance. Gedo does not advocate this approach as universally applicable, and acknowledges that "if all of this is not needed and one does it, then all of those criticisms are certainly in order." (I.e., overlooking the "hidden negative transference.") Gedo views the nature of his crucial "interpretations" as relevant precisely to the point that he would "not be fooled" by the patient's maladaptive fraudulence, and would attempt to provide a reliable reality not subject to depreciation: an authentic relationship not marred by hidden agendas or covert manipulation for other motives. Analytic neutrality, he continues, is not a fixed position for the analyst, but floats with the conditions prevalent in the patient's psyche: in this instance, the assessment that the patient's ability to analyze the transference was so impaired as to require this form of active intervention: "I performed certain functions on his behalf that were impaired for him," and acknowledges that this "foreclosed the possibility of [a mother transference] by acting so different from her." At least for the time being, this analysis sacrificed the working-through of a negative mother transference—seen by Gedo as an impossibility, given the extent of the damage—in order that certain critical functions (such as reality testing) be permitted to grow in the interaction between patient and analyst.

A comment from a seminar participant about self psychology stirred a discussion of issues which are frequently raised in the context of the analysis of patients characteristic of the "widening scope." Gedo felt that his interactions with the patient were not characterized by the evolution of an idealizing (selfobject) transference, nor would he characterize the transference that did evolve as the "therapeutic mobilization of the idealized object" (Kohut, 1971). By contrast, Gedo sees the process as one involving a "terrific struggle to overcome the defenses against idealization." This refers to his direct interference with the characterological "fraudulence" with which this patient warded off idealization. Gedo referred to this as the "nursemaid transference," because "even though he knows I am of value to him he hasn't been able to idealize [the relationship]." Gedo also feels that in this instance self-esteem regulation was not the focal issue, but rather the capacity of the patient to deal with "practical matters." His patient suffered from extensive "apraxia": the "failure to develop skills that normally are autonomous" (Gedo, 1988, p. 3). The "failure to learn adaptively essential skills" is what caused this patient to resort to "modes of behavior regulation of more archaic origin." The analyst's interventions might be characterized as "optimal disillusionment": "intended to assist the analysand in accepting the realities of his existence without being traumatized" (Gedo, 1988, p. 168). "Those things I did [for him] are unprecedented in his experience . . . he wouldn't let the nursemaid do it (i.e., teach him about reality), because he thought that let his mother off the hook." In sum, Gedo [1988] has stated:

> I realized that the psychopathology consists of more than a regressive potential that brings to the fore a mental organization that requires external assistance (Kohut's "selfobject"): most of the persons prone to regress to these archaic modes in the analytic situation have never mastered the psychological skills in question. . . . Once a holding environment has been established, we must help the analysand to *overcome* his apraxia [pp. 168–169].

To the extent that the patient "shares his father's cynicism and his mother's commitment to injustice," these early identifications form the most profound barrier against his ability to deal with reality in a more adaptive mode and form the core of the kind of issue that Gedo's approach attempts to address.

Clarifications and Addenda (Gedo)

a. The question of patient-analyst "match"

It is perfectly true, as Dr. Gehrie implies, that one source of the gratification I have continued to feel about performing this analysis is the mark of esteem that it represented on the part of the colleague who made the referral. In this regard, it is relevant that, although this was the only person this analyst ever referred to me, one of the analysands I described in detail in *Beyond Interpretation* (Gedo, 1979) had previously been in therapy with this colleague's spouse. *That* patient was widely recognized as a man of enormous talent who was unable to collaborate with anyone who was either manifestly less competent intellectually than he or felt intimidated by him. My 1979 account included some consideration of these issues, and I am confident that the referrer of *this* prospective analysand was familiar with that work. Hence, it was implicitly understood between us that I was once again being called upon to cope with the special problem of analyzing a person who might turn out to have "genius."

As I tried to show in a monograph on the problem of creativity (Gedo, 1983, see esp. chap. 6), it is expectable that the analyst (or psychotherapist) of a person capable of creative achievements will have to struggle with (possibly unconscious) envy of the patient's potentialities. This problem often leads to hostile/depreciating attitudes (analogous to those discussed in chapter 1)—these frequently echo the worst aspects of a traumatic childhood!—and a therapeutic impasse may therefore eventuate. I believe that it was information the referrer had about my previous freedom from this difficulty that led him to believe that he could "match" this patient with me. If I possess any unusual talents (to quote Gehrie), the relevant one is the pleasure I take in promoting the creativity of others.

On a more general level, I believe that the notion that the match between the participants in an analysis may be good, bad, or indifferent is a sound one. In my own case, I have been chagrined to note that I did markedly less well in assisting patients from certain demographic subgroups than I managed to do with my clientele as a whole. The idea that matching analyst and patient is an important consideration in terms of outcome is supported by the studies of Kantrowitz (1986).

b. A clinical update in mid-1992

To date, this treatment has lasted 10½ years, with no end in sight, although there have been some dreams hinting that the patient hopes to be ready to dispense with psychological assistance in the not too distant future. Obviously, progress has been excruciatingly slow, but it has been continuous, so that neither participant has ever experienced significant discouragement about prognosis. In terms of external adaptation, there have been dramatic improvements, now going well beyond the encouraging developments I tried to summarize at the end of the first session of the seminar. The major increment in well-being to take place since that report has been the consolidation of a satisfactory network of social relations (with both men and women), significantly including several friends engaged in creative endeavors, a fact suggesting that the patient is on his way to master his competitive envy. He has even succeeded in having a couple of essays published in respected journals. He is currently in love with a woman he respects, they treat each other well and are seriously discussing the possibility of getting married.

c. Masochistic submission and the course of the analysis

My initial reaction to the patient's accounts of how a sadistic virago was mistreating him was to ask for the reasons that impelled him to tolerate such abuse. In a response that proved to be quite typical for this man, he misperceived these questions as a set of explicit and concrete instructions for future conduct and abruptly severed the relationship to his tormentor. Throughout the seven years following this intervention, and about two years beyond this seminar, the patient carefully refrained from allowing anyone to abuse him—at the price of remaining emotionally distant from everyone.

Finally, he began an affair with a young woman whom he had admired (and pitied!) for many years and rapidly "fell in love" with this cold, egocentric, and controlling person. In this context, it became possible to correlate his propensity for masochistic bondage (especially vis-à-vis women who elicited pity) with his childhood relationship to his mother. Although as yet these issues have not been repeated within the analytic transference, much insight has been gained into his early life. In terms of current adaptation, this self-knowledge has led to the cessation of his (retaliatory) abuse of women. In addition, in his complex financial dealings with his father, he has become much better able to assert his rights without infringing on those of others. In parallel with this achievement, he was able to separate from his lover without much rancor. Subsequently, he has been able to enter nonmasochistic relationships with women.

d. On treating the sisters as nonexistent

Reviewing the record of the seminar, I am struck by my failure to say anything about the patient's two sisters—and the willingness of the class participants to let the matter rest there. Outwardly, the sisters led conventional lives as upper middle-class married women with children; if they were adversely affected by the family environment, this deleterious influence manifested itself only in the form of their adherence to rather unusual religious beliefs and rituals without precedent in the family. Both women, however, appeared very childlike to my patient. He regarded them as naive, unsophisticated, and unnaturally dependent on their parents (and spouses). Consequently, he felt both pity and contempt for them; in his eyes, they counted for nothing.

It was this attitude that was mirrored in the seminar by my implicit choice to treat the sisters as people not worth mentioning. Needless to say, the patient's attitude of superiority vis-à-vis most women can be seen as a sister transference.

e. A basic defect in the psychological repertory

In terms of fulfilling any of his genuine aspirations, the patient has been incapacitated by a severe learning block manifested as an inability to study, especially to read. As he kept reporting his repeated attempts to overcome this problem, it gradually became clear that this difficulty did not simply reflect his negativism. It is true that, in response to external pressures, he was almost always uncooperative. He did not, however, regard the task of confronting literary classics as *assignments*—mostly, he was not conflicted about wanting to tackle these readings. All too often, though, he found that he fell asleep within a few minutes of starting such work.

It took many years of analytic observation finally to reach the conclusion that the crucial factor affecting his ability to read was the emotional effect of the material involved. He was able to continue only if that effect was congruent with his predominant psychological needs of the moment. As an example, much of the time he felt in urgent need of being *soothed*; if the text he was reading (or music to which he was exposed) was not suited to this aim, he was utterly unable to attend to it. In other words, his somnolence was an avoidant defense, one focused on perception itself. He seldom had the luxury of being able to allow himself to be swayed by the emotions works of art are intended to evoke.

As I understand this syndrome, it is the legacy of dire failures in early emotional attunement that leave the person with practically no margin for accommodation to extrinsic emotional stimulation. His consequent handicaps as a student constitute the kind of limitation in psychological skills that I call an "apraxia" (Gedo, 1988, chaps. 12-14). In my judgment, as long as such a person is so handicapped, he is likely to resort to grandiose fantasies to restore self-esteem. Hence I have concluded that, in cases with

significant apraxic difficulties, therapeutic success is contingent on
helping the patient to identify and overcome the deficiencies in psychological skills. With this particular patient, the necessary first step in this
process was to help him to focus on his baseline emotional state, thereby
to avoid putting himself in the impossible position of attempting to do
intellectual work while in the throes of a psychological emergency to
which he has refused to attend.

*f. The necessity to repair apraxia and the analysand's freedom
of choice*

One candidate's comment that dealing with the characterological obsta-
cles to the performance of the analytic task amounts to *interference* with
the analysand's freedom of action is a fairly common response to the
recommendation to deal with certain resistances and destructive enactments not by means of interpreting the motives for them (or not by such
measures exclusively), but through various measures intended to set
limits. Frequent though responses such as this candidate's are, they
amount to a serious misconception—one I tried to overcome by pointing
out that, for someone incapable of appropriate self-regulation, the offer of
external limits provides a welcome potentiality to master perplexity.

Should the *analysand* experience the delineation of reasonable limits as
interference with his or her autonomy—a complication I have encountered on occasion, although not frequently—it is relatively easy to make
clear that the choice is (naturally!) entirely up to the patient, but that the
expectable consequences of abiding by the limits proposed increase the
chances of analytic success. The situation is entirely homologous with our
routine recommendations for such features of the psychoanalytic setting
as the use of the couch or the importance of frequent appointments. As
general experience has demonstrated, it is rare for analysands to defy
such dictates of common sense or to experience these prescriptions as
infringements on their autonomy. Ultimately, users of professional services do understand that either one accepts the advice of an expert or, if
one will not, it makes sense to abandon the collaboration.

As for the rationale for my particular recommendation to this patient
to simplify his life in order to avoid filling his sessions with empty
obsessing about a superfluity of choices, my own intolerance for disor-
dered thought processes of that kind was only one reason among many. It
was equally important to provide this man with tools he did not possess to
help him to cut short the endless spinning of this broken record. As Gehrie
points out in his Commentary, my intervention was based on having
decided (on grounds I shall specify later) that the obsessional phenomena

did not constitute resistance: they were the end-products of disorganization. In other words, this patient needed to learn better ways to reorganize himself than this version of the "he loves me/he loves me not" ritual.
Hence, when I outlined ways in which he could cut short his obsessing, I
gave him new opportunities to overcome an apraxia.

g. *Diagnosis of the nadir of the regressive potential*

I had heard about the patient's disorganization when he went abroad, as
well as a number of similar stories about episodes of regressive incapac-
itation in circumstances that presented him with a novel challenge he had
to face on his own, before I felt confident that the obsessional behavior I
was observing in my consulting room amounted to a regressive collapse
rather than a successful defensive effort. It is, of course, impossible to cite
the innumerable bits of evidence that pointed toward this conclusion;
suffice it to note here that no amount of such evidence can be *conclusive*.
Our choice of intervention cannot be based on convincing proofs—nor is
it terribly important to make the right choice on one's first attempt.

What *is* essential—and this is just as true if we choose to make an
interpretation of the defensive motive behind a pattern of behavior as it is
if we decide on an intervention "beyond interpretation" (Gedo, 1979)—is
to observe carefully the effects of one's intervention. The nature of these
effects will generally show whether the choice of therapeutic modality is
correct or not. If a patient is mired in helpless perplexity, interpretations
of motives for such behavior must of necessity fall on deaf ears, whereas
effective guidelines for clearing up the confusion will be eagerly espoused. (Witness, for example, the manner in which my patient perceived
my question about reasons for tolerating abuse as if it had been a
prescription to avoid it, thereby short-circuiting a pattern of destructive
enactments. In that instance, I had not intended to relieve his perplexity,
but he was able to use the *purport* of my question as an indication of the
dictates of common sense.) If, on the other hand, one extends concrete
assistance to someone who could cope without it (i.e., someone who
actually needs to grasp the defensive significance of apparent helplessness), sooner or later a reaction to the depreciation of the analysand
implicit in such underestimation of his or her resources should surface—
most likely in the form of a dream.

Conversely, when an interpretation of defense is on the mark, the
behavior in question is usually altered as a result of the intervention; if the
interpretation is based on an overestimation of the analysand's resources,
what will soon surface is profound anger (and/or disappointment in
analysis). Unfortunately, it is all too easy to deny that such reactions are
appropriate responses to our therapeutic errors.

h. Competitive issues in the transference

In connection with the patient's emulation of my interest in the visual arts, we have gained insight into certain aspects of the father transference, for he experienced some anxiety about the fact that he had at his disposal many more resources for his activities as a collector than I had been able (or at least willing) to devote to the acquisition of the art he saw in my office. In this context, he was able to share with me his gleeful fantasies that his activities as a Don Juan far outshone his father's sexual experiences. To date, these traces of anxiety-laden phallic competitiveness have constituted derivatives of the most mature level of psychosexual development he appears to have attained. It is therefore most likely that he suffered an arrest in development at early stages of the oedipal period. In terms of the hierarchical model of psychic functioning (Gedo and Goldberg, 1973), he seemed to be arrested at the level of transition between modes III and IV.

Incidentally, the manner in which these issues came to light is a good illustration of what makes this man intimidating: it is, indeed, easy enough to fall into envy (and malice!) vis-à-vis someone who can outbid the Louvre at a public auction. Perhaps it was fortunate that I do not happen to prefer the kind of art the patient chose to buy—or, to put this differently, that I am satisfied that in my own collecting I have obtained value for my money . . .

i. The question of the typical situation of danger

My statement that the patient's severe anxiety when he is challenged to behave in an adult manner could not "exactly" be pinned down to the developmental level wherein castration is the typical situation of danger (mode III in the hierarchical schema) is entirely reasonable when one is dealing with isolated segments of behavior—the mode of psychic functioning that yields a specific behavioral result is always very difficult to ascertain. I was confident that the patient did not experience anxiety concerning the violation of internal standards (typical of mode IV), because through seven years of analytic observation I had never encountered such a conflict on his part. Behind his seeming fear of retaliation, however, this man appears to harbor more primitive anxieties: he was unable to imagine any possibility of existence outside the orbit of his family of origin, as if he were bound to be overwhelmed by such a challenge. (Anxieties about such issues are referable to mode I and/or II.)

My impression at the time of the seminar has been more than substantiated by the evidence brought to light more recently. We have encountered the severe problem of *separation guilt* (Modell, 1965) that produced the developmental arrest in early childhood. The conflict inherent in such a problem is not the intersystemic tension postulated in Freud's (1923) tripartite model (i.e., it is not referable to mode IV): in such cases, a symbiotic mode of existence is one of the basic building-blocks of identity. (In my preferred vocabulary, a lack of autonomous functioning has high priority in the self-organization.) Hence, any necessity to behave in an autonomous manner threatens the integrity of the personality; because the differentiation between self and object has been compromised, this threat is automatically externalized and mobilizes whatever restraints on hostile aggression have been acquired. (In this sense, the term "separation guilt" is something of a misnomer.)

j. Grandiosity and the incapacity to learn

Apparently the patient was unable to learn from his previous analysts because he armored himself against their influence through a fantasied merger with a grandiose, glamorous world. (The emotional situation was comparable to that in which narcissistically injured people are able to boost their self-esteem by joining movements such as National Socialism.) I have ever looked upon the particular milieu this analysand had joined as pretentious, phony, and worthless, so that no effort on my part was needed to convey that I was *unfavorably* impressed by such an identification. Because it was *my* attitude to which he was steadily exposed, the patient was unable to withstand this negative reinforcement, and his grandiosity was thereby undermined. In order to accomplish this noninterpretive maneuver, it is necessary to feel free to make certain value judgments and to share these with one's patients: "Joining the Ship of Fools is as dangerous as using cocaine!"

Obviously, puncturing one specific grandiose fantasy will not do away with a person's need to boost self-esteem through fantasied mergers with idealized others, and the manner in which I punctured this patient's grandiosity allowed him temporarily to place me in the position of an adopted *guru*. In the course of our lengthy collaboration, there have been numerous opportunities to attempt to undo this "parameter of technique" (Eissler, 1953) by means of interpretation (including explicit statements of the rationale for discrediting his previous *gurus* in this manner). In the meantime, the analysand was more or less willing to use me as a resource person from whom he could learn. I emphasize that this readiness to be instructed was limited and tenuous, because the patient's idealization of his parents (reactive to a prior disillusionment) continued unbroken. Adherence to the Ship of Fools had merely patched this adaptation in a few places where it had broken down. Ultimately, he began to show contempt for me as a major transference development; this contempt turned out to constitute an early identification with his mother's megalomania.

k. A hierarchical view of the clinical situation

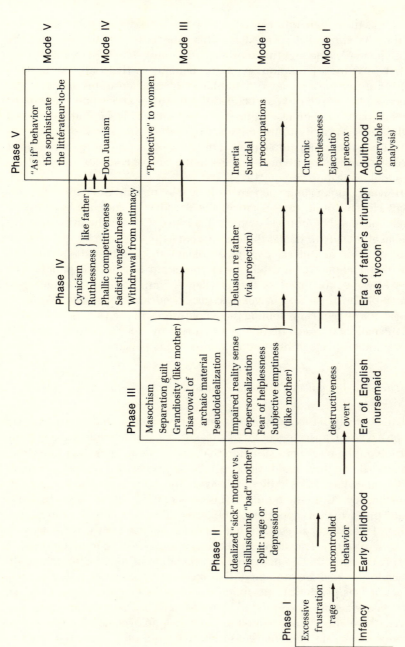

Figure 1. A Hierarchical View of the Clinical Data in Gedo's Case

l. Pseudoidealization and its consequences

Insofar as the patient differentiated his parents from each other, it was his mother he continued to idealize. This differentiation was in part the consequence of the fact that mother had always shared her caustic view of her husband's limitations with the patient, so that only the father's success in business escaped debunking. (In this sense, my irony at the expense of the Ship of Fools echoed the mother's attacks on the father.) For her part, mother was utterly intolerant of criticism and responded with intense hostility to the mildest implication that she was imperfect. Thus the patient had ample reason to erect a reaction formation against his disillusionment with her—leading to the kind of complex attitude I call "pseudoidealization" (Gedo, 1975).

However ambivalent such an attitude may be (and the patient's grievances clearly found expression in the decades of guerrilla warfare he waged against his mother—witness his murder of her beloved dog!), at one level it leads to denial that the parent's qualities are less than ideal. Thus the mother's severe psychopathology—the fact that she had lapsed into being almost completely inert sometime during the patient's latency—was rationalized as the privilege of an aristocrat; a failure to remember to tip a taxi driver was disguised as the prerogative to be capricious or arbitrary. Joining the whole family in such a denial of reality led the patient to assert his own entitlements by identifying with the most devastating aspects of his mother's impaired behavior.

m. The issue of choice in evoking a particular transference

Relatively early in this analysis, I gained the conviction that the emergence of the earliest transferences (involving either parent) would put a greater burden on the treatment situation than the patient's shaky confidence in the analytic method could support. I therefore decided that, if it were at all feasible, I would tilt the analysis in the direction of some *positive* transference. At the time I made this choice, I did not yet know that this would prove to be a repetition of the transactions with the English nanny. In fact, I was not at all certain that I could avoid the early emergence of a difficult negative transference, however I chose to conduct myself. I merely believed that, pending the consolidation of the analysand's confidence in the analytic method and in me as a reliable and skilled professional, it was prudent to postpone the stresses of reliving the patient's early years, which I expected to prove to have been nightmarish.

As I have already mentioned (see note c.), an archaic maternal transference eventually did emerge; in line with the tilt I had introduced in assuming the role of "reliable caretaker," both the erotic and the hostile aspects of these early transactions were relived in relation to a third person. Even at that relatively late stage of the treatment, it was barely possible to transcend this transference crisis without an actual catastrophe (most likely a suicide attempt), and I am not at all certain that the outcome would have been favorable if the analysand had reexperienced his childhood despair as a result of *my* disappointing him. Whether the therapeutic outcome will be fully satisfactory if these issues are dealt with only in this "displaced" manner is an empirical question the answer to which must await termination.

n. The struggle against idealization

As I have mentioned, as a child this patient refused to acknowledge his mother's severe impairment as a caretaker, erected reaction formations against his disappointment, turned against potential mother substitutes, and identified with mother's pathological behavior on the basis of the delusion that it represented superiority. This fantastic (and disastrous!) misconstruction of the world coexisted with the split-off disillusionment and the boundless rage this disillusionment provoked, much of which was acted out without conscious awareness of what this activity was about. It was this complex set of psychological dispositions that was repeated in the analytic transference—a circumstance to which the term "transference of defense," much used in the Chicago psychoanalytic community a generation ago, applies rather well.

Although the patient acknowledged that I was helpful and competent, and therefore superior to the false prophets he had followed to New York, his attitudes toward me did not reflect early childhood idealization. He was very much aware of my manifold imperfections and, on balance, more embarrassed about having such a prosaic and old-fashioned person as an instructor than he was gratified by our association. This was particularly true early in the analysis, when, because of his financial uncertainties, I charged him a very modest fee. In the world of his father, *only* money can talk!

o. Primary identifications and the issue of apraxia

I do not mean to imply that this analysand's parents were less effective than are other people in transmitting their way of life to their children. Of course he *had* learned their procedures in using the services of interior decorators (or doctors, lawyers, and Indian chiefs). In following their methods, however, my patient got into a great deal of trouble: the top-flight professionals he now wanted to employ were simply unwilling to be capriciously second-guessed, cynically treated as commercially fraudulent, arbitrarily overruled, and so on. He eventually asked me to specify a better way of conducting these transactions because I was consistent in confronting him with the ill effects of using his faulty methods.

At the same time, these faulty interpersonal relationships were simply the consequences of his primary identifications with his parents, and, in order to learn better ways, he had to acknowledge that his family's dealings with people were bizarre and counterproductive. Hence, my focus on the patient's difficulties about elementary practical matters led very directly to central issues in his psychological makeup: his pseudoidealization of his family and his struggle against idealizing worthier individuals. This analytic work did not directly lead to his idealizing either me or his architect—but he did get along sufficiently well with the latter to have formed a valuable friendship. Neither of his parents had ever made friends with anyone outside of the extended family.

p. The compulsion to be helpful to needy women

In the love affair that echoed the patient's early relationship to his mother, it became clear that the distress of someone he loved filled him with pity and impelled him to rescue the other person by asking nothing and giving whatever the afflicted person demanded. An expectable complication of such a pattern of relating is that the patient's self-esteem depends on his success in these hopeless endeavors.

By dint of persistent analytic work, we have been able to clarify that the source of the patient's boundless anger is his grievance about the indefinite prolongation of a lack of mutuality in *caring* in these relationships. This is the dynamic that then fuels his sadistic perversion.

The next attempt the patient made to form a stable relationship to a woman involved a decent but very inhibited person who, once again, was unable to reciprocate his affection. In this instance, the patient became keenly aware of the negative side of his ambivalence; instead of erecting loving reaction formations, he was inwardly enraged by his partner's inability to satisfy his longings for warmth and overt expressions of personal regard. At the same time, he was able to contain his anger and to refrain from taking revenge through spitefulness, as he had always done vis-à-vis his mother. He understood quite clearly that his expectations, though perfectly routine and reasonable, lay beyond his lover's capacity to fulfill. Consequently, he was able to discontinue this affair without rancor or injury to anyone's self-esteem.

q. Addressing the behavior disorder

As Mark Gehrie points out, I am opposed to the therapeutic tactic, strongly endorsed by many self psychologists, of focusing on the (subjectively justified) grievances that lead to rageful destructiveness. These tactics are generally recommended because they are alleged to be more "empathic" than are other choices at the analyst's disposal. Naturally, most patients are highly gratified by such an endorsement of their position (and sanction for their vengefulness), and this satisfaction is likely momentarily to dispel their rage—particularly in the analytic setting. At the same time, such a transaction tends to encourage the continued acting out of hostile impulses. Hence I regard the policy of endorsing the analysand's entitlement to rageful misbehavior as the siren song of unreason—and therefore as an instance of pseudoempathy.

In my view, the task of analysis is to assist patients to cope better with stressful situations (even those that echo the stresses of early childhood). Such a program cannot be fulfilled simply by providing a stress-free milieu in the treatment setting, however helpful and soothing a diminution of stress may be in the short run. In this connection, it is well to recall the follow-up studies of the Kantrowitz group (1990), who found that analyses conducted in what they termed a "soft" manner had a tendency to undermine superego standards. In other words, as regards outcome of treatment, one should assess the totality of adaptive changes (including the unfavorable ones) instead of focusing exclusively on the patient's subjective state.

Having said all that, I must also emphasize that a focus on a patient's behavior disorder does not preclude consideration of the childhood circumstances that gave rise to it (parental neglect, for example). It is also reasonable to point out that neither in childhood nor in the present (i.e., within the transference) is misbehavior likely to attain the aims the child may naively have had in mind for it (such as my patient's effort to force his mother to stop delegating caretaking functions to the hired help).

r. The authenticity of experience

With patients as close to complete depersonalization as my analysand was, it is urgent to establish as quickly as possible which experiences yield genuine pleasure or pain. This knowledge permits the analyst to begin to challenge those activities that are inauthentic—those carried on merely for their connotations, "as if" the patient were someone else. In the case under discussion, success as a Don Juan did not represent genuine sexual excitement or pleasure, but it did yield some real gratification of competitive strivings, and it was a direct expression of profound sadism. Similarly, the patient's athletic activities gave him real pleasure, both bodily and psychologically, but these considerations were outweighed by his humilation as a result of departing from the meretricious ideals he had adopted.

s. The nature of psychopathology and the choice of analytic technique

Despite the accumulation of evidence about the archaic nature of the patient's difficulties and the complete absence of useful behaviors referable to more mature modes of functioning, the decision to conduct this analysis on the assumption that the overall problem was best conceptualized as an arrest of development (as I have already stated, at the point of transition between modes III and IV) remained a matter of clinical judgment. Because an absence of evidence does not correspond to proof of a null hypothesis, the possibility of more mature sectors of the personality being masked by a regression can *never* be ruled out.

Therefore, the choice of analytic strategy must be dictated by a consideration of the relative risks entailed by making the wrong choice in either direction. My own clinical experiences (as well as follow-up studies such as that of Firestein [1978; see also Gedo, 1980]) have led me to conclude that it is more dangerous to overlook archaic pathology than it is to underestimate the analysand's capacities. Consequently, whenever the ultimate diagnosis is still in doubt, I choose what I regard as the more prudent and conservative course, that of assuming the worst of the severity of pathology. I have found that if such a choice proves to be in error—a conclusion that will emerge sooner or later if one is alert to indications in the material that the analysand feels depreciated or infantilized—it is relatively easy to acknowledge one's mistake and to change tactics. In my experience, such minor misadventures have never interfered with carrying analyses to successful termination. I believe that all of my analytic failures came about because I *underestimated* the severity of the psychopathology and adhered too closely to traditional techniques.

3

An Analytic Approach to the Treatment of Massive Developmental Arrest

Introduction (Gehrie)

Apart from the case offered by Gedo, this presentation is the only one in this volume made by a graduate analyst. About two and a half years after the original seminar, the same case was discussed in a faculty study group; that recorded session is included as a "follow-up."

In this case, the borderlands of analytic territory are explored. Every ordinary venue of the analytic context is challenged and breached, every usual indication for analysis is set aside. As suggested in the transcript of the seminar discussion, the question of whether such a relation can be correctly characterized as analysis at all is properly raised. In the process of examining the nature of our doubts, however, a number of central issues arise about analysis in the more general sense, and we are forced to address pivotal questions about technique that we often manage to side-step.

At the outset, the patient was "about 40," a woman who "thought she wanted analysis" and who was in the midst of her graduate studies in social work. Her training was clinically oriented, but her dissertation research was "not therapeutic." She was divorced, with two daughters in their early and midteens. Apparently, the fact that someone the patient respected had recommended analysis for her and had referred her to this analyst was of paramount importance—as will be gleaned from the discussion. "Someone" had said that this was what she needed, and in that emotional context the transference to the analyst was immediate and consistent with what we will come to understand as this woman's global orientation in close relations: an overarching need to feel taken care of and responded to without reservation. Her needs in this dimension were for an unencumbered realness of responsiveness from the analyst, a realness measurable in terms of the analyst's emotionality and distinctly not in his devotion to the analytic task as he (at least initially) understood it. This issue of "what is real" forms a core for the understanding of the task of this treatment, and the analyst's attempt to address it while maintaining analytic goals becomes the focus of the technical questions.

The patient has one sibling, a brother three years and two months younger. Shortly after the brother's birth, the father, who had been inducted into the army, was sent overseas for seven or eight months; during this period he had an acute psychotic episode. For some substantial interval during this time, there was no contact with the father, and the mother presumed him to be dead or missing. Upon the father's return from overseas, he was psychiatrically hospitalized for several weeks. It seems clear that during this time of trouble immediately following the birth of the brother and father's departure, both the patient and her mother suffered critical depressive reactions.

First Session

> PRESENTER: I picked this woman [for discussion] because she presents a number of technical difficulties and challenges. I met her over five years ago; she was about 40 at that time. I think I was out of the Institute about two years, and a private analytic case was not the commonest [event in] my career at that point.
>
> She thought she wanted analysis. Someone she respected had recommended that to her; that's who referred her to me. But she said it as if she [hoped] I would help her find somebody because, clearly, I was far too busy myself—being such a prominent person— to have time for her, but perhaps I knew [someone]. And I wasn't thinking in those terms myself, but I happened to have some time to start with her. I think that this is an important aspect of her presentation of her character, of her style of interaction: maybe I might have some time for her, but probably not.
>
> She's a very pleasant looking, sort of pretty, but somewhat undistinguished looking, woman, unremarkable looking. At the time she started with me she was in the midst of her Ph.D. work in social service. I think she had finished her courses and was working on some research. After that she started to do some clinical work in therapy, but her research was not therapeutic; it wasn't a clinical matter that she was working on.

She was divorced, and she had two children, girls. The older must have been 16 and the younger about 13 or 14. She lived in the same neighborhood I lived in, [but] I didn't know her and never heard of her, didn't know anything about her. The thing that stands out in my mind in terms of events was the first vacation, which would have been about five months [after starting]. As was her usual routine, she went to visit her mother who lived in the southwest; this woman grew up there, in a small town. She would always visit her mother for vacations, and there was an expectation that she would at some time return [there] and look after her mother in [the latter's] old age. [It was also expected] that she should spend all her vacation time with her mother, so that's what she did. The mother was a widow at this point. The patient has a younger brother, three years younger, who lives within maybe 200 miles of the mother.

So she went back to the town where she grew up, I don't remember exactly how it happened—she must have looked up a man she had gone out with in high school whom she hadn't seen since college; it was 20 years since she had seen [him]. And this man was married; he was unhappy or at least frustrated in his mar-riage—he could have no children with his wife. And the upshot of it was that he had a houseboat on a lake nearby, and they spent time together and she went to bed with him. I think she had been sexually involved with him in college but had had no contact since. When she came back, one of the interpretations I made was that this [man] was a substitute for me. She was somewhat insulted by this but wasn't really angry and didn't believe it or see it as a useful [intervention].

A period went on with this woman in which the most important [transaction] was that I "forgot" her. I would forget about her. I would never forget things about her when she was there, but she would never come to mind in the thinking about one's patients that one does, wondering about sessions, and wondering what did this mean and that mean, and so on. [Alone] of all the patients I saw, she would somehow be in the shadows of my mind, a rather undistin-guished, unremarkable woman.

Somewhere, a year and a half into the analysis, she discovered that she had a small mass in one breast. She had a biopsy. The mass was malignant, and so she had a mastectomy on one side and then, several months later, she had to have a mastectomy on the other side, and then she had reconstructive surgery. So we went through a period of maybe a year and a half in which I continued to see her four times a week, but the mode of operation really changed very drastically. I visited her in the hospital; she was surprised that I would want to do that. When I went to visit her—I think I went twice—one of the times I didn't prearrange that I would come to see her, but I called her from the front desk to make sure that she wanted me to come up at that point, because I felt that it would be very intrusive suddenly to appear. She said no, that she was very uncomfortable physically and this was not a good time. I did see her subsequently and that was fine.

There were two things about this experience that she talked about in retrospect. One was that I [had thought] about how she might be feeling, that that was a relevant consideration, and that she had the right to say that it wasn't a very good [time]. The other was that of all the people who visited her in the hospital, and there were many, there were only three who would move the chair that was there closer to the bed. Her two children were the other two, and I was the third.

She had a very difficult time around this surgery. She had, in fact, some very serious physical reactions postoperatively, with precipitous blood pressure drops, and she felt reluctant to have the second [operation]. She felt, "Why fight this?"; it's probably going to kill her, she's going to die of cancer. And I took [the] stance that she shouldn't do that; she should do what she could for herself. The prognosis was not so bad. In fact, that's what her surgeons told her, that the lesions were small. I think she had some metastasis to the lymph nodes, but not very much, and [the doctors] were optimistic. Similar things came up around the reconstructive surgery, that that felt horribly humiliating to her, she could do it only by almost depersonalizing herself, that she'd go through it, let the surgeon do whatever he thought he should do. But she went through that. She had trouble for a couple of years in keeping the follow-up appointments. There were some issues around bleeding from the cervix, and there was concern that there would be metastasis to the uterus. So there was quite a bit of reluctance, but she stuck with it, and I think she's probably at the point [now] where she's out of danger. I don't know that it's been an issue for several years. But there was a period of time [when] I think that was the main focus.

Another complication was that inadvertently our lives began to be a little more connected. One of her daughters, who was a year older than my daughter, turned up in the same high school. Although they were [in different classes] they were in the choir together. And they both befriended a man, a young fellow who played the piano for the choir, so he would be at our house because my daughter would have him over, and he'd be at their house because her daughter would have him home. And then somehow or other they figured out that I was her therapist. I don't think my daughter ever knew anything about this, but the patient's daughter and this fellow knew. And then there was a choir concert; actually it was a dinner at Christmas time. They had a dinner, with the choir singing, and I sat at the same long table with my wife and I don't remember who else, my mother-in-law, I'm not sure. And the patient and her mother—we were at a table roughly [six feet long] and we saw each other and said hello. When the analysis refocused *as* an analysis, the issue . . .

GEDO: I object, I object![a]

PRESENTER: Okay. I knew you would. There's one other event [that was] very important to her. There was a meeting at the Drake Hotel, the Analytic Society's regional meeting. I can't remember which one it was, but I had some official role. And I remember going for a walk around the Drake Hotel during one of the breaks, walking along very preoccupied, and it turned out—I didn't see her. The patient and her mother were coming out of her plastic surgeon's office just as I walked by, and she had an [almost] overwhelming, but not quite overwhelming, urge to reach out her hand toward me. She wanted to, but she didn't, and she also felt I didn't want to see her because I gave her no recognition at all. I remember puzzling over that. I had no awareness that she was there.

But the really difficult matters were the following. One was the gifts. She began to bring me a gift at Christmas, and the [gift was] flowers. For two or three years she brought me roses at Christmastime, the number of roses matching the number of years we had been working together. And then she discovered a flower shop that had [particularly] lovely and unusual flowers, and she stopped the roses and brought some of these particularly exquisite flowers at Christmas. There had been a fantasy since she learned from [her daughter's friend] about my interest in the piano that she was going to buy me a wonderful piano. When I began to make interpretations to her about feelings about me that I thought were [repeating] feelings from her past, her response was and almost to this day remains, "Oh, that means it's a transference. That means it's not real. That means we have no relationship. This would also be tied up in what happens after I finish with you. That means if we ever meet again, we never have any contact whatsoever, if I can't talk with you about a case" (her work had gotten her more into work that's comparable to what I'm doing), "I can't see you, I can't do anything with you. That means we have no relationship now," which gets connected to feeling that she's going to kill herself, that she has no connection to anybody and that she never did have any connection to anyone.[b]

Frequently, when she [was] in this frame of mind, she would tell me about her intentions—[perhaps] not her intentions, but her very clear notion about driving her car into a concrete pillar or whatever. She had told me that as a teenager she would race her car 100 miles an hour on a back road, and she was very envious of the boys who would drag race out on the back roads. I later learned that, [with] tremendous effort on her part, she had hoarded 100 [sleeping] pills, that she had these. And that she had had the thought for a long time that she was going to kill herself, long before she met me [but] that she had an obligation, really a sacred duty and an obligation to see her children to their 21st year and then she was going to kill herself.

GEDO: So how old is the youngest now?

PRESENTER: Eighteen. I don't think she's in danger. [Let me go] back into history. She had, I think, truly been in love with a fellow, not the man that she slept with that one time, but she had been in love with another man in high school and in college. There was a great deal of back and forth between them, [but] she wouldn't marry him because she didn't trust herself to be able to really love him reliably and be a wife to him in the way she felt that he deserved. And so she did not marry him. He persisted in trying to persuade her, but he couldn't; she wouldn't marry him.

She went to college in the south. She became a social worker. She went north and got a master's degree in psychiatric social work. She did some special studies with someone who's written a fair amount about schizophrenia and had a substantial reputation. She did very well. She was involved in some group therapy because she did erratically as a student in graduate school and someone suggested it. In the midst of the therapy she got involved sexually with one of the other patients. I remember [that] when I heard that I started thinking about her tendency to act out and whether she's really a treatable patient. I think I was very concerned about doing things according to the book and whether she was capable of doing that.

She married a man about ten years older who had been married before. His wife had left him abruptly; I think the wife was pretty sick. It was very devastating because she took their son, and he didn't get to see his son for a long time. He sounds [as if] he was a very rigid, rather cold man. I don't think [the patient] ever loved him. She was dutiful, and certainly she experienced sex as a duty. This was similar to her mother's view about sex: it was the wife's duty, but men are really barbaric. They have these needs, which shows that women are stronger than men, and you just let them have their way periodically, not too often, but periodically. That was what mother would say. At some point [the patient] found the marriage more and more intolerable; [her husband] seemed to care less and less about her, [about] what was interesting to her. He [belittled] her efforts when she decided to return to school when her children were old enough for her to do that. Yet, she did *extremely* well in graduate school.

COMMENT: May I ask a question? Did she derive any pleasure or satisfaction or any excitement [from] her children growing up?

PRESENTER: I think she derived satisfaction, I don't know about excitement.

COMMENT: Well, excitement is the word I'm interested in.

PRESENTER: No, I don't think excitement. I didn't see any excitement. Pleasure. Her children, especially the older one, did extremely well in many ways; she was very, very well regarded, a very nice girl. So [the patient] gets pleasure and some satisfaction; she could give, but not receive. I think she could feel important and valuable. She can clearly see the contribution she was making to her children's lives; that was good, but not excitement. But she felt the marriage became more and more intolerable and insisted that he leave, and she felt very guilty about that; [she felt] that she was a very, very bad person, that she had taken his family away from him and that she shouldn't have done it.

There was a lot of discussion about how she managed the divorce proceedings, that she just wanted him to leave and she wanted nothing from him, nothing. And he was doing very well; he was making a lot of money. He's continued to make a great deal of money. And she had no income and had no prospects of an income at that point, but she wanted to be on her own entirely to raise these children. Fortunately her lawyer protected her against [her self-restrictions], because she couldn't possibly have done it. He forced her to take a different position, and he would have to coach her as to what to say and what not to say, and she would have to steel herself to act the role that he had prescribed for her so that they could work out that the husband would in fact pay child support and whatever else. And the husband has. He never spoke to her again, but he has honored every agreement to the letter. She made a few overtures to [resume] some kind of relationship. She's continued to be friendly with her ex-husband's mother, and, in fact, they go to the opera together.

Now, the other thing [to be mentioned] is her past relationships, with her family and her parents. One of the major themes was her rage at her mother, her terrible anger toward mother and her thinking [that] her mother was just worthless. [Yet these statements] felt very unconvincing to me. I couldn't find a way to believe this or understand it or connect with it.

COMMENT: You mean you don't believe she really felt that way?

PRESENTER: Oh, I believe she felt that way, though it wasn't even said quite in a way that one would immediately believe that she felt that way. This woman doesn't kid around. I mean she doesn't tell stories, she tells you what is [what], and I believed her. But she never could recreate anything that would let me [feel my way] into how she felt and let me identify with her, the way other people do, [to] get a better sense of what she felt. She felt the mother was neglectful of her and was indifferent to her. She would quote her mother [talking] to some relative or other, a grandmother or an aunt, when they would ask, "Where's [the patient]?" when she was out playing, "Where is she? She's been gone for an hour and a half or two." "Oh, it doesn't matter. She'll come back when she's hungry," her mother said as if she meant "Who cares? We needn't give her any thought."

Her mother [obviously] liked her brother better. The brother was a happy, responsive child, and [the patient] was a grumpy, grouchy, difficult child. She would climb trees and also would abuse the brother, who was [several] years younger and couldn't climb trees as well as she, and he would cry and get upset. And then she would take the tack that she, in fact, was a miserable person, was an evil person, and she had done these terrible things and caused problems. Should I keep going? Do you want to hear about the father, or should I stop?

GEDO: I threw up my hands because I wondered whether there *was* a father. You have presented this [woman] as the result of an immaculate conception—thus far.

PRESENTER: The father . . . there certainly was a father. Her father died, I'd, say maybe four, five years before the analysis started; so she was in the mid-30s when her father died. The father constantly yelled at the mother. That was the relationship. He belittled the mother and took nothing that the mother did seriously. He wanted a hot meal at lunch at 12:00 o'clock, and he wanted his dinner at 5:30; and if it's not there at 12:00 o'clock it's because the mother's a failure. There's no reason in the world for it not to have come about; she was just wasting her time talking with her friends. Apparently the mother would sometimes go fishing by herself, and she would stay there too long. This was the gist of the relationship between the parents as the patient understood it. The father had some sort of cancer, so he died over a period of time, and the patient learned that the father was not going to leave a penny to the mother. She said that was intolerable, and they had a big confrontation, and she said he had to make provisions for the mother, and he did. He responded.

The father worked all his life for the Federal government as a bureaucrat. He was a college-educated man, but he was a loner. He had [only] one friend. He would always do what was "right," according to the rules. He was willing to quit several times when he got into some kind of a conflict with a superior. In fact, his one friend would be the person to persuade him to back down and take a more reasonable position. He liked the patient; he seemed to [have] the patient as a favorite. He was very critical of the brother, saw him as a bumbler and not a terribly adequate person. The only time he'd be angry with the patient was when she was a teenager; he felt that she was acting too wild, too sexual, [that] she wore too revealing outfits, and [that] she was going out with the wrong sort of boys. That was essentially it.

What turned out to be the crucial events in this patient's life [from the point of view of] helping us to understand her reactions in the analysis, are the following: The patient's brother was born when she was three years and two months old. The father had already been inducted into the army. He was to be shipped overseas [but had been] given permission to stay until this child was born. About a month later, he was shipped overseas, and he was sent to New Guinea, which would have been in early 1943. As she later learned, [for some time] the family received no word from the father, and they could not contact him. Where he was was a secret. I think there were some efforts through the Red Cross to try and reach him— there was no channel made available. For some period of time, the mother was concerned that the father was dead or missing. They did learn he was alive.

The father was overseas for seven or eight months, and he had an acute psychotic episode while there. I've in fact seen his VA records [because the patient] brought them in. He was not actually in direct combat, although they were very close to the lines; he was in charge of supplies, and he was trying very hard to organize whatever his responsibilities were. He was working very long hours; he could not do it successfully. He became more and more obsessed, he became withdrawn, he became depressed, he stopped eating, he would stare off into space, and he was sent back to the United States and was hospitalized for a time—not terribly long, several weeks. He made something of a recovery, although I think his personality was certainly damaged. He never had any relapses; he was never rehospitalized. I don't think he ever saw a psychiatrist after his experience in the service. He was first in a hospital [on the West Coast], and the mother took the patient (but not the younger brother) and visited the father while he was there, and then she moved the family there. They lived in a hotel while he was still in the hospital, and then he lived with them. Later he was discharged [from the hospital]. He was still in the service, and then they were at a base somewhere near there for several months.

While the father was overseas, the mother and the two children lived in several different places. They lived with a grandmother; they lived with an aunt and uncle, I don't think they had a home of their own. I think they had been living with the grandmother before the father went into the service. And then after the time [near the army base], they lived in different places before they settled into a house in a small town. What we've done, I think, that has [proved] most effective in the treatment is to reconstruct the amount of depression and feeling of isolation and disconnection from her mother that the patient experienced at the time of the brother's birth and in the few months after the brother's birth. She brought in some pictures that were taken when the brother was roughly three, four, five months old, and they're remarkable pictures. The mother looks like the happiest woman you can imagine with this infant, not [such a] tiny [baby anymore], and the patient is looking over there, this very depressed looking little girl. And there seems to be no evidence of any contact between the [patient and her mother] in this picture, in those two or three pictures. Well, let me stop here.

GEDO: Well, that's quite a handful. Many of you must have all sorts of questions. I do too. Who would like to start?

COMMENT: I have a question about the time when the brother was born and there was the loss of the mother, but I guess I'm obsessed with the idea of excitement in her involvement with men and in human relationships in general. Wouldn't it more be that the loss was [that of] the father who wasn't there? Therefore, he couldn't derive any excitement or pleasure from her burgeoning femininity at that time, which was at the beginning of, or middle of the phallic phase of development (to lapse into jargon). Therefore, she could never really be excited about being a woman or give excitement to a man about being a woman. And the mother—as I heard it in your first statement, she goes down to see mother and she's planning on taking care of mother. I thought of it again in terms of excitement in establishing something for herself.

PRESENTER: I lost you.

COMMENT: Well, maybe to be more concrete would be helpful. Since she has to go back to take care of mother anyway, either for vacations or when mother gets older, there's no point to her of establishing a good, exciting, sensible relationship with a man, meaning you, in terms of her analysis, or her husband, in terms of the father of her children. Of course it would be too painful to lose . . .

COMMENT: Lose the man?

COMMENT: Yeah. And, you know, I heard her a tad differently, in terms of much more about the father and the son, and things like that.

GEDO: Well, anything is possible. I am always very uneasy about formulations based on the amount of evidence that we have heard, [especially if they] go beyond what the analyst tells us. You have the story, you have a text, you don't have a patient. [The presenter] could have given us a number of alternative texts. He knows infinitely more about this than we do. So if he says [that] thus far the mother [has been] the focus of attention, we'd better take his word for it. That doesn't mean that what you say may not in fact turn out to be crucially important. It's around the corner, if so, and we have to understand why it's so out of sight. I mean, it cannot be a coincidence that we didn't hear about the father until so late in the presentation.

COMMENT: I'm thinking about the other comment that you made about not being able to remember her. I wonder why that happens, because obviously her story is so sad and moving and profound. So what is it that's operating that makes it hard to [remember] or [to explain why] she doesn't come up in your thoughts?

PRESENTER: Well, I think this has all shifted a lot too, and that is no longer the case. I think that it was true for a long period of time. I think part of that is [that] this woman is determined to be fiercely independent and unconnected, independent, *not* dependent; I think that's one reason. I think another [reason] is that she [has to play a part]; she went through the divorce as though forcing herself to play a role that was not hers: she was doing what she was convinced was the right thing to do. I think there's that quality about being in analysis, that she had the idea "this is the right thing for me to do," but she's not entirely there.[c]

She saw me for four or five years in one office, where, as she would walk to the couch, there was a wall of bookcases that she would see every single time. She couldn't help but see it. She had a dream I recall about moving books, and I spoke of these books in my office. She had no conscious awareness that there was a bookcase, not just a little one, but a big wall of books. The other thing that she said, with a lot of feeling, is that she hates to lie down. She hated it for five years and never gave me any indication that she hates it. I mean she really *hates* it! [But] she would do it!

I think that indicates [that she is determined to show that] she doesn't need anybody. She's here on her own, and she has these pacts with herself. Her telling me how she feels about me puts her in jeopardy of having to kill herself. She has a pact with herself that we don't really quite understand, but it is that by letting me know and letting herself know how important I am to her and how much she feels for me she is in great danger of having to kill herself. Whatever the rules of this pact are, she finds some way through it, some of the time. But we're skidding on—when we do this, when we get to this, we are right at the edge of—I don't know how to put it, but we're just walking right on the edge of that.

Not too many months ago, she didn't come in. There were a few times she didn't come in. I mean she'd never done anything like that before. But she also felt she couldn't ever let herself not come in until she realized that I would still charge her for the missed session. If she were to not come in and I were to not charge her, then she would have to kill herself. That would be absolutely "impossible." So [she must make certain] she's not hurting me. She doesn't want to hurt me, that's another aspect.

GEDO: Fascinating. Could you explain what cued you in to the fact that you had to go visit her in the hospital? You said that wasn't analysis, and I objected. At the time you said that my objection was based on pure prejudice, but now that you have told us how frightening her illness is, it doesn't sound so much like prejudice. In fact, you told us that she would have allowed herself to die of cancer without your intervention, so that you have literally been her lifeline. Although she had these almost thought-disordered rationales for denying this . . . [she would claim that] there's no real relationship between [these things], so even though you supply her with oxygen, she's not dependent upon you in her mind—[just like her] father. Something must have tipped you off very early that the need for you was a fantastically desperate one, which is why you [must have] made the unacceptable interpretation that the affair with the man on the boat was somehow a displacement.

PRESENTER: I don't know that I could give you much of an answer, except that I thought that she couldn't possibly go through [the surgery] and come back without my having made some contact with her. That the issue of this being proscribed would be too much [of a repetition of past traumata]—I guess I thought I'd be just like the husband, who, as far as I could tell, couldn't make contact with this woman. And I think it's true, I don't think he was capable. I think she picked someone who was not capable of making contact with her.

COMMENT: That was my thought. That you felt compelled to demonstrate to her that you were different, a different kind of man, and that you were going to be available to her in a way that she had not up to this point experienced.[d]

GEDO: Now, what's the theory of technique behind such [an approach]?

PRESENTER: Well, that she had not, up to this point, been able to develop this capacity to relate to men because she simply had not had the opportunity to do so.

GEDO: Well, but if this patient were in treatment with Charles Brenner—don't laugh, he's very good, he really is *very* good—how would he handle it? I mean, according to his writings. How he handles it behind closed doors, only Charles Brenner knows. But in accord with his public position, presumably he would handle it through words. He wouldn't go to the hospital.

COMMENT: Yes.

GEDO: But we all know what his theory of technique is, behind that. He assumes that this is an intrapsychic conflict that is symbolically encoded and that is capable of resolution if explicated clearly; that both the motive and the countermotive [should be] brought into consciousness. [Let us try to make] explicit an alternative theory behind the procedures followed in this case.

PRESENTER: Yes, that she could not have used, meaningfully used, intervention at that level. It would not have been experienced by her as meaningful, it seems to me, because it would not have had anything to [resonate with]. That is, [an interpretive approach] presumes that information or experience can be brought to the surface; in this case, it doesn't appear to be possible [to proceed] that way . . .

GEDO: Well, why is it impossible? Why did you feel it wouldn't be possible to deal with this at the level of verbal communication?

PRESENTER: Well, it wasn't working. I think that would be my theory of it . . .

GEDO: You had seen her for about two years at that point?

PRESENTER: Yeah. This was clearly an emergency. I don't think she was at her best, but I don't think that's the issue. I think [interpretation] would have felt to her [like] going through the motions. She needs some *demonstration*, not some kind of flagrant or unacceptable demonstration, although sometimes [I was afraid that she might need that]. That she would demand that I do things I can't do, [that I should] get involved with her sexually, or something else [of that sort]. But to pick up on the idea about excitement, there needs to be something more "living" than words.

COMMENT: Why didn't she have to kill herself though?

PRESENTER: Because I don't *make* her say anything.

COMMENT: You mean it's only in speaking?

PRESENTER: Yes. If I make her tell me what she feels, that's what's unacceptable. It's all right to feel it, and it's even all right to respond to it, but it's not all right to tell me.

COMMENT: In [terms of] feeling, is she aware of it?

PRESENTER: Oh yeah, oh yeah. Well, the loving feelings, yes. Those are . . . now I don't know what feelings she would have had around my coming to see her. I don't think it would be the same sort of loving feelings.

COMMENT: And what if you speak the words that she's afraid to speak to you?

PRESENTER: I think that's violating the rules. She's as much as told me [that in that case] I've read her mind or she's told me too much.

COMMENT: So you can act it, but you can't speak it?

PRESENTER: Right. I can act it, but I can't speak it. At that point, and for quite a while . . .

COMMENT: But that's a different thing than whether or not it's verbally encoded in her mind.

GEDO: Yes, it's more complicated. We just learned something new in response to your question. Even more fascinating.

PRESENTER: Well, this was not the case—I don't think this was understood. I'm sure it wasn't understood at the time of the surgery, when I went to see her. I think what I was responding to then was her being a lonely soldier, the isolated soldier, and she was going to go through this obviously horrible experience. It was a great deal. I had to convince her to call her mother to come up and help her. She wasn't going to have anyone at home after the surgery. She'd do it herself. "You *can't* do it yourself. You have to get help." "All right, if you say so, I'll do it."

GEDO: Like the divorce lawyer.

PRESENTER: Yes. Right. Well that was another model I had—that she would [be self-destructive if someone didn't intervene], and I have no reason to disbelieve her. I don't think this is bravado or an act on this woman's part. She would have said to the husband, "All right, I know I'm destroying your life, I don't deserve a penny from you, I don't want a penny. I can work at McDonald's, pumping gas, I don't know, but I'll do whatever I have to do."

COMMENT: But then it seems it takes on more the flavor of a sort of brief collusion in the service of helping her get beyond this point of difficulty, but it's not the same as the other.

GEDO: Well, you call it brief, but in fact it was continued over the years, ever since they reached this modus operandi. We might say it's a fantastical apparatus that makes this treatment possible, but before they developed this Rube Goldberg device, nothing was possible. It's really a baroque arrangement, isn't it? I mean, whatever it is, it seems to be crucial. Every part of it seems to be weighted with issues of life and death. If you say things that are not to be spoken, you murder her. This preceded the analysis: if she does certain things in a way for which she takes responsibility and it's all made explicit, she has to kill herself. If she is forced to do it, as though she were an automaton, then it's alright.

COMMENT: Couldn't you say that counterbalanced with that, which sounds accurate and sensible, but counterbalanced with that [there] is on her part a very subtle driving of a sense of closeness that starts preverbal and then [becomes] verbal, and then [comes] the visit to the hospital. Maybe it hasn't been explicit, but she is unconsciously setting up a line of communication with you in terms of closeness. After all, the only way the piano teacher could have known that you were the mother's therapist was if mother told her daughter to tell the teacher. It had to come from mother in some way; so that there is also a very subtle movement or line where she is allowing communication and closeness to develop. The issue of technique becomes how to see [this], how to pick up on it and interpret it, so that it can be made explicit.

GEDO: Except [that] she doesn't allow interpretation.

PRESENTER: Yeah, well she's not there yet. The line is developed, and the way the line is manifesting itself now is [in] discussion of her clinical work. She's involved in clinical work, and she takes on very difficult cases; and a lot of the sessions sound very much like supervision or discussion between colleagues about the clinical material. She said, "This is great. You know we really are close, and this is okay with me."

COMMENT: [to presenter]: How did you find out that you and her two children were the only people who drew their chairs up [in the hospital]?

PRESENTER: She told me, she told me.

COMMENT: Is that an observation, or is that an interpretation?

PRESENTER: On her part?

COMMENT: Yeah.

PRESENTER: Well, I think it certainly is an interpretation. It's an observation, and it's something that she can acknowledge as meaning a greater closeness between us—if that's what you mean by an interpretation.

COMMENT: I'm not sure. I don't know exactly what to make of this. I'm rather puzzled by the technical problems here. I can't formulate. . . .

PRESENTER: When she says that she noticed this and this means something—oh, and, further, that mother did not do that when mother would visit her in the hospital—it's as if there [were] a slip. It doesn't speak to another aspect of herself about what our relationship in fact is; of course, it means there is something different than her version, and she's referred to this many times. She's said, "Oh, what you just said comes right from the analyst's handbook, doesn't it?" And so she has a notion of what a stereotyped analytic response would be.

GEDO: Well, now I'm going to [say something so speculative that it is] illegitimate; this sounds like she is saying to you that the usual channels of communication, the usual content, and the usual manner of conveying that content are not to be trusted, that she can accept from you only those things that you have spontaneously devised.

PRESENTER: *For her.*

GEDO: For her, for her! Which suggests that she's trying to master something, change it. She's enacting certain circumstances, she's reenacting certain circumstances from the past and trying to impose a new, happier ending on them. Repetition in the service of mastery, but it can only be done by two people. It's something interpersonal from the past that needs to be repeated. We don't yet know who the other person was in the past, or maybe it was even more than one person. A succession of people in the past. Some experience in the past that involves another person and the fact that she will not allow anything conventional to transpire suggests to me that she was treated correctly in conventional ways and that all of that was fraudulent. When the words are "right" it's fraudulent, and she has learned not to trust them. [I assume] that nobody made an overt misstep. If you transcribe it on paper it sounds great and then [it turns out to be] nothing. In fact, it's worse than nothing because it boggles the mind.

PRESENTER: Yeah, I think that certainly would put into words my [long-held] position of not understanding her rage at the mother, because the mother didn't sound that bad. All right, that statement [of the mother's], "She'll come home when she's hungry," may not be very empathic . . .

GEDO: Oh, listen, that's what the suburban police told me when my dog ran away and I was worried. "Why are you worried? In our experience, they always come back."

PRESENTER: Yeah, right.

GEDO: I mean, this wasn't Chicago. This was some small rural town.

PRESENTER: Yeah, and she was out on the farm somewhere. And, in fact, mother has helped a number of times—loaned her money, did come up and was reasonable after her surgery in helping to nurse her, and so forth. And the examples [of the mother's behavior] never matched the intensity of [the patient's negative] feeling.

COMMENT: But what about the couch? Her hatred of the couch and not reporting it for a long time. Is there any understanding of what the hatred or what the feelings about this are, or what goes with it?

PRESENTER: Well, I think [that] on the couch she is somewhat less in control of herself. Her emotions are stronger, and she can't suppress them. She hates to cry—she *hates* to cry. Now she cries, but as sort of a joke she said, "I can't cry today because I have a silk blouse on and the tears stain the blouse and I can't afford to send it to the cleaners." So I said, "How about some Kleenex?" So that the feelings are stronger and she's less in charge of herself.

GEDO: And is she willing to put them into words now? Is she beginning to be willing?

PRESENTER: Yes, she puts the feelings into words, and we know what the dangers are, but I have to be very careful not to say very much. I certainly cannot interpret. I cannot make a standard kind of interpretation at all, because that "ruins the analysis." And if I'm not exquisitely careful, I ruin it, and that will send her out in a suicidal state.

COMMENT: What sort of standard interpretations are you talking about?

PRESENTER: Well, if I were to say something about her loving feelings for me and make any connection to the past—[that it was] something she had felt before—you know, there would be talk about father or even talk about a boyfriend, and that these things seemed to come in sequence.

COMMENT: But if you only said half of that, would she also reject it? The half which is the feeling, the loving feelings toward you. Forget the father.

PRESENTER: Oh, yeah, she tells me that the feelings are there.

COMMENT: So you can comment about that, and it doesn't send her into a suicidal spiral?

PRESENTER: Oh no, no.

COMMENT: So when [the interpretation is] genetic, when there's a piece of it that's genetic . . .

PRESENTER: When it's genetic, or when it isn't something that we're *living* together, a *real* thing between us. She doesn't want me to tell her that I love her—that's not important to her—but that we are there together with her feelings and her feelings have meaning between us.

GEDO: That begins to support [the observation one of you made] that something wasn't genuine in the relation with the father; maybe with the mother too, earlier, but certainly with the father.

COMMENT: But your earlier point about technique is that the analyst must continue to adjust the technique, to edge up on her gradually, increasing her capacity to tolerate closeness, to this level that was originally traumatic for her.

GEDO: If our collective conjectures are approaching the truth, [the pathogenic circumstance] was not that her feelings as a child didn't take place. It's not that the experiences with the father were missing, as we originally speculated, but that, although they were present, they were somehow contaminated or rendered worthless by some sort of miscommunication. Communication is the crux of this analysis. And from the beginning, communication through wordless actions has been the safest.

COMMENT: More reliable.

GEDO: Now, to draw the chair closer is more than acceptable to her, and then she's allowed to speak about it. But it's the words of the other that are dangerous, because they might not be genuine. And when she says that you will ruin everything if you say that it's a repetition of the past, it's even possible that that's literally true, that you'll ruin everything, because, in fact, it's not a repetition.

PRESENTER: Well, yes, I understood it may not be a repetition in any case.

GEDO: That's correct. It may be that this is a new experience. Like your quasi-supervision of her work is certainly a new experience. That's the kind of experience that I think Kohut was trying to get at when he conceived a "twinship transference." I think it is a very equivocal idea, sort of a metaphor that ran away with itself, because obviously the analyst is not being a twin in teaching her what he's teaching her. But he's not too far ahead of her. Presumably his teaching is acceptable, and she's not humiliated. He's only half a step ahead of her, and she's able to accept that from him, and that's something new and infinitely valuable. And, of course, what is essential for a person like this is to avoid the transference, because (as she stated it repeatedly) if the past were repeated she would have to kill herself. Whether that's literally true or only 99% true, I don't think that anybody would want to test it in action. I would guess that it's only 99% true and that that statement is in itself the transference. But I would say that when she is saying that she is "in the past," she's sunk into the desperation of early childhood and [that] the feeling "I must kill myself" is a quotation from the past and probably the only actual repetition of the worst moments of childhood that you have permitted. Thank goodness, no? A little of that goes a long way.

Now you know, of course, when I say it's mostly new experience and you haven't permitted transference, that's a fantastic oversimplification. You haven't permitted the most dangerous of the transferences; there are all sorts of other transferences. One assumes that the disappointment in the parents wouldn't be so utterly devastating if there had been no attachment to begin with. [In that case] she might have developed into a frozen, aloof person, but she wouldn't be so angry and she wouldn't constantly be trying to show that the name of the game is to be able to love. The early enactment on the boat was a message—I must say, you might have had better luck if instead of telling the truth that it was a displacement—it's true, it's true!—you [would] have said, "Wow, is this a message? It's a living dream and a dream you enacted, like"—I'm incorrigible; I would have said—"like the first act of *Tristan and Isolde*. Twenty years ago you took a love potion," I suppose it's the *second* act of *Tristan and Isolde*. The first act is on a boat; that's when they drink the love potion. They actually have intercourse in the magical garden in the second act.

PRESENTER: Well, in 1982 I wasn't quite ready . . .

GEDO: To think it, or say it? Well, at any rate, you know if you emphasized its function as a communication, as something that has to be paid very close attention to, particularly in terms of its formal elements (it's a communication, like a ballet—it's not the words that were spoken between her and this man that she's reporting, but their actions), I suspect she would not have spat that out.

PRESENTER: I think it does bring to mind another thing as I'm listening to this. It undoubtedly was in my mind for a good period of time with her that she's dangerous. Not the self-destructiveness, but the acting out, is dangerous. Either it's dangerous to the analysis, as analysis is supposed to be done, as I understood it at that point, or she's going to get herself involved with various men that she shouldn't be getting involved with and get into all kinds of difficulties. There were a few things like that, and I think that I may have been responding without being aware of it in some punitive way, that she shouldn't be doing this. But I think that she could be dangerous. I also think that may also be a sense of what she took out of her childhood, that she was thought to be in some way troublesome or a problem, more than just an ordinary kid is a problem.

GEDO: Well, and of course she *is* a problem. *What* a problem she is to you, huh? And when does she start to be such a problem? Probably relatively early on. At the time those [childhood] photographs were taken. You say you were concerned about purity in your analytic technique. Well, but if you're going to approach it from that point of view, then we have to ask how is it that she persuaded the original referring analyst—and I assume somebody who had some knowledge of analysis—and you, too, that she was suitable? Were you surprised at what was in Count Bluebeard's back room when you opened the door?

PRESENTER: I've never discussed her with the person who referred her. I think he would be flabbergasted.

GEDO: So to the outside world she presents some kind of a false self that's very engaging and . . .

PRESENTER: Well, nice, friendly, not very engaging. Actually more engaging, maybe more engaging, because she's always surprised [for instance, that] she has a woman friend whose work takes her out of the country for long periods, and, of all the people she knows, on her brief visits back she always seeks out the patient and has a very warm relationship. The patient is surprised that people react [well] to her.

GEDO: Well, so, in terms of the theory of technique, what this problem illustrates first of all is that one must be very alert to the existence of real splits in the mind. When such a split in the very deepest layers of the mind is present, then depending on what one does one can engage the person on one side of the split or on the other side of the split. How many of you have come across Margaret Little's 1985 article on her analysis with Winnicott? It's quite a remarkable document, [illustrating such a split between an adequate social being and a quasi-psychotic inner core].

Second Session

PRESENTER: There are some things we haven't [covered]; certainly, there's a lot that hasn't been said. One thing that occurred to me was the nature of her research for her Ph.D. Completing [the degree] and considering herself to be a worthy and adequate student was often discussed [in the analysis]. A feeling of inadequacy as a student was with her, although she did extremely well. She would measure herself against someone who was extraordinarily good and find herself to be not up to that level, and then [she would] decide that she was really not competent at all. But she did very well and [her] work is well regarded. She was interested in mothers' attitudes toward children. That is certainly relevant to our discussion.

There have been two relationships that she's had since I've known her. One started while she was still married. She started an affair which she kept secret. As far as she knows, this was never known by her husband. She felt terribly guilty that she was doing this, because it is wrong; you shouldn't do that. It was the only time she had an affair during the marriage. It was with a man, about ten years younger than she, whom she had met at the university. I think there was some pleasure and some gratification in this affair, and there certainly was no pleasure in her marriage. And then this man [contracted a potentially fatal] disease, was hospitalized, was treated with steroids, and [developed] a psychosis. I think this occurred after the divorce, so that the relationship could [become] public. And she played some role in helping him get treatment. I think he was suicidal; this was all before I met her. She [helped him to get] to psychiatric treatment, [and he stopped] doing crazy things. Then he got better; he went into remission from the original illness, and the relationship [between them] was on again off again. Then he again developed signs of the [primary illness] and the psychosis along with it. And then he rejected her. He pushed away any of her concern and certainly broke off any romantic involvement with her and married somebody else, rather precipitously.

Again he became suicidal, and [the patient] played some role. She was very impatient with everybody, including his psychiatrist, who didn't seem to take this as seriously as she thought he should be taking it. And then he died of the [primary] illness. He left her a $100,000 life insurance policy. He also had written several different wills, one of which left her a large amount of money. That will was thought to be not valid, and there was a lot of fighting within this man's family about money and the wills. She found it all horribly distasteful, she certainly wanted none of his money whatsoever.

And we talked in great detail about the insurance policy; that it had been taken out when he was sane seemed pretty clear. It was [at] no great cost to him; he had paid the premiums. I think I persuaded her that she should retain that [insurance money], that she had played a large role in his life in several different ways, and that his purchasing that insurance was in response to [his] feelings about her and appreciation of her efforts on his behalf, and also because they had a relationship. And so she did keep that money, and she, in fact, used [it] to help support herself. I don't think I browbeat her into doing that, but I tried to be persuasive and we discussed it in great detail. The other money she never came into, and that just eventually quieted down.

More recently she has [again] gotten involved with a man. After her surgery, she had felt that she would never be involved with a man sexually, that she [was] disfigured and no longer a woman [that] she couldn't offer herself to a man in a sexual relationship. But less than a year ago a friend of hers fixed her up with a man who was again about ten years younger than she, and who's Jewish.

COMMENT: Excuse me, how is she disfigured?

PRESENTER: She had breast cancer; she had a bilateral mastectomy. [Yet] she fairly quickly developed a sexual relationship with this man. There was a fairly intense, but short-lived, trepidation about doing it. Despite many inadequacies, this man seems to have been a very good partner for this particular experience, to revive a sexual life for her. The first or second time they went to bed together she fainted the next morning, but that was it. After that there were no difficulties, and they have an enjoyable sexual relationship. I think she's fond of him, but he's a troubled man. He seems very much caught up in conflicts [between] setting off on his own in life and remaining entwined in a family business and in family relationships. He can't find his way out of that and can't get help, even though she's been trying to help him get help. So at the moment she's rather pessimistic and doesn't feel she should commit herself to him further because he's so tied up in his own difficulties.

COMMENT: Backing up to the insurance policy, [what] did you think about her hesitation to take it? Then, what made you take the approach that you took, to encourage her to take [the money]?

PRESENTER: Well, I understood it in terms of her intense guilt about having the affair, her guilt about hurting her husband, even though it never came to his attention, and also in terms of her feelings of being undeserving and a person for whom nothing [good] should come her way.

COMMENT: I'm thinking about what [we] talked about two weeks ago; about the nonverbal exchanges and her not being able to accept anything verbally. Now you seem to be talking on a very different level, [saying] that this is operating on a different psychological organizational level. More guilt as opposed to something else. Is that true? I mean, her inability to accept words and her guilt conflicts are not the same thing; they're different.

PRESENTER: No, I think that what you're saying is true.

COMMENT: I'm just thinking, I'm almost 99.99% certain that I'm the psychiatrist who treated the first guy, who was floridly psychotic with grandiose ideas of going naked to the United Nations . . .

PRESENTER: Correct, this is the same person.

COMMENT: . . . to solve the Iran crisis. She really served to organize him and helped him tremendously, through a long period. As his illness became more and more severe, he became more psychotic, involved with women whom he got through massage parlors, the *Reader*, and things like that. By the time he died, in a very crazy way he had wills being set up to distribute money. In fact, the estate is still being litigated to this day.

GEDO: Are you one of the creditors?

COMMENT: I'm one of the trivial creditors. The condition of his death and the deterioration in the psychosis would have had a tremendous [influence] on anybody accepting money or being involved in this afterwards, independent of whatever dynamic issues there were. This was real chaotic, bizarre!

GEDO: Well, let's not get too hung up on him. [Let us return to] the technical questions. What determines [that the analyst should] throw his weight into the balance of her conflicts, and what persuades him that it's an analytic thing to do to help her to take this money? What [makes him decide] that it's an analytic thing to do to go to the hospital when she's having her mastectomy? I am putting it in my terms, but of course he started off his account by apologizing for the "nonanalytic" things he had done. If this is an analysis (and he presents it here because it's an analysis; otherwise it wouldn't belong in the seminar, right?), then everything he has done is part of this analysis. This is the one and only treatment that she has had. He tells us that most recently she [has been spending] much of her time in the sessions giving him accounts about her therapeutic work and evoking from him responses such as a supervisor or consultant is more likely to give. She is using him in some such capacity; this is what her analysis is like at this stage. These are terribly unusual circumstances; I assume that is why we have been presented with this material.

Of course, the big unanswered question after [the last seminar] was, what had convinced [the analyst] that this was the proper way to go? It's a very difficult question to answer. Whenever anybody asks me what convinces me to do anything in an analysis, I respond (I hope with some irony) that it's the Muses who lead me in that direction, or I get a message from Apollo, or something like that. So which of the Muses has led you?

PRESENTER: Which of the Muses? [pause] I don't have a quick response to that. I think that my sense of her is that she would not have taken the money if we had not made that a topic, and if I had not tried to persuade her, to show her the . . .

GEDO: Well, presumably you didn't simply say, "Take the money, take the money, take the money. How are you going to pay my fee if you don't take the money, so take the money, and I can raise my fees." It was on some other basis. You must have determined that good reality testing would lead her to take the money.

PRESENTER: Right! I tried to imply that [accepting the insurance] was not stealing money, [that] this is not money that she's not entitled to. This money was not illegal, and the reasons for not taking it were irrational. They were not based on the reality of her relationship with him and the reality of exchanges between adults.

GEDO: In other words, in our technical vocabulary, you decided that her temptation to refuse the money would have been major, self-destructive acting out.

COMMENT: But I think [with regard to the previous] question, that given that [truth], it might also be possible to see the technique you would use in handling that somewhat differently, for example, by interpreting the problems that she had in taking the money, rather than actively encouraging her to take it. So the question is, what made you decide to *tell* her that you thought she should take it?

PRESENTER: Oh, that I think [goes] back to the issues raised last time, that if I were to rely on interpretation, regardless of what comes of that, that would be [experienced as] an unspoken message of [lack of concern], of disregard for her welfare. [She would feel] that whatever happens to her is fine with me; to hope that interpretation is in some way useful in resolving her conflict would feel to her to [mean] "I don't care what you do, do what you want to do."

GEDO: Am I hearing correctly that you decided that, although there is a guilt conflict about whether to take the money or not, in the transference that's not what you were dealing with?

PRESENTER: Right, right. That's right.

GEDO: [Two things were] going on at the same time: she was talking about [her conflict], but in the transference you were somewhere else. In the transference the issue was, "Will you rescue me from myself?"

PRESENTER: I think that's correct.

COMMENT: Last time you were talking about the pact she had made . . .

PRESENTER: Yes, a private pact with herself.

COMMENT: A private pact, and that if she didn't keep it, she would have to punish herself in some fashion, in a major fashion.

PRESENTER: Kill herself.

COMMENT: She would kill herself.

PRESENTER: Kill herself. She'd have to destroy herself.

COMMENT: I still don't understand what your function was when you intervened in that "pact." You said, "You don't have to keep that"?

PRESENTER: "I won't permit you to keep that pact. I can't rely on saying to you that it is not reasonable to adhere to that pact, that won't do it. I have to intervene so you won't, in fact, keep that pact."

COMMENT: There is some sort of schema of values that she has, which is organizing her to act in ways that we would consider to be irrational. [For example], she's just going to get the divorce and not get any money, or she isn't going to take the insurance; she either doesn't need those things, or shouldn't take those things, or shouldn't rely on anyone. I still have a lot of questions about how she accounts for this sort of behavior.

PRESENTER: You mean these attitudes?

COMMENT: Yeah, the refusal to acknowledge normal needs and the insistence on being radically independent. Alternatively, the insistence on enlisting other people—the lawyer, you—to take responsibility for rescuing her from that particular schema. I'm not clear on why she has to do that, how she experiences that she has to do that.

PRESENTER: I think you're right that she certainly feels that she has to conduct herself in an exemplary way, according to a peculiar set of ideals. Because she is never able to carry that out perfectly, she is undeserving, she is totally undeserving. That seems to be operating.

GEDO: How would Otto Kernberg formulate such a problem? Or the self psychologists? How would a Winnicottian formulate such a problem? They would talk about some sort of introject, huh? Some sort of malign introject, the origins of which have not yet come to light in this analysis, so that it is this introject that whispers into her ear that she should throw herself off the cliff, and she can't say, "Get thee behind me, Satan," and the analyst has literally to grab a hold of her and say, "I won't let you do that." And if he merely says, "Oh, there's a malign introject in your head, and you are going to throw yourself off the cliff if you don't say no to these things," presumably she would feel like the victim in the joke about the Rogerian therapist, you know, the plop joke.

PRESENTER: I don't know the joke.

GEDO: Well, the joke is that the Rogerian therapist is echoing what the patient is feeling, and then the patient is standing on a window ledge and when the patient jumps, he says, "Plop."

COMMENT: Even to say the thing about the malign introject (that particular vocabulary) would put this whole thing in some *language*. I'm not clear about how much you should put things like that into language.

PRESENTER: I certainly did put things like that into language, and it was always a failure. I could feel, "Oh, my God, now I got it," or, "I'm eloquent today," and I gave her my best, and it was the worst. I would certainly say things [relating to the influence] of her mother, or that's a representation of her mother, and go to some piece of history about the relationship with mother. Or after she brought me [those] very poignant pictures [of her early childhood], I could accurately say that we were duplicating something, just by the look on her face.

GEHRIE: Let me just offer a vignette about a patient of my own who can also be characterized as suffering from a negative introject. Every time I would say something to her that she experienced as correct and hopeful for her, without fail the reaction, whether it [occurred] right then or in the next hour, would be devastating. And then I would interpret to her that she suffered an overwhelming sense of loss because her hopefulness had to bring her into contact with the loss of an object tie critical for her. That she would lose the mother, if you want to put it so literally, if she allowed herself to feel better and go forward. Therefore she was in an unbearable bind. Anytime there was positive hopefulness, she would have to give up what to her was most precious on this deep core level, and the only thing to do at that time, as far as I was concerned, and apparently as far as [the analyst of this patient] is concerned, would be somehow to make an attempt at an alternative kind of intervention, to grab onto her when that occurred, because [the usual] interpretation of [the problem] simply caused [a repetition of the sense of loss].

In the case of my patient, the early relationship to the mother was overwhelmingly negative. It was based on negativity and on hostility. [She could] either [experience] the mother in this hostile form, or there was no mother, in which case [she experienced chaos] and oblivion. When you think of a young child, the alternative to this hostile relationship with the early object is oblivion, and this is what gets recreated [if the analysis separates them] from that early object.

GEDO: The patient [presented here] is not exactly like your patient. She is like the little girl [in the news] whose mother abandoned her in Gary, who responds so positively to the hospital that everybody falls in love with her, although she says, "Please call my mother."

GEHRIE: Healthier than my patient.

GEDO: One step up from your patient. Your patient accepts no assistance. The patient [presented] accepts the analyst as a substitute for the mother, but only if he really mothers her, not if he remains a therapist.

PRESENTER: [Some] of the most gratifying moments for her [occurred]—this is very much more recent—when a couple of times she left the session [after] bursting into tears and being unable to speak. A couple of times she wouldn't be able to come back to the next session, though she said she realized that I would charge her; that allowed her to do it, because she couldn't miss the session [if she thought I would] miss my income. She would feel so guilty about doing that; she couldn't do that. When she was sure I'd charge her, then she could miss the session. But at one time when she was in the midst of being very upset and about to become silent . . .

GEDO: Excuse me. Please, everybody *remember* that. You're not being kind to people by not taking your fee.

PRESENTER: I said to her, whatever her name is, "If you just lie there silent, I'm going to hit you with the Kleenex box," and she lit up. This was the most loving thing I'd done since the time I'd visited her in the hospital—that I would do something, I would actually be willing to have contact with her, to get . . .

GEDO: To get your guts in an uproar.

PRESENTER: Right, right. Get in an uproar and be with her, really have contact with her.

COMMENT: Well, this poses a real [ethical] problem with patients where it seems that contact is required and words and distance are not [sufficient].   *Bill*

PRESENTER: I didn't touch her.

COMMENT: No, I know, but this patient is also healthy enough to participate in the process. A lot of people present themselves as patients who are not that healthy.

GEDO: Would you recommend analysis for *any* of those people?

COMMENT: No.

GEDO: No. Okay. So fortunately we don't have to worry about this contingency.

COMMENT: But we may get them as control cases.

GEDO: I've done a fair amount of supervision by now, and I must say I have not encountered any instance in which the patient demanded some specific action on the part of the analyst and was unable to tolerate the frustration of that demand. Note that [in this case there] was only an implicit demand, and it's not a demand for action, it's a demand for feeling. And I think that's the frontier between a treatment that can still be conceived of as an analysis and something else. God only knows what the future will hold, but I think in 1988 we can say that that's the frontier. Of course, many people will disagree with that.[e] Many people would simply say that what [was done in this case] is not analysis. The world is full of analysts who are much more worried about what is not analysis than what analysis is. Still and all, it's the only conceivable treatment for this woman. We could ask [the presenter] to specify what he thinks would happen if this person were seen on a sitting basis once or twice a week.

PRESENTER: I don't know.

GEDO: And of course none of us can *know*, but in my experience with problems where the interpretation of unconscious contents was not the name of the game, if the patients are analyzed then you get at the material, [but] only after they've given up their defenses through the institution of the iatrogenic regression [set in motion by] the analytic method. On a once or twice a week basis, you get endless intellectualizations in one set of these patients, and in another set you get chaos. [With such a schedule] every interruption produces a traumatic state in the next session; [at best, you] deal with that traumatic state. You're not quite finished with that at the end of the session, and then it's the same the next time, and so on. A nightmare of difficulties, where you are barely able to keep your head above water. So I think that if the patient really wants [to overcome the problem], an analytic effort is usually justified, but obviously one has to meet the patient half way and not impose a technique on the patient but devise a technique the patient can use.

PRESENTER: I don't know. I think this woman would have quit if I had said that she should be seen in something other than an analysis. I think that she really was trying to change her life. I think that's one reason why she divorced and didn't live out a life of servitude to [her husband] and his needs. I think she had some idea that either she should find a way to have a more gratifying life or she should kill herself. Simply to be what he wanted her to be was unacceptable. As her children got older the role [of being a mother began] to diminish in importance. So she went back to graduate school and did extremely well. I think that she must have had some idea that she could have something of a life for herself for the first time. I think the other thing that may have been very important [was that] the person who recommended me to her (and I think she was given only my name) said that I was a very *good* person. He didn't say that I was a great analyst, but a very decent person. That's my friend's view of me. I think that must have had a lot of significance, in retrospect, that she was after *somebody*, as much as some *technique*.

GEDO: Well, but somebody who is admirable in a certain way and not necessarily in other ways. You didn't have to be intellectually brilliant, for instance, as far as she was concerned, but you had to be decent enough. And she indicated to you in an affectively persuasive manner that she had an absolute need for you to embark in a small boat, without a compass, to cross the ocean, [and you made her feel] that you'd do it for her. I use that image because when I published my 1979 book I had a seminar like this with a bunch of candidates. I was telling them that they were applying a technique which was useful for only a limited number of people, and [that] they were also applying the same technique in a blind way to still other people, and that with most people we don't know what sort of technique is applicable. One has to devise a new one in every instance. One of the candidates cried out in great pain, "You expect me to embark on a transatlantic voyage in a small boat without a compass!" *That's right.*

I haven't had an experience exactly like this [case]. The patient I've had whom this case reminds me of the most is the person I reported on in *Beyond Interpretation*, the third case there. A man who had had a lot of treatment on a once or twice a week basis and decided that it was unable to come close to what concerned him and where his feelings were. He came in and said, "Unless you can really do something about this, I'll commit suicide, or should I commit suicide right now?" I'm paraphrasing, but essentially that was the question. And first of all you have to take these people maximally seriously. In my experience, if the story doesn't *upset* you, you're useless to the person. So that these are people who cannot settle for neutrality. I mean they don't require you to touch them, that's not it. They require you to be *touched* by them.[f]

I had an experience about two weeks ago with a very difficult person. It's a long, long story, I don't want to go into the antecedents of all this, but, like the $100,000 here, he was about to piss away something terribly important, more important than a sum of money. [He] wouldn't hear anything I said about it, although I was getting more and more firm and definite in trying to state what the realities of the situation were. But he developed a paranoia about a person whose good will represented his entire future. And he just kept on being quite provocative during the session. I got a little provoked (although not as much as I made myself sound), and near the close of the session I said with great insistence—I won't quote myself, it's too shocking. [The message was that] he was a stupid man who was going to destroy himself because he wouldn't listen to anybody. So he sat up, and he saw that I was really affected by this happening, and he started to cry. He said, "I'll never be able to repay you for what you have just done." And the paranoia just melted away. But, of course, the issue was not what was going on between him and this patron of his about whom he had become paranoid.

The issue was what was going on between *us*. If I had just continued to say, "Well, you opened the window. Are you going to jump? It's a free country; you're perfectly free to destroy yourself," [he would have jumped].

COMMENT: When you said that, were you effectively [helping him to master a childhood trauma]?

GEDO: Much depends on the genetics of the situation. I would assume that the difference between Dr. Gehrie's case and the case [presented here] is that in Gehrie's case the child never turned to anybody else. Either there was nobody else, or the mother made sure that it was unthinkable to turn to anybody else. It was the mother or nothing. I assume that in [the present] case there was always a glimmer of hope that someone would intervene. Nobody did effectively. Can you tell us about the background of it?

PRESENTER: Not really. It would be hard to say very much about that. We have the history; we know a great deal about the events. I don't know how to reconstruct her early [life] to prove any point. I can say one thing about the [present] that fits very well with what you've said: in her therapeutic work, she saw one of the children as a patient along with the mother, and I guess it's never been clear whether the [child had been abused sexually]. She took the position that there was a great deal of abuse; but the point is that she was going to be a spokesman for this child, as it were, that he should be taken seriously and that he should be helped out of whatever psychological state he was in, presumably because he had been mistreated and abused. But even if he hadn't been abused, he was in a state as if he had been abused, and so she should play that role.

Currently she's involved in another very, very difficult situation in which the senior people where she works turn to her to help them with a horrendous family situation. [It's] a very prominent and wealthy family who throw their weight around and in the process handled two little children very badly, so she is again the advocate of small children. She personifies the hope of the child, of the over-whelmed and [helpless] child.

GEDO: Okay, so you represent that hope to her, and that's a transference position. Now, whether it represents the transference of the hope or the transference of a relationship from the past remains to be determined.

PRESENTER: It's been very difficult to determine [because she op-poses my efforts] to make statements about the past [whenever I try]. It didn't really elucidate the past and it disrupted the present.

GEDO: Of course, it's partly because reality testing itself was impaired by the past. [The analysand decides,] Let's not take the $100,000, or (in my case) let us get paranoid about our political sponsor. So the past is a nightmare about which the patient has no conception, really; so you don't know, [and] she knows you don't know. That's simply not a useful avenue to pursue. I must say, in the vignette I just gave you about the man who was paranoid about his sponsor, I worked with him for a very long time, in fact in two separate periods of analysis, and so I know him very well. And it's only after untold years of work that he was able to share with me the split-off series of memories from the past having to do with the fact that the most important love relationship of his childhood was with an older brother, four or five years older than himself, to whom the mother entrusted him "Take him out to the park. Be the babysitter," [she] essentially [said].

And this brother was a sadist, not so much [using] physical tortures (although that was part of it too), but the favorite game was to undermine reality testing: spin him around until he lost his bearings and then say, "We're lost, we're lost. We'll never get home. I don't know which way to go," until the patient would get panicked.

Well, one has to be very careful not to spin such people around. I mean, the closer they feel to you, the more you evoke the brother transference. It's a very serious matter to make incorrect interpretations to such people, very serious. They are always a hair's breadth away from being paranoid about you, and one might say that the name of the game is to avoid *that* transference, that *crucial* transference, for as long as possible—to work around it as much as possible. It's very convenient if the patient develops such a transference about [a politician] instead, and [you can] work with that and prepare the ground. After three or four years the patient knows that he has a paranoia. Then, when he becomes paranoid about you, you can refer to that.

I'm not saying that this is the only way to go, but that [offers] one possibility of being able to deal with such a thing. Of course, [the presenter] hasn't told us that his patient has a propensity to be paranoid, but she [also] certainly has a strong prejudice that makes her presume that when there is an accusation of child abuse, the child has in fact been abused.

PRESENTER: Well, it's approaching it.

COMMENT: In what you've been saying just now, it seems like the key word is "transference." The way you use it and the way self psychologists use it [are] very different. I bring up self psychologists because I've tried to think of this in different ways. When you demonstrate your affectivity to this patient, that allows the patient to develop the transference, or the transference to emerge, you're not . . .

GEDO: Why would you put it quite *that* way? I think I am [implicated] in a transference even at that point; that [merely] allows the transference to shift to a more mature level. You see, I think [the presenter] in his case, and Dr. Gehrie in his, and I in the case of my paranoid patient (at least at the stages of the analyses that we have each reported on) are operating at a level more primitive and more archaic than anything Heinz Kohut was ever concerned with. Kohut said, essentially, "If you don't watch out, people will regress to that, to those awful positions. They'll become crazy." That's what he said, that there are no borderline *patients*, there's [only] a borderline. You're on one side of that line or on the other side of the line. The patients he was reporting on, at least when he started his work, were people who were on the more integrated side of the border; and the technical difficulties had to do with certain traumatic events, the unavailability of the analyst or a failure of empathy, which made them "fragment." In other words, cross the border. And Kohut says quite specifically that he's not interested in the details of what then happens, and he says that it's a technical error to go into those details, that you should concentrate on the genesis of the regression. "What have I done wrong to cause you to have this catastrophe?"

I have no objection to that whatsoever. If the patient has been for the most part in an integrated mode, if you haven't tilted the work in any specific direction, it seems as if that's what the patient needs to work on, this integrated mode; and if you do something, if you foul it up and cause a regression, I think Kohut's recommendation makes absolutely good sense. You correct your error; the patient returns to the level that he needs to be working on. So at that point the phenomenology of the fragmentation is like vomitus. You don't worry about the content of the vomitus, you worry about why the patient is vomiting, right?

That's not the case here. Certainly not in the case I was telling you about, and even less so in Gehrie's case. The patient was *never* integrated. The patient is permanently suicidal, and in order for her not to continue on her slow, self-destructive course, the analyst has to take actions: not literally to stop her from jumping out the window, but commitments in the analytic space. And that amounts to entering the patient's world.

Kohut would say it's a selfobject function. I don't like that vocabulary, but this is not the time to go into that. We all understand, I hope, what Kohut meant by the term. So [the analyst] is permanently the selfobject that keeps her from destroying herself, that actively intervenes in her self-destructive behaviors. In my case, the patient has a sadistic older brother and in fact he very closely identified with his older brother, and was a child abuser for many years, literally. And his sexual organization is that of a sadistic perversion, although he has not permitted himself to do anything about that in decades. Essentially, in the transference we've gone back to the origins of his sadistic perversion and his pedophilia, and now he is in the role of the older brother and is, of course, torturing me. Unless I express the affect that he felt as a small child, when he was being tortured, the whole thing is like a fiction, because he's utterly confused about everything except what he can perceive in the external world.

COMMENT: The only way that he knows is by seeing you experiencing your experience?

GEDO: The only way he knows that we're talking about something meaningful to him is if somebody is beside himself because of the pain of being driven crazy. Then we are in the right ball park, and then the past is lived again. As long as you say words about the past, you are only kidding him, as the brother did. Words have been utterly discredited. Of course, I am oversimplifying. Life is never that simple; and, of course, it wasn't just he and his brother, there were parents there too—a large family. Words were not what they ought to have been for either the mother or the father. The father would get up on a beautiful morning like today, not quite as cold as this, and would say, we'll go to the zoo today. And then he'd go to the bathroom and emerge after lunch. "It's too late to go to the zoo." I won't go into [parallel] activities of the mother that also discredited verbal communication.

COMMENT: When a patient does that, it forces you to take the role of the abuser, or he treats you as he was treated in order to convey the experience that he can't articulate, right?

GEDO: Well, okay, some people say it's a message, that he's conveying a message. That's not quite true; I think it's a *transference*, but it's such a primitive transference that the issue of who did what to whom is not yet relevant. Only the feeling is relevant.

COMMENT: Yeah, the feeling is relevant, but is it because you will not abuse him and he's forced into the position of abusing you? Is that the reason why it developed in that form as opposed to the other way around?

GEDO: Sure.

COMMENT: That's the reason.

GEDO: Well, isn't it? He certainly tries very hard over a long period of time to evoke the abuse. [His patron, the politician,] comes closer to it than I do. There are vast cultural gaps between this man and his patron, and the way organizations such as the one they are functioning in do things is by my patient's standards abusive, so naturally there he experiences the past with relatively few changes. How can any of us at our worst come close to that?

Let me give you an example why he was being paranoid about [the politician]. His arrangement is that he gets a modest salary and then he gets an almost equal amount of money out of this politician's campaign chest. So for 1987 he was supposed to get X amount of money, and along about September or October this politician says to him, "Say, how would you like to get your money in 1988, when your tax rate is going to go down because of the tax law change?" "Oh, how considerate of you, how wonderful, wonderful. Right. 1988." So the second week of January he gets about a quarter of his money, and he says, "What's this?" And they say to him, "Well, the other fellow with whom we had this arrangement is about to get a divorce, so we can't give him any money because then his wife will get a better settlement, so could you wait until that has been settled?" And so on, and so on, and so on. Well, of course he feels he's in the grip of an abusive system, and he encourages the abuse by never saying what he wants. My therapeutic activity, like [the presenter's] in his patient's treatment, has been the supervision of how one deals with a political organization. I tell him, "You're doing this preposterously. That's not the way to deal with the Irish. Let me tell you; I'm one of the world's experts in dealing with the Irish." And so on, and so on, and so on.

COMMENT: Well, that's very vivid. Hypothetically, when [the analyst] gets further on in this case, she's going to start mistreating him in some way.

GEDO: That might happen, or it might not. She might start mistreating somebody else. She might find somebody who will mistreat her.

PRESENTER: She's probably mistreating the boyfriend by not breaking off with him.

COMMENT: Well, then do you interpret that? You force that in some way or really focus on that?

PRESENTER: She focuses on it. I haven't taken a stand on that. That's her own self-reflection about the situation. Even if she doesn't resolve it, she certainly seems to be aware of what she's doing, but she's making unreasonable demands on him that she knows he can't fulfill. She feels terribly dissatisfied with him, but she feels she doesn't want the loneliness that goes with breaking off with him completely. So she sees all the different elements. It would be much fairer to him to say, this isn't going anywhere and in fairness to both of us we should break it off. That would be the mature thing to do, but she won't do that. And she's grumpy. She said, "How does he stand that? I'm so grumpy, and I turn a cold shoulder to him." So I think that she's in some sense mistreating and taking advantage of him, but she has awareness of that, and I don't know that I need to intervene.

GEDO: Let me try to respond to the question you asked just before this last one, about which transferences follow in what sequence. [The presenter] is maintaining what Kohut called the idealizing transference by being the good selfobject who tells her everything she needs to know about dealing with her patients in a nonabusive manner—dealing with herself in a nonabusive manner and dealing with her patients in a nonabusive manner. So he represents her childhood hopes or, if you will, the scraps of childhood experience where some third person intervened on the right side of the conflict and helped her to be the kind of person she wanted to be, and she admired the decency of that person. He has to be decent. He has to be decent because no one else has ever been decent; and fundamentally she isn't decent, or she suspects herself of not being decent. When she says she's not smart enough to get a Ph.D. from her university, that's ludicrous. She knows very well she's smarter than most, but she's not decent enough. She doesn't deserve it. Well, okay, so during the session they're in—we call it an idealizing transference—she's not traumatized, and she absorbs the decency, and it lasts her for 24 hours. Or if it's four sessions a week, 45 weeks a year, it lasts her essentially all the time and she is in equilibrium. She is both decent and integrated, except in the episodes with the two boyfriends, plus God knows what other episodes, [including episodes with] the husband too. After all, she was abusive to the husband; she cheated on him in more ways than one.

PRESENTER: In marrying him, she cheated him. She misrepresented herself.

GEDO: She said so, she said so. As you know, these self-accusations have to be taken *very* seriously, very, very seriously. And we can't say, "Oh, you're too hard on yourself" [because the patients know better]. In these relationships where she's so abusive, she is reexperiencing a transference, too, in which all that counts is that familiar feeling, the familiar feeling that is so important to Dr. Gehrie's patient that everything else, *everything else* is insignificant. You know, if it's a choice between that and anything else, she'll opt for that, she'll opt for that. He only hears reports of this more primitive state of being, but in fact it characterizes her life much of the time unless she is thrown a lifesaver and pulled out of the ditch, which is what we do. What has pulled her out of the ditch far enough so that she feels she deserves to live is that she doesn't have to be as indecent as otherwise she would be compelled to be. The art of it all is that you can't pull her out all the way. At least I'd say you can't pull her out all the way and analyze the problem. If you always keep her above that most primitive level of her being, all you are doing is putting a patch over it., the patch that Kohut called compensatory structure.

That is why I was in such sharp disagreement with him about his statement about what a satisfactory analytic termination is. Whether we were talking about the same cases or not we'll never know, since he's dead, although we did have an opportunity to talk about some specific cases, most of all the case that is reported on Goldberg's 1978 casebook, and that Kohut then wrote the first chapter of his 1977 book about. I was part of the casebook group then, and I was in sharp disagreement with the rest of them. Kohut said that the case was not amenable to further work because the man was so abusive. This was the man who noticed a "physical disability" of his analyst and developed sadistic fantasies about it. At any rate, I think his sadism was never analyzed. And he was allowed to leave with this silent pact that "we'll all be decent together and we won't touch your sadism." Well, as many of you know, it was supposedly a great therapeutic success. There's no question about it. If you can be inspiring enough so that people remember how inspiring you were and lead a decent life ever after, you have been a successful therapist, and that's great. But by my definition that's not an analysis.

COMMENT: How does her idealization of [the analyst] keep her functioning?—a ridiculous question . . .

GEDO: No, I didn't say that. I said it the other way around. I think [the analyst] actually intervenes and helps her to be decent to herself and decent to her patient. He tells her, "Hey, that's indecent! Don't do that! Don't do that. Don't throw away the $100,000. You're being indecent to yourself." And he's only [doing] the same about her therapeutic work. As a consequence, she idealizes him. In that sense, the idealization is an epiphenomenon, in my judgment. That's another way in which I am in total disagreement with the self psychologists who see these as developmental necessities, as the crux of the matter, as the motor of human psychology. [In self psychology], both the grandiosity and the idealization are seen as primary. I see idealization as [the sum of] the sentiments that [are evoked when someone does] a good job as a parent or as a therapist. He's doing a good job in keeping her [from] repeating the horrors of her childhood or passing them on to other people in an indecent way. He has managed it so that she is able to feel that she deserves to live, at least temporarily, like Kafka's K in *The Trial*. His sentence was postponed indefinitely, [as you recall]. According to Kafka, that's the best thing one can hope for in life, that one's sentence of death is postponed. Well, so is hers. Still, he has permitted her to dip into her "savings account" in the relationship with this man, so they can begin to talk about the fact that her self-accusations are not without foundation.

PRESENTER: Well, she's in a better integrated state. She has a place that's relatively safe and stable from which to view [things]. I also think that everything doesn't hinge on the relationship with this man.

COMMENT: Your decency to her allows her to turn around.

GEDO: It seems to me that [the analyst] has gone beyond being decent to her, although, of course, he started out that way. He has elevated decency into an abstract principle. "Everybody must be decent to everybody else," [that] is what he has conveyed to her. She must even be decent to *herself*. "You have no right to turn down the $100,000."

COMMENT: That's an *affective* decency, because when we talk, make interpretations to the patient without affect like that, we're being decent in doing our regular daily work, but there's something more to *this*.

PRESENTER: Well, she took that position long before she met me: with her father. I mentioned last time that her father, who was a paranoid man, was going to leave her mother nothing. Whatever one would say about their relationship, she stayed by the father throughout his life. She said to him, "You can't do that to her! That's indecent and I won't stand for it." And the father said okay—one of the few times in his life he ever simply said, "Oh, I guess you're right," and changed his behavior. So she had that as an ideal before she met me.

GEDO: It can't be coincidental that she managed to get an analyst whose reputation for decency precedes him. But when she did [that] with her father, it wasn't in the service of an abstract ideal; she was protecting her mother.

PRESENTER: Oh, right, yeah, yeah.

GEDO: So, she's been doing it on the outside too, in flashes. But when some sort of routine analytic intervention [has taken place] and she starts by saying how worthless it is, that's very indecent. Wouldn't a decent response be that he's a good man and he's doing his best and unfortunately something else seems to be necessary? She attacks him for it, and that's indecent.

PRESENTER: She mocks me for being an analyst, and she certainly knows how much of my adult life has been involved in becoming an analyst and trying to master it, and she mocks me. She says, "Oh, you read that in the handbook, didn't you?" Or, "That's what you were trained to say." She doesn't say, "I don't think this is so helpful. We should try another tactic." She spits it out, mockingly.

GEDO: Poisonous, huh? Like her father's paranoia. So it's not that the core of the psychopathology, the beginnings of the psychopathology, don't show up in the analytic situation, but the organized transference is something else. She responds poisonously when [the analyst] is imperfect. He tries to be relatively satisfactory. I must say one reason for opting for my technical position is that the alternative is unendurable. Anybody who pretends that he can put up with a paranoid person's abuse over long periods of time is a fool, or a knave, or both. I don't think that we're obliged to put up with any abuse in any treatment.[g] In fact, it's just as unacceptable as not to take the fee when a patient cancels, and this patient couldn't tolerate it if you tolerated being abused, because for some reason we haven't heard about yet she did incorporate a conscience. And when she is wicked, she condemns herself to death; so to allow the patient to be wicked with you is intolerable for both.

PRESENTER: There are some genetic [data] that come to mind. The father certainly had a conscience. The father was a highly principled man. I think I mentioned that he worked for the government, and I think he was quite good at what he did. But there were issues with superiors; he was intolerant of their ways of doing things. I don't know whether they were breaking laws or stretching this or that, and he would threaten to quit. There was a man who was his friend (this was the only relationship outside the home that I ever heard about) who would counsel the father and calm him down and say, "You can't do that. You can't quit, You have to be more concerned about your own welfare than about your principles." So there's [the] model for the patient's [pattern of behavior]. There's something of that which I'm duplicating with her, [telling her] "You can't destroy yourself because of your principles." She saw that transaction take place in childhood.

GEDO: We can say, "I totally agree with you that you must pay my fee because you are in fact the kind of conscientious person who otherwise couldn't tolerate the implicit frustrations that you impose on me. And for the same reason, if anything happens here that I find too difficult to bear, I'll let you know." Because of the special dynamic here, you can't much use genetic reconstructions, but you'll get there. It will all begin to fit.

Cases like this raise the technical issue that Heinz Kohut made the center of his work in the last 15 years or so [of his career]. Is it really true that the mutative interpretation is the transference interpretation within the analytic setting? Well, I don't know. If that were true, then one suspects that with cases like this one would never get there. I mean, there isn't going to be an organized transference in which [this analyst] abuses this person in the way that her caretakers abused her as a child, and I cannot imagine that he would put up with that kind of abuse on his own behalf for long enough so that in fact it would constitute the kind of reliving that we witness in the transference neurosis. And I suspect that the closest they'll come to it is through enactments outside of the treatment situation.

GEHRIE: But wouldn't you also say that even if it were possible for [an analyst] to provide that kind of an environment and tolerate that kind of an enactment, that would not necessarily also provide the opportunity for [a] resolution in the way there is a model for the resolution of the transference neurosis? That is, because of the features involved in such an enactment, the separation of the enactment from the rest of the personality would be extremely difficult, if at all possible.

Gedo: That's even more true in the case that you alluded to. Although we heard relatively little about it, [we did] agree that [your case is] on a [somewhat] more primitive level. So what is the therapeutic task in these instances? It's not repetition, because, in fact, these people never cease repeating their relevant issues. They come in the first place because their life consists of a [series of] repetition[s] of terribly primitive things that on some level they can't stand either. So, on one hand, you have to try to transform the enactments into verbal statements. And one hope is that, once it can be stated in words, it doesn't have to be continuously repeated in action. At least that was Freud's thought. He said that even about the transference neurosis, of course. I think there's something to that, don't you? We all hope there's something to that. So if that is true, then in fact the treatment consists in teaching the person a new language.[h]

Comment: Then is she teaching herself a new language? How is she able to do that?

Gedo: Well, [the presenter] is excessively modest. I think he's doing more of that than he's permitted himself to claim.

Comment: So your assumption is that he is actually helping her to see that she is treating her boyfriend sadistically and this is what the articulation of the core psychopathology has been. She will never be able to really relive it directly within the transference.

Gedo: Well, I don't know whether that particular set of transactions has been articulated. You know, learning a language is a very complicated matter, and it's not necessarily that tightly correlated with specific issues in focus in the analysis. Let me get back to my patient, because I can provide illustrations more easily from [my own work]. He's not getting his money [from the politician], and he keeps forgetting the check that he has written out to me. He has been very prompt in paying me, because we had a difficulty about that some years ago, not a trivial difficulty. He wrote out the check as soon as he got the bill, and for several days running he didn't bring it with him. I tried to put into words the issue between him and [the politician], because he tried to say the issue between them is money. And I said, "Oh no, oh no. That's not it. You and your brothers use money as a metaphor for everything, but that's not it.

The issues between you and [your mentor are] love, friendship, and being made to wait. As you know, I don't like to wait." Now, of course, when I say we try to teach people a new language, I'm not saying that he doesn't know the meaning of the word "to wait." Obviously he's a very, very, very articulate man, in fact, something of an orator. I'm making a connection for him between the words "to wait" and the terrible pain when somebody makes you wait on purpose, to torture you.

COMMENT: I would argue that that's a very different example from [the presenter's] case, because you were talking about the dynamic between you and him, not something outside—[that factor] makes it much more immediate.

GEDO: [But between us] it happened a long time ago—I won't tell you how many years ago—in the first period of treatment and, in fact, led to an interruption. For years he was quite paranoid about it. [This time, I] merely said, "*As you know,* I don't like to wait," which is not an interpretation. In fact, it's not a statement about him at all except . . .

COMMENT: Yes it is.

COMMENT: But he's doing it to you.

GEDO: Well, he's the one who is waiting now.

COMMENT: On the outside.

GEDO: Yes. You see, he says, "I forgot to bring the check," but after all, it's only the fifth of the month when this is happening, so it's no problem. He knows that our agreement is that he will pay by, whatever, the tenth. These things are terribly, terribly complicated. Every statement we make has a thousand functions, right? And ten thousand meanings. But very gradually, over the years, it should become possible for him to be able to say, when he feels like that, "What you deserve is that I should pay you at midnight on the tenth, with sacks of pennies."

COMMENT: That makes complete sense to me. I understand that. I don't understand [the presenter's] patient, because [the cases] feel very different. I don't understand how she can get a grip on what she's doing without [its] being exposed in the way in which you're exposing what [your patient is] doing to you. I mean, she says, "I'm doing this," and she's brilliant in that regard; as you say, she's very talented. But is that all there is that allows her to do that? Are some people just smarter, so they can identify this aspect of themselves?

GEDO: Well, some people are smarter than others, and some people are very psychologically minded . . .

PRESENTER: You start off with this woman growing up in a home in the [backwoods] where people are doing things to each other continuously and seemingly have no awareness of this. She now has a Ph.D. in social work and is getting clinical experience; she must have a great talent. And she's smart with words, even though she pooh-poohs that. So I think she does have a lot of talent. She's very good at understanding and also with [tolerating difficulties]. I think she does have a particular talent. I haven't thought about what I would do if she didn't. And I may have taken it for granted to some degree, and I'm happy to do it.

GEDO: The problem is that we don't have a learning theory. We teach people all sorts of things, and we don't know how we do that. So he's not able to tell us how he's teaching her, but he's teaching her. Don't you believe his disclaimers. And the best methods of instruction are probably the least direct ones. The real problem is not in connecting for her these various symbolic systems that for her don't translate into each other. They'll manage that between them. The crux of the matter is going to come when the problem that Dr. Gehrie brought to your attention becomes focal. Can she give up abuse as the center of her life? Gehrie's patient probably cannot, and it sounds [as though] it might become an interminable treatment.

COMMENT: Would it be possible if Gehrie became a benign, positive introject that she could rely on in order to replace the loss of the negative mother? The same thing in [the presenter's] case . . .

GEDO: That's what all the optimists say, and there are more psychoanalysts who believe that sort of thing than any other kind. But I stick to Freud's position that adding things to the bouillabaisse doesn't remove any poison.

COMMENT: I'm not sure that that analogy translates.

GEDO: Well, Freud didn't use the bouillabaisse metaphor; he used the sculpture versus painting metaphor, as you recall. He said that psychoanalysis is like sculpting in stone—you have to remove what's there. Adding benign introjects, becoming a selfobject—somewhat different conceptualizations, perhaps somewhat different proce-dures—is simply an intent to neutralize the poisonous behavior and is essentially an interminable task. It's perfectly possible that he doesn't have to see her four or five times a week interminably, and if you get sufficiently inspiring—you know, as one gets older, one is given credit for being inspiring automatically—it may be possible. If you have a concentration camp tattoo on your forearm, and you let your patients see it, it's entirely possible that they'll get well on your behalf just by virtue of that. And you don't have to see them very often, or ever. Now don't get me wrong, it's entirely possible that all of us will obtain our results in large measure through such unintended psychotherapeutic effects. But we're talking theory, and [in theory] what you're proposing is not an analytic solution.

The analytic solution is to remove the poison, which means to remove the patient's sense that the very core of existence is torturing or being tortured. And if that's really the core of existence, if it's *really* the core of existence, if there's very little else, it's not possible to give it up. I mean that's the kind of situation that Dr. Gehrie is alluding to: To [remove] the pathology is to disembowel the patient. There are such instances. It's possible that in addition to the torture there were other things. In that case, the other things can continue to serve as the crux of [future existence]. One can always reassure one's patients by reminding them that life is the pits and that if they want to wait a little while, they'll have terrible, unpleasant experiences without tilting the wheel of fortune against themselves. The main thing for your patient is to be able to stop herself from abusing others. Then she can think of herself as a decent person, deserving of good things in life.

PRESENTER: Well, she is still abusing herself at the same time.

GEDO: Okay, that's next, that's next. You see, she doesn't complain that she has been self-abusive, from what you've told us. She complains that she doesn't deserve to live, because she's a poisonous snake. We must stop.

Follow-up Session in 1991

PRESENTER: A lot of the work with this woman has been to try to reconstruct a very disrupted and chaotic early childhood. And it's led to one unusual event, and that is that I met with her mother about a year or so ago to discuss some of [the patient's] early experiences. The other thing that's made this treatment very complicated is that about a year and a half into the treatment, malignancy [was detected] in both breasts. Now she's more than five years postcancer surgery and has been clear. So certainly that was an ongoing concern for a number of years—whether she was going to live or not—which fits this woman's character. [She feels] that she isn't going to live anyway, and she's going to die because she can't sustain her own life.

She was referred to me [as] a classic hysteric [who] needed analysis. What I remember of her [is that] she looked depressed and tentative and frightened. She said she hoped that I would be willing to see her—would I accept her? She gave me opportunities to say no, that I was too busy or I didn't want to be bothered.

QUESTION: What did she give as reasons for wanting treatment?

PRESENTER: I'm not even sure. I think she felt depressed. I don't know precisely what she had in mind for treatment.

QUESTION: I was asking something like, "Why at that point in her life?"

PRESENTER: That's a good question. She had to have someone help her. She had no one to look after her. She [usually dealt] with her need to be looked after by looking after somebody else, but that was disappearing from her life. She also had an absolute conviction that she wouldn't be able to make it in life, that she could not look after herself. Now, I don't think that she could have enunciated that at that time, but it was announced by her manner of saying, "Will you take me? 'Cause I need someone to take me." One of the first things she told me about was her relationships with men, that they all come apart. The one love of her life [had been] in high school, a fellow who wanted to marry her and persisted through high school and college, trying to get her to say that she would marry him. He was a decent fellow, a nice fellow, an upstanding citizen. She wanted to marry him, but she was convinced that she would get very depressed at some point and couldn't be a wife to him, so she didn't want to saddle him with her[self].

A major theme in treatment [has been] that if I interpret anything as something else, that's unbearable. That makes what she does meaningless, not genuine, not real. And it was intolerable. And we went around and around on this for quite a while: I would make "transference interpretations," and it was clear enough that she had feelings for me that she hoped to have, that she felt she had. If I were to interpret anything as having another kind of meaning, it made for no relationship between us. I had a lot of trouble with this: I didn't know what to do with it for a long time.

Now one of the things that she began to see was how much of a struggle this was for me, to know what to do with it.

QUESTION: Did you come to restructure the style of your interpretations?

PRESENTER: Absolutely. I didn't make interpretations. We talked about things. I didn't interpret.

GEDO: It's a sign of some kind of profound disturbance in the process of language acquisition, that somehow the connection between the concept and the words that go with that concept is so tenuous that if you blow on it, it collapses.

QUESTION: Is it more that to use language puts [the transaction] into another way of relating?

PRESENTER: I haven't seen it in terms of language.

QUESTION: Does your purpose deviate from what she thinks you ought to be doing?

PRESENTER: Well, to jump right into one of the main themes, there's no sense of connection. How to put that together with language?

QUESTION: There is no other connection? Or if the connection is not proper on the affective level, it's words that have to make the connection?

QUESTION: What do you mean there was no connection?

PRESENTER: She would be concerned if I'd say, "You're feeling this way about me because . . . this is very much like you felt about so and so." That means that we have no relationship.

COMMENT: But up until you said "because," she definitely did feel you have a relationship.

PRESENTER: Absolutely, but then [if I give a reason], I am denying the relationship. Right then and there I'm saying, "There's nothing between us," by making an interpretation. I can intervene all I want. But by translating, by saying, "This in some way resembles that," that means "This is nothing."

COMMENT: But if you didn't say that part, if you just said, "You feel angry at me," or, "You love me," or whatever it is, she most certainly did feel that to be true. It was a very clear cut . . .

COMMENT: I think the introduction of the word "because" in that sentence just negates everything, because, as you were saying, John, the underlying connection, which is nonverbal, the nonverbal part of the communication, is negated by the verbal part of the

communication. I think John's thinking of it developmentally because the sequence was, first, before we have words, we have
nonverbal communication. And our emotional connectedness to
others is based on that. It's based on affective signals, not a verbal
signal, not a syntactical, verbal signal. This woman doesn't make
that connection. She tries to make it [by way of] some other meaning. For [some] reason she can't *think* [without a] threat to the
relationship, even if [the thinking merely consisted of] translating
feelings, pointing out a parallel. To her it means it's nothing. There's
nothing there.

PRESENTER: I think what developed over time is that first, at some
point, she had an appreciation of what a struggle I've gone through
to be able to comply with her enough so that she could stay in
treatment and still be an analyst as I conceived of being an analyst.
She would say, in a sort of sympathetic way, "Oh, you read that out
of the analyst's handbook." And then she would say, "All right, now
I've learned [you] have to do that; okay, I've learned enough about
[you to know] that we have to go through that, but I don't have to
take it seriously. That doesn't mean that the tie is broken. You don't
mean me any harm, or things aren't always perfect between people.
That doesn't mean the relationship is over."

GEDO: "Not all that verbiage that I take so seriously is disturbing.
It's just hot air and can be safely disregarded, and I can rely on my
feelings."

COMMENT: "The valuable part is valuable enough, so I'll put up with
this."

PRESENTER: I know I went through a period, maybe in the second or
third year, [when] I couldn't keep this woman in mind at all. I
couldn't remember her. In my thinking about patients, I neglected
her. Every other patient would get some kind of "just due" in my
reflection of my work and understanding what's going on, and
whatever. But she just sort of disappeared. She just sort of faded into
the woodwork. Another aspect of her demeanor is that she could be
very bland and accepting—she could look very bland. People sort of
[overlook] her.

QUESTION: If you lost your interest in her, relatively, at some time
more than another time, would she pick it up and react to it?

PRESENTER: I don't think she picked it up. No, I don't think she
picked it up. She may have reacted to it. I'm sure she reacted to it,
but I don't think she realized what she was reacting to. She didn't

call me on that. But the sort of thing that would fit with that were periods when she was a latency-age child, when [her] grand-mother, who was a stroke victim, was lying comatose in the bed-room. She would go into the grandmother's bedroom and the grandmother was not conscious, and she would lie down on the bed in the room. This would be the family farm and there were cousins and aunts and uncles around, and no one else was paying any attention to this comatose grandmother, except for the patient. So the idea of being still and practicing being dead was an aspect of what she did.

QUESTION: Is that her view of what she was doing? Or was it the view that she was with somebody who [was dead]?

PRESENTER: That could be true, but . . . *she* wanted to be still. It was all part of her relationship with her mother; she wanted to be away from the mother. Desperately! But she couldn't sustain the separa-tion from the mother, and she would be very threatened.

QUESTION: Did she want to be away from the mother in the sense of being able to avoid some intrusiveness, something coming from the mother, or what?

PRESENTER: That's what we are learning, what she wants to be away from. The way she talked about it for quite a while was that the mother preferred the brother—because he was a jolly baby, he would smile, and he was happy and compliant. [The mother] did not like the patient because the patient was a tomboy; she was a lot of trouble for the mother. That was on one level. More seriously, she felt that the mother didn't want her. The mother used to humiliate her [by acting as if the patient did not count]. Yet she felt completely tied to her mother. She was furious with her, even into adult life. And forever. Her plan was that when the mother became old and feeble, she would give up her life in Chicago and move back to look after her mother.

COMMENT: That means that she can say "because," which is a real development. We're talking about developmental achievement.

PRESENTER: I think I became a supporter of hers. She makes her living being a therapist. I would be, in essence, supervising her cases. We talked about her cases and I'd encourage her, remind her of her abilities, and point out her misperceptions about herself or her misperceptions about other people. So I think those themes cemented our relationship. Also, she could give me gifts, and I learned to be able to accept them. Every Christmas she would bring me a flower. Would I permit her to do this? Would I allow her to have that much contact with me? One rose, an orchid. And I would accept it. It would sit on my desk for that session. But she never asked me further about it.

She got involved with cases of children who had been abused. Sexual abuse or sadistic physical abuse. She became obsessed with this topic, had dreams about it, and went on and on and on about it. And we spent a lot of time trying to decide whether or not she had been abused. She had no [such] memory at all. We looked very carefully at the time the father was away, and what we discovered was that there was nothing that she or I could latch on to, [No] "Oh, I bet something actually did happen." No memory of any sort, nothing that was even circumstantial. We learned two things from this. One is that that year (or nine months) when the father was gone was chaotic, absolutely chaotic. The brother was born, the father was called overseas, and the mother became virtually psychotic. The father stayed a few weeks after the brother was born. Because she didn't hear from him when the father went overseas, the mother instantly decided he was dead. In contrast to the way that she would say that the daughter will come back when she's hungry, the mother thought that the father was dead.

COMMENT: We don't know what the mother's state was when she said, "She'll come back when she's hungry." That can look like a cute thing to say, but it could cover over [anything].

PRESENTER: They must have lived in five or six different places in that nine month period. The patient brought me some pictures of herself and the mother, and the patient and the brother, from the time the father was away. And as much as a picture can capture what a person is like, [it was an image of] this woman whom I would forget. The mother is beaming, the little baby brother is a chubby little baby bouncing on the mother's lap, and this child is sitting looking off into space, totally unconnected to the mother. Disappearing into thin air. What we did reconstruct from all the concern about sexual abuse was the mother's toilet training procedure with the patient, which was, from some time around age one, to strap her to a potty and leave her there until she produced. This went on for at least a year.

COMMENT: That's *very* abusive!

PRESENTER: We had some questions about whether enemas were given or not, from some dreams. We don't know; we never could establish whether enemas were given. The patient had a lot of trouble holding on to [these] facts. Could we believe this? We had the mother's testimony, and then the patient thought, "Well, maybe it wasn't true," that she's making it all up. So she's having a great deal of trouble.

COMMENT: Well, let me interrupt you, because her perception of what is real and what isn't is one of the areas of her deficit. That's what she's telling you. She doesn't know what is real. Is it the same thing as [a deficit in language development]?

GEDO: She doesn't know what's real on the basis of *feeling*. Right? So she has to pay attention to language. There's some problem with language, too. Because she doesn't understand the difference between causality and negation.

COMMENT: Because of similar pathology emanating from the same kind of crazy mother, I mentioned to one patient that she had been abused, and she almost quit the analysis. This is years into a good treatment. Why was I saying she was abused? She had never used that word for her experience. She detailed the experience; it wasn't that she forgot it. But the language, in terms of the reality of the abuse, [is not available to permit] my patient's reality testing.

PRESENTER: Oh, this has tremendous relevance! For four years my office was arranged so that right behind my chair there was a bookcase that filled up the whole space. Every time she walked to the couch, she would face that bookcase because it was right behind me. She never saw that bookcase. It appeared in one of her dreams. When I pointed it out in her dream, she didn't know what the hell I was talking about. Just a few weeks ago, she said, "You've got a new lamp on your desk." Well, this was very good; it's only been there a month. "Where's the other one?" which has been gone a year. Knowing what's real. She also can't process very much, at least in the regression in the treatment. But, in any event, she became uncertain about the facts of her abuse, and because of that, when the mother was visiting, I said that I would see the mother and discuss things with her so that we could nail this down.

COMMENT: Although it was she who came up with [the fact] that she had been strapped to the potty chair.

PRESENTER: She had come up with it. I don't remember where she had heard it. She probably confirmed it with the mother by phone, but then the mother started to deny it. So, of course, the mother's confirmation and denial are driving her crazy. I offered [to talk to the mother] as a way of helping nail this down. "I would be willing to see your mother if you would like me to. Maybe this will help you and maybe I can confirm for you her inability to hold on to a story herself."

COMMENT: And her response was, "Fine, if you would do that. Yes, that would be fine."

COMMENT: I just came back from [a meeting] where this kind of stuff would mean, "You're under arrest!"

QUESTION: Do you think [that those who feel that way] would think she's analyzable?

COMMENT: Well, [they would say] this is psychotherapy, so it doesn't make any difference. They would start thinking about the analyst's countertransference problems in doing something like this.

GEDO: That's very complicated. If they agreed that she has real trouble in reality testing, then they should say she should not be in analysis, she should be in psychotherapy, and they would be perfectly comfortable [about meeting a relative].

COMMENT: I am concerned myself [about] what your motivation was and how [your action] would be experienced by her, given her earlier [objections when you tried] to make interpretations like an analyst—[she saw that] as breaking up something between you. However, *this* she experiences as enhancing something between you. This woman is a professional, and she certainly knows that analysts don't do [such] things—so it must be that you're doing it out of concern for her.

GEDO: Because she has a special need, because she is in perpetual doubt about her reality testing.

COMMENT: I'm not concerned [about] the technique per se. I'm talking about what she must be experiencing when the analyst does this.

COMMENT: I think the treatment would not be possible without her conviction on that point.

COMMENT: I have had two kinds of experiences with this sort of intervention. One person went berserk at every interpretation, [but] he would think that when I [intervened noninterpretively] that's not being an analyst. Another person, [once] you did things like this, demanded that you do *only* things like this. Both of them were reasonably sophisticated. So I'm curious [about why] she read this as "help."

PRESENTER: The mother changed her story about the toilet training. [The child] had been strapped. "Well, it wasn't that way," and she was angry with me, [she claimed] I misunderstood her and that I was a schmuck. The mother was angry because I was pinning her down; she felt I was accusing her of being a neglectful and hostile [parent]. So I only pushed her so far. She started to deny that [those events] ever happened, and she didn't know where the patient had gotten such an idea.

The other thing the mother did at the interview was to tell me how desperate she had been when the father was overseas and that she should have gone to Florida. I don't know why that particular place, but she should have gone and had a little apartment with her two children, but she couldn't do it. She couldn't make a home; she couldn't find a home. I think she said that to me eight times, what a terrible time that had been for her, and she wanted some sympathy, because after all she hadn't known if her husband was dead, and it was very hard for everyone, it was *very* hard, and so forth. And I granted that it was very hard, it was a very difficult thing to manage.

[Two other matters about the patient should be mentioned]: One has to do with her ability to hold onto herself, her integration. She became obsessed with multiple personalities and a movie [about one]. She's never been able to watch the whole movie. Recently, she's become obsessed with a case of a child being lowered into a well. I think that it must be her way of trying to approach her own failure of reality testing or integration—some sense of a loss of integration that she has to contend with, which we've never really identified as such.

The other issue we had a lot of discussion about, in the face of her recent surgery, was whether she would slip away from me, from the contact with me, [because] the relationship was a way to stay alive. She had a great deal of trouble holding on to the idea of staying alive. She had a pact with herself that she would see her children to the age of 21 and then she would kill herself. That she revealed to me somewhere in the middle of our work, that she had this pact.

QUESTION: How old were the children at that time when she revealed it to you? Approximately.

PRESENTER: The younger one has just graduated from college, so she must be about 21; she was then maybe 18 or 17. The older one was approaching 21. She had a very good relationship with her children, I think she was warm with them. She was certainly caring and concerned; she had warmth that showed up nowhere else in her life. And her kids have turned out pretty well. The patient revealed at that time that she had a collection of pills at home.

GEDO: Then getting into treatment was like challenging you to change that [pact].

COMMENT: You're the executioner, unless you save her.

PRESENTER: At some point along the way, on the way to a session, she was going to run the car as fast as she could and drive into an embankment. But she threw away the pills, [feeling that] she owed it to me to not do it. And one of the ways I dealt with that was to say, under John's influence, that—*I said*, "Well, if you were to do that, if you were to kill yourself now; if you were to do that, that's your business, but at your funeral I'm going to call you every name I can think of." And she thought that was wonderful, that I really cared about her. That and threatening to hit her with the Kleenex box.

Around this last surgery, she had a lot of trouble again. I visited her in the hospital, and she was enormously anxious and somewhat paranoid. She was very grateful that I came, and she latched onto me. She was quite disorganized and almost paranoid, and she needed help—the environment was hostile, disrupted. She was very angry with the nursing staff for no real reason. She couldn't sleep, she was very irritable, very angry. But she also knew that she was just agitated and very anxious, and she didn't know why, and I prescribed some Valium. I told the surgeon she should have some Valium, and she was better in 24 hours or 48 hours. I saw her twice.

[Some time] ago, she started a relationship, I think somewhat at my urging, with a man. She had had none. He was quite a bit younger than she, a very obsessive, contained fellow. After her first surgery she had had no dealings with men. She felt herself [to be] mutilated, and she couldn't bear the idea. She's very bland in her manner and appearance. She's a pretty woman, and she has a nice figure, [which she had flaunted] and [losing that] obviously hurt her. And again she felt that it wasn't fair, she couldn't offer a full woman, so how could she ask a man to be in a relationship with her? She had this sense of equity and fairness.

[Finally] she did get involved with this fellow; he treated her pretty nicely and she was able to have a sexual relationship with him. It was very difficult for her to initiate it, to get into it, but they did. She found it very difficult to sustain a relationship because he was so obsessive and he would withdraw, and he was very messy and careless in a variety of ways. It troubled her greatly. So they would go on and off, on and off. And she urged him [to get help] and he got into some treatment. But what's happened is that he suddenly became an Orthodox Jew, and she's just broken up with him. She can't tolerate the absolute separation [of the sexes] that he insists on. Whenever there's a holiday, he refuses to have contact with her. He started this about a year ago. And she can't bear it. I tried to interpret this in terms of the father, who was probably psychotic, briefly, overseas.[i] [Afterwards] he was "different." That's what we're trying to determine. Did he ever come back? She has testimony from relatives that he had some spirit and would fight with her as a child. But when he came back, he was bitter, paranoid, isolated, and fought with the mother constantly. That's all they would do—bicker and fight. He liked the patient. He was sort of pleased by her, but he didn't have very much to give. [That's what we are trying to deal with at present.]

Commentary (Gehrie)

It is apparent at the outset, from the form of the analyst's report, that primitive transference longings were in the forefront of this patient's self-presentation, that the regressive opportunity of the analytic situation was not required for the emergence of these archaic states. The patient consciously thought of the analyst as a figure of considerable significance, likely without "room" for her as a patient. By contrast, the analyst reports that in this period "the most important transaction was that I forgot her . . . she remained in the shadows of my mind [alone] of all the patients I saw." Remarking on the events of the first interruption in the treatment, five months after beginning, the analyst reports that he attempted to interpret her having an affair during the break as an acting out—that is, as a displacement from the transference—and that this interpretation "was not utilizable by the patient."

This apparent transference/countertransference dynamic, however, was soon to change: the patient as helpless and needy of constant guidance in life, and the analyst as guide—initially disinterested, but suddenly galvanized into active and involved caring following the discovery of the patient's breast cancer and her surgeries. "I visited her in the hospital . . . she was surprised that I would want to do that." The analyst reports that their "mode of operations changed very drastically," but it seems more accurate to suggest that it was he who changed in relation to his patient, that the diagnosis of her illness made it possible for him to permit himself to become engaged with her. He, besides the patient's own children, "was the only one who would move his chair closer to her bed." As the intensity grew, the analyst began actively to argue with her about the necessity of clinging to her own life: "I took the stance that she shouldn't [allow herself to feel she was going to die]." This form of relatedness—the sincere, passionate involvement of the analyst as helper and healer—was to become the central bulwark of the treatment, and its main issue. It appears safe,however, to suggest that at the outset,the source of responsibility for the emphasis on this issue may belong not to the patient alone and that what follows in the treatment should perhaps not be characterized as solely the emergence of an archaic state projected onto or into an environment of analytic neutrality.[j]

Following these interactions, and the increased contact outside of the hours (including some in familial contexts), the analyst attempts to make transference interpretations about the patient's fantasies regarding gifts for him, to which she responds with disbelief and self-destructive fantasies. In other words, is this patient simply intolerant of reality? Or is the central point the shift in the analyst's posture from the proferral and acceptance of "real" emotional interplay to a position more reminiscent of an analytic context in which interpretations about that emotional interplay suggest some reality other than that in which both parties had until that moment participated. Certainly a subject of frequent argument has been that the opportunity to make transference interpretations relies on an atmosphere that makes it possible for such implications (past versus present) to be heard, an atmosphere in which there is a minimum of confusion about what the reality of the analytic environment is. At the height of the transference repetition, these distinctions become as blurred as we dare as a matter of course, but such blurring is permitted in the service of analytic teaching and learning.

In this vein, it is interesting that the analyst reports that this patient, earlier as a member of a therapy group, "got involved sexually with one of the other patients," and it was this fact that caused the analyst to question "whether she's really a treatable patient." Here, again, it is arguable that the patient's ability to recognize transference, or, more properly speaking, to reflect on her own primitive or regressed experience, is poor, but not necessarily a structural flaw of the personality. It is not clear from this event that she is unable to make such a distinction, but only that the context may not have provided her with adequate opportunity to do so.

Related to these questions is the analyst's difficulty shortly thereafter in grasping how this patient felt: "She never could recreate anything that would let me feel my way into how she felt, and let me identify with her." From the patient's description of her ex-husband, as well as her distance from her father (who died five years prior to the analysis), it is unclear to what extent the patient manages her relationship to the analyst through a seamless repetition of her early adaptive solutions, and to what extent the countertransference factor plays a role in the analyst's experience of this. The early absence of the father (in the patient's fourth year), his psychosis, and the multiple family moves during his absence are undoubtedly factors in the patient's management of the transference and in her experience of the analyst. They unquestionably influence her ability to communicate her affects in such a way as to establish clearly her emotional states—that is, the risks involved in the repetition of the early traumata require her distancing, forcing the analyst to step over into the active position of re-creation:

> What we've done, I think, that has [proved] most effective in the treatment is to reconstruct the amount of depression and feeling of isolation and disconnection from her mother that the patient experienced at the time of the brother's birth and in the few months after the brother's birth. She brought in some pictures that were taken when the brother was roughly three, four, five months old and they're remarkable pictures. The mother looks like the happiest woman you can imagine with this infant, not [such a] tiny [baby anymore], and the patient is looking over there, this very depressed looking little girl. And there seems to be no evidence of contact between the [patient and her mother] in this picture. . . .

Surprisingly, considering the patient's anxiety about transference interpretations, reconstructions by the analyst are experienced as helpful and calming insofar as they clarify early emotional states and acknowledge the meaning of the early experience. Such a response by the patient suggests that the analyst's countertransference of active intervention to mitigate the patient's helplessness—viewed as an unplanned form of interpretive assistance—had an effect both therapeutic and analytic. To the extent that an opportunity for understanding was possibly created, or at least preserved by it, the intervention permitted the patient to maintain her fantasy of independence while simultaneously accepting (and depending on) emotional involvement. These events are consistent with the analyst's acknowledgment that his patient was "not entirely there" and would not notice things in his office while simultaneously her dependence on him grew. For this patient to do otherwise is too dangerous: "Her telling me how she feels about me puts her in jeopardy of having to kill herself."[k]

Gedo inquires about what cued the analyst "to the fact that you had to go visit her in the hospital?" The analyst's response is revelatory of the utility of the countertransference for the management of such archaic transference configurations:

> I thought that she couldn't possibly go through [the surgery] and come back without my having made some contact with her. That the issue of this

being proscribed would be too much [of a repetition of past traumata]—I guess I thought I'd be just like the husband, who, as far as I could tell, couldn't make contact with this woman.

The next question must, of course, arise: "What is the theory of technique behind such an approach?" Classical theory, Gedo notes, would presume an intrapsychic conflict, symbolically encoded, "that is capable of resolution if explicated clearly." In this case, the analyst insists that the patient "could not have used intervention at that level." This patient, he insists, needed "demonstration" (of the analyst's emotions); she required that the analyst respond to her without the intervening "processing" of that response that she felt as emotional distance, and hence he could "act it but not speak it." Gedo remarks that this "collusion" is "a fantastical apparatus that makes this treatment possible . . . [it is] crucial." What, though, is it that prevents this patient from accepting interpretation (in the usual sense)? Gedo's reply is that in the global context of this enactment, the patient is, by way of repetition in the service of mastery, "trying to impose a happier ending" onto circumstances that were once unbearable: a sense of fundamental "fraudulence" about conventional interaction: that in her central family relationships, the underlying reasons for the great intensity of her emotions were not likely to be understood by her. Note, for instance, the analyst's remark that "the example of mother's behavior never matched the intensity of the patient's negative feeling."

A central point, and a confusing one, is that the underlying damage was as much a product of the patient's confusion about her own affects as it was about real events in her history. She was unable to understand why she felt so angry at her mother and distant from her father, and she fell back on a sense of being out of control and bad and on her desires for vengeance. It was this experience she sought most strongly to avoid. Owing to its nature, it was not amenable to ordinary interpretation, since ordinary interpretation replicated this experience for her. She could not grasp why she felt so intensely: "If you transcribe it [reality] on paper it sounds great, and then it turns out to be nothing. In fact, it's worse than nothing, because it boggles the mind." The key to interpretation under such circumstances appears to be a foothold in current, "actual" experience of the moment, which reveals that "her feelings have meaning between us." Gedo adds that the implication is that the patient's early experiences "were somehow contaminated or rendered worthless by some sort of miscommunication." The problem with interpretation of the present solely in terms of the past (i.e., as a "repetition") is that the present "is not a repetition" but is "a new experience." In other words, success with a patient such as this requires that the analysis be a new experience, rather than solely a new context for words that might prove to be fraudulent once again, and in that sense repeat the pathogenic circumstances. Words are dangerous because they might not be genuine.[1]

It is in the second session of the seminar that we are introduced in more depth to the evolution of the analyst's involvement with the patient. Of particular interest is his conviction that the reason the patient resisted the idea of accepting the insurance money was because of her "guilt about hurting her husband" and that his attempts to "persuade" her to take the money seemed intended to help her overcome that anxiety. In reply to the question about why he took this approach, the analyst said,

> I understood it in terms of her intense guilt about having the affair, her guilt about hurting her husband, even though it never came to his attention, and also in terms of her feelings of being undeserving and a person for whom nothing [good] should come her way.

The question that naturally arises about this point is raised by Gedo:

> What determines [that the analyst should] throw his weight into the balance of her conflicts, and what persuades him that it's an analytic thing to do to help her to take this money? What [made him] decide that it's an analytic thing to do to go to the hospital when she's having her mastectomy? . . . What had convinced [the analyst] that this was the proper way to go?

Discussion of this issue leads to a most interesting point: that more fundamental than the patient's guilt conflict about taking the money was the analyst's conviction that to "rely on interpretation" would be taken by the patient as "an unspoken message of unconcern" and that therefore the primary transference issue was not the conflict about her guilt feelings. The primary issue in the transference remained the maintaining of experienced realness in the emotional tie, and this depended on the analyst's taking passionate action on the patient's behalf, for instance, insisting that the patient take the money or not kill herself. As Gedo remarks, "[This] patient accepts the analyst as a substitute for the mother, but only if he really mothers her, not if he remains a therapist." Like a "real" mother, the analyst must "get [his] guts in an uproar" over the patient.

The discussion of this essential and controversial interaction—actually

---

[1]It might be argued at this juncture that this patient's insistence on demonstration and spontaneity of affects constitutes a defense against dealing with the reliably disappointing nature of ordinary communications, which always contain the possibility of fraudulence. Although this is true, it misses the main point that it is the very possibility of fraudulence that overwhelms this patient's ability to remain in emotional contact. To call this avoidance a "defense" would be functionally valid but would in practice be technically ineffective because such an interpretation would not be usable by the patient.

an ongoing series of interactions in this case—leads to the fundamental question of the nature of *analysis per se*. Gedo comments:

> I've done a fair amount of supervision by now, and I must say I have not encountered any instance in which the patient demanded some specific action on the part of the analyst and was unable to tolerate the frustration of that demand. Note that [in this case there] was only an implicit demand, and it's not a demand for action, it's a demand for feeling. And I think that's the frontier between a treatment that can still be conceived of as an analysis and something else.

Several questions are raised by this perspective on the "frontier of analysis."

First, it was not clear that in this case there was "not a demand for action." It seemed that the requirement for passionateness included an implicit demand for specific actions having to do with the active management of the patient's guilt as well as of the more primitive dependence on the analyst for the maintenance of the patient's sense of genuineness in the interaction. Although the countertransference dimension is significant, it seemed in any case that the analyst's response to the patient's hospitalization, for example, was at least partly to his perception of her need for his passionate action; the expression of feeling alone in such instances might not have had the same result and might have engaged the patient's anxiety about the "realness" of the analyst's feeling. It should be noted that the "interpretation of unconscious contents" is not the only, or even main, use of symbolic interpretation. Especially in cases like this one, the interpretation of the ongoing process and dynamics of the interaction would seem to be central.[1]

Gedo's comments that we must "not impose a technique on the patient but devise a technique that the patient can use" is manifestly applicable in this case, and in essence applies to every case. Technique must reflect the unique elements that present themselves in each instance, or else we consign ourselves to addressing only a predetermined universe of psychological phenomena, while everything else goes by the wayside. It is also true, however, that this flexible approach to technique has its limits and is not endlessly expandable while simultaneously preserving an analytic environment. This case strongly supports the idea of the need for the analyst's passionate response that "she had an absolute need for you [the analyst] to embark in a small boat, without a compass, across the ocean, [and you made her feel] that you'd do it for her. . . . [Such patients] require you to be *touched* by them." The question must arise, however, as to the purpose and sequelae of such interventions.

If the purpose is solely to maintain emotional contact, then the sequelae will be psychotherapeutic at best; if the purpose is to maintain emotional contact in order that analytic goals of exploration, understanding, and increased mastery may eventually be achieved, then the sequelae may be analytic. It appears, however, that the analyst must have an extraordinary view of process and of countertransference before venturing "across the ocean in a small boat without a compass." In this case, for example, was it true that "there was always a glimmer of hope that someone would intervene"? Or could it be that true hopelessness may be represented in the unmitigatable need for a passionate response from the analyst, which may never be reflected upon (Since reflection presumes the loss of passion or a distance from it)? If true reflection can never be reliably engaged, what hope is there for an analytic result as distinct from psychotherapy? If it is to be argued that the technique in this case is a way station—a preparation—for the eventual engagement of reflection and the subsequent attempt to expand the patient's repertoire of capacities for relating, then there is hope for an analytic result.[m]

Gedo's argument about the power and significance of the underlying paranoid transference in such cases—and in the additional clinical example that he gives—suggests that the basic disturbance in reality testing lies in the critical failures of early caretakers combined with traumatic overstimulation. When early symbiotic attachments are damaged in this way, the adaptive response is paranoid in nature and therefore requires—perhaps more than anything else at the outset—a genuineness, a passionateness, in response. This demonstrable realness is the only avenue of access in such states, but in analysis this must not be permitted to remain as the sole product; rather, it must be utilized as groundwork for further development.

A comment in the seminar raises a question about the distinctions between Gedo's approach and that of self psychology. For Gedo, the archaic transference exists prior to the analyst's "demonstration of affectivity" and the subsequent emergence of what Kohut called the selfobject transference. In such instances as this there is a "preexisting condition" (a preintegrated state) that must be addressed actively by "entering the patient's world." In other words, Gedo holds, the patient's "fragmented" state (in instances such as the case under discussion) is not a result of the analyst's empathic failure(s), but rather exists from the outset and therefore requires a technique that addresses this condition. The patient's "poisonous" response, which recurs in the context of any selfobject failure, is the core of the pathology; this potentiality is not caused by that failure, in Gedo's view. Should a patient present in "the integrated mode," Gedo has no disagreement with Kohut: if the cause of the regression is an empathic failure, then "you correct your error, [and] the patient returns to the level that he needs to be working on."

Perhaps the crux of Gedo's point is that for patients such as these, who exist primarily in a chronic, unintegrated (and possibly overstimulated) state, the transference, such as it is, is so primitive "that the issue of who did what to whom is not yet relevant. Only the feeling is relevant." Gedo's technique involves gaining access to this feeling state through any possible means. It is informed by the hypothesis that symbolic interpretations at this point are likely to exceed the patient's capacity for understanding; therefore they are likely to agitate the underlying condition in one form or another (such agitation may take the form of behavioral or cognitive compliance, for example). The heart of the disagreement with Kohut appears to be, in Gedo's view, that maintaining an empathically organized selfobject transference in the analysis may keep patients "above their most primitive level" and that there may be a danger of encouraging what Gedo considers to be a "patch" over such disturbed underlayment.[2] The issue seems to focus on which is the relevant layer of pathology, which are the relevant means by which to address it, and what constitutes truly analytic repair.[n]

On the level of more general clinical theory, Gedo questions the emergence of idealization and grandiosity as primary developmental phenomena and sees them as more "epiphenomenal." Although it is not clear that he is referring to the same type of cases as are under discussion here, there remains the question of the nature of the analytic approach to the developmental distortions subsequent to early developmental traumata. In the analytic environment, are we seeing the reemergence of normal developmental stages or the results of the skewed development that followed upon the early failures? In the case under discussion, Gedo suggests, the patient's idealization is secondary to her recognition of the analyst's caretaking response. "He tells her, 'Hey . . . don't throw away the $100,000. You're being indecent to yourself.' " He "rescues" her from her guilt, and "as a consequence, she idealizes him." It is not certain, however, that this idealization may not also be characterized as that which emerges as a result of the reinstatement of the selfobject bond, that is, as a developmentally relevant phenomenon, even if not the reappearance of a "normal" developmental stage.[o]

---

[2]Kohut's (1977) use of the term "compensatory structure" has been the source of some confusion in this area. In his definition of the term as distinct from "defensive structure," he said, "I call a structure compensatory when, rather than merely covering a defect in the self, it compensates for this defect . . . it brings about a functional rehabilitation of the self by making up for the weakness in one pole of the self through the strengthening of the other pole" (pp. 3–4). Discussing the conditions at termination, Kohut added, "the compensatory structures have now become functionally reliable . . ." (p. 4). "This functional rehabilitation might have been achieved predominantly through improvements in the area of the primary defect, or through the analysis of the vicissitudes of the compensatory structures (including the healing of their structural deficiencies through transmuting internalizations), or through the patient's increased mastery resulting from his comprehension of the interrelation of primary defect and compensatory structures, or through success in some or all of these areas" (pp. 4–5).

The issue is further elaborated in the discussion of the "mutative interpretation." Since, for the reasons described, in this case it appears unlikely that a classical transference neurosis is to become the focal point of interpretation, everything in the process must shift: the therapeutic task is not the evolution, interpretation, and transformation of symptomatic repetitions (since the repetition is global), but rather the attempt to transfer enactments into verbal statements, which implies "teaching the person a new language." For Gedo, this means employing a "method of instruction" that is developmentally appropriate to the level of the patient's pathology and in so doing to "remove the poison . . . which means to remove the patient's sense [in Gedo's description of this case] that the very core of existence is torturing or being tortured." This approach is differentiated from the view of treatment as an attempt "to neutralize the poisonous behavior" by "adding benign introjects."[p]

In the follow-up session a number of years later, the analyst reiterated some of the earlier issues and emphasized that interpretive work in the usual sense was not the focus of the treatment. Rather, the analyst stressed that because this patient felt simultaneously "completely tied to mother," humiliated by her, and furious with her, his attempt was to "become a supporter of hers . . . encourage her, remind her of her abilities." These activities, he reports, "cemented our relationship." This supportive, reliable constancy was essential to maintaining a relationship, especially in view of mother's unreliability, her "confirmation and denial" of history. The enormous deficit in reality testing may be measured by this patient's utter reliance on words, for "she doesn't know what's real on the basis of feeling."[q]

In conclusion, it may be properly asked if this patient will indeed be able to be analyzed, given the steps that her analyst has had to take in order to maintain even a primitive tie. Will this enactment with him ever rise close enough to the reflective surface as to be processable in verbal terms? Will the analyst's attempt to bring a stable reality to this patient's life ever result in the development of a capacity to process reality? Much remains dependent on the analyst's abilities at various levels, as well as on the as yet unanswered questions of this patient's ability to relinquish any aspect of the enactment.

Clarification and Addenda: The Heart of the Matter (Gedo)

a. What constitutes a psychoanalysis?

Psychoanalysts have never been able to define precisely the procedures that qualify as an authentic psychoanalytic treatment. Whenever the process is conceived as a set of technical prescriptions for analyst and analysand, the observed consequences turn out to be infinitely variable, from optimal processes that follow theoretical expectations to empty exercises that go through the motions in a useless manner. The opposite extreme is represented by impostors who wish to call any form of a "talking cure" an analysis.

Despite the difficulty of determining the limits of an authentic psycho-analysis, it is a matter of real consequence to attempt to do so, for it is only by clarifying the principles underlying one's definition that it is possible to avoid the twin pitfalls of the chaos of *ad hoc* improvisation and the ritualism of unthinking adherence to rules of thumb. Such principles were embodied in Freud's celebrated aphorisms about the goals of ana-lytic treatment, "Make the unconscious conscious," and, later, "Where id was there shall ego be." These mottos summarize the technical conse-quences of Freud's successive models of the mind, those portraying his topographic theory of 1900 and the structural theory of 1923, respec-tively.

What, then, are the implications for the theory of technique of the hierarchical model of mental functioning I have espoused? Because the model conceives of every possible mental disposition in terms of progres-sion, arrest, or regression along parallel developmental lines, the funda-mental goal of psychoanalytic treatment (in accord with such a model) can only be the expansion of the repertory of modes of functioning available to the individual through the resumption of interrupted developmental processes. As I have tried to demonstrate elsewhere (Gedo, 1988, Epi-logue), developmental progress can occur only through the acquisition of new psychological skills—in other words, it is a matter of learning.

From such a view it follows that psychoanalysis should be aimed at filling lacunae in the analysand's repertory of skills (i.e., overcoming a variety of "apraxias") and correcting the maladaptive consequences of faulty learning in the past (i.e., removing "dyspraxic" structuralizations in behavior). As Mark Gehrie (in press) has outlined, in order to carry out such an ambitious agenda, it is often necessary to create a holding environment, that is, an analytic situation that will facilitate (or even make possible for the first time) the analysand's cooperation with the requisite procedure. The steps required to create such an environment are the apparent departures from standard technique that K.R. Eissler (1953) named "parameters."

In the case under discussion, the analyst decided that, to ensure the patient's cooperation in the medical procedures necessary to save her life, he had to intervene in a vigorous manner, a decision that clearly indicated his primary commitment to her survival. His decision was apparently dictated by the analysand's dangerous, overt attitude of choosing to allow her malignancy to destroy her by her failure to do everything possible to fight it. In the seminar, I objected to the analyst's characterization of these essential therapeutic measures as nonanalytic. In my view, these interventions may or may not have been as necessary as the analyst believed, but they were "analytic" in either case because they were based on a reasoned assumption that, left to her own devices, the patient was too regressed to make rational choices about her own survival.

In my experience, whenever analogous measures have been employed (whether they proved to have been truly essential or unnecessarily cautious), the subsequent course of the analysis has always brought into focus the rationale that impelled me to use them. At that time, it was possible to "reduce the parameter," as Eissler (1953) put it, by interpreting the effect it had on the unfolding of transferences. In other words, the specific consequences of all analytic interventions are mere grist for the analytic mill,

The analysand whose case was presented in this seminar expressed her recognition of the significance of the analyst's commitment to her survival in the "language of flowers," as we were to hear in response to my objection to the idea that intervening to save her life was not "analytic."

b. The analytic relationship as lifeline

That the analyst's genuine commitment to the patient's welfare overcame her suicidal tendencies was shortly confirmed by her announcement that she would be kept alive only if she could feel connected to him by a genuine relationship. She experienced their relationship as authentic only insofar as it was a new experience—*not* a transference repetition. The analyst's efforts to find childhood precedents for the transactions between them were therefore both technically misguided (because they threatened to cut an essential lifeline) and fundamentally invalid: only manifestations of "negative" transference (which were obviously few and far between) would have constituted repetitions of the childhood past. Any such developments would have necessitated prompt interpretive intervention to eliminate the resistance they inevitably produce. What the analyst understood as "positive" transference was essentially unprecedented in the experience of this analysand.

As we were soon to learn in the course of the seminar, this patient experienced the relationship to her analyst as something entirely new, but only when she felt he was proceeding on the basis of his authentic personal responses to her. She was correct in this judgment: however her parents behaved toward her when she was a child, their actions did not reflect their affects in a genuine manner. I suspect that the patient was intolerant of interpretations that seemed to be drawn from standard analytic texts because she experienced them as echoes of her parents' communications, which generally followed some conventional schema instead of their own feelings.

c. On "having a right to a life"

This patient (like the one discussed in the previous chapter) illustrates the problem first described by Modell (1965) in his pivotal contribution on "separation guilt." In order to get well, she needs to establish a relationship to someone that is different from those with her parents; but in everyday life she has shied away from every opportunity of that kind, and she can accept an analysis, her last chance to save herself by such means, only if someone else takes the responsibility for that decision. According to Modell, self-restrictions of this kind are dictated by unbearable guilt about the possibility of separating from a vulnerable and needy person. In this case, the issue is likely to be that of abandoning mother after reaching an accurate assessment of the mother's exploitativeness and egocentricity. Modell summed up the conflict, as subjectively experienced, in the evocative phrase that such patients do not feel they "have a right to a life." They are caught in a dilemma they are unable to resolve: whether they are justified in defending their own vital interests if there is a risk that in the process someone else might be damaged.

    In contingencies of this kind, the analyst becomes the arbiter of what is just—and justifiable. Thus, it was only on his recommendation that the patient was able to act in her own best interest. There was a helpful precedent for this pattern in the story of the divorce attorney's skillful intervention in inducing this woman to permit him to do an optimal professional job on her behalf.

d. On corrective emotional experiences

One of the participants in the seminar proposed the hypothesis that, in intervening to safeguard the analysand from the consequences of her self-restrictions, the analyst was trying to differentiate himself from the childhood parental imagoes. One implication of such a statement is that a relationship of a novel kind will provide patients with what Alexander and French (1946) called a "corrective experience." There can be no question that the analyst's policy facilitated the elimination of resistances based on negative transference; as I have already stated, I believe he thereby provided his analysand with the means to avoid self-destruction. This concrete assistance did not correct the legacies of the past, however (as

Alexander naively assumed could be done by the provision of construc-
tive interpersonal transactions). The impossibility of such a simplistic
notion of cure is, in fact, demonstrated by the subsequent course of this
case: no matter how often the analyst rescued her, this patient continued
for many years to repeat her self-destructive behaviors.

It is inescapable to conclude that the psychopathology consisted of
structured mental dispositions as legacies of a traumatic childhood past.
Specific behavioral consequences of these structures could be over-
ridden—and had to be, merely to keep the patient alive!—but character
change could occur only as a result of mastery through insight. In other
words, this patient could become self-sustaining only if she could eventually make use of analysis as a learning experience—most importantly,
about the mistaken nature of the views of herself and her caretakers she
had accepted in her childhood. It was insufficient to *assert* that she had
the right to survive a malignancy (or, later, that she could with honor
accept reciprocation in the form of money for her kindness to a friend); it
would be necessary to explain precisely why her sense that she had no
right to protect her interests was in error, how her childhood experiences
had led her into that error, and how she could probably master the
irrational guilt that had always decided her to sacrifice herself for the
sake of others.

e. The current frontier of psychoanalysis as therapy

Nobody has disputed the fact that, since the death of Freud, psychoanalysis has widened its scope (to borrow Leo Stone's [1954] phrase). Contro-
versy has centered on the question of the extent and kind of technical
modifications, necessitated by the specific requirements of unusual cases
such as the one under discussion, that one may introduce without fatally
compromising the essence of psychoanalysis. Traditionalists have always
defined that essence in terms of technical criteria, so that, in cases for
which they do not dispute the need for flexibility, they simply avoid the
problem by classifying the work as "*not* psychoanalysis." If one were to
call the case presented in this seminar a psychotherapy conducted in
accord with analytic principles, few would quarrel with the appropriateness of the analyst's procedures.

Starting with the technical experimentation of Ferenczi (for details, see
Gedo, 1967, 1986, in press-a), there has always been a dissenting minority
of analysts who insist that psychoanalysis should be defined in terms of its
goals rather than its technical procedures. For the past 30 years, I have
been one of the most active champions of this viewpoint (see Gedo, 1979,
1981a, 1984, 1988, 1991). From the perspective of the theory of technique

I espouse (first adumbrated in Gedo and Goldberg, 1973; see also Gedo, 1981b, 1991, in press-b), the relevant question becomes that of empirically determining whether particular modifications of technique do or do not permit the attainment of termination with the achievement of analytic goals. Among these, the most crucial are the ability to process all relevant insights by means of consensual communicative channels (mostly *verbal* ones) and the achievement of affective mastery.

For this reason, I look to the ability of the analysand in this case to make do with transactions that communicated authentic affect (to be sure, at the time of the seminar, this communication had to avoid the use of words as much as possible!) as the indicator that analytic goals are feasible for her. In my experience, whenever such communication is the crux of the matter, it is possible to find a way to effect it without engaging in actions that one finds unacceptable accoring to professional standards. For example, this patient devised a way to express her positive feelings for her analyst through the language of flowers.

In the seminar, I said that patients can be expected to tolerate the frustration of any specific demand they might make for an action on the part of the analyst. (This is, of course, different from claiming that all patients are able to tolerate the frustration of a *series* of demands of this kind—this is precisely why I have followed Ferenczi's [1908-1933] example in terms of flexibility in technique.) In recent years, as the traditional technique of psychoanalysis has gradually lost support because it is suitable for a relatively small proportion of cases (for evidence about this, see Erle and Goldberg, 1984), many analysts have been afraid to be overly inflexible and have consequently jumped from the frying pan into the fire: in a masochistic mode, they tend to submit to the tyranny of demanding patients. As justification for their policy, they cite the patients' rageful responses when frustrated. Obviously, those who cannot stand the heat must get out of the kitchen—but containing such rageful assaults is the prerequisite for being able to analyze people who suffer from problems referable to archaic stages of development.

f. Neutrality and the affectivity of the analyst

The case under discussion strikingly illustrates that certain patients, for whom verbal communication was compromised in childhood, can be reached only through affective channels. In my experience, analytic interventions are always better understood if they are presented in a manner laden with appropriate affect; hardly anyone can fully grasp the lexical meanings of a message devoid of emotional coloring. In other words, if analysts want to maximize the effectiveness of their communications, they must pay attention to the paraverbal aspects of speech—the music has to be congruent with the words (see Gedo, 1984, chaps. 8 and 9: in press-a).

Unfortunately, prevailing opinion holds that it is technically desirable for an analyst to avoid any display of emotion. This erroneous judgment is generally rationalized on the ground that a flat and colorless manner of communication is most consonant with the analytic role of "neutrality." Such a view is based on confusing a pseudoobjective manner with that desirable equidistance from the conflicting sides of an intrapsychic struggle that the concept of neutrality properly refers to. It should be noted that "neutrality" is the appropriate prescription for the analyst to follow only when the material in focus is safely contained in the realm of fantasies alone, that is, when there is full structuralization of the agencies of the mind Freud (1923) postulated in "The Ego and the Id." In circumstances that reflect a more primitive mode of organization (modes I through III in the hierarchical model), the concept of neutrality becomes meaningless.

g. What constitutes abuse of the analyst?

Probably in response to the realization that rigid adherence to any inflexible technique is traumatically unempathic for many patients, analysts in recent years have shown some confusion about the boundaries between helpful flexibility and masochistic submission to abuse—submission that ultimately proves to be equally damaging to both participants. In this regard, it is important to differentiate unintended injuries from sadistic mistreatment. Whenever an analysand's behavior is damaging to the analyst through inadvertence, calling attention to the issue is generally sufficient to motivate the patient to be more careful to avoid harm. If the behavior in question is driven by sadism, however, such statements about its effects seldom suffice to alter it—even the threat of sanctions (such as abandonment of the analytic effort) may fail to deter certain provocative individuals. Obviously, interpretations of the functions and meanings of the sadism are indicated, but the correct ones may be difficult to find. In the meantime, it is best to be maximally firm that the abuse will not be tolerated.

My own best indicator that abuse is taking place is my emotional response of spontaneous outrage. I am fairly confident that it is a reliable indicator, because I am generally quite willing to go out of my way to accommodate the special needs of patients. Clearly, so was the analyst of the case discussed in this seminar, so that he would have been more than justified to respond to the patient's indecent mockery with indignation. (In this connection, it may be helpful to recall that when better integrated analysands have hostile and cruel thoughts about their analyst, they report these with great shame, guilt, or anxiety. It is the absence of such indications that the ideation in question is repudiated by the reality ego that differentiates it from routine associations.) Thus, it would have been both legitimate and helpful to pinpoint the illegitimacy of the patient's verbal assaultiveness; it could have led directly to analysis of her identification with her father's paranoid behavior.

In my view, any effort by patients to force analysts either to perform an action against their will or to experience some emotion or bodily reaction (such as humiliation or sexual excitement) is abusive. It is also intolerable to have to submit to the undermining of one's reality testing ("brainwashing") or to subversion of the commonly accepted groundrules of professional transactions (e.g., refusing to leave at the agreed-upon time, invading the analyst's privacy, withholding fees, and so on).

I do not mean to imply that analysands who do any of these things should be dismissed as untreatable. Rather, they should be informed at the earliest opportunity that such behaviors cannot and will not be accepted, and that the inclination to engage in such conduct is in itself gravely pathological and in need of urgent examination. I have found that most patients do grasp rather promptly that it is dangerously self-destructive to assault the very person on whom they rely for vital assistance.

h. Psychoanalysis as a learning experience

The heart of the matter is that psychoanalysis as a therapeutic modality differs from other types of treatment in that its mode of action consists of new learning, particularly in the realm of information processing itself. This point has always been widely understood, although it was often stated in an unacceptably reductionistic manner, claiming that analysis works by providing "insight." It has long been realized, however, that insight provided by the analyst is hardly ever lasting and sufficient; to ensure continuing adaptive success, it is desirable for analysands to acquire the skill of introspective self-inquiry (see Gardner, 1983) so that they may attain their own insights. Thus, the crux of analytic success is the acquisition of new psychological skills, especially those extending the realm of conscious thinking. Nor is the capacity for insight the only skill required; it has been acknowledged from the inception of our treatment efforts that cure depends on some kind of mastery of affectivity, to be achieved by means of "working through."

The hierarchical view of psychic functioning (Gedo and Goldberg,

1973) has illuminated the fact that interpretation is not the sole thera-peutic tool of psychoanalysis, for the inability to achieve insights via introspection is not the only skill missing from the psychological reper-tory of most patients. In recent years, I have proposed that we designate all deficiencies in essential skills as "apraxias" (Gedo, 1988, chaps. 11-14). Treatment must aim at enabling patients to overcome these deficits by means of new learning, a difficult process because character structure is generally designed to maintain the status quo. For this reason, character change is often a prerequisite for any willingness to abandon old ways, no matter how maladaptive, in favor of learning better ones. Hence, for these developmental disturbances, psychoanalysis is the treatment of choice; I regard the technical problems encountered in the analytic work as obsta-cles to a program of instruction (Gedo, 1988, Epilogue).

i. The effects of remedial instruction in the course of analysis

The most damaging of the apraxias suffered by the patient discussed in this seminar was her inability to make use of verbally encoded messages for self-understanding. It took many years of devoted effort circum-venting this obstacle to reach a point where the analysand became able to hear the analyst's words as they were intended. At the time of the follow-up session, it was possible to attempt to explain some of the analysand's reactions to a new lover in terms of precedents in the child-hood past—in other words, she had learned to listen to the analyst's verbal communications for whatever valid information they might contain. It is unclear from the data presented whether she could have tolerated an interpretation had it been offered about her transference to the analyst.

j. The evocation of an archaic transference

There no question that the analyst's decision to intervene consistently "as helper and healer" (to quote Gehrie), on the assumption that this policy was the only safe one in view of the patient's suicidal threats and near-suicidal behavior, decisively tilted the transaction in the direction of the most archaic potentialities for transference relatedness of which the analysand was capable. Such a contingency is optimal in any case, for the best results are obtained only if the patient's more archaic problems have been addressed. Moreover, the resolution of issues at relatively less primitive levels is likely to be easier and more lasting if residual problems referable to earlier phases of development have already been dealt with. It follows from the principle of epigenesis that the solution of later challenges in adaptation is largely dependent on the success of the solutions of those of earlier developmental phases.

It is worth noting, however, that the analyst's moves in this matter did not constitute the initial events in setting in motion the tilt in the direction of an archaic transference. From the beginning of the analysis, this patient was transmitting messages, often nonverbal ones, alerting the analyst to her primitive needs. As he reported the treatment, the analyst laid heaviest emphasis on two considerations: first, that the patient induced him to "forget her" between sessions, and, second, that his own input had the greatest significance for the nature of what followed. From these clues I infer that he was receiving the information that the primary problem was that this woman had never had her emotional needs met (even remembered!) and that the analyst's capacity to respond to *that* issue was a matter of life and death for her.

From that perspective, the archaic transference was ready to become manifest as soon as this analysand-to-be accepted the referral to someone advertised as exceptionally decent—someone she could hardly imagine as having the time to deal with her!

k. The silent unfolding of an archaic transference

Although it could not be interpreted at the time it occurred, the meaning of the analysand's acknowledgment that she had profound feelings about the analyst is that the archaic transference (see Gedo, 1977), potentially in evidence all along, had by then reached full flower. Overtly, it manifested itself in the statement that articulating the feelings involved would provoke in her an impulse to kill herself. I take such a message to mean that she would, once again, experience unbearable guilt about burdening a caretaker with full responsibility for her fate—and I assume that she had felt the same way about the possibility of burdening her mother (perhaps both parents) in childhood.

It is in *this* regard that the analyst will have to pass a crucial test: if, like the mother, he were to feel overburdened by his difficult patient, she would probably lose all hope, and the suicidal risk would be great, indeed. However, passing the test is, by itself, never curative (in practice, the test is repeated *ad infinitum*); in other words, new experience is never truly corrective. If anything, patients tend to look upon those aspects of analysis that are unprecedented for them as strange irrelevancies: *only* the repetition of the past has actual emotional meaning for them. *Passing* the test makes it possible to begin the task of clarifying for the patient that she was testing, that she needed to do this for the weightiest of reasons, that the entire transaction is the central issue for her analysis, and for her life as a whole. Gradually, it should even become possible to clarify which aspects of the relationship repeat something from the past and which aspects are in the nature of new experience.

l. The demand for action and the limits of a psychoanalytic procedure

When Gehrie implies that the pressure of the patient's needs in itself constitutes a "demand for action," he is correct, but that is not the point I was addressing in the seminar. In the sense I meant, the patient discussed never demanded *anything*, and that was the core of her pathology. She was in desperate need of insight about the legitimacy of expecting help— insight she was capable of comprehending only if instead of being encoded verbally it was communicated through nonverbal (mostly affective) channels. Implicitly, of course, complying with her communicative requirements was the action on which therapeutic success depended.

I believe analytic work becomes impossible if a patient truly cannot tolerate it when clinical requirements frustrate the demand for some specific piece of behavior. In 35 years of clinical work as an analyst, I have (to repeat part of what I said in the seminar) never lost a patient or halted the progress of an analysis by refusing to comply with an irrational demand. I am not claiming that I have never made a temporary compromise in this regard; but when I put a stop to such a concession, my analysands have *always* been able to tolerate it. Moreover, I have always found that the compromise accomplished little beyond postponing an inevitable showdown on the issue.

I *have* encountered patients who initially sought analysis but proved to be unsuitable for the procedure precisely because they insisted on operating within a set of idiosyncratic groundrules at variance with my conception of "treatment." Such a conflict of minimum requirements invariably came to light during the period of preanalytic consultation or immediately after treatment was instituted.

m. How widespread is the inability to use symbolic thought?

Gehrie is right to raise the question whether this patient can ever become capable of "reflection" about her transference expectations. Her need to deal with these issues on a nonsymbolic level (i.e., like a toddler who either has no linguistic skills or is unable to attend to words when strongly aroused) is the best possible illustration of the kind of psychological deficit that I have called an apraxia. The answer to Gehrie's question cannot be stated with any certainty at this time, but, as a matter of principle, patients deserve the benefit of the doubt. In other words, we are obliged to proceed on the assumption that, until proved otherwise, their defects are remediable.

In this case, however, it is even possible that the apraxia may have been perpetuated by a specific transference constellation. Because, in relation to her primary caretaker, this patient had to focus on the affective realities, to the exclusion of paying attention to the verbal interchange between them, the defect is probably not so much a matter of being unable to *reflect*. Rather, it consists of giving too much weight to some of the information she is provided and too little to the rest. The technical problem, if that proves to be the case, is how to make this transference interpretation to someone who is unable to make use of verbal communication about such matters!

n. A hierarchical view of psychopathology

To be precise, the hierarchical model implies that, in those cases which reveal pathology referable to various developmental levels (probably these constitute a very high proportion of patients who need psychoanalysis), all the "layers" of maladaptation are *equally* relevant. In practice, this means that to effect lasting repair it is dangerous to neglect any of the layers; even if focus on some of the problems does suffice to patch over the others, failure to address them leaves the analysand in a state of vulnerability. I believe it was such an outcome Kohut (1979) illustrated in his case report on "The Two Analyses of Mr. Z."

For the most part, the more archaic layers of pathology tend to be given short shrift, often on the assumption that they only represent (negligible) regressive retreats from the anxieties generated by the challenge of problems at later phases of development. In my clinical experience, if problems referable to more archaic levels remain unresolved, it is extremely difficult to deal successfully with issues from later phases, for it is precisely the maladaptive legacies of earlier vicissitudes that have always made it impossible to meet the challenges of subsequent problems in adaptation.

o. Is the idealization of the analyst developmentally relevant?

Gehrie is undoubtedly correct in pointing out that, whatever the analyst contributed to evoke the patient's idealization of him, that reaction was a *transference*, that is, a repetition of a developmental universal from earliest childhood, akin to the blind confidence toddlers have in the capacities of their primary caretakers. (Those very few infants who never achieve such trust in parental figures become severely impaired in their capacity to relate to other humans, far more impaired than the patient under discussion, who, it will be recalled, was an excellent mother and a devoted friend.)

Although it is true that some analysands develop an idealizing transference spontaneously, as Kohut (1971, chap. 2; see also Gedo, 1975) was the first to point out, patients who suffered traumatic disillusionment in previously trusted caretakers early in childhood are extremely reluctant to risk its repetition by lending themselves to a type of relationship that renders them vulnerable once again. It is with people of this kind that a considerable period of effective helpfulness on the part of the analyst is likely to tilt the situation in the direction of idealization. For the emergence of a transference of any particular type, it is always helpful if the analyst can be "typecast" (see Gedo, 1991, chap. 7).

p. Instruction versus the provision of benign introjects

The hypothesis that damaging experiences from the past can be neutralized through the provision of good experiences in the present (which are allegedly capable of forming new object representations, the so-called benign introjects) is an outgrowth of Ferenczi's technical experiments ca. 1930, codified by Balint (1968) in the notion of a "new beginning." Most psychoanalysts have rejected this proposition because their clinical work has led them to conclude that such additions to mental structure do not eliminate previous structuralizations and their pathogenic consequences (see note d.).

I am in full agreement with the skeptics who see no value in promoting the formation of new introjects. Hence I have been at pains to spell out that, in advocating that the analyst should expand the repertory of patients' psychological skills (if necessary by actual instruction within the analytic setting), I do not propose to provide a model for introjection. It is true that the analyst who becomes an effective teacher will often be seen as a benign and admirable figure, a point equally valid for any kind of satisfactory instructor. Such a development, however, is merely a minor complication (not too difficult to deal with by means of timely interpretations); the actual effect to be aimed for is to make the patient more self-sufficient through new learning.

In the case discussed in the seminar, teaching the analysand a consensual *verbal* language that would enable her to reflect about human transactions, instead of enacting the alternatives of helplessness and dominance, should lead to the ability to control her guilt-driven self-destructiveness without having to rely on the analyst to do so. As Bucci

(1992) has shown, the crucial step such a person has to master is to be able to link words (which she has had at her command all along) with affectively charged human transactions.

q. Language and the issue of testing reality

As long as affectivity remains divorced from consensually understood verbal symbols, it is not *possible* to make valid assessments about "reality." Hence, the patient continued to need external confirmation about the validity of her judgments about human relationships. The analyst performed this task in a reliable manner throughout this long treatment: he supported the proper assessments of the patient's functioning against the latter's tendency to accept the capricious and unreliable judgments of her childhood caretakers. At last report, he was finally able to begin to focus on the crucial fact that the parents had borne false witness against his analysand. If he succeeded in getting the patient to accept this bitter truth, the ultimate prognosis may actually be quite good!

Follow-up: August 1992

Analytic work continues; there have been adaptive gains in the sphere of professional life. For a lengthy period, the patient insisted on attending only three sessions a week and felt moderately depressed; she rationalized her choice on the ground that she did not have the "energy" to come more often. She has not been involved with any man recently.

The dominant content of her associations has been the sadistic mistreatment of helpless victims (women, children, Jews). The patient's attitude toward this material was that of fascinated abhorrence. Often she fantasied either being victimized or being the protector of a threatened child, but she disavowed any personal responsibility for these preoccupations. It was not possible to correlate the material to vicissitudes of the analytic relationship or to past events in the patient's life. To overcome this impasse, the analyst strongly recommended the resumption of more frequent visits.

Once a four-times-a-week schedule was reestablished, the patient regained a sense of "having energy." She also began to see that the contents of her fantasies reflect something about her inner world, and she has been able to acknowledge that the relationship to the analyst had transference significance. She still resorts, however, to defensive disavowal of the meaning of conflict-laden associations. In recent dreams, she portrayed the analyst as a witness of her passively endured anal erotic experiences. She has connected this material to her father's failure to interfere with the patient's mistreatment by her mother, but she has as yet been unable to acknowledge the pleasurable aspects of those experiences.

4

Idealization, Fantasy, and the Denial of Reality in Analysis

Introduction (Gehrie)

This difficult case is presented as a medium for the consideration of the complex interplay between developmental requirements and the struggle to integrate reality. The patient, referred to become the second supervised case of a young female analyst in training, presented with "career choice" problems. Trained as a ballet dancer, she was unable to achieve her desired level of success and was forced to return home with what appeared to be psychosomatic abdominal reactions, which had led to an "unwarranted" appendectomy. The [youngest] of three girls, she had made a suicide attempt in high school, and she had engaged in multiple trials of short-term therapy since college. At the outset, the analyst was concerned about this feature of the patient's history, "that she could act out that much"; indeed, the analytic relationship almost immediately became involved with enactments on several levels. These enactments not only posed immediate technical problems, but also heightened the complexity of considerations involving the management of the transference and the nature of interventions over the long term.

The presenter chose to bring this case to the seminar because the patient, who had terminated the analysis some years earlier, had recently returned to the analyst for assistance with the same problems that had brought her for help originally.

144

First Session

PRESENTER: I am going to present a case that was my second [supervised experience]. The reason I would like to do it is because she has "convicted" me.

COMMENT: Many people do.

PRESENTER: Yes [laughter]. I understand that. I obviously think that there are other ways to think about her than I did the first time around. I will try to present this in the way that I learned about her. As I recall, I wasn't totally thrilled with [her] phone call when I got it. This was a woman who had gone through the interviews at the Institute clinic and then had decided with the social worker that [analysis] was not for her because she could not make a commitment to it. She had gone through psychotherapy for somewhere between six months and a year with an analyst or psychotherapist who recommended strongly that she get into [more intensive treatment].

She came in with an initial complaint that she could not get her career choices in line. She felt that there was a tremendous conflict about whether she could follow her creative choices or have to do something that was, in her mind, [lacking in] creativity. She was trained as a ballet dancer; she had been to New York three times by the time I saw her to attempt to break into the ballet world there. The first time she had been greeted reasonably enthusiastically but then began to run into trouble. She wasn't getting parts—she was left off the cast list.

But what brought her home was that before one tryout she began to have abdominal symptoms and actually ended up having an appendectomy that [turned out to be] unwarranted. She came home briefly, and then she went back and tried again, and again had stomach pains. At that time her parents basically told her to call it quits. She had some therapy here, and then she decided to give it one more try. But really she was not getting a lot of good feedback, so she decided to give it up.

She came back here, and by the time she saw me she was involved in all sorts of things. She was working part time for her father, who is a very successful lawyer. She was working as office manager, doing things like filing, computer work—doing about a half a dozen things.

She was the third of three girls; actually, there were four, I found out later. There was a fourth girl born between the first two who had died at birth. She has a sister seven years older than she and a sister four years older. The mother is a housewife, although she got a master's degree in teaching, but she never used it. She got the degree while my patient was in high school.

The most [questionable] thing she told me about in the beginning was what she called a suicide attempt when she was in high school. She described that she was very involved in the arts in high school but also felt that she had to stay a straight-A student. She was playing the piano and dancing in contests.

COMMENT: She was in private school?

PRESENTER: No, in the suburbs, a public school. Around her junior year she decided that what she wanted to do for her life's work was to be on Broadway and go into musical comedy. She became very involved with all her extracurricular activities and started getting Ds. Apparently her mother was the one who then said that she had to curtail her activities. This would not do; they were not going to tolerate her career choice if it led to that kind of work. And apparently there was a hue and cry about it, and as usual her father sided with her mother. And she obviously felt very abandoned [because of] this. She felt that she could not please her parents. So she superficially scratched one of her wrists with a razor blade and then decided the whole thing was pretty ridiculous. She covered up her wrists and wore long-sleeved shirts and did not tell anybody until she was in college.

One of the things that she wanted to do in analysis was to understand her suicide attempt. When she went to college she started to major in psychology; after two years she switched schools and had training in dancing.

GEDO: Did she go to a real ballet school or a dance department in a university?

PRESENTER: She went to a ballet school. It was not one of the famous ones or I would remember its name. She always felt [as if] she was behind [her peers] there. Everybody knew something that she didn't know. She was always trying to make up for something.

GEDO: [That was] probably not unrealistic.

PRESENTER: Oh, right! She [started] late; she was a step behind her classmates; and she would get some encouragement about her abilities but then would find certain little things, barriers that sometimes she couldn't quite break. Couldn't always be a soloist, that kind of thing—she was always [close] but couldn't quite take featured roles in ballet and couldn't quite switch to modern dance either. Yet she was aware that she was good, and people would confirm that she could dance very well and had talent.

GEDO: Was there some reason for her changing her ambition from Broadway to ballet?

PRESENTER: Well, later on in the analysis [we discussed] that it was a change of ideals or mentor. She said that when she was in high school she really looked up to Ginger Rogers; that was her ideal. And when she went into ballet, it was Maria Tallchief. What she said to me was that there was something about ballet that was more "legit." There was always conflict about her going into musicals or something more "serious."

Her parents are both patrons of the arts. And when she was a small child, she would go to performances of music or dance, so that there was a great deal of emphasis on the arts. Her mother was involved with the Art Institute. But all the girls went to [music and dance] classes. Each of the girls was given some affirmation by the father; the oldest one was the smart one, the second was the musician, and my patient was the dancer.

GEDO: What became of her sisters?

PRESENTER: The oldest one became a lawyer. She is married and has two or three children; she lives on the East Coast. The second one attempted to go into singing but ended up doing occupational therapy. She married, divorced, and has one child. The patient is the only one who really felt that she wanted to pursue the arts. I think that all three were given opportunities as children, but only my patient was totally turned on by the experience.

GEDO: Well, then, it sounds like the oldest one did it the way the parents might have imagined, and the second one accepted a more modest solution. Well, are we satisfied enough about the background to plunge into an account of the treatment? Any comments or questions?

COMMENT: [She sounds like a] perfect analytic patient!

PRESENTER: Lucky me! [laughter]

COMMENT: Especially for your second analytic experience.

PRESENTER: Right! I asked my supervisor when I got the call—all of this conflict going on, and the suicide attempt, all of these symptoms—well what do you think about it?

QUESTION: What was [the reason for] your reluctance?

PRESENTER: The suicide attempt frightened me, that she could act out that much.

QUESTION: Was her intention to kill herself?

PRESENTER: In her mind, that is what she called it—her suicide attempt. So I don't know. I had no idea.

COMMENT: I have a question about the gastrointestinal thing. Were there some earlier childhood experiences like that, or illnesses in the family that would explain why she reacted like that?

PRESENTER: She herself was very sickly as a kid; she had asthma as a child.

COMMENT: She was not old when she came to you. Did you ask her why she wanted low-cost analysis?

PRESENTER: She was 28. She says she can't afford [a full fee].

GEDO: We can only offer low-cost analysis. But we may ask why we spend our hard-earned donations on a family like this.

PRESENTER: Obviously, she was very well aware of all that. It was very important for her. She was doing all of this totally [without] the knowledge of her family. They did not know about this.

GEDO: She asked you to lower the fee?

PRESENTER: And she didn't want to take anything from the family for herself. She was going to do this on her own.

QUESTION: Did her parents tell her to give up [dancing after] the stomach stuff? [Did they have some] recognition that it was stirring up some kind of emotional obstacle with her?

PRESENTER: Well, I would have to answer that in two different ways. From my *patient's* [vantage] point at that time, she really came in with her mind set that life was a struggle with her mother. Period. This was a fight with her mother, and everything that she wanted to do her mother did not want her to do. So even when they said, "Come home," she experienced it as an external conflict. [She felt] that they were still opposing her choices, that they were telling her to come home and get a job and stop all of this "nonsense."

GEDO: Is the analysis more "nonsense?" Is that why it has to be kept secret?

PRESENTER: Yes—being psychological is "nonsense."

GEDO: Well, there are many ways of skinning a cat. I have a personal distaste for such transactions: I couldn't do it that way. Even if I were tempted to agree to treat her, I [would be] unwilling to agree [to participate] in this enactment of [keeping a secret] that would make it seem like psychoanalysis was either a rebellious act or shameful nonsense.

Maybe this should not become an issue in *this* case. But you don't want to get into a situation with her wherein you become her "secret sharer." She externalizes the internal conflict, so that you [are forced into] taking the position of the devil, or the serpent [in the Garden of Eden]. That can cause a lot of trouble.[a]

COMMENT: The part that I have trouble with is that whatever her motivation, she is an adult who is making a decision not to involve her parents about her need for analysis. That means that she has to pay a low fee because of limited resources. At the beginning [of this] contract, it is impossible to know what it means for her to set it up that way. I know that I would be hesitant to [proceed that way] without having a discussion with her about what it might mean. But I would not necessarily assume that she should pay a higher fee because of her parents' [resources].

GEDO: Absolutely. One can't challenge that to begin with. Hopefully, if you have a suspicion that this is only the tip of the iceberg, that this is a more complicated story than you can discern from the beginning, [you make clear that] when things come to light which would put a different construction on the whole matter, it will [have to] be re-negotiated. It is a good idea to state that in [every] case.

I shall never forget a lady who came to see me whose husband was a very successful man, and she wanted to negotiate a rather modest fee because he had lost a lot of money on some of his investments. After three years I discovered that the "loss" [was actually his failure] to make an investment that [would have] yielded a large gain. [This may serve as a cautionary tale.]

QUESTION: Did you ask for restitution—with interest?

GEDO: I won't tell you the rest of the story [now]. But I felt violated for having been so naive.

PRESENTER: With this woman, I actually think something interesting happened in [her setting up the analysis as an act of] "autonomy". One needs in some way to accept that she needed a piece of separate, autonomous behavior.

Gedo: You're quite correct. You can accept that by going along with her preference to pay for it herself. Other things being equal, [her being financially responsible is the] better alternative, in any case. But she has to be consistent, if she is an autonomous person. This means she cannot make a secret of the fact that she has decided to have an analysis. By going along with the secret, you are undermining the striving to be autonomous. Of course, the fact that she simultaneously set up these [contradictory] conditions [shows that she has a conflict about autonomy versus symbiosis].

Presenter: Well, we got into that pretty quickly, anyway.

Gedo: All right, tell us what happened.

Presenter: Well, it was very clear that her whole motivation for coming [for help was to decide between] her mother's choices and her [own]. She said to me very clearly that relationships weren't particularly very important to her. Marriage and children were her mother's choices and thereby [they were compromised in her eyes]. What happened was that the first time she saw me—at the very end of the session—she asked me whether she would still be able to travel as much as she had, to do her work as a performer. They were going all over the midwest. I was sort of taken aback, so I said, "Well, it's not optimum." That is a quote. She flew out of my office in a huff and said, "I knew it. You are going to be just like my parents. You are going to make sure that I have to take a 9 to 5 job. I was looking for a creative solution, and I'm not going to find it here." And then out the door.

Gedo: How many of you would proceed after that? We know that the work was "completed." There was a beginning, a middle, and an end—but that [initial reaction would, for me, be] very discouraging.[b]

Presenter: Well, I was a little flabbergasted myself. Then she came back the next day—we had an appointment set—this [outburst] was an "extraanalytic" transaction.

Gedo: There are *no* extraanalytic transactions! In private practice you would have said, "My dear, you are a free agent. If you don't use the time, I'll be happy to take a nice walk along Michigan Avenue!" But you can't do that when [you are not getting the fee for a clinic patient.]

Presenter: The only thing that calmed me down was that she said she would come back the next time. She had the ability in the interim to calm herself down. She did not realize that [her statement] was a distortion, but [she felt] that something [of value] was coming for her, and if she was to do this she had to make a commitment. She had already begun to rearrange her schedule so that she could be in town [for the analysis]. So, with that, I calmed down too. She put herself back in order and then we proceeded. She actually began to look for work within a three block area of my office.

Question: Initially, did she [merely] comply with your demands? Why did she come back?

Presenter: Are you asking me what she said to me consciously or what I believe her motives were? Consciously she saw it as an act of reasonableness.

Question: I have a question about how she experienced this. Did you confront her [that it was unrealistic to think] that she could pop in when she was in town and the analysis would still be successful? Or was she hearing you saying that you would not be flexible in trying to work around her schedule—you would not accommodate to her but she would have to accommodate you?

Gedo: Apparently you agreed silently not to explore this flare up. She [behaved] like a rubber ball, bouncing up and soaring away. Beyond whatever you discussed in her treatment, there remained this issue of [entitlement to some kind of special handling in accommodating her, whatever the requirements of an analytic treatment may be]. If one is lucky enough to establish a really good working relationship, that [may temporarily neutralize] such demands. Even after termination, such a relationship may persist in some way [and serve] to guarantee this person against fresh outbreaks of these aggressions. Of course, [the masking of such problems] is the reason many people do come back [for further assistance] after termination. I'm not saying there is anything the matter with that. The best we can do is what we *can* do, and that is to handle their other problems, and if from time to time this [intractable residual] has to be dealt with later, so be it.

Comment: What would be the reason it could not be dealt with in analysis in the first place? No matter how sustaining a relationship is [the problem] is always [present]; [it manifests itself] right off the bat.[c]

Gedo: I had a patient once who came [to me] after a suicide attempt somewhat more serious than that of your patient. We did an analysis in less than three years. This was 25 years ago. [Both of us had great confidence that we had dealt with everything she could verbalize.] She had been a graduate student. She was offered a splendid academic job on the East Coast, where she originally came from, so we decided to terminate, and so she left. She wrote a novel about her analysis [where] she describes leaving her last session and coming out [of the building] across from the Chicago Public Library. She was struck with the thought, "I wonder why I never told him I'm going to write." She proceeded to write—a lot of poetry, and then the book about her treatment. Like your patient, she came back; I referred her to a colleague out East. The remainder of the story is not my responsibility. Too many cooks sometimes spoil the broth. The patient did keep in touch with me, and she kept assuring me that the things that she had learned in the first analysis were true and useful. And all of the issues that came up in the second analysis were quite different. Well, let's hear more about your case.

COMMENT: About *this* woman, this issue of some clash between her view of what she wants to do and what somebody else wants her to do. It seems like something that was created very quickly in this analysis. It would seem like this is something that there would be plenty of opportunity to experience. I don't understand why analysis would just go on, and she would simply experience a sense of support, given how quickly she mobilizes that issue and [the likelihood] that this issue would be repeatedly engaged.

GEDO: I was giving a worst-case scenario, [one that] is probable, but it doesn't happen every time.

COMMENT: I have had patients who go through aggressive [outbursts] that they explain on a basis other than something in the relationship to me—but I haven't seen people who have those kinds of vulnerabilities and are able to use the relationship in such a totally sustaining way that the problem doesn't recur during the course of treatment.

PRESENTER: Well, I think [it depends on whether one produces] regressions—whether they come up or not. I think this did actually happen in this woman's analysis. I think there are a lot of people like this. The first part of the analysis [consisted of] working through a lot of defensive aspects. She arranged her life in order to come in and see me, but in the office she was very provocative, very angry all the time, very obsessional. She would ask me questions all the time, and she would begin to get furious if I didn't answer her. She would pick at everything I said: it was not quite right, or "What did I mean by that?" or, "This did not exactly fit her experience." As a new analyst, I was basically stirred up, not knowing what in the world to do with this woman.

GEDO: What was the advice from your supervisor?

PRESENTER: He basically supported my tactics. What she accused me of was being just like her mother, that I was the one who was cold and I was the one who was distant. My refusal to answer questions or not giving her exactly what she "needed" or thought she needed [meant] I was being as demanding of her as her mother was, etc., etc., etc. I should say one other thing because it comes up in the process of the analysis. Just as she began the analysis she also started to date someone in her father's firm, a young attorney a couple of years younger than she was—described as the office clown. This was somebody neither her mother nor father could stomach. They couldn't understand why she was going out with him. That becomes a part of the analysis.

GEDO: What did your supervisor advise about answering her questions?

PRESENTER: I'm not sure he was ever clear about it. I didn't have the most active supervisor in the world. I think he basically felt that his stance with me was to support what I did unless he thought I was doing something that was really out of bounds. But he didn't really say much. It was me with the patient and whatever we could make of all of this. And what I did was to attempt to take an interpretive stand, to see what her thoughts were about me, and eventually to interpret it as defensive. This was a repetition with me, [the function of which was] not to be involved in the analysis, not to make a commitment, to keep a distance between us. She came to acknowledge [that]. When [she stated what] she felt, I didn't fight with her, but I would be furious with her; and there would be these long pauses. Then she would get into these scraps.

GEDO: Did you tell her you were silent because you were too irritated with her to say anything?

PRESENTER: No, I did not.

GEDO: Well, of course that is one of those crucial issues about which analysts differ. I think there are three different points of view. One is the one you took. The other is to respond to everything by sharing with the patient [your impression of] the experience she is having. "Your experience must be such and such; I think you feel such and such." That's all; gradually and very, very, very slowly to attract the patient into cooperation with such measures. And, of course, the third alternative is the countertransference interpretation. "You make me feel such and such." I think each of these approaches can work [in selected instances]; but you don't get through the next phase of the analysis if you make the wrong choice. You have to be in the room with the person to get an affective sense [about] which is the optimal way to go.

I suspect that I would have told [your patient] that I was upset by her attacks and that it would be very useful for her to consider whether she had that kind of effect wherever she goes. One brings to the attention of the patient that [in analysis] there is only one canoe, and when it springs a leak at either end we are in terrible trouble. Deal with that issue: the madness of not seeing [the danger of attacking the analytic work itself]. It takes all kinds to make a world. I'm not saying that I disbelieve that [you are] calm in absorbing the insults; but if you don't feel comfortable taking the insults, don't feel like you have failed in the psychoanalysis.

PRESENTER: I made an assumption that these were all identifications with a demanding person. That's the way I interpreted it. [She was repeating] her own traumatic experiences and how obnoxious they felt to her; [I assumed] that a lot of this was [a reversal of childhood events]. She had a need to keep herself strong and [to shake up] someone whom she saw as uncaring and untrustworthy. She said to me that her primary concern was about my commitment to her on [the issue of helping her to achieve] creativity. [Her offensive behaviors] were defense mechanisms to protect her until she could have what she really wanted. She was wondering if she was strong and capable; she felt she was the one who had to go out and slay the dragon, and if I was one of the dragons, so be it. It was fireworks—I felt [barely] adequate to deal with [her]. Eventually, for whatever reason, she could tell me about it. I felt the earlier issues about commitment needed to be dealt with until she could be committed to me also.

GEDO: How long did this treatment take altogether? Are we ready to go on with the next phase, or do we know enough about the opening moves?

COMMENT: You threw me when you shifted to the issue of commitment. I was thinking you understood her in terms of a mobilized maternal transference: her need to prove she is strong by doing to you what her mother did to her. Which would make you do things that you did not want to do: to see her under unreasonable conditions or answer questions for whatever reason, when you weren't prepared to do so. [It seems] that there was coercion in the transference, an attempt to force you. So I'm having trouble shifting the perspective to "commitment." Maybe she makes a commitment through the enactment?

PRESENTER: Well, if she is making this reversal, it is an identification with the mother, but there is also identification with the father.

COMMENT: He was coerced by the mother too; you said that earlier.

PRESENTER: She was coerced by him, too. Okay. I said commitment [because] as she began to calm down and feel more attached to me and feel some hope in the relationship (she would say to me, "This will work!"), she also felt that we will have this nice comfy relationship, but it ain't gonna last. It's only going to last a day, two days, three days; something is going to interfere with it, and the interference is going to come from my side. That's what I mean by "commitment." [She needed guarantees against] interference by some kind of traumatic event. But, early on, the way she and I talked about it was "commitment."

COMMENT: It seems she was trying to defend against an attachment to a care-giving individual. That means she had to give up herself, twist herself or not do whatever her own [needs dictated]. That in itself is very life threatening, not to attach to any kind of caregiver. Is that correct?

PRESENTER: The last part, yes. What happened over the first year, she sort of settled down. She was able to talk about lack of confidence—told me about her parents going off when she was little, and her sadness. Another thing that came up was this: she is the youngest child, and she felt that she had no line to her parents, that she was this isolated figure who was not able to engage in an alliance; no one was on her side.

GEDO: Was there domestic help?

PRESENTER: No. There was, but not a permanent figure; someone came in one or two days a week. The mother did not go back to school until my patient was in high school.

QUESTION: Was she close to her mother?

PRESENTER: No, none of the girls were close to their mother.

GEDO: Were there other children in their world?

PRESENTER: There weren't any when she was very small. They lived in [a poor part] of the city then. She describes herself as not having friends close to her. [When they were quite young] these kids were doing what happens to all of us: they were really "booked." There was not a lot of free time to go to the playground. Even by the time these kids were kindergarten age they were going to all those lessons. They lived very structured lives. Friends were made but only in dance classes. The other thing is that this was one of those families that was very large; all the grandparents were still alive and so the family was the structure of their lives. There wasn't a lot of permission [for alternate experiences]—the structure was already provided. She didn't really have a lot of cousins close to her age whom she could [relate to], [except at family parties, where she could perform].

GEDO: Oh, she was already doing the clown.

PRESENTER: Very early.

GEDO: Well, before we run out of time—so we won't be in suspense for two weeks—give us a hint about what happened.

PRESENTER: Well, do you want the next four years in five minutes?

GEDO: However you think it is best for us to learn.

PRESENTER: Basically, the second major event that happened [between us] was around her plan to take her boyfriend home with her at Thanksgiving. She was expressing that it would be absolutely terrible and her mother was going to give her holy hell. She had a fantasy about me being available to deal with this, so she called me on Thanksgiving. I was at my family's house, and a lot of things were going on in the background. She called my service, and I called her back. I basically handled it in a quiet, supportive way. She told me how painful it was to hear the difference between her home and mine. I told her we would talk about it on Monday. She asked me about my family, about the family makeup that made it possible for me to be the kind of person [she believed me to be].

GEDO: Obviously [getting information about your family] is what she was trying to achieve.

PRESENTER: Right. I think that is true. As she [came to] feel more comfortable with me, what would come up is her saying, "I know you are there, but underneath all of that you are not with me." She would feel sort of comfortable with me, and then she would have anxiety dreams. The first one involved being with her mother in a bath-house; some sort of "Valley of the Dolls" scene. She would talk about her concerns about her own sexuality and the thought that she might be lesbian, especially when she was close to a maternal figure. What I interpreted was that it had an exciting effect to her, so stimulating that she would erotize it. She would get over that and then go back to fighting with me. Then she told me that she had to be the boy for her mother, that she was devoted to the parents, and she was supposed to be available for her mother.

GEDO: She was a "depression baby."

Second Session

GEDO: Why don't we start with a really brief reprise of what this was all about.

PRESENTER: Okay. This is my second control case. We started in, I think, 1979 or 1980. At that point she was a 29-year-old, single, white female. She came in absolutely insisting that the only thing that she wanted to do anything about was her choice of a career. She'd been trained as a ballet dancer, had been to New York several times to try to break into the big companies there, had been stopped by psychosomatic reactions twice, the first time with an unnecessary appendectomy. Finally, her parents convinced her to [give] it up and head home, which she did. She tried it one other time on her own but did not really get anywhere with her auditions and again decided to come home.

She said that children and marriage were absolutely irrelevant to her, that those were her mother's wishes. A lot of what she talked about were issues around an open conflict between herself and her mother. This had started when she was an adolescent and had first had ideas of doing musical comedy; her grades began to drop and there was a confrontation between her and her parents, that she had to get straight "A's" and she had to curtail her activities, and this would not do for a career. And there was a suicidal gesture at that point.

She made multiple attempts at short-term therapies since college. Actually, I [didn't say] this last time, [but] her first encounter in therapy was [when she went] to a school counselor who sent her to a psychiatrist who apparently was an analyst and told her that he thought that she was absolutely normal and she should go back to school.

Then there were some therapies with a psychologist or social worker when she was getting ballet training. Actually, they even had a couple of sessions with her mother in which her mother actually disavowed her own depression and said everything was fine, that she didn't see what the problem was.

When [the patient] first came to the clinic, she decided not to go into analysis because of the time commitment. This woman was absolutely busy: she was clowning, puppeteering, dancing; she was just spread all over the place. I mean she really was what her mother called her—sort of a jack-of-all-trades and a master of none. So she had at that time been referred out by the clinic, was in therapy for about six months; then her therapist recommended that she get into analysis, and that's when she came back.

The beginning of the analysis was very stormy. She asked me at the end of the first session whether she would be able to continue to puppeteer, which would take her out of town for stretches of time. I said, "That would not be optimum," and she sort of huffed out of my office saying that she knew I was going to be just like her parents and I wasn't going to help her find the "creative solution" she was looking for. But she was able to reintegrate herself by the next session, calm down, and realize that if she was in fact going to make a commitment she had to be in town.

So, that's where we started. There was a very stormy year, when she was continually angry at me, always accusing me of not standing by her and being just like her parents, that I was cold, distant, and demanding, and I wouldn't answer her questions, and on and on and on. Over that first year I think that a basic therapeutic alliance was built. She needed an ally, and she really did not see me as capable of being that. Finally she called me on Thanksgiving and could hear my family in the background; you know, there were just sort of family noises going on, and she took that as a sign not only that I could be available to her but that I came from a different kind of family [from hers], I had a different kind of parenting experience than she had, and because of that I could be a different kind of parent to her, and she calmed down.

GEDO: She came to this herself?

PRESENTER: Yeah. That's what she said to me after the whole thing.

GEDO: You have no reason to doubt that in retrospect?

PRESENTER: No. As a matter of fact, I think that it becomes very clear toward the end of the analysis that out of that event she formed a whole host of fantasies about me—not only that I could perhaps be a different kind of mother, one [who] was more supportive, more gentle, less intrusive, but a whole set of fantasies about my whole family. You know, where I was in the family, where my family lived, what my position was in the family, all sorts of things that didn't come out until much later. I think that she actually formed a silent idealization of me at that point, seeing me as caring and on her side.

GEDO: Insofar as you feel that that was a genuine phenomenon, genuine in the sense that it was fated—[that is], it was the kind of transference that, if one didn't screw it up, was fated to develop— the difficulties of the first year [need to be explained]. That raises the question, did the [negative transference] just evaporate, or did you do something to work it through? If so, what, and what other alternatives might there have been? You know, how could it have been expedited?

PRESENTER: How could what have been expedited? You mean, her forming [an idealizing] transference with me?

GEDO: Whether instead of 200 sessions of noise, it could have been reduced to 20.

PRESENTER: Hmmm. [laughs] Well, that's an interesting question. I haven't really thought about that one.

GEDO: You know, if you can reduce [the noise] to one [session], you're not doing analytic work, you have a crystal ball. [Several voices speaking at the same time.] How could anyone have known . . . ?

GEHRIE: [interrupting] That first session [revealed] the tip of the iceberg. It was there. [Several people speaking at once.]

GEDO: Of course, *of course* it was there! [The analyst] said something neutral, "wouldn't be optimum." I mean, we all have these little pat phrases which are in our file; somebody pushes a button and out pops a sign on our computer screen. I would have said, "I think the work cannot be done in absentia." That's my stock phrase for these situations, although I think early on I would probably take the trouble to say that of course it's entirely up to her and that the only obligation she owes me is financial, huh?

PRESENTER: [laughing] Except that as a candidate at that point . . . I suppose that's still so.

GEDO: It's still so. And the fact that you are a candidate and therefore are very anxious if she doesn't show up all the time is a terrible handicap with this kind of patient, so much so that it can increase a 20-session noise to a 200-session noise.

PRESENTER: Oh, I think that's true! I mean . . .

GEHRIE: [interrupting] Well, with respect to Dr. Gedo's question, did you try to interpret all of the noisy complaints about how imperfect you are as covering something, and were there hints of perhaps an idealization, or a more loving, admiring . . . ?

PRESENTER: [interrupting] No, I didn't see it as really covering up an idealization at that point. I think that what I interpreted was that I thought that she was very afraid of the commitment and . . .

GEDO: Of course that's a correct statement, but not an interpretation of the specifics of why the commitment to you is so frightening; [there was] something about you that's frightening, as it turns out, huh? It is that you have a halo around your head, an aura, huh? And that she's going to have some kind of really embarrassingly childlike feelings for you. Well, anyway, you didn't smell it. So how did you conduct yourself during this first year when she said, "You don't answer my questions, it's intolerable!" What did you do?

PRESENTER: [pause] I'm pausing because it's so long ago . . .

GEDO: [interrupting] Well, you asked your supervisor? What did your supervisor advise?

PRESENTER: [laughs]

GEDO: We don't know who it is. You can be frank.

PRESENTER: No, no, no! I'm giving you a look because my supervisor was very neutral. I mean he said very little to me except if he really felt I was falling off the track someplace. So anything that was not blatantly incorrect he didn't say much about. I don't really recall his giving me a whole lot of technical advice. With this woman, a lot of the time I felt very taken aback because she was so [confrontational], and I bit my tongue a lot. You know, I attempted to stay neutral, and I think I consistently tried, particularly around weekends and [other interruptions] to interpret the feistiness and the anger as an identification with belligerent, demanding, intrusive caretakers. [I told her] that they were the feelings that she was more frightened about.

GEDO: Well, that's unexceptionable, of course; again absolutely correct. You helped her to work through the defensive posture if you confronted her with those feelings.

PRESENTER: Eventually, when she began to talk to me about the breaks, it wasn't just that she would miss me. This woman was quite prone to an underlying depression which she just didn't want to get into. A lot of her associations around the breaks were about herself as a widow and left out. She felt like this little, youngest kid who really didn't have much of a say in this world [especially] about her affects and about her having much effect on anybody.

GEHRIE: That was her first remark to you, wasn't it? That it's just going to be just like with her mother, that you were going to have it your way and she wasn't going to have any control over it, and that was going to be that.

GEDO: It never occurred to you that this was love?

PRESENTER: Yes, eventually I interpreted it as that. Not at that point.

GEDO: But before Thanksgiving?

PRESENTER: [pauses] No. I think it must have been after that, because her reaction to that Thanksgiving really was a tremendous softening. What she would do is walk in the door with this smiling, beaming face that was very engaging and loving, and then she would lie down and just be belligerent again, and then I could say to her, "You know, I think this is your way of loving." I think we said something about this before, that this was actually an identification with her father. We were going to have this intellectual battle, and that's what I wanted. And she should be that way, that she wasn't supposed to be this sweet, loving thing; she's supposed to be like Oscar Madison, that was her reference to herself.

GEDO: Alas, I don't know who Oscar Madison is.

GEHRIE: "The Odd Couple."

PRESENTER: Yeah, "The Odd Couple," right. And Oscar Madison is this sort of bumbling guy who's into sports and really doesn't keep his room very straight . . .

GEHRIE: The messy one. On the other hand, he's also the one who's a lot more human than his [roommate].

COMMENT: I got a little confused when you said, "It's love." Are you then equating her view of [the analyst] as having the perfect life, the halo, [with] love?

GEDO: I'm not using the word in a technical sense.

COMMENT: Okay, because [it matters] in terms of what kind of experience does the fighting ward off, what experience of herself, and what kind of view of [the analyst]?

COMMENT: Worshipful.

COMMENT: Okay, right. [Worshiping] is different; worshiping is perhaps a kind of love but . . .

GEDO: [interrupting] Yet, of course, you know it's the love of a seven-year-old for the idealized mentor.

COMMENT: Right, okay, but when you say, "It's love," that could mean something other than that kind of hero worship. So, as you say, we need to know what exactly is the warded-off experience.

GEDO: But [the presenter] has already told us. So we can't demonstrate how intuitive we are, because she gave us the answer.

PRESENTER: Well, I have to say that I did not experience it as that early on. I did not pick up that meaning from her response, that this was sort of idealizing. I forgot to look in the mirror, and I did not see the halo [laughing and speaking at the same time]. . . .

COMMENT: But it isn't just worship in the more positive sense of looking up. She still kept secret from you some of those fantasies about how great your family was. Why does the shift happen when you give her something like the phone call and the connection? It must be that the fantasy really was not *just* admiration, but admiration of someone who doesn't give you something. Does this make any sense?

PRESENTER: Try again, I . . .

COMMENT: Well, we have the theory that there's a fighting, argumentative defense against an idealizing transference, okay? Or an idealizing state where she's the little kid looking up to the person with the halo. The question still remains, why does this enactment of your availability suddenly lead to the shift? It wasn't interpretation; you didn't say, "I think you're afraid to look up to me. That's why you've been fighting with me the entire year." Instead, it gives way at a point of your giving her something; then she allows a particular fantasy to emerge that may have been there all along. What I'm suggesting is that the reason it did was that there was some more negative fantasy. The relationship to the idealized person can't be *just* good, it's not just a good deal. You understand what I'm saying?

GEDO: I think I begin to understand what you are getting at, and that's probably quite cogent. That she's been disappointed in the past, she's a burnt child, and therefore she's afraid to idealize people, but that fear too has a content which is projected onto you, huh? So that her initial fantasy about you, in the first session when she has this blow-up, is that you're a very disappointing person and that it took a year to get over that. We're not hearing the details of the daily work. It's not likely to be this single event that demonstrated that the worst fears are not realized and that she can begin to hope that you are the kind of person she wants.

PRESENTER: Yes. I should add two things. I have tried to [present the material] in chronological [order], but there's no use [keeping to that]. The way I felt when she called me that Thanksgiving was that she was making a pretty clear statement. She said, "My mother is going to be awful on Thanksgiving, and so I'm going to call you." Basically [she was saying], "I just need a different kind of mother, period," and she would spend time during the analysis later on saying that she felt a developmental glitch [because of] her mother. "My mother could get me to 'L,' but she couldn't get me to 'M,' and I need somebody to get me there." There was this absolute search for a different kind of object, and she created a situation where she could start that kind of idealization.

GEDO: Well, you tipped us off last time about what sort of object she was looking for. Because we don't have the sequence of the material, we don't know when you learned that information, but you told us that as an adolescent she idealized Ginger Rogers and that during college she switched to Maria Tallchief, okay? So, if you knew that during this first year, it might have been possible to use that to figure out what the nature of her loves is. She's looking for a star, hopefully a superstar. It's hard, when one is a first-year candidate, to accommodate to the fact that one is going to be seen as a superstar.

PRESENTER: Very much so, yeah!

GEDO: A more experienced person might not have had that difficulty.

PRESENTER: Right, I don't have to look in the mirror any more. [laughter by all]

GEDO: You know the famous anecdote about Louis Shapiro and the tall Texan?[1] You know, he picked up *immediately* that he needed to be a superstar. [The presenter] might have been able to say after [the patient's] first temper tantrum, "Oh my, oh my, oh my, you're really on edge here. Every word has to be just perfect. So apparently you feel that we are going to have a performance of a great ballet." It would be more up my alley as opera, because I'm such an opera buff. In that case, I would say, "You think this is going to be *Die Walküre*, and I'm supposed to be Brunhilde. That's a *hard* role, and if my voice cracks a couple of times, you know, really there's no audience out there. It's not a catastrophe or a disgrace." You know what I'm alluding to?

PRESENTER: No . . .

GEDO: Brunhilde is the one who magically fixes everything for the other girl. [pause] Well, you got her to stop fighting. So what happened next?

PRESENTER: Well, okay, but I think that there is another aspect to all of this. I realized that some of her complaints were right. I *was* being distant and "analytical," so she really was experiencing the . . .

GEDO: [interrupting] Well, we can't let that go by. We can't let that go by! You were being distant and therefore *un*-analytical!

PRESENTER: Right, okay! Pseudoanalytical. I mean, as in intellectual distancing.

GEDO: You should talk to Charles Brenner about what it takes to use his technique. It takes a merry look in one's eyes! Or it takes a certain presence. He has that; he has that! He's a wonderful gentleman. And everybody who meets him experiences that. I've talked to patients of his. He's not distant. He's there, he's *there*. It's in the French literature that they talked about this, although the first author who proposed this, Sacha Nacht, was not a purist as far as technique is concerned, so the concept got a bit mixed up. They used the word *présence*—the analyst has to be present so that the analysand has to feel that you're *there*. You can be there silently if you have this *présence*.

GEHRIE: You would agree, I think, that this *présence* is an affective communication of great power, so that he's not really silent in a withdrawn way, he's just not saying anything and he encourages

---

[1]When the tall Texan looked disappointed on meeting the 5'4" Shapiro, the latter said, "Come in anyway!"

you to agree to and tolerate this technical requirement of his in part because emotionally he is so apparently present.

GEDO: Yes, yes! I don't think I'm telling tales out of school. When the series of articles appeared in *The New Yorker* counterposing Brenner and Stone as the "good guy-bad guy" in terms of analytic technique, I ran into Charles Brenner at a meeting and I started to tease him about what it must feel like to be written up in *The New Yorker* as the bad guy. And he started to giggle and said, "It's so funny. They tried to make out that Stone and I are so different; but we are in complete agreement and we do everything the same way!"

COMMENT: In my own analysis, I think that one of the absolutely essential things has been the sense of the analyst's presence while he's not talking. I mean, it's just crucial; when you put it into words it doesn't quite carry the same meaning of really feeling someone to be there. Sometimes I almost feel [as if] he is on the edge of his chair and ready to go, but not talking. And how that gets conveyed or what process you have to work through in order for the person to begin to feel, that is an interesting question. It does seem like it was an affective experience. I mean, it is the twinkle in an eye, the smile when you come in, the tone of voice when he is speaking.

GEDO: Well, I remember the moment in my own analysis, when I had reached a certain [pitch] of negative transference, and I felt I was in the presence of an enemy, and I was very anxious. Then I suddenly turned around, and the man was smiling and there was a twinkle in his eye. I mean, nobody could take him for anything but a friend. It was a decisive experience. From then on I could go forward with a negative transference.

COMMENT: So it [wasn't only] this patient [who needed] that amount of time, it took [the analyst] that amount of time also to permit herself to be *there* in this way.

COMMENT: The Wolf Man had to [go through a long period of idealizing Freud before the true problems came to the fore as a delusional negative transference].

GEDO: Well, you talk about the Wolf Man, and that's the prototypical case, alas. But that was a complicated, difficult, special problem. Thus far we have no reason to believe that this lady is going to be a special problem. We'll see.

PRESENTER: [laughing] They're all special problems!

GEDO: When I was a candidate, we had a class called "Special Problems." Literally. [general laughter]

PRESENTER: And everyone came.

GEDO: We had no choice about it; it was required. Only suckers teach electives like this. There are special problems, but then there are *real* special problems. [general laughter] This lady does not yet sound like a real special problem, although she's putting you under pressure. If that pressure hadn't come in the first year of your experience as an analyst, you might have reached the point where you could accommodate it with ease in less time. If she were paying you a regular fee, you would have responded to her initial question in a different way; and, instead of falling into a rage, she might have fallen into worshipful admiration of you immediately. As someone implied, it can be done in one session—sometimes. I mean through sheer luck, of course. Since you have told us how it went on, it is very easy to say what might have won the game sooner, right? And that's not fair; but you might have won the game sooner if you had demonstrated a strong interest in the ballet and some knowledge about it, if you had been able to use dance or at least musical metaphors in all your communications, if you had been able to sing or whistle a few relevant musical associations to her. In fact, it's very hard to think of this sort of a transaction in a ballet; a classic transaction of this kind is in the Shakespeare play "Much Ado About Nothing." And, of course that's the correct interpretation. "This [behavior] is much ado about nothing. You don't hate me, you love me!" But how quickly can one formulate that? That proves to be the crux of the matter.

Are we ready to go on to the second year?

PRESENTER: I was just going to comment that if I could have taken her as a private patient and made a statement about her money, it would have bypassed a complication. [As it was, I could not clearly convey] that I did not have an agenda for her. [When I told her that frequent absences are] not optimum, I made a very fuzzy statement. [It implies that I have an idea about] how an analysis should go and that I have an agenda. For this woman, the question of whose agenda is really [to be followed was very crucial].

GEDO: Okay, let me give, on the third time around, the perfect response for [the patient's question]. The perfect response for this patient would have been to say, "Listen, you put me in an impossible situation. You put me in an impossible situation: you want me to do 32 fouettés. You know the answer perfectly well. You know one cannot do the work in absentia. But you want me to sing you an aria like Baron Ochs sings to the young bride in *Rosenkavalier*. 'Without me the nights are long. But with me, you are going to be happy.' How could I possibly say a thing like that? Whom do you take me for? Your mother?" [laughter by all]

COMMENT: [to the Presenter] You *thought* of that, right? [more laughter]

PRESENTER: I thought it was a premature interpretation.

GEDO: Well, I thought of it the third time around, right? Ten years later. But that would have been the perfect response for this lady.

PRESENTER: Yeah. Yes, I think that I could have just as usefully said, "Who do you think I am, your father?" Certainly a lot of the positive, romanticized stuff comes out around her dad.

We began to shift to a transference neurosis after we'd worked through a lot of the defense transference and she could respond to me as an ally. When she saw me as a different kind of mother, then I could interpret the defensive stance, [the meaning of] the fighting and carrying on. It was an identification with her father; she said that she needed to be a Sabra, just like her father was, sweet on the inside and prickly on the outside.

COMMENT: [to Gedo] In the middle part of your perfect interpretation, you're saying that your sense of what she wants is to be loved by the worshipped mother even when what she wants is to separate from her.

GEDO: Well, I didn't quite say that much, but what you say may be true. In the material we have heard thus far, we have only heard one side of it; we don't hear how she wants the mother to feel about her, but she wants her mother to be a more admirable person.

PRESENTER: I think that the interpretation would say that if she had some perfect love with the mother, perfect triumphal love with the mother, then she could have a perfect and triumphal separation; she wouldn't have all the problems. If that were possible, then she wouldn't have gotten caught in this morass. At any rate, during the first two phases [there was] this back and forth movement: she would feel more comfortable with me; [there would follow] outbreaks of anxiety dreams, usually around a maternal transference. [She dreamed of] women in bathhouses, steamy scenes, "Valley of the Dolls" pictures, and we would talk about her feeling that to be close to me was a very dangerous proposition.

GEDO: Now we can go back to the use of the word "love" in this connection. Actually, this too came up in the original presentation two weeks ago, so I was not being as intuitive as all that. One uses a vague word like "love" to the patient because in fact what she wants is ambiguous and is ever in danger of being erotized, as these homosexual fantasies demonstrate. They involve a great need to idealize or at least to disavow some disappointment.

COMMENT: To disavow [disappointment], they always involve the need for an ideal, or what?

GEDO: Or, at the very least, to say, "This person is not as bad as I thought."

COMMENT: Are you saying that the idealization fills in for the disappointment?

GEDO: No, I don't say that, although that's been proposed in the self-psychological literature. I suspect that a need to idealize or the capacity to idealize is based on transactions that take place extremely early and that the child comes to the disappointment with this capacity already in place. That would be my assumption, but obviously these are still open questions. I mean it's just a correlation that when you get a homosexual fixation there are problems of disappointment.

PRESENTER: We were able to talk, at least on an initial level, about the meaning of those dreams, about her feeling that if she loved me she worried about getting endlessly stuck with me, like a bad addiction. She had conscious concerns about whether she was lesbian or not; [she felt] she was stuck with women and couldn't form a relationship with a man.

There was a shift that occurred around a particular event, as we were talking about all this. I had to cancel, pretty precipitously, for two days; I forget exactly what happened, but I came back depressed. Not bad, but preoccupied, and she very clearly picked it up. She saw me not only as depressed and preoccupied but as weak, incapable. She took a very staunch stance with me, that now she was going to have to take care of me. We could, then, begin to work on the defensive aspect of the relationship with the mother again. She was going to have to be the boy again, [the one who] carried the groceries for mother and stepped in when Dad couldn't be there.

GEDO: Now, this all came out of her without too much intervention on your part?

PRESENTER: Nooo, I don't think so. I think I was probably pretty active at that point and interpreting her behavior, [especially] within the analysis. Instead of her being regressed and my being worried about dangerous [possibilities], all of a sudden I had this [patient with] much less affect. I interpreted [the change] as a reaction to how she was experiencing me, and with my acknowledgment that something was really going on, she could say, "Yeah, I don't think you're doing so hot."

GEDO: So we can begin to draw the picture together: "The nights are long without me" is an inversion of the actual truth, "the nights are long without you because I'm depressed, and if you want to meet with me you must be available, you can't be in New York, you can't be puppeteering out of town. I need you."[d]

PRESENTER: Well, it went both ways; it was not just her having to be that capable. It's interesting—she was acting capable, her behavior was very different. As I said, she was much less regressive, but what she would *talk* about was her failures in ballet, that she never really got to be the lead. She always was the understudy, or something happened. I remember interpreting that to her as being disappointed that when I was in that [preoccupied] state, she could not feel special to me in the way that she wanted. My depression came first and she came second. She responded to that by again becoming more comfortable, giving up [her defensiveness], and she asked me for a fifth session.

GEDO: And did you agree to that?

PRESENTER: I did.

GEDO: And from then on it went to five times a week?

PRESENTER: No, as a matter of fact, I can't remember when it changed. Later she wanted to go back to four because of her schedule. But she saw me five times a week for quite a bit of time.

GEDO: That's an indication that you were doing very well indeed, that she got enthusiastic and she couldn't get too much of this good stuff.

PRESENTER: [It seemed that she did not have the terrible exhibitionistic conflict about doing well as an analytic patient; that conflict had interfered with her career.]

GEDO: It was not to be taken seriously that one might become the star of the New York City Ballet. She was supposed to be splashy in *this* community, right? [Her talent is] not to be [used in the service of] a career.

PRESENTER: That's right. You do it for me, at home; don't do it for a living.

GEDO: So, if you are representing your activities accurately in this summary (it's so hard, so many years later and in summarizing, to convey exactly what you did), it strikes me that you went a little too fast.[e]

And it seems to me that's the issue [your patient was] acting out. She is not good enough: to be an understudy, that does not justify doing it to her mother. I mean, if she were the next Margot Fonteyn, then she would feel justified; she would give the mother enough satisfaction "long distance" so it would make up for having deserted her. That's the issue. That's why I would go into, "Why wasn't it good enough to have the smallest role? God, it sounds like such fun. Wowee! Wowee! My God! I'd pay $300 a night just to stay in New York!" [laughter by all]

GEHRIE: However, might not an intervention like that be heard as telling her that her [ambitions] are unreachable, that she cannot have the relationship [with the analyst] that she desires, and that she'd better get used to [the idea] now because otherwise she's in for a real rude awakening?

GEDO: Does everybody follow exactly what Mark has in mind?

COMMENT: Please expand on it.

GEHRIE: Well, it seems to me possible that [in her present] state of mind, "What's the matter with the understudy role" could be heard in a number of ways. One is the way John described. It is also possible that she would hear that as a veiled assessment of the fact that she really doesn't have the capacities or shouldn't have the hopes and ambitions that she seems to have, and that furthermore she's not entitled to the relationship with the analyst that she aspires to.

PRESENTER: That she'd feel it—and I think this is true—that she'd feel that she was being told to settle.

GEHRIE: Yes, "Cool it, baby, cool it!"

GEDO: Well, to be sure. You're responding to what I say here in the seminar as if that's what I recommend people should say to the patient. Clearly, you have to frame the intervention in such a way that it will be understood [as you intended], that you don't mean that she will forever remain an understudy. She gave up a promising beginning before it was demonstrated that in fact she could not go any further.

PRESENTER: Uh huh, that's right.

GEHRIE: So then you *would* include some communication of her promise.

GEDO: Well, I would be careful, because I don't know how much promise she has. I would say, "Personally, for the chance to be a hanger-on in one of the great dance companies, I would be very happy to devote five years of my life to that, and it would be just a fantastically enriching experience *even* if nothing further came up. But who knows what might come of it?" If nothing else, maybe she could, in this city, turn into a ballet impresario. Carol Fox [the founder of Lyric Opera] was just such a person, Ardis Krainik [her successor] was just such a person. So if she puts in her experience, supposing she isn't Margot Fonteyn, there's lots she can do with that experience. I mean, gosh, it's an entrée into the ballet world. Why did she have to give it up? And then I'd go on to say [she gave up] because she did not have the immediate, huge success she needed in order to appease her mother.

COMMENT: [to Presenter] I don't understand your comment about this, because I can't see why she wouldn't hear the message of "What's wrong with just being involved in whatever your actual level of talent is?" as a statement that, "You can have me as a mother without any of the shenanigans that are required in your relationship with your actual mother." I don't see how that can be misconstrued.

PRESENTER: You're only talking about it on one level, I think, when you do that. The whole idea of the comment is that what needs to be looked at and understood is the drivenness, to bypass being the understudy and get to being the star. You know, that nothing else will do.

GEDO: I think that's what she is doing to you. I know that if you take Merton Gill literally you would see her talking about the ballet after this transaction with you, in which she sees you as being depressed, as the reemergence of a resistance. She is trying to displace to a topic that's a little less heated. I think that that is likely not to be true in this case, and because it's not true in *many* cases, I see Gill's proposal as one sided and technically not prudent. It leaves out the need for her to work through the consequences of her insight in terms of practical purposes.

Her life has been blasted! She came in and told you that the problem is vocational—"I wanted to be a prominent ballet dancer and I blew it"—and now you're beginning to hear why she blew it. So she comes back to that trauma. That's where it hurts, that's where she's hurting. I can't quote any more who said it, but it's a wonderful line: "No pain is as acute as the pain of lying fallow." That's what she's complaining about. So she's going to be a puppeteer, so she's going to be a housewife, this, that, or the other thing; she wanted to be a major artist, all of that is only a ghost of a life, and she died when she had her appendectomy. [pause] Not to allow her to talk about that circumstance [would be monstrous]. At this point, one of the options you have is to say, "It's never too late, never too late. We can get you into analysis with the most reliable people wherever you go." That's not merely a practical suggestion; it's framing the treatment as exactly the opposite of what she assumed it was in the first session, [an anticreative enterprise].

PRESENTER: That's right. I think one of the reasons she's talking about dancing here is that it really was her best attempt at making an adaptive solution to the relationship with her mother. She basically said to me, at the beginning, "I wanted to be able to find *my* own solution to my dilemma. I don't want to accept somebody else's." And for her to accept my timetable meant, in her mind, that she was accepting having to end up with my solutions, not hers.

GEDO: [interrupting] When she chose the timetable issue to make a stand on, she painted herself into a corner, because if she's puppeteering in Kokomo you can't do the work, and that's preposterous. You have to demonstrate that it's only through *this* work that a solution of her *own* is conceivable. Unless the work is successful, she is going to be a housewife in Glencoe before you can get up there on the Eden's Expressway.

PRESENTER: Well, the problem for her is that [creative success] may have been her best chance at an adaptive solution, but there's so much aggression involved in it that she tripped herself up.

GEDO: Real aggression or fantasy aggression?

PRESENTER: Well, I think that she went to New York with a vengeance.

GEDO: We haven't heard about that. You must tell us about that part.

PRESENTER: Well, we don't get to that until termination, so I'd better hurry up. Do you want me to skip?

GEDO: Well, we can wait. You're telling us that what I've just said is too simple, that she really went vengefully and therefore the whole effort was foredoomed from the start.

COMMENT: It wasn't just that she quit too soon, or that she can't stand to be an understudy or the youngest daughter, but there was some actual . . .

PRESENTER: [interrupting] But there was something she was doing [to defeat herself]. I didn't really understand why she wasn't successful [the time she didn't quit]. You know, the first two times, actually she was getting enough encouragement to stay, and it really was the somatic reactions that forced her home. The third time she really did not get the encouragement, and she was told that her chances of breaking in were not that great. She always knew that there was more work to do, that she had certain liabilities that she could not seem to overcome.

GEDO: So she wasn't going to be the Sleeping Beauty. She could have danced smaller parts; she could have remained an artist.

PRESENTER: Right, well, that's what she came back here to do.

GEDO: But she's become a puppeteer—that's awful!

PRESENTER: She's dancing too. It's just not enough to sustain her.

QUESTION: [to Gedo] When you commented about the vengeance, were you questioning whether or not dancing was ever a genuine aim?

GEDO: I'm not questioning anything. I had assumed that it was a genuine aim, but later in the analysis it came out that doing what she was doing was hostile.

PRESENTER: Well, we already know it was a compromise of sorts. You know, Maria Tallchief came later; [the patient originally] wanted to be Ginger Rogers. But she talked about herself as the Fanny Brice type, one who wasn't particularly gorgeous, but who through her flamboyance and her skill and her being an entertainer could win the hearts of millions. She has a broken heart, *but* her career will sustain her.

COMMENT: Right. Her abilities are what count, yeah!

GEDO: Just what she is good for is not for *us* to determine. That's not your job. And to what degree she gave up after these misadventures in New York is not entirely clear. You don't have to give us the material about the hostile intent behind the dancing until you come to that part in the analysis; we'll keep it in mind. Still and all, the technical point that all this started with is valid. She wants to talk about her professional concerns, and she says to you once again what she said at the beginning of the analysis: "I am here because I have a practical problem to solve about making use of my talents. Now that's my chief complaint, so don't you forget it." And to say, "Let's talk about you and me, kid," makes you sound like the mother again. Look, people, be careful! Give Merton Gill credit; he's quite explicit about the fact that we must keep in mind very carefully what our course should be and the effects on the transaction of what we actually do. And to confine one's purview to the relationship between the two people in the analytic room is a very, *very* powerful enactment.[f]

COMMENT: The perspective on what happened between the two of them would allow [the analyst] to interpret how the relationship with the mother was felt as a constrictive force on the pursuit of her ambitions. So it's not that focusing on "you and me, baby" takes you down a blind alley. Here we've talked about how that initial transaction, if we really understood it at that time, could really have opened up the mother transference.

GEDO: But let me just remind you of the wonderful Mike Nichols/ Elaine May record about the analyst who cries when the patient won't make an appointment for Christmas. [general laughter] Talking about the genetics will not undo the destructive effects of that sort of ongoing countertransference.

QUESTION: You don't think it would have helped the patient for [the analyst] to have said something to the effect that the patient was reenacting her experience with her mother?

GEDO: Oh, yes, yes, but then the patient starts talking about dancing, dancing, dancing. And [we should not] treat that as "resistance." I am saying treat that as a return to a consideration of the adaptive dilemma of a very talented person who's not all that interested in human relationships.

You might not think that musical comedy is all that spiritual, but of course that's an unfair judgment, because for those who do it [it may be]. You remember (she's actually a puppeteer) that wonderful,

wonderful story, "The Juggler of Notre Dame"? It is repeated many, many times in French literature. It was a medieval legend: everybody had brought presents for the Virgin on her Feast Day. The juggler came to put on his act before the statue of the Virgin, and the statue started to cry. To the juggler, that's the most spiritual thing. So don't give even her puppeteering short shrift. The solution, whatever it is, is going to be in that channel, because that's the channel that she used in adolescence and up to the age of 20 or so.

PRESENTER: I think talking about this interaction the way we are points up where something was not attended to. [The patient and I] took a long, circuitous route and reenacted the whole business [that she had to become someone] special to impress mother. What that meant [was that she felt] caught and trapped within the confines of a family that leaves one feeling limited, second rate. Her dismay that only certain solutions seem available to her came out at termination.

QUESTION: [to Gedo] When you say that interpreting the genetics is not enough, [do] you mean that she actually has to come to a different solution, she has to do something in this area of her ambitions?

GEDO: I think we're talking somewhat at cross-purposes. All I meant was that even though you offer her a genetic interpretation, which makes it sound like your emphasis on the transference was strictly in the service of insight, such an exclusive emphasis on the transference will be taken by this sort of a patient as chopping off her ambition.

PRESENTER: I think the interpretation that could have been made as she talked about dancing was [about her underlying affect]: she was depressed. There was a sense of dismay and futility that she would never be able to be special or important or the star of the show to anybody else but me because of *my* depression, that she would never be able to disengage herself from me and really do what she wanted to do.

GEDO: Well, of course, what she wants to do is to make use of specific talents which are not called upon in treating the depression of a family member. Why should she be any good at that? It's a hopeless task—the task of Sisyphus. It never ends. You may get close to the top, but then the rock will tumble down again. And it's an endless, hopeless task which will defeat her.

Shall we stop at this point?

Third Session

GEDO: It's been a while. Try to summarize rather briefly what we should remember.

PRESENTER: As I recall, we only got to talk about the emergence of what I called "the transference neurosis" and some evidence about an emerging paternal transference.

GEDO: Well, tell us what you covered in the analysis.

PRESENTER: There were a significant number of events, really traumatic events, that may have had a lot to do with what happened and did not happen in the analysis. Before those events came up, what I saw was an emerging paternal, really romantic, transference with me. She would have all sorts of dreams about spending an evening with me, and it was very romantic [with] breezes blowing; but there was always a sense [that] it would never last, that it was just for one night. There were other people in the wings; she had to wait her turn. [She always felt she got] short shrift as far as this went; she was never really the best or the chosen one.

GEDO: And how did you know the precedent for this was the [relationship to] father?

PRESENTER: Well, [pause and then laughs] you've got me stuck, because in thinking about this I can tell you the assumptions I made. We spent a lot of time interpreting dreams. [In retrospect] that may have been [due to her] compliance. At any rate, when she would get more attached to me for a while, anxiety would come up. It was clearly a homosexual anxiety, because she would have dreams about women in bathhouses and things that were sort of cloudy, but dangerous, and . . .

GEDO: [interrupting] Was she reading Proust at the time?

PRESENTER: [laughing] No. But there was a shift in her dream material. It came around another event: she came in one day and said that she was going to get married, and she was absolutely tearful. I said, most people who are going to be married are not feeling so bad about it. When she began to try to separate from this boyfriend, there would be an increase in anxiety around me. One time, when she was thinking of separating from the boyfriend, she attended a meeting out of town where she would be surrounded by men, so there was this possibility of things happening. She had a dream then about standing with a bouquet of flowers, but it was made of candy, ribbons of candy, and there were four of them. As she was standing there, there was a man standing in a doorway beckoning to her to come into a cafe that was dimly lit. It was a red-light district. Her associations [referred to feelings of being] overstimulated about going [where there were] possibilities of meeting people, particularly if she were free. [We interpreted that she felt that my support for] her getting away from the boyfriend [made me into a] licentious seller of secrets, that I was beckoning her into something that seemed a lot more dangerous that had to do with her own sexuality.

GEDO: I don't get it. You know, the reason I asked my question is that I've had the experience of doing a number of second and third analyses, and with women, in particular, it often turns out that the first analysis didn't go "deeply enough" because this kind of material was assumed to be referable to father. This often amounts to an unwarranted assumption, although it [refers to] the correct age range—the reconstruction goes to the right era of childhood. This child had not had an adequate development up to that point; she was not age appropriate in object relations. So, that's one of the questions we have to keep on the back burner until we hear about what's happening currently. Did the first analysis promote her on relatively thin grounds to a more differentiated level of development than was strictly warranted? Now, you know one can't do that if there isn't some truth to it; if one is making grossly inaccurate reconstructions, the patient isn't going to get it. But insofar as there is some truth to it, that truth can screen a more important one.[g]

PRESENTER: Well, I think that's absolutely right. I don't want to jump around too much, but lately we have been talking about [the fact that she] brought to every developmental level a particular defect that we never addressed during the analysis.

GEDO: [interrupting] Okay, more of that when we get to it. So tell us what the sequence was.

COMMENT: Question: you said that this is not leading in the direction of the father . . .

GEDO: [interrupting] Well, what has been said in the last three minutes since I interrupted [the presenter] all sounded like infantile material—the conflict between candy, presumably the nursemaid, whatever, and sexuality, men, leaving town.

PRESENTER: As I saw it, there would be this sort of engaging, overexcited, yet sort of dismayed, state and then regression to seeing me as depressed, unavailable, [which meant that] she had to be the caretaker. This was a shift to a more regressed, maternal transference, trapped by a depressed mother. She felt that she really had missed something with her mother, that there really was something wrong with her, and that she didn't have the equipment really to understand and get through later developmental stages. We spent [much of the analysis] in working through a very difficult, entrenched maternal transference with me and the multiple layers of identification with a depressed mother. She changed a lot with that, over time. She began to make shifts in a number of things. As she became less depressed herself, she made a decision that she really didn't want to take care of sick people any longer. What she wanted to do was work with healthy people. In the transference she saw me as less adequate than herself; I was somebody who had to be bolstered or held together and sort of brought along. She had a habit of making friends with women who had brittle adaptations, were quite depressed underneath; and she would play Sir Walter Raleigh with all of them. She realized what a self-defeating habit that was and that it really had to do with her mother and . . .

GEDO: [interrupting] Excuse me for interrupting a moment. This particular metaphor you use is like an association to the dream you told us about. So on one level she's having an assignation with a paternal figure. That's manifest content, but this association points to a latent dream thought, dream wish, wherein she is the phallic lover of the mother. As you all know, one of the favorite childhood fantasies of the daughters of depressed mothers is that it's only the magic phallus that can cure the depression, [the phallus] the father doesn't have. The consequences of that fantasy system determine the outcome of character formation.

COMMENT: The perfect-man fantasy, is that what you mean?

GEDO: Well, the perfect phallic being fantasy. The father, though phallic, is grossly deficient because the mother is depressed. That's the evidence. So one is going to become a magical being. If a boy falls into such a trap, he can have fantasies of being bigger and better than the father in a more or less conventional way; it just fuels his oedipal competitiveness. But if a girl is in that position, it amounts to a grandiose fantasy.

COMMENT: The fantasy could be anything that would make the mother feel better. Rather than the competitiveness with the father, or around being a bigger man, it [could be that] mom needed a woman.

GEDO: [interrupting and speaking over] Oh, absolutely, absolutely, that's an alternative infantile fantasy, but [the presenter] tells us that [in this case] it was a phallic one.

PRESENTER: I think most girls actually have both, back and forth; whatever will make the mother better, and I think that she did have both. Early in the analysis, in the stage of defense, and later, [I heard] that she really needed to be a boy and that that's really what was expected of her and that's what was needed in the household . . .

GEDO: [interrupting] Remind us. There were no brothers?

PRESENTER: There were no boys. She's the last of three girls and there was a neonatal death between the two older girls and herself. She felt [she needed to] make up for that for her mother.

GEDO: Well, that's a double whammy. Not a boy and a replacement child.

PRESENTER: She was supposed to be the boy, to be the better child, or be the stronger child. All of that led to this confused mass of fantasies.

COMMENT: Could I ask a general question? This raises a big [quandary] for me in terms of the mother—the issue of deficit because the kid has not been loved enough. I have found it extremely helpful in treating the children of depressed mothers to help them work along the lines of what was their role in the family. For instance, one woman had to stay depressed, stay at home, be with mom, be in tune with mom, and not rock the boat. Of course, in adult life, when she does this and keeps enacting the same deal with other depressed people or needy people, it keeps her in a depressed, unenthusiastic state. As we've analyzed that, that's helped quite a bit. Other people had to be the man [for mother]. But I've often heard, "Well, look, these people were not loved," [as if to say] that they have the defect because the mother didn't love them. I don't know how you resolve this . . .

GEDO: Well, I must say that that has to be resolved on empirical grounds. The assumption that these people were not loved is an exceedingly improbable one. You know, I have had a fair amount of experience with family constellations of this sort, and I don't think depressed mothers love their babies less than nondepressed mothers [do]. If you can quantify loving, it seems to me that, if anything, they love the babies more. I had one patient who was called by her mother, "my depression baby." It was a fierce, extraordinary love. Of course, you can say it's poison. So the people [you quote] who talk like that, are incurable romantics who think that what matters in human relations is sentiment. That's a big topic, and we shouldn't go off into that at length here, now. But let me just assert flatly that in human affairs sentiment is trivial. It counts for nothing. It counts for *nothing*. It's like salad dressing.

COMMENT: I was thinking in terms of "defect psychology"; some people talk [as though] the ultimate cure [must deal with the fact that] the person did not feel loved and [in response] developed an infantile theory, for instance, [of being] unlovable because unloved, or [being] a girl . . .

GEDO: [interrupting] But the word "love" in those sentences is just so vague! Let me give you one concrete illustration: depressed mother, only son; an excessive attachment and an excessive need on the part of the mother. What is the mother's unconscious fantasy about this, her only son? The only son is the replacement for the dead father. That father died when the son was five, except of course the father had his flaws too, so the son was perfect, and the son is worshipped. It's "love, love, love, love," as Charlie Chaplin put it. But what kind of love is it? It's in the narcissistic realm. What a delusion! Poison! But how long does it take a child to grasp that this isn't good? Of course, it depends on the intellectual level of the individual concerned, but it's unthinkable that any child could grasp that this is bad stuff until 12, 13, 14. So, what does love do? What I'm counterposing to this need for love that people talk about is what Old King Cole wanted—he wanted his slippers and he wanted his pipe. Practical things. "The *real* empathy."

QUESTION: *Real* empathy?

GEDO: *Real* empathy. In terms of [defects in structure] sentiment is like [*Schlag*]. [laughter]

PRESENTER: The other thing that happened was that her mother had a miscarriage when [the patient] was about two and a half. We went over this, over and over and over again in the latter part of the analysis. She had told me about it early on, but it came up around her realizing that there was a repetition of her getting depressed every year at the same time; it had been at that same time that she had been depressed when she was an adolescent and had the wrist-scratching episode. It really happened in the transference: she was absolutely sure that I was abysmally depressed. As we explored this, [we concluded] that it really had to do with her mother's miscarriage, a precipitous, out-of-the-blue event. She had been shipped off to her grandparents' house for a couple of days and really wasn't told what was going on, and then her mother really came back quite depressed, which would be understandable, having lost a second child. I'm sure that in [the patient's fantasy] that was the boy [who was needed]. We ended up focusing on that, but I don't think it was correct. [We saw it as the ultimate source of] her feeling that her mother left her in the lurch; [her] sense of deficit came from around that time. Her mother really was gone, unavailable, not ministering to her in any kind of adaptive way. She felt she really missed something and felt it was owed to her, and if her mother wasn't going to give it to her, her father [had to do so].

GEDO: Did you challenge that?

PRESENTER: No. That's what I'm saying. No, [I did not].

COMMENT: This is the line of patient talk that I was trying to [ask about]. The patient says, "I didn't get something . . ."

GEDO: [interrupting] Well, okay, it's now very popular not to challenge that but to say, "Yeah, you got a bad break and collectively we understand how you felt and how you feel." And that's said to be empathic; that attitude is often defined as the empathic one. And, of course, that *can* be correct. I'm not saying that it isn't, but there is a differential diagnosis to be made, because that kind of talk can, of course, cover over any dynamic you care to name. Let's say arbitrarily, as an example: supposing that at two and a half she was somewhat prematurely involved in a hostile transaction with her mother and wished her dead or wished the baby dead, on the basis of whatever, competitiveness with the mother's reproductive function or jealousy of the pregnancy, whatever. Then the hostile wishes magically come true, and the child is flooded with guilt. The kind of story that we're talking about can be an elaborate avoidance of the rage and the guilt.

COMMENT: One of the ways that discussions get really vague is that it is often argued that there must be truth to the other side also, because the mother failed to recognize the dynamic in the child and that this was the real loss.

GEDO: Well, that's perfectly true, except it's based on a preposterous definition of what is the average expectable environment. It assumes that mothers ought to be child analysts. That's the way to lead people into attitudes of really unreasonable entitlement and feed their rage and . . .

COMMENT: . . . conceal their guilt.

GEDO: Of course, they can't cope with their guilt because now to be guilty will produce guilt vis-à-vis the therapist.

PRESENTER: Will produce what?

GEDO: Guilt vis-à-vis the therapist; so guilt has become *verboten*. I mean, that's a nightmare! That's not to say that the discoveries of Kohut about matters of this kind are incorrect; they were perfectly correct in particular clinical instances, but they're not universals.

GEHRIE: I think what you're saying is that the issue of differential diagnosis at that level is extraordinarily complex and takes a lot of data that we often fail either to get or properly to assess.

GEDO: And *whatever* interpretation we are talking about, no interpretation and no reconstruction should be made on the basis of a patient's statements either about current attitudes or childhood attitudes.

COMMENT: About the parent.

GEDO: Or about an internal state. It's entirely possible that at age three this child felt, "I've been fucked by the fickle finger of fate." I mean children reach all sorts of conclusions, but they're not necessarily correct. The task of the analysis is not merely to determine what the child concluded at age three—that's one task—but also to determine what the realities were at that time.

GEHRIE: This is critical. What you say runs through [everything] that you've written, and it's probably the most misunderstood part. Most ideas about this have to do with the representation of the child's experience as a priori "correct" and [the assumption] that the approach to the child's experience has to start from that premise; otherwise nothing can proceed.

GEDO: Well, I agree, of course, that it has to *start* from that premise. It is terribly important to determine the child's internal state at such crucial junctures and then to talk about what followed from that. And that can only be understood from the child's internal point of view, but one cannot endorse an infantile view of the world and do an analysis. In this regard, even Kohut—I'm not talking only of his followers—even Kohut, as he was dying, was on the threshold of endorsing an infantile view of the world. He called the usual analytic position a "maturation morality," which, he said, was illegitimate. I think such an argument cannot be resolved. One's position is a question of one's own value system. I am perfectly willing to accept the charge that I adhere to a maturation morality; I do. I most certainly do, and I'm not going to throw garbage at people who don't share my value system, but when they do treatment they're engaged in a different enterprise from what I try to do. And insofar as self psychologists espouse Kohut's opposition to a maturation morality, I think they have split away from other psychoanalysts and have founded a different therapeutic discipline.

COMMENT: Along that line of thought, I wanted to ask a question about this girl: what role did the older sisters play for her? It's very frequent that latency age girls just love to play with toddlers and interact with them.

PRESENTER: I have no evidence for that. At least in her internal world, they had very little to do with her. Her next older sister is seven years older than she. When [the patient] was an adolescent, she attempted to get closer to the oldest sister, who was then married and living out East. She attempted to make some kind of relationship with her. She ended by feeling that her sister was really just a chip off the old block and really was not available to her. It was like going to a carbon copy of her mother and father, and I think this was actually true.

COMMENT: That does make it pretty bleak.

PRESENTER: Well, yes, I think so. Let me jump and tell you some things that she's told me in the therapy [we started when she came back after the analysis was terminated]. It's [legitimate] to jump because all that we can talk about between [what I have already described] and the end of analysis is a lot of content, going through a certain layer of development. I understand now that the deficit, or the difficulty for her, really started much earlier than I was willing to place it or understand it [during the analysis] and much earlier than she was willing to place it. The first thing that she said was that she came back because she was still having trouble being successful. She thought that in her analysis she had let her father off the hook. She hasn't really been able to explain this to me. She said that she thought that she still had him on a pedestal and that she focused all of her rage and her hatred on her mother. A lot was resolved: she got along a lot better with her mother, she was less depressed, she could handle things; but there still was something missing. The other thing that she told me was that she had realized in speaking with her mother just lately what had been her mother's agenda. It's interesting; this contradicts her claim "It's my dad's fault" because he believed that success was everything, and one kept working to avoid unhappiness, and that should be the cure to all one's ills, etc., etc., etc. Then she said, "You know what? I finally realized that this was my mother's agenda too, she just never said anything."

GEDO: I'm sorry I have to interrupt you, but you have to tell us in connection with this whether during the analysis, in the transference, she experienced some kind of burning hostility toward you.

PRESENTER: [Yes.]

GEDO: Did she want to damage you, or kill you?

PRESENTER: It was never directed directly at me. It was directed at my office, not at me personally. I'll go back and tell you what happened. She really seemed to improve greatly, symptomatically. She gave up a lot of her phallic identifications, really decided that she wanted to be a wife and mother, became a lot more feminine, less strident, less angry, really began to bloom, got her life to calm down. She was busy doing 20 things; she decided to do only five at a time instead of 20. Things got better for her, and as she . . .

GEDO: [interrupting] You're saying that you analyzed her phallic competitiveness and her wishes to castrate you as the father?

PRESENTER: No. I think what we analyzed was actually more the idea of having to be the phallic replacement of the father for the mother.

GEDO: Well, okay. That's what I was asking about. Because, going back to what she presents with when she returns, one of the items of the differential diagnosis is that she's still guilty because she wants to castrate men, on competitive grounds. You know, after all, when you're dealing with a "success neurosis," that's the area that you would think of first. With a woman patient and a woman analyst, it's not easy to get to the bottom of that aspect of the father transference. Now, I don't know whether that's significant in this case, but until you have demonstrated that it ain't, one has to wonder whether you can get at that without getting her back into analysis.

PRESENTER: Oh, I think she needs a second analysis! She would love to make this second encounter a sort of intellectual psychotherapy, but . . .

GEDO: Well, and if she gets back into a second analysis, just on the chance that this is the crucial issue, there might be some advantage in her going to a man, because in this regard—how shall I put it? It takes less imagination to reexperience this particular matter with a male analyst.

PRESENTER: Well, I think you might be right, because something did happen in the analysis that I think I really misunderstood, and it may have something to do with this. The first thing that happened was that her mother was hospitalized psychiatrically, and the patient attempted to get hold of me to help with the referral. She was not able to [reach] me, so she was disappointed. In some ways she handled it very nicely—she felt that she handled her whole family much more adaptively and was accepted as an adult. It really did help to resolve something about having a more realistic [view] of her mother.

QUESTION: What was wrong? Depressed?

PRESENTER: Yeah, she was depressed. She had an agitated depression. She basically "lost it." She just said, "I can't do this any more. You know, somebody has to take care of me." And they put her in a hospital, and she sort of recouped. About six weeks later, my dad died, and I was out of the office for about a week. [My patient] read the obituary; a friend of hers showed it to her. During the time that I was away, she was in the hospital for three days for kidney stones. Her reaction to my dad's death was never adequately worked out, but her reaction to the obituary was very interesting. Her reaction was to feel absolutely mortified; one of the reasons she felt that way was that it destroyed a fantasy that she had had about me for a long time that I knew nothing about. It was that she had made me a nice little home-town girl from a family in Wisconsin; [she imagined] that I had been able to break away from this family and become an absolute pioneer and come to the big city to slay dragons. She'd always kept this vision of me in her head as something to emulate; it was a very idealized view of me. I can't tell you at this point whether that was a paternal or a maternal image of me or maybe it's the phallic-woman image—a combination of both of them. She described it as my being a woman who could do this, who could break away from the family and do great things, which was what she wanted to do.

GEDO: Do great things that are different from the family's preconceptions?

PRESENTER: Sure, yeah.

GEDO: But the obituary must have stated what your father did, and so she knew that . . .

PRESENTER: She [learned that] I'd followed in my dad's footsteps. She also figured out that I was divorced. I didn't change my name for nothin', so she put two and two together.

GEDO: She knew you were single.

PRESENTER: Yeah.

GEDO: So she had assumed you were never married.

PRESENTER: Right.

QUESTION: Was she mortified that she found out about the death through somebody else?

PRESENTER: I can't answer that. She didn't express that. In retrospect, I think that might have had something to do with [making this] so traumatic; it [could have been that] the disappointment was passively inflicted; it felt like it was done *to* her. She didn't have any control over it; it just was overwhelming. The day I came back, she told me she was quitting her job. Probably, retrospectively, it was a good thing to do. She told me that she had decided that she was going to become an actress. I remember being very startled, "Oh, Jeez! Now what?" Actually, I was as overwhelmed as she was. We associated her deciding to do acting as part of her disillusionment with me as "the pioneer." If I wasn't going to be it, goddamit, she was going to do it. Enough of this [looking upon creative work as a] forbidden career; no one was going to stop her.

GEDO: That has a flavor behind it of her being really competitive with you.

PRESENTER: Oh, yeah. She always was, underneath—that's what we kept trying to work at under these layers of "Oh, you know, you're so depressed; I have to take care of you."

GEDO: The depressed mother.

COMMENT: What is interesting is, are you the *man* she's competing with? That would be the . . .

COMMENT: That's what Dr. Gedo was talking about a while back.

GEDO: Well, it can be on both levels, of course. Let me try to state this clearly. The fact that she takes care of the mother, which looks like a pregenital tie, blah, blah, blah, can in fact be [a function of] competitiveness. It's a way of putting mother down. "You're nothing but a sick gork."

PRESENTER: Oh, that's come out. She said to me that in her head was a real depreciation of me; that is still there. When she came back to see me again, she was looking at me and said, "I was looking at your clothes. The thing that popped into my head was 'all dressed up and no place to go.'" [laughter] Like her mother [laughter]. So, yes, that's still there.

GEDO: You say, "Like her mother." You mean it's her childhood attitude about mother. So the mother got upset one time for reasons that we don't know anything about and was hospitalized; you know, the very fact that they hospitalized her can be an act of hostility and depreciation. What does it mean that the mother has "no place to go?" You know, she is the Duchess of Glencoe, no?

PRESENTER: Riverside.

GEDO: So, what kind of deficit have you found in her? The more we talk, the more it looks like what wasn't covered in the first analysis were the negative attitudes.

PRESENTER: [sighs] You know, I think that's all true, but I think that there is something earlier that she brings to every one of these situations. Her mother wanted this absolutely independent girl, [but, at the same time, she] really never allowed the kids anything like teddy bears, blankets, dolls, anything. You begin to get a picture of the kind of mother who either consciously or unconsciously really had an agenda for her girls. The mother had a fantasy that *Erin's mom?* then was shared by all the girls. They were supposed to be some kind of replacement for her sense of inadequacy in this world; they would be the pioneers that she could not be. That early [deprivation] of transitional objects has left this woman with a real vulnerability. She has no sense of anything to turn to except real people, who then disappoint her.

She demonstrated something over and over and over again, whether in her acting classes or in the analysis. Over and over again; she talks about it as "missing an affective space." She will be distressed or upset in a situation, and she has no sense that she can influence anybody, change anything. It goes from feeling persecuted, with a very small "p," to a sense of rage that one has to fight for everything. The only thing that you can do is to confront [people] and argue and make sure that you [insist] the wrongs are righted.

This is what she did with me over and over again in the analysis. It doesn't matter which of these developmental issues that we're talking about [she may be dealing with,] she reacts in the same way. She even explained that she felt that she's very good at complying with people and that she felt she did that in the analysis with me. That I would say something, or point a direction, or ask a question, and she would say, "Sure, I can do that for you." She experienced a lot of it as a sort of passively endured, subdued relationship with me, where there's this kind of passive submission, and then she would have to fight it. She either [submitted] or she had to fight for her rights.

COMMENT: It's almost as if she's [felt herself to be] a narcissistic extension of the mother rather than having any sense of her own initiative being able to guide her, either affectively or in terms of behavior. You know, she had to passively endure mother's wish, mother's fantasy, for what these girls ought to do.

GEDO: Well, there again, that's *her* claim, and I would be hesitant to accept that claim. I must say I'm a little bewildered by [something said earlier]. This is a woman who comes into the analysis as a puppeteer; so how can you say that she has no transitional object? She wanted to be Ginger Rogers, and maybe she was only an understudy, but she actually had jobs in ballet companies in New York, and now she's an actress. So what really matters to her are these transitional experiences.

PRESENTER: Right. I think she's searching for them. I don't know that she can do them well. There's a difference. She has a deficit when it comes to all this stuff, and I think it just keeps catching up with her. Even about the acting, she's been told that she's good, that she has what it takes, but she's not a natural. She takes lots and lots and lots of classes, and she says that she needs input all the time; that she can't do things very often the first time around.

COMMENT: But she's not put off by that. She goes ahead and does it. She doesn't accept the judgment against her, it seems. She doesn't back off and withdraw and say, "Well, it's hopeless and I can't do it."

GEDO: Let me approach it from another point of view. When she reads your father's obituary in the newspaper, after several years of analysis, she for the first time reveals this elaborate fantasy which has been kept secret. So *that's* a transitional experience. She created an imaginative world; she didn't share it with you. Based on the mother's intrusiveness, we can understand that she has learned to keep those things very private indeed. But it's not that there is a deficit of transitional space; it's constantly threatened by the mother, but she successfully resisted.

PRESENTER: Okay.

COMMENT: I'm thinking of my third control case. [She relived] this idealizing kind of thing with her father in the transference, a very erotic transference. We worked through this, and what ultimately has come out is much more hostile, competitive stuff. It's almost like there are two analyses. I was thinking about what gets "unanalyzed." Your [comment] on the people who come back for a second analysis—one thing you often hear is, it's the relationship with the mother or the earlier stuff that was not covered. [Another possibility]—and this is my actual experience—was [overlooking] the competitiveness with men, anger with men. The woman I'm thinking of talks very much like this, "I've got to fight for my rights. Nobody's going to be there for me, in the law firm." A lot of this does turn out to have to do with her relationship with her father. The real lacuna in your presentation [that causes our confusion] is, what do you think of as her relationships with men? What are they like? Are they competitive? Does she only see devalued men whom she can dominate? Are there some data that would help you? Because this would be a very different kind of formulation than going back to real early stuff and saying that she can't manage to soothe herself . . .

PRESENTER: I think you can talk about it in both ways. Yes, I think that there's a lot about competitiveness with men. In the latter part of the analysis, she started a relationship with a guy that she clung to for almost two years. She was a good girl with me for a long time, when I was acutely depressed, and she set up this thing with this guy. She was going to make him love her, come hell or high water. She would not let it go; she wouldn't accept what he said to her. If she wasn't the most beautiful, she was going to be the best directed, or the most exciting, or the most flamboyant, or whatever. She was going to get into this man's bedroom and make something of this relationship. She just would not take no for an answer. But the reality comes in at a certain point, and she had to stop.

COMMENT: She wanted to win his love. But what did she want to do with him when she got him?

PRESENTER: I have no idea.

GEDO: Wear him in her boutonniere. But, again, these are fantasies based on highly condensed selections from the material. You present the picture of somebody who doesn't treat men as real human beings, but as puppets. She's a puppeteer; he's got to do what she wants. Probably that's an identification with the mother's terribly intrusive, domineering style, but it's part of her character. So one of the sectors that the first analysis did not alter sufficiently is her relationship with men, the primitive cast to her relationships. I must say that, contrary to your impression that her life is lacking in transitional experience, I would formulate this in an aphorism to the effect that, alas, she has *only* transitional experiences. [pause] You can't treat people as though they were dolls.

PRESENTER: I suppose that in essence people are her transitional objects. As a matter of fact, she calls her father "a big thing."

GEDO: Winnicott didn't say that transitional experiences have to be brought about through material things. The first transitional experience is with the baby's tongue, right? The tongue games that babies of three, four, five months of age play are already transitional experiences.

QUESTION: Why would that be a transitional experience? You mean interactive?

GEDO: The baby will play with its tongue as though it were . . .

COMMENT: As if it were somebody else's. All right, okay.

GEDO: Yeah, it's an absolutely independent activity and nobody can take that away from the baby. Her mother can try to intrude, but she can't. This girl has demonstrated that she had an imaginative world, and she knew how to keep it to herself. The Wisconsin fantasy.

PRESENTER: So [this girl as a child] wasn't sure whether [independent activity could be] accepted by the mother, right? And so it then becomes secret or private.

GEDO: I'm not wedded to Winnicott's vocabulary all that much. I am tempted to say that here is a case where Melanie Klein's vocabulary would be singularly apposite. This is a woman who lives in a world of part objects. [pause] In that sense you're correct to say that there is a primitive deficit in her capacity for object relations, and therefore both the positive and negative Oedipus remain unresolved, because the only question is who's the puppet and who's the puppeteer. [pause] It's interesting that she goes into professions where you need a coach, so that you have to be a puppet and the coach is the puppeteer. But she doesn't quite make it. And I would be very suspicious that she defeats the coaches the way she defeated you. She covers her rebelliousness with this pseudocompliance, and she's still claiming that she's compliant; but the "compliant" patient in analysis *never* really complies, because we're so explicit that [compliance is] *verboten*. I assume that even beginners say to their analysands relatively early, "Do me a favor, don't do me any favors." [pause]

Well, I think she does need to go into analysis to deal with this matter, if we are even close to the truth. It's not clear why her object relationships are so grossly defective. Can you give us any hints?

PRESENTER: More than we've talked about? I'm not sure that I can.

GEDO: Her siblings' object relationships aren't that grossly defective, are they?

PRESENTER: Well, no, that's not true. The oldest sister has managed to stay married and has three kids, although the kids are having trouble, the boy in the family, in particular, apparently. I remember [the patient] telling me during the analysis that this preadolescent boy was having tics at that time but the family refused to allow him to go into therapy. Now, this same boy is a late adolescent, and she's convinced he's homosexual. There's a girl of about 18 who seems to identify with my patient a lot and [struggles with] the same issues, which is understandable if she grew up in a carbon copy family. The other sister actually has had a tremendous amount of difficulty. She went into dance therapy and then into physical therapy; married against her parents' wishes, was married for about five years, divorced, has one son. She is very isolated and lives out of town; has not that much to do with the family. As a matter of fact, my patient's talked about her some because she said that she was worried about her because very clearly her sister is depressed. She's not talking to anyone, doesn't want anybody to know her business, and my patient feels that she's at considerable risk.

GEDO: Now, does either of the sisters have a vocation?

PRESENTER: [They both work professionally.] The middle sister, in particular, continues to be in open rebellion against the family in whatever choices she makes. My patient has always managed to have a decent core group of women friends, most of whom are in the arts. But her relationships with men really stay very problematic. She goes through this same cycle that I'm talking about: she manages very quickly to get involved with men, becomes intimate with them very quickly, and then finds herself really enraged at them for some slight. She says that she believes that she scares men away, that she's too intense. Which is true.

GEDO: Well, we can't carry this any further. These are questions which could only be answered by another analysis that covers this particular aspect of the waterfront. Let me ask a different question. How on earth did you manage to terminate the first analysis?

PRESENTER: [laughs] Well . . . what happened was this. About three months after my dad died I got better, and she started to detach from her boyfriend. She then came into my office in an absolute rage, absolute rage, and began to do things like refuse to lie down. She walked around my office. She wanted to see certain private parts of it, what was in the closets, what was in the drawers, and this went on for a month. You know, she would stand behind me and I. . . .

GEDO: [interrupting] Well, what are you saying? She was crazy?

PRESENTER: No! Absolutely not! She was just in this haughty rage. There was a reversal [in operation]: she was very clear that she wanted me to feel what she had felt, helpless and dominated, and that she knew that she wasn't going to be in analysis forever. She was going to make sure that she satisfied some fantasies that she had always had [about our] changing positions or about knowing private things about me. The only thing that got her to calm down was when I started pointing out to her how much fun she was having, that underneath the rage she was just having a ball. I started pointing out her smile, and she began to say, "Well, yeah, you know, I am getting a kick out of this," and "I don't want to stop because I know if I stop I'm going to have to settle down and grow up. That means I'll have to finish the analysis, I can't do this forever, I know I can't be a child." [This pattern began with] a phone call to me in the middle of the night; she had just broken up with a boyfriend for the umpteenth time, and really only wanted one response from me, to tell her to continue to pursue this, that it was worthwhile.

GEDO: At 2:00 A.M.?

PRESENTER: Yeah. And I said to her instead, "This is not an appropriate time to talk about this. We'll talk about it in the office." And that's when she came in in a rage, you know. She was beginning to do with me what she had done with the boyfriend. I mean, she was being absolutely insistent that she was going to get into my life and nothing was going to stop her.

GEDO: She had gone into your bedroom.

PRESENTER: That's right. That's what I interpreted. I interpreted it as a primal scene enactment. You know, that she wanted to see and she wanted to know, and this also had to do with her reaction to [my father's] obituary, which had a primal scene meaning to her. That the door to my life had been flung open and she was totally overstimulated by what she found inside, and it wasn't what she had wanted.

GEDO: A love affair between father and daughter?

PRESENTER: That's right. That I was . . .

GEDO: Well, so how did you manage to quit, to terminate?

PRESENTER: Well, as soon as she began to calm down and I interpreted that it grew out of the trauma of seeing inside my life, she said, "I know you're right and I know I have to stop this"; but also, "I don't want to accept the limits." And she promptly got depressed. Not *really* depressed, sad. She began to mourn; [she felt] this was the position she never wanted to accept . . .

GEDO: [interrupting] That's fascinating. It really begins to sound like she raped you. She was enjoying raping you. And that this is a grandiose enactment in the mother transference of a fantasy that she is the puppeteer and phallic being. And when she "grows up" she has to give up the unreality of the fantasy of being capable of doing that.

PRESENTER: I think you may be right. The way that she presented herself when she came back is that she's still stuck despite this brittle idea about self-sufficiency. She sort of mumbles to herself, "Why can't I do this myself?" I think I have missed even this time that it's so easy to pin it on the parents and that this has been taught [by mother]. [She enacts a] grandiose fantasy of being the perfect male.

GEDO: That's right. What you can pin on the parents, I think in this instance the mother, is that they didn't puncture this balloon. We can't be sure; this second treatment is not an analysis, and we don't have the kind of data that would make us absolutely confident of all this; so we are guessing. But I think it's very likely that the ultimate truth will turn out to be that, like Hamlet, she was too much loved. Too much loved. This depressed mother made her feel like she was the magic phallus. Her totality was the magic phallus; that she can do anything. She can do *anything*. That she can get away with anything because the mother needs her and loves her in a way that she doesn't need anybody else. So at the point [where she enacts this] you have a delusional transference. You say she wasn't crazy. Well, outside of your office, she is not a psychotic character; but at that moment in your office, in the transference, that's a psychotic transference—she's not accepting reality. She can do *anything*. I mean, at one's most optimistic, one can say that she's enacting a primary behavior disorder. You look blank. This is such an old-fashioned term that you haven't heard it anymore?

COMMENT: It doesn't sound like it was completely contained in the room, because she did call at two in the morning.

GEDO: Well, not literally in the room, but in the analytic space.

COMMENT: Okay.

GEDO: You're perfectly right. She does not observe the time constraints; she does not observe the space constraints; she has never observed the basic rule, right?

PRESENTER: To a certain degree that's right.

GEDO: Well, to a certain degree she had this "secret," and it's only when that particular delinquency was punctured that all this crazy behavior came into the open. She has contained the craziness within that fantasy. The fact that she acts like it's an outrage that you're not the girl from Wisconsin shows how far out in left field she is. "What do you mean by being the daughter of an eminent man?" says she, with outrage.

QUESTION: Isn't part of the outrage too that she isn't the analyst's only lover?

GEDO: Yes, yes, absolutely, absolutely. So she gets into her drawers. In the good old days, that would have been considered a pun. Now, at what developmental level is this pathology? Very early, huh? It's not that she wasn't given transitional experiences; she wasn't taught reality testing! The content is at the oedipal level: she is crazily competitive with the father (and by displacement with all other men) and she is delusionally certain that she is the mother's only love.

PRESENTER: It's probably true.

COMMENT: So why did she come back? I don't understand . . .

PRESENTER: [interrupting] Well, I actually think she came back because she was called up to do [a follow-up at the Institute Clinic]. As soon as she was called, she got herself into a car accident—minor. For all the other rationalizations she gave me, I think she was just really stirred up by the call and got into a rage at me again. So she probably came back to get me to calm her down.

GEDO: Well, I must say, that's very interesting too, because you and she agreed to terminate and everybody presumably reached a consensus that this was a reasonable end. She didn't say, "You're selling me out and I'm not well," and *you* didn't say, "You're leaving to escape analyzing the real problem." You agree to the fiction that the analysis is a reasonable success, but when she's called for the follow-up that fiction can no longer be maintained. The analysis ended in a denial of reality, [just as] her primary pathology is a denial of reality. That is not an unusual outcome, by the way. I don't know how many of you have read the Steven Firestein termination book. It's a very important book. It's now about ten years old, but there are eight well-documented, complete analyses described, every one of which was terminated to the satisfaction of the candidate analyst and the supervisor at the New York Institute. Then Firestein did the follow-ups, and none of the results were any better than this. None of them, although they conscientiously analyzed certain issues, by and large pretty much the same issues that you succeeded in analyzing. We're most familiar with that territory so we do best at it, and patients are relatively at ease with that territory. And that's not useless. Those gains are not lost. I mean, she's better, she's better.

PRESENTER: [Yes,] she's better.

GEDO: And so were the patients that Firestein did the follow-ups on. They were better, but they were still sick. And so she says, "I'm still not successful." Well . . .

QUESTION: What would you say to her at this point? Do you feel she's interested in another analysis?

PRESENTER: She'd like to do without it. [She'd prefer for] somebody to say to her, "Go ahead, you can do whatever you please. You don't have to come back and go through all this business." But I also think that she's frustrated enough that, yes, she would probably do it.

GEDO: Well, the practicalities are not easy to solve at this stage of the game. You're not going to do it at a trivial fee, I assume.

PRESENTER: She would have to do something about her life and change it around again in order to do an analysis. But you really think that it probably would be easier with a man. [laughs]

GEDO: Well . . .

PRESENTER: Because depending on who it is, she can just go over the same ground again, you know. [laughing]

GEDO: I think it would have a slightly different flavor with a man. I think she'd have a harder time in concealing her competitive frustrations. She kept her fantasies secret, which makes it even more difficult to deal with [the problem]. She defended herself against the competitive frustrations through the secret fantasy: that you'd never been married, and you were just a little girl from Little Rock. Well, of course, she can . . .

PRESENTER: [interrupting] You can tell by my down-home twang, right?

GEDO: Obviously, if she's imaginative enough, she can construct a similarly depreciating fantasy about anybody, but I must say she doesn't sound all that clever, and . . .

PRESENTER: She isn't; she's dogged.

GEDO: Not all that imaginative, and therefore I would assume that if she were in analysis with Richard Baer and she discovered that Richard's wife is a television announcer, the fat would be in the fire! [pause] It's not a suggestion for a referral. [laughter]

Commentary (Gehrie)

First Session

The first seminar session begins with a discussion of some salient features pertaining to the beginning of the analysis, in particular, the question of this patient's capacity to make a commitment, the history of the "suicide attempt" in high school, and the introduction of the role of ideals in her career choice. In reply to Gedo's question, it is revealed that the patient changed her ambition from musical comedy to ballet between high school and college, apparently under pressure that she experienced from her mother. This struggle had a history in her parents' long-standing involvement as "patrons of the arts," yet the patient was the only one of the children to aspire to an artistic career. The patient's concerns about her aspirations, however, seemed from the first to be bound up with her entry into the analysis. Although she came from a well-to-do family, she sought low-fee analysis in order that her family would not discover that she was in treatment. She saw this as a kind of independence, according to the analyst: "She didn't want to take anything from the family for herself. She was going to do this on her own." Shortly, however, it becomes apparent that there was more to it than this: "She really came in with her mind set that life was a struggle with her mother; period. This was a fight with her mother, and everything she wanted to do her mother did not want her to do."

The analysis, of course, becomes the center of the issue, leading to an immediate pressure for enactment: the patient's need for the analyst to agree to participate in keeping the analysis a secret from mother. Gedo suggests that to agree to this secrecy (as the analyst did) was tantamount to accepting the patient's implicit judgment that the analysis "was either a rebellious act or shameful nonsense." This emphasis on not permitting the analysis to be the patient's "secret"—even at the outset—is founded on Gedo's view that the analyst must not accept the patient's externalization of the conflict and that some "reality assessment" of the situation is indicated. He stresses that to go along with the patient's view is to be undermining:

> She has to be consistent, if she is an autonomous person. This means she cannot make a secret of the fact that she has decided to have an analysis. By going along with the secret, you are undermining the striving to be autonomous. Of course, the fact that she simultaneously set up these [contradictory] conditions [shows that she has a conflict about autonomy versus symbiosis].

This view is a fundamental departure from the idea that the patient's experience of the moment—albeit within the context of the enactment—must be the central focus of the analyst's contact.[h]

This young analyst seemed to feel that accepting the patient's requirements (i.e., participating in the enactment) was essential for engaging the patient in the analysis. Hence, her reply to the patient's critical inquiry about traveling while in analysis was clearly an equivocal attempt to address reality but also demonstrated an awareness of the underlying anxiety about feeling trapped (in the transference): "Well, it's not optimum." Significantly, the patient's response revealed an acceptance of the underlying reality issue—"she had already begun to rearrange her schedule so that she could be in town for the analysis"—despite the initial accusatory outburst. This action, of course, also helped the analyst to "calm down," because now there would be an analysis or at least an attempt at one; but the concern remains that the critical meaning of this opening transaction was not explored. As Gedo notes, "Apparently you agreed silently not to explore this flare-up. . . . Beyond whatever you discussed in her treatment, there remained this issue of [entitlement to some kind of special handling in accommodating her, whatever the requirements of an analytic treatment may be]."

It must also be considered, however, that the analyst may have felt that such an exploration might have been premature and could interfere with the critical balance that permitted the patient to accept the limitations and restrictions of an analysis at that moment, given the overwhelming anxiety in the negative mother transference. Certainly Gedo is correct that this engagement leaves a significant "residual," which must, at some point, be analyzed if there is to be a truly analytic termination, but at this point in the analysis there seems to be some technical justification for not insisting upon its immediate investigation.[i]

The analyst begins her description of the opening-phase process by indirectly acknowledging this same point—that the patient "arranged her life" for the analysis, while simultaneously being "very provocative, very angry."

> She would ask me questions all the time, and she would begin to get furious if I didn't answer her. She would pick at everything I said: it was not quite right, or "What did I mean by that?", or, "This did not exactly fit her experience."

In the absence of supervisory advice to the contrary, the analyst took "an interpretive stand" and eventually "interpreted it as defensive." The patient experienced this posture of the analyst as a repetition in the negative mother transference, and an uncomfortable struggle seemed to develop between the two of them—the patient angry and feeling unresponded to, and the analyst feeling helpless and, as Gedo suggests, also angry, feeling pushed away, and accused by the patient of failing her. Gedo elaborates three approaches that might be taken at such a juncture, including the one taken by the analyst (neutral and interpretive), or "responding to everything . . . by sharing with the patient the experience you think she is having," or, third, that of "countertransference interpretation." Gedo offers the view that the countertransference interpretation might have been most useful; but it could also be argued that the second alternative, in which the analyst (empathically) directly addresses the experience of the patient, might also have been effective, insofar as the patient's main experience of the interaction was of the analyst's purposeful failure to address her experience and to focus on her own agenda (interpretation) instead.

Under conditions such as those which quickly evolved in this analysis, it is arguable that any affectively meaningful engagement—organized around the experience of the patient through either empathic "attunement" or countertransference response—would improve the analytic venue, that is, "attract the patient into cooperation with" the analysis. In this instance, the analyst's technique was too much of a repetition of the patient's childhood past and had the unintended effect of re-creating certain essential features of the pathogenic relation to mother. The countertransference component of this position is also evident in the analyst's interpretation of the patient's negativism as "identification with a demanding person."

Despite the analyst's concealed anger toward the patient, her underlying capacity for a (preconscious) orientation toward an empathic position is revealed in "the second major event that happened between us." The patient called the analyst on Thanksgiving Day and was obviously very relieved that the analyst would return the patient's call from her family's home, thus showing herself to be emotionally available. This increased closeness led to some sexualized anxiety in the transference. The anxiety gave way to the angry fighting again when the analyst interpreted it, not an incorrect interpretation perhaps, but likely premature. It may have been experienced by the patient as a hostile withdrawal by the analyst. Such moments highlight the relationship between technique and the state of the transference: a theory of technique must take such dynamics into account lest technique become a slave to the ongoing enactment.

Second Session

Delving back into the discussion of the Thanksgiving Day phone call, the analyst elaborated on the powerful effects of the patient's experience of the moment:

> I think that it becomes very clear toward the end of the analysis that out of that event she formed a whole host of fantasies about me, not only that I could perhaps be a different kind of mother, one [who] was more supportive, more gentle, less intrusive, but a whole set of fantasies about my whole family. . . . I think that she actually formed a silent idealization of me at that point, seeing me as caring and on her side.

Numerous questions are raised about this occurrence. Is such a (silent) idealization genuine? What is its role in the analysis? What happened to the negative transference? These are complex and interrelated questions. A view based on the process suggests as one possibility that the analyst's responsiveness at a critical moment (the Thanksgiving Day phone call) enabled—for the first time in the analysis—a (temporary) healing of the underlying, chronically fragmented self, permitting the evolution of the developmentally significant idealizing transference. From this perspective, the hypothesis assumes that the analyst finally permitted herself to respond (empathically) to this level of the patient's experience, rather than maintaining the distant, "interpretive" position that had the effect of repeatedly retraumatizing the patient in this dimension. In this view, the idealization is not only genuine, but is a developmental necessity, forming a foundation for further growth.[k]

The negativity expressed earlier would be understood as the result of the analyst's (repetitive) failures to grasp this aspect of the patient's experience, thus aggravating the narcissistic injury to which the patient responded with narcissistic rage. The analyst's studied attempts at "neutrality" could be seen as an example of such failure, as well as her attempts to interpret the patient's anger as "identification with belligerent, demanding, intrusive caretakers." In the countertransference, the analyst clearly felt unreasonably demanded of and intruded upon by the patient's depressively organized longings.

Another view, suggested by Gedo's comment that "it never occurred to you that this was love?" suggests that, due to the overwhelmingness of the early negative maternal identifications, this rageful demandingness was the only way in which the patient could express an intense connection with the analyst in the transference. This early characterological adaptation is what was available to the patient and formed the entirety of her basis for relating. The patient's negativity, from this perspective, is not the result of an empathic failure by the analyst, but the emergence of the underlying adaptive organization of the self. As to the question of "why does the enactment of your [the analyst's] availability (i.e., the Thanksgiving Day phone call) suddenly lead to the shift?" Gedo suggests that the patient's history of disappointments—the "burnt child"—made it impossible for her to permit the idealization to emerge earlier, and that it took a year of work to begin to ameliorate her anxiety. He suggests that "it's not likely to be this single event that demonstrated that the worst fears are not realized and that she can begin to hope that you are the kind of person she wants."

Both of these views of process retain the perspective on the patient's idealization as not fundamentally defensive in nature; the critical distinction between these views lies in the explanations of its emergence and in the view of the relationship of negative affects to technique. In the ensuing discussion, the analyst acknowledges that "some of her (the patient's) complaints were right. I was being distant. . . ." This is a crucial realization that includes the notion that emotional presence is not theory dependent. The idea that classical analytic technique demands emotional distance, for example, is rejected by Gedo, who then gives an example of the role of emotional presence in the management of the negative transference in his own analysis. Gedo's view implies that the analysand's ability to recognize the negative transference as transference is an important component of analyzability; that while the empathic failures of the analyst must be acknowledged, the opportunity for the analysis of the negative transferences must also be preserved. Gedo's subsequent remarks emphasize that, given expectable analytic conditions and proper technique, the idealization might have emerged sooner, especially since it is now clearer that "she wants her mother to be a more admirable person." In this view, the idealization is not defensive: the patient requires this form of relationship for an aspect of her own self development.[1]

It is also true, however, that these feelings of closeness arouse the patient's homosexual anxiety—a sexualized version of her fears about being disappointed by her ideal—that is, that the idealization would lead to disaster:

> [H]er feeling that if she loved me she worried about getting endlessly stuck with me, like a bad addiction. She had conscious concerns about whether she was a lesbian or not; [she felt] she was stuck with women and couldn't form a relationship with a man.

The incident in which the analyst had to cancel and "came back depressed" was handled very differently from the way similar events had previously been dealt with in the analysis and had different results. The analyst acknowledged that "something was really going on" (in her own life), and this admission freed the patient to "talk about her failures." In this environment, the analysand was able to "give up her defensiveness" in this area of great vulnerability and even asked for a fifth session. This dramatic shift in the patient's affect and availability for the analysis can be seen as a direct consequence of the shift in the analyst's own emotional presence. Gedo suggests that despite the "wonderfulness" of this, the analyst may have gone "too fast" that is, that her efforts to explore the material were not sufficiently thorough and painstaking, "because the question to ask is, what the hell is the matter with being understudy for the star of a major ballet company?"

Again, more than one perspective on this process presents itself. Although Gedo is indeed asking a critical question, there may also be something to gain by allowing the patient to evoke fully the losses and anxiety she experienced in the mother transference as a way of letting her begin to question her need to be the star. To interfere with her sense of wonderfulness with the analyst at this point may be precisely to suggest "that she really doesn't have the capacities, or shouldn't have the hopes and ambitions that she seems to have." Gedo would be "careful" about communicating about the patient's "promise . . . because I don't know how much promise she has."

This is a central point: on one hand is the view that the patient's "drivenness" to be the star is of functional, developmental significance beyond the issue of her career and that the disappointments she has suffered relate intimately to her experience of having failed with her mother—that is, having failed to evoke adequately the proverbial "gleam" in mother's eye. This perspective would be consistent with the idea that what precipitated the engagement of her feelings about the failures and disappointments in her life was precisely the shift in the emotional availability of the analyst. On the other hand, Gedo emphasizes the "practical matters"; beyond his disagreement with Gill's view that after the interaction with the analyst, the patient's perception of the analyst's depression might be seen as a "resistance," Gedo sees the work of the analysis as including a "practical" dimension in which reality testing is a necessary part. The patient must understand, in other words, that the work of the analysis must underlay any truly successful solutions, including providing an opportunity for the expression of her ambitions.

Such understanding, however, is a point of some difficulty since, as the analyst remarks, it is not clear whether the patient's attempt to "solve" the dilemma with mother was simply an adaptive, creative endeavor or whether it was also an expression of "vengeance." Further, it was possible that, beyond the patient's experience of the analysis itself as anything other than a kind of career counseling, she felt regularly manipulated in the negative mother transference; that in order to get what she wanted, she had to take a lot that she didn't want. Gedo remarks that the patient's agreement to participate in the analysis came from the practical side; to shift the emphasis to the relationship with the analyst "makes you sound like the mother again." At the same time, it was also powerfully evident that the analyst's availability provided an antidote to this anxiety, and supplied a venue for the exploration of previously unavailable feelings. Gedo's concern appears to focus on the possible consequences of too narrow a focus on the enactment in the transference alone, without adequate consideration of "the adaptive dilemma." The danger from this vantage point is that "exclusive emphasis on the transference will be taken by this sort of a patient as a chopping off of her ambition."[m]

Third Session

At the beginning of the third session, the analyst reports developments that she understood as the elaboration of the father transference, evidence for which was cited in the patient's anxiety in her attachment to the analyst. Next, there was a dream in which the patient's associations led to an interpretation of the patient's feeling "overstimulated" by the analyst as a "licentious seller of secrets." Eventually, however, this position gave way to the view that underlying this "engaging and excited" state was "a shift to a more regressed, maternal transference [of feeling] trapped by a depressed mother. . . . In the transference she saw me as less adequate than herself; I was somebody who had to be bolstered or held together and sort of brought along. . . ."

There follows a discussion of the various possible characterological consequences of the girl's need to save her mother from her depression and of the notion that somehow psychological defects can be accounted for by the absence of love. Gedo stresses that it is not the absence of "love" which is the issue, but rather "what kind of love is it." When excessive and inappropriate attachments become—in the name of love—intrusive and damaging in various ways, such dynamics are most unlikely to be apprehended and understood prior to the early teen years, if they are grasped at all. Gedo prefers to recognize the role of "practical things" in human relationships; an analytic stance that he characterizes as having true ("real") empathy. These are actualities of interaction that pertain to the acquisition of psychological skills.

The discussion continues to evoke questions about the relationship of the patient's subjective experience of reality to the analysis and about the fundamental differences in definitions about what sort of hypotheses underlie that process. In this case, the analyst accepted the patient's views that the mother's depression had left the patient having "really missed something" that was "owed" to her. The patient's experience was clearly that she had been short-changed and accounts for her own anger and depression, which had only been partially concealed by her hypomanic attempts to stimulate her mother.

Although Gedo acknowledges that to accept the patient's experience about this can, in certain instances, be "correct empathy," he feels that there is a "differential diagnosis" to be made. The implication is that, properly speaking, empathy is functionally reliant on a form of reality testing and furthermore that the analyst must come to a judgment about the nature of the patient's experience prior to deciding whether to accept it as a valid response. But even in the context of the kind of example that Gedo cites as problematic—a child's attempt to avoid rage and guilt about negative feelings—does it necessarily follow that (a) the analyst must have come to some reality judgement about this prior to taking an empathic position; (b) that if the analyst does take an empathic position, the guilt and rage will be ultimately and successfully avoided (i.e., that proper empathy may constitute accepting a fraudulent or at least infantile view of the world); and (c) that, handled properly, an empathic position may "lead people into attitudes of really unreasonable entitlement and . . . feed their rage"? It seems essential here to distinguish broadly between appropriate and inappropriate uses of empathy;[n] as a data-gathering tool it must not be confused with the active attempt to interfere with or protect a patient from negative experience in the transference. Gedo notes that "children can reach all sorts of conclusions, but they're not necessarily correct" and that "the task of the analysis is not merely to determine what the child concluded at age three."

The appropriate use of empathy is not tantamount to "endorsing an infantile view of the world," and there are also deleterious consequences if the analyst fails, at critical moments, to convey to the patient an ability to grasp the patient's subjective experience of his or her [infantile] view of the world. Finally, it appears risky for the analyst to attempt to "determine the realities" of the patient's early life, although the doubt must cut both ways: perhaps neither the past nor the present need be assigned with a fixed certainty without possibility for changes in understanding.

In this case, it seems likely that the struggle that engaged the first year of the analysis, prior to the Thanksgiving Day phone call, was largely a result of the analyst's failure to utilize an empathic approach. Perhaps an enabling acceptance of the patient's experience in the archaic transference during that period might have enhanced her ability for reflection, which ultimately might have led to a more positive analytic result (Gehrie, in press). Instead, the enactment in the negative mother transference engaged the analyst's countertransference rage, and this kept the struggle alive. Not until the phone call, which the analyst was able to manage differently, was the power of the enactment interfered with and could the beginning of the analysis of the enactment proceed. This shift was not tantamount to endorsing an infantile view of the world, although, clearly, the development of the analytic process depended on the subsequent evolution of the analyst's technique.[o]

Gedo acknowledges that we must begin from the premise that the child's experience is "correct." The technical procedures that emerge from that perspective, however, must constantly evolve in concert with the developmental goals of the analysis. To insist that the analyst must never diverge from the patient's infantile views would be absurd, but it would also be unreasonable to assert that such a program is advocated by those who appropriately use empathic engagement as a fundamental tool in the establishment and maintenance of an analytic process.

The analyst goes on to describe that the negative transference was never directly brought into focus in the analysis, and Gedo remarks that the patient "is still guilty because she wants to castrate men, on competitive grounds." According to the analyst, this was only analyzed as the patient's wish "to be the phallic replacement of the father, for the mother," and not in terms of the more directly competitive strivings with the analyst in the father transference. All of this could also be seen as an aspect of the failure to recognize the patient's need for an idealizing transference: she was unable to feel that she had succeeded in engaging the analyst (except for moments) and therefore felt she "had to fight for everything." The idealization could not occur so long as the negative mother transference (and the associated perception of the analyst as depressed and in need of the patient's support) was enacted and not analyzed.[P]

The analysand's "negative attitudes" are not solely a result of the analyst's empathic failures—they are organized around early negative identifications and form the basis of her characterological adaptations. But, in the analysis, the failure of the analyst to be available consistently in an empathic way cemented the analytic difficulties. On several levels, these conditions led to a kind of endless compliance, a "passively endured . . . passive submission" that would become engaged periodically. Thus, her "deficit" was reflected in her utter dependence on the analyst's empathic availability, without which she was caught in the helpless repetition of the (doomed) attempt to restart her failed development by archaic means. As Gedo notes, she attempted to achieve a new beginning by constructing an imaginary world belonging to the analyst, but this effort was unable to be transformed into analytic work. These "transitional experiences" are kept secret in an effort to preserve at least some sense of autonomous existence, although her attempts to form relationships on this level remain arrested: "the only question is who's the puppet and who's the puppeteer."

On the subject of how the analysis was terminated, the analyst remarks on the amelioration of her own depression and on the patient's rageful refusal to participate in the analysis in the usual way. The rage had been precipitated by a telephone interaction with the analyst, one very unlike the Thanksgiving Day phone call. During this call, the analyst refused to discuss an immediate problem with her, and the patient became angry at the limits. In the seminar, this incident was discussed in terms of a primal scene enactment, although there is also evidence that the patient's reaction was secondary to her intense disappointment at feeling once again rejected by the analyst.

For Gedo, the patient's reaction to the phone call and to the limits set by the analyst was evidence of the primary pathology—the defects in reality testing: "she is delusionally certain that she is the mother's only love." The analysis ended with this "denial of reality" still intact. Gedo sees this pathology as a failure of learning (and of teaching) that was not repaired in the analysis. In several instances, the imposition of the analyst's reality prompted intense rage reactions, which Gedo sees as the grandiose enactment in the negative mother transference that is a developmental product of the parents' failure to teach their child about reality. The "depressed" mother needed this "magical" child. From a self-psychological perspective, the rage may be seen as partly reactive to the failure of the analyst to recognize the patient's need for idealization as part of the process, which would encompass phase-appropriate opportunities for disillusionment. In this view, beginnings in this direction were, regrettably, lost to the reinstatement of the analyst's more distant posture, forcing the issue to be sealed over. From both viewpoints, however, reality is a central concern, and both viewpoints permit the conclusion that the fundamental analytic tasks were not accomplished.

Clarification and Addenda: Colloquy with a Self-Psychological Critic (Gedo)

a. Collusion with pathological enactments or empathy?

Joseph Conrad described the role of a "secret sharer" as that of a mirror in which the protagonist may see his own reflection; I believe Kohut (1968) chose the term "mirror transference" on the model of Conrad's metaphor. Many analysands spontaneously develop transference expectations for such "mirroring," and (in the wake of Kohut's impact on the psychoanalytic world) large segments of the analytic community hesitate to inflict traumatically unempathic experiences on patients who request some specific compliance (such as that of the analysand presented here for a fee low enough to enable her to keep her analysis "secret") with their preferred conditions for treatment.

Despite my general concurrence with Kohut's (1971) recommendation that, when in doubt, it is safer to comply "reluctantly" with poorly understood demands for such unconditional acceptance than to start an analysis by frustrating them (thereby risking the early onset of a negative transference marked by what Kohut [1972] called "narcissistic rage"), I believe it is a serious technical error to collude with enactments if their pathological nature is clear from the first—as it was in this case. This patient was asking for an unwarranted subsidy so that she would not have to reveal to her parents that she was undertaking an analysis. The situation would have been quite different if she had asked the parents to help with the cost of treatment and they had refused to do so: in that case, a low-cost analysis through the Clinic would have been indicated. By allowing the prospective patient to conceal her intention to be analyzed, the candidate was affirming that it was necessary for this woman to continue to behave like a small child vis-à-vis her parents, that is, like a child who dare not reveal a difference of opinion with them.

Because the patient was in overt conflict between such a childlike attitude and her assertion of autonomy (a conflict that she externalized by allegedly fighting maternal authority), whatever practical choice the analyst made, she could not simultaneously empathize with both attitudes. Her actual choice, to go along with the reenactment of a childhood situation, amounted to collusion with the patient's pathological need to externalize the problem. It seems to me that true empathy would have called for an interpretation of the defensive function of the behavior the patient wanted to adopt—or, if you will, an attempt to interfere with the illusion that one can assert one's independence while acting like a child fearful of punishment. The failure to challenge the patient on this score aligned the analyst with her analysand's unconscious wish to have her symbiotic cake while eating it rebelliously—an invitation to poor reality testing by means of disavowal.

It should be noted that, if the presentation is to be credited with accuracy, the parameter of collaborating in the foregoing reenactment was never alluded to through the subsequent course of the treatment.

b. The prognostic significance of an early temper tantrum

What I regard as an unfavorable prognostic sign is not the patient's anger about the inevitable frustrations of treatment but the fact that she was unable simply to put into words what she was experiencing. Instead, she communicated her overall reaction by means of a dramatic scenario in which the words failed to communicate the complexity of her attitudes: what she said equated the analyst's input with the pathogenic aspects of transactions with her mother, but (as she revealed in the next session) she knew perfectly well that this was untrue. Whether she spoke as she did as an aspect of her manipulativeness or simply because one part of her did not know what another part was thinking, she was functioning in an extremely primitive mode (probably mode II of the hierarchical model, in which mutually contradictory thought processes are tolerated without inner discomfort).

Persons presenting themselves for psychological help who lack the adaptive resources to fend off such primitive potentialities in the midst of an important negotiation about vital practical matters are seldom prepared for the rigors of an analytic procedure: on the contrary, they are urgently in need of symbiotic assistance to patch over those handicaps in adaptation. A period of supportive therapy, relying on measures often called "ego building," may be the safest course of action on their behalf. If an analysis is attempted, it is most likely to be successful if the analyst offers immediate help to remedy the deficits in the patient's repertory of skills—in the manner I try to demonstrate in the case discussed in chapter 2.

c. The failure to deal with the significance of an untoward event

In an effort to be tactful to the presenter, I did not pursue the significance of her failure to explore the meaning of the patient's irrational outburst. Obviously, the best she had been able to do at that stage of her training was far from our expectations for a seasoned practitioner. Ideally, the analysand needed to learn that her rageful behavior was in fact the crux of her psychopathology. That this issue was never dealt with in the treatment was a serious error of omission, even a silent compact to ignore the most primitive aspects of the pathology in favor of a focus on less difficult matters, such as the meaning of the mental contents that produced the outburst. This is an invitation to handle maladaptation through the mechanism of outright denial.

Instead of spelling out this viewpoint in the seminar, I chose to recount an excerpt from one of my own clinical encounters. The point of this anecdote was to illustrate that even seemingly quite successful analytic processes deal only with the specific segments of psychic life that are explicitly considered in the therapeutic dialogue. In other words, even if we do pursue the significance of whatever an analysand communicates to us, we are in no position to process those issues about which a defensive silence is maintained. (In the case I was summarizing, I believe the defense was operating without conscious violations of the basic rule of free association.) If either patient or analyst neglects the requirement of thoroughgoing inquiry into the meaning of manifest behaviors, the analytic task becomes hopeless.

d. Transference repetition and reconstruction

The material presented in the second session lends itself to a clear demonstration of the manner in which the unfolding of a sequence of transferences may be used as evidence that permits a reconstruction of past events in the analysand's *inner world.* (It is often assumed, erroneously, that reconstructions are attempts to reach conclusions about "historical truth" only on the stage of actual events and overt behavior.) The analysis began with a traumatic disappointment, repetitions of which were then warded off by a defensive withdrawal that took the form of fighting and obnoxiousness. Ultimately, interpretations of the defenses led to the establishment of an idealizing relationship. We may infer that idealization was well established in early childhood, only to be disrupted by severe disillusionment. When the analyst's inner state lent itself to the reliving of the disillusionment, the disillusionment was relived in a non-traumatic manner.

The presenter failed to make clear whether or not she had made use of these transference vicissitudes to reconstruct the past history of the patient's inner experience, but she did relate that what made it possible to deal successfully with these fluctuations in the quality of the transference was her willingness to confirm in the treatment that the analysand's perception of the change in the analyst was valid. This demonstration of *competence* led to a fresh upsurge of idealization, indicated by a request for a fifth weekly session.

e. The necessity of correlating past and present

I characterized the analyst's technical procedure as "too fast" because she did not bother to take the time to spell out the lessons to be learned from the dynamics of the transference about the etiology of the deformation of the patient's character. In other words, she expected structural change to follow from a corrective emotional experience, that of avoiding the traumatic repetition of the past. Obviously, such change is contingent on *not* repeating the original traumata, but that happy condition is by itself insufficient to produce any alteration in the structured consequences of the past. In order to overcome the potential of fresh traumatization (and the character defenses erected to ward it off), it is essential to pinpoint the childhood vulnerability and the specific consequences of the transactions that initiated the trauma. To put this differently, if the analysand experiences the treatment as a situation of relative safety, it should be possible to focus on what the original danger situation might have been, so that it may be faced and (perhaps gradually) accepted as tolerable, without resort to defensive behaviors.

In the case under discussion, genetic interpretations about the analysand's disappointment about the mother's egocentricity and needfulness should have been made, thus clarifying that she had retreated from facing the truth about her mother and substituted for the pathetic reality that her mother was too pitiful to be left to her own devices the myth that she was controlling. In this way, the issue of separation guilt would have become available for detailed examination.

*f. An exclusive focus on the vicissitudes of the analyst–patient
transaction*

I have no disagreement with the widely held view that transference
interpretations are enormously powerful therapeutic tools, probably the
most important ingredients of our armamentarium. What I do object to is
an extrapolation from this conclusion that narrows our analytic technique to an all-but-exclusive use of transference interpretation, to the
(relative) neglect of paying attention to the detailed implications of these
dynamics in the adaptive sphere (see Gill, 1983). In the case under
discussion, the analysand was rightly insistent that attention be paid to
the actual problems that had led her to seek assistance. Whenever the
analyst shifted the focus to the transference proper, the patient experienced this as a repetition of her mother's need to put herself into the
spotlight vis-à-vis the daughter.

In my experience, such unintended consequences of excessive emphasis on the centrality of transference are not uncommon. Even in cases
where such a narrow focus does not threaten to repeat a pathologic
aspect of the past, it constitutes a subtle seduction, enticing the patient
away from seeking satisfactions on the stage of everyday life and in the
direction of deriving self-esteem from becoming the ideal analytic patient.
Moreover, if it is the analyst who actively promotes an exclusive attention
to the transference, this circumstance may obscure from the patient the
very fact that the development of transferences reflects his or her own
unconscious desires.

g. The positive Oedipus as a screen for a negative one

Insofar as children enter the oedipal arena, it is always to be expected that
they will develop conflicts about triangular relationships involving both
mother and father. If the analytic work neglects either of these constellations in favor of the other, this lack of exactitude in interpretation will
lead to a therapeutic impasse. The Presenter implied that such a lack of
precision may have determined the unsatisfactory outcome of her work.
It is particularly easy for the positive Oedipus to screen its negative
counterpart, because the latter is usually more laden with shame, as a
result of its primitive connotations. Analysts (of both sexes) are probably
also more conflicted about the wishes concerning the parent of the same
sex, so that it is easier for them, too, to deal with the positive version of the
Oedipus complex.

As we learned late in the third session of this presentation, this
analysand was fixated on a very archaic psychosexual level; her sexual

relations were actually perverse, performed in a fetishistic manner. In order to understand the meanings of such behavior, it would be necessary to elicit the erotic aspects of the transference and on that basis arrive at valid reconstructions of the patient's earliest fantasies about phallicity. This kind of work was not undertaken, in large measure because all of sexuality was arbitrarily classified as an aspect of the childhood attachment to father.

h. The centrality of the analysand's subjective experience

I don't completely agree with Gehrie's statements about this issue: I believe the views I expressed in the seminar do not cast doubt on the need to start from the patient's subjective experience or the desirability of making it the central focus of the analytic contact. Contrary to the position espoused by Evelyne Schwaber (1981, 1983), however, I believe it is seldom if ever necessary to *confine* our purview to this subjective viewpoint. If a patient asserts that $2 + 2 = 3.9$, we should not hesitate to interject that that is a very unusual opinion, indeed, and that we are personally wedded to the validity of the assertion that $2 + 2 = 4.0$. The analysand discussed in this seminar was giving voice to an analogous absurdity; one could have made *genuine* contact with her (especially the person she proved to be in the termination phase, when it was too late to reach her!) only by letting her know that her communications felt like assaults on one's sanity. As Modell (1990) has cogently discussed, that everyone's subjective experience is unique does not constitute an insurmountable obstacle to the achievement of a "shared reality," which is a prerequisite for fruitful dialogue.

i. How do we gauge whether it is safe to explore certain matters?

In the seminar, I expressed no opinion about when it might have been optimal to confront the issue of the patient's irrational outburst about having to conform to an analytic routine. Gehrie, assuming that the tantrum was caused by "overwhelming anxiety in the negative mother transference," comes down on the side of recommending delay. There are, however, other possible explanations, and I am not at all sure that any delay was necessary or desirable. It would have been possible to determine how far one could safely go in exploring the significance of this behavior only by making some attempt to do so and assessing the nature of the analysand's response. I must add that I am not primarily guided by patients' emotional reactions to my efforts (these are grist for the analytic mill, provided we are prepared to absorb them)—I would conclude that a line of inquiry is untimely only if it fails to produce further associative material.

Another way to put my concern about Gehrie's cautious policy is that I do not accept the patient's accusation that the analyst is just like mother as a pathognomonic indicator of a mother transference. As I stated in the seminar, I believe the analysand was trying to externalize her internal conflict (about autonomy versus symbiosis); thus her view that *either* mother or the analyst tried to control her was overtly preposterous. As we know from the material presented later in the seminar, the mother transference actually focused on issues of disillusionment and separation guilt. Hence I suspect that the outburst was simply an early indication of the patient's grandiose propensities. If so, there would have been no danger whatsoever in making inquiries about the purport of her unusual behavior.

j. How does an ill timed interpretation constitute an assault?

Gehrie is stressing an essential point in stating that even valid interpretations may be experienced as hostile if they are ill timed. Many patients will say, as Gehrie reports, that if they feel assaulted by an analytic intervention, the analyst has lost empathic contact with them—in Gehrie's words, has "withdrawn." Of course, the analyst seldom makes interpretations for hostile reasons, and it is often possible to clarify that the felt effect of the intervention was unintended. In my experience, the most frequent cause of such an empathic break is the analyst's inability to assess correctly how much therapeutic activity is tolerable for the analysand at a specific time. Correct interpretations are experienced as assaultive if they put the analysand in a position of unacceptable passivity—in terms, for example, of causing excessive anxiety or even pleasurable overstimulation. In other words, interpretations are worse than useless if the analysand is regressed to a mode of organization more primitive than mode IV.

k. Idealizing transference as a "new beginning"?

Gehrie has skillfully summarized the assumptions of self psychology about the conditions for the establishment of an idealizing transference and its possible consequences. There are several problems with formulating the data of this case (and many others, I believe!) in this manner. First, the state that supervened did not duplicate the patient's infantile idealization of her mother before she was disillusioned; as her anxiety about later disappointment (or abandonment), as well as her transference response to the analyst's brief depression (that of volunteering to become the latter's caretaker) demonstrate, her loving admiration was based on disavowal of her mistrust. In the past, I have labeled such conditions as "pseudoidealization" (Gedo, 1975). Note that in establishing this state, after a lengthy period of rageful mistrust, the patient was in all likelihood repeating an identical sequence from childhood.

Second, "further growth" based on such unstable foundations scarcely provides a "new beginning" (Balint, 1968). As subsequent events showed, it is merely a prelude to the repetition of the next step in the childhood sequence, the erection of a false self of unruffled competence following the next disappointment in a maternal figure. Even if the analyst is able to postpone such a development by performing flawlessly for a long period, the emotional equilibrium provided by such a honeymoon can do nothing to minimize the patient's vulnerability to fresh disappointment. In other words, the onset of that state of transference Gehrie calls "idealizing," however helpful in transcending the fruitless distancing maneuvers that preceded it, merely sets the stage for the analytic work that needs to be done.

It is well to remember in this connection that Kohut (1971) made it clear that he did not believe that the establishment of an idealizing transference would be curative per se. He continued to insist that analytic results (according to him obtained through "transmuting internalization") would only follow if the consequences of subsequent disillusionments (on the occasion of relatively minor breaks in the analyst's empathic availability) were properly understood and thus mastered. The hypothesis articulated by Gehrie is a much more radical version of self psychology—one that I totally reject (see Gedo, 1989).

l. Idealization and "self-development"

Once again, Gehrie formulates the material in terms of self-psychological hypotheses that I do not accept. When he states that the patient requires a relationship that permits idealization "for an aspect of her own self-development," he uses concepts I do not endorse. As Modell (1992) has shown, the concept of "self" in Kohut's work (and I would extrapolate this to Gehrie's commentary) is a purely phenomenological one; I do not find such a definition useful or sufficient. In those terms, the "self-development" Gehrie writes about amounts to nothing more than a subjective phenomenon, poorly correlated with the underlying organization of personality.

In my view, it is not idealization that promotes development—idealization is, in fact, merely a designation referring to the expectable cognitive errors of young children about their caretakers, errors that are best eliminated as quickly as possible and replaced my more realistic assessments. In any case, the designation refers to mere contents of thoughts, which are always epiphenomenal with regard to development. Psychological growth refers only to an expansion in the repertory of *skills*, that is, of the variety of ways in which mental contents may be processed. The learning of new skills is impeded by traumatic experiences, and it is the absence of experiences such as during these periods that Gehrie characterizes as periods of idealization that permits development to proceed.

m. Does exploration of psychopathology interfere with idealization?

About the issue of exploring the patient's anxiety-driven ambitions, Gehrie misunderstood my meaning, as did some other participants in the seminar. I advocate agnosticism about patients' actual degree of talent or promise; I would exercise great caution in either underestimating or overestimating these. (In fact, it is best to state and restate that an analyst has no way of assessing what people are good for outside of the consulting room.) Gehrie writes as if an attempt by the analyst to pin down the fact that, in order to be free to pursue her vocation, the patient felt she had to become a star (thereby to buttress her mother) would interfere with the analysand's admiration and trust. In my experience, any piece of superior analytic work tends to reinforce analysands' idealizing propensities.

The point I wanted to make in the seminar (but obviously failed to put clearly enough) is that a genetic interpretation of the childhood need to prop up mother by succumbing to her symbiotic demands should permit clarification of the continuing influence of separation guilt in the form of having to justify autonomous activities on the ground of their great public success. Consensus on this point would, in turn, make possible more precise reconstruction of the childhood vicissitudes that made such excessive ambitions necessary. I prefer to approach such an issue by asking questions that challenge analysands' unexamined assumptions. In this case, I felt the most fruitful point to raise might have been that of the patient's lack of freedom to pursue more modest enterprises.

Thus, I do not believe that my technical recommendation is an *alternative* to analysis of the significance of the patient's need to become a star, as Gehrie goes on to suggest; on the contrary, I consider it to be the most promising avenue for elucidating that issue.

n. Empathy and reality testing

I am in complete agreement with Gehrie that appropriate empathy is a sine qua non of psychoanalytic success, and my comments in the seminar were intended to indicate what in my view such an attitude would amount to in the case under discussion. I do believe that, if the analyst (in the guise of accepting the patient's subjective viewpoint) erroneously thinks it is "empathic" to endorse persistent infantile notions of entitlement (such as this analysand's arbitrary judgment that she did not receive sufficient "love"), this technical error is likely to increase the patient's ragefulness. Obviously, Gehrie is correct in his conclusion that I regard "proper empathy" as a function of adequate assessment of the realities.

To put this differently, it is appropriate to focus analytic empathy on the actual emotional position of the child at crucial junctures in the past; it is neither necessary nor truly empathic to *endorse* the subjective viewpoints of adult analysands whenever they are manifestly unrealistic. If we are not in a position to judge whether the analysand's subjective viewpoint is congruent with the actualities, the properly empathic position for us to take is to ascertain that we have accurately understood the nature of that viewpoint and then to state that, for the moment, we remain *puzzled* about the reasons for it. Gehrie also asks whether an "empathic position" would compromise the possibility of ultimately elucidating unconscious rage and guilt. My answer is that it may often do so if what the analyst regards as correct empathy is, instead, only the acceptance of illusions.

o. Empathic failure in the case under discussion

There is no disagreement about the fact that an analyst caught up in a "dyadic enactment" (Gedo, 1988, chap. 9), such as this presenter described to characterize the first year of this analysis, does not command the empathy requisite for effective analytic work. Obviously, such a failure of empathy could have been caused by the candidate's inexperience, the supervisor's passivity, and their joint decision to adhere to a standard (or "classical") interpretive approach. As Gehrie stated earlier, the analyst showed flashes of better understanding of the patient's actual needs even before the pivotal Thanksgiving turning point.

It would be a gross oversimplification to assert that the return of the patient's holiday telephone call could, by itself, correct a longstanding countertransference impasse. On the contrary, I am confident that this analysand would dare to make such a call only because she understood that her analyst's angry incomprehension was yielding to a more appropriate attitude of insightful responsiveness. To put my point in a different way, it is almost certain that the telephone contact became the vehicle of affirming the transformation of the hitherto unstable analytic situation into a "holding environment" (Winnicott, 1954); in this sense, the transaction would never have arisen if the analyst had from the first shown the proper helpfulness to her primitively organized patient (see note b).

While it is perfectly legitimate to discuss these issues in terms of the organizing framework of "empathy," as Gehrie has done, this is neither the only way to understand them nor necessarily the most illuminating one. The avenue of apprehending the crux of analytic situations through empathy is always difficult and uncertain; in contrast, a differential diagnosis based on relatively objective, cognitive criteria is preferable, if the information on which one can base it is available. In the case presented here, it was possible from the very first session onward to make a reasonably reliable structural diagnosis that the patient was functioning in a primitive manner (let us say, fluctuating between modes II and III in the hierarchical schema). Primed by such a conclusion, the analyst would not have had to rely on empathy to conclude that interpretations were not in order (see Gedo, 1979) and that the crux of the matter was to convey appropriate concern about the patient's impairment. (That was the probable meaning of the Thanksgiving transaction: the analyst was conceding, in action if not in words, that her interpretive technique had overestimated the patient's level of integration.)

Ultimately, that is why in the seminar I stressed that to be *really* empathic with this woman, the analyst had to offer her concrete help with the adaptive problems that were of acute concern to her. If we provide such assistance, even the sickest patients are able to tolerate our efforts to provide alternatives for their unrealistic illusions. In the case in question, these illusions involve not only idealization of the mother/analyst, but grandiose fantasies as well (especially about her power to remedy the caretaker's depressive vulnerabilities). Another way to put this is that, ultimately, the analyst's empathic efforts proved to be insufficient—not because she ran out of empathy, as Gehrie implies, but because her technique did not permit her to challenge the patient's grandiosity.

p. Adventitious vicissitudes affecting the analyst's presence

Gehrie is certainly correct in noting that the fluctuations of the mother transference between idealization and a grandiose assertion that a reversal of roles was feasible was not "analyzed" (i.e., put into consensually meaningful secondary process terms) but was merely reenacted over and over again. He may, however, be unduly critical in attributing this circumstance to empathic failure on the analyst's part—after all, as the presenter finally reveals, she was still working with this material when the patient broke off treatment in reaction to learning certain facts about the analyst's private life through coming across the obituary of the analyst's father. I do not mean to imply that better management of the entire treatment would not have made such an untoward reaction less likely, but we should not overlook the fact that the publication of the information in question was an adventitious event beyond the analyst's control.

Ideally, the analysis should have brought to light the patient's secret fantasy that the analyst was a prototype whose example she could emulate, thus rendering innocuous the kind of information she blundered across in the obituary. But the analyst cannot be blamed for the fact that *this* disappointment occurred as it did, traumatically and without preparation, and this coincidence probably determined the unfortunate outcome. Neither analysts nor parents can be expected to protect their charges from deleterious acts of God.

Gehrie ends his discussion by expressing the opinion that the patient broke off treatment because of the rage that was generated following interactions, like the late-night telephone call, in which the patient felt rejected, and which were not processed in the analysis. Such an assumption runs contrary to my clinical experience: I have never worked with any patient, no matter how impaired, who was unable to accept such limits. In fact, no analysand of mine has ever called me at an ungodly hour; they all understand perfectly well that such an action is always an angry provocation. In other words, in my judgment, the phone call was already part of the behavior I called a "psychotic transference" in the seminar. It was this potentiality that showed up in the very first session of the treatment, and it was the failure to address *that* issue that constituted a lack of empathy, not the analyst's legitimate refusal to lend herself to abuse.

Distortion versus Subjective Reality

Technical Divergence in the Management of Severe Regression

Introduction (Gehrie)

This case provides an unusual opportunity to witness the transformation of technique in the mind of the analyst and the impact of that change in the management of an analytic case. It also continues the discussion on technique from the previous chapter. As the transcript reveals, from the outset the analyst had associations to dealing with her own small child, with the reverberations emanating from her experience in dealing with her child's struggle to grasp "reality," an issue that was also of major concern in the case owing especially to the severity of the presenting regression. Accordingly, the issues involved in the choice of technique and the role of the analyst are the central point of the discussion that follows.

The patient was a 33-year-old female journalist of Hispanic descent who was separated from her husband of eight years at the time she requested analysis. She said that she felt "vulnerable and unprotected" and reported marital difficulties and problems relating to men, the onset of all of these dating to the death of her father two years previously. The father had died while away on vacation with the patient's mother.

First Session

PRESENTER: I thought of an analogy [to characterize the analysis I want to present]: when my son was two-and-a-half years old and things were maximally difficult with him (because he always wanted to do things in his own way), he would not want to get dressed and I would say to him, "Absolutely the last thing I want you to do is get dressed," and then he would be perfectly cooperative and do exactly what I wanted him to do. And I always felt somewhat guilty because I thought, "Oh, I'm going to teach him to disobey. [He'll think] that he will always have to do the wrong thing," until I realized that really the issue was not obeying or disobeying; it had to do with his needing to feel like an independent person and to do it himself. Once I addressed the proper level of organization, things went quite smoothly with him.

When she came to analysis two years ago, the patient was 33 years old, a woman separated from her husband of eight years. She is of Hispanic descent and employed as a journalist. She said that she had been feeling vulnerable and unprotected and thought that [these feelings were] linked to the death of her father two years previously. She also dated her marital problems to that time. She described her father as very controlling and more interested in his needs than hers, but she'd always felt that in some fashion he protected her. They had had a very difficult relationship because it had often been an opposition of wills, and she had a particularly stormy adolescence. She felt that when he died she had never had the chance to resolve some of these issues with him.

She talked about the way in which their arguments went: he would remain extremely cool and self-possessed, although [in other contexts] he was wild and out of control. With her he would remain cool and insist that she show no emotions, and when she would become emotional he would say to her, "Come back when you've calmed down." So she developed the ability to make air-tight arguments—well, anyway, air-tight for a kid and a teenager—and would come back to him with very rational arguments and then she would lose anyway because he would ultimately make a decision based on being her parent. She related her current anxiety and lack of self-esteem to these exchanges.

Her father had died two years before she came to me, while he was on vacation with her mother. She felt that he had chosen the way in which he died, that this was part of the way in which he withheld himself from her and the way in which she felt distanced from him. She also felt that he could have chosen to stay alive somehow. And she also felt that because of that she hadn't been able to say good-bye. She described feeling devastated after her father died . . .

GEDO: [interrupting] What did he die of?

PRESENTER: He had a cardiac arrest. He'd had a history of heart problems since she was eight years old. How it affected her when he died was that she [became] unable to tolerate the extended unavailability of her husband.

I'll go back a little bit. She met her husband while she was in college and eventually married him after he moved to Chicago to work for his father. She was originally from San Antonio. Eventually she went back to school, got her degree; although she took some time out and worked to support him, as he had a business venture of his own. The business required his working at night and then working in the daytime to do paper work. So he was really both "not there" and exhausted when he was at home. After her father died, she felt she couldn't tolerate this. She had had a brief affair when she was in journalism school. That first affair was with a fellow student and they parted very amicably, both attributing their involvement with each other to [their being] extremely anxious about school. But just before she came to the Institute, she found herself about to get into another affair, and she was so distressed by that as a [sign] that there was something wrong with her marriage that she decided that she had better get some help.

The other concern she had was that she had difficulty being intimate with men, which she also related to her relationship with her father. Each time she got close to a man she would feel that he was manipulating her or controlling her; she would become angry, distrustful and feel compelled, usually on some pretense or another, to discontinue the relationship. She was afraid that that would happen with the man with whom she was currently involved. [She gave] some very clear examples of what would happen with him. Generally they involved an expression of love on either his or her part, followed by something she would interpret as an indication that he really didn't care about her. Then she would erupt into an absolute rage. He would become defensive, and she would feel there was no hope, that she had seriously misevaluated this person and had no other choice but to leave. She would storm out in some way. At the same time, she castigated herself and she'd end up feeling bad about herself because, if she had misjudged the man, then it was she who had picked out the wrong man and therefore she was at fault. However it went, she ended up feeling completely responsible and completely bad about herself for [spoiling] the relationship.

The patient was one of five children. She had an older brother, 18 months her senior, a younger brother, 18 months her junior, and then there was a nine-year gap to a sister, and then another sister who was 13 years younger. [The patient] felt that she had had a very close relationship with her father until the age of six, when she felt her father had withdrawn—withdrawn in order to focus on his career. I'm not quite sure what her father did up until that time. I think he was an educator of sorts. When she was seven, her parents, who were Catholics and involved in some Catholic organization along a missionary line, took the opportunity to move to Peru, where she lived from age seven to age thirteen.

She also attributed her father's withdrawal from her to her increased sexuality, or sensuality, and felt that he was frightened of that. She [listed] a number of ways in which she felt that her father couldn't deal with her developing as a woman. His focus was always on a career and on independence, and how she looked was not important. He was very strict about dating and so forth and always, always drilled into her head that anything that ever happened with a man was partially her responsibility, that "it takes two to tango." Her older brother and her father had also had an extremely stormy relationship and were constantly battling. The father had a first heart attack when the patient was eight years old, in South America. But the second heart attack she remembers much more clearly, because it occurred back here when she was a teenager, and it occurred in the middle of one of these fights that her brother and father were having. She witnessed one of their battles in the kitchen, and the father fell on the floor. The brother ran to telephone the police; her mother went into the bathroom to get the nitroglycerine, and she went to comfort her sisters. It was to the fact that her brother and her father had such a difficult relationship that she attributed her brother's problems.

When she was six years old there were only three children, who were sharing a room, and the parents were in the dining room with a curtain strung across to make their bedroom. The brother invited her up to his bunk in his bed and invited her to masturbate him. And he was very reassuring to her, saying, "It's perfectly all right, come on, come on." She remembers this very clearly. She believes she felt this pit of anxiety and some hesitancy to do it, but she adored her brother because she felt her father was no longer available. This is all her reconstruction of it. She felt that she would go along with whatever [her brother] said, [but] the instant that she participated in this event she felt culpable. [Although] she felt guilty, she would not betray her brother; so she never told her parents. As she recounted this, she had some feeling that her parents must have known. She's observed the families of juveniles and has seen how parents know but don't acknowledge that they know and allow something to go on; so she believes that her parents must have known. [The patient and her brother] continued to have this kind of a relationship until she was 13 years old. There was never any more than her masturbating him: but when she was 13 years old she was asleep and woke up to find him fondling her; and she felt [that he had the] intention to have intercourse. At that point she became enraged with him and said that if he ever came near her again she would tell her parents, and from that point on she refused to be alone with him. From that time on she has always had a man around to protect her.

[I have not told] you what she looks like actually, and what she's like. She's very attractive, and she's very sophisticated looking. She really looks like [professional women portrayed in movies]. You know, she's sensual, but not overt, so she's pretty neat looking.

Initially I didn't get too much information about her mother. She felt that her mother had always stood between her and her father, that her mother had sort of hogged the relationship with the father for herself. Her mother had gone back to school sometime and gotten a degree in social work, and she currently works for a couple of psychiatrists [doing] therapy. She describes her mother and these psychiatrists as of the "touchy-feely" school.

The early issues of the analysis had to do with fear: her fear of her intensity; her fear that she would overwhelm me and herself and everyone. [pause] She was so afraid she would overwhelm people [that] she ended up being extraordinarily provocative everywhere she went, and got into quick, rather amazing fights, often even physical fights, with people. Certainly with men. She would provoke them into rages with her, and then she would be the cool, calm, rational person with them. I remember that very early [in the analysis] she went down to the laundry room in the building where she was living and someone had taken her laundry out of the dryer [when it] stopped, and her outrage about having been abused in this fashion stimulated the other person to punch her, at which point she went and called the police. The police came, and she was hysterical. The police then responded to her hysteria [by telling] her to calm down and "chill out"; [they said] she was overreacting. And she was so incensed that the police could only react to her emotions rather than to the way in which she had been injured. That's how it ended; she was very upset and distraught about the whole thing.

She had a recurrent dream all through her life, over and over again. She told the dream [when] talking about her fear of opening up in the analysis; basically, she was afraid that if she started to cry she would never stop. And she was afraid that she was an excessively needy person and that I wouldn't want to see her in [analysis for that reason]. In that context she told me about [her] recurring dream of a very dark house that had many, many rooms. In the attic was a secret room to which she could go. Her associations were to Anne Frank and to hiding. Later on she realized that it was the house of the school [she had attended] in South America. She'd always had the sense that this house was something very real for her. [Once, when she was] very upset, she said to her husband, "Well, we can always go to the house." And he looked at her and said, "What house?" At that moment she realized that the house was not real, that it was a dream.

[In the analytic setting, she needed to be] in control and conscious of everything that was going on all the time with me. So it was hard for her even to report dreams as they occurred. [The report] would often be several days after they occurred or she wouldn't report events as they occurred, or feelings that were occurring in the analytic hours. It was often after the fact.

GEDO: Did she know that she was withholding this information, or did this occur automatically?

PRESENTER: I can only answer that by saying that after she had missed one session she felt [that her motivation] was conscious. But she had a dream about frantically trying to get to my office because she thought she was going to miss another session, and [that consequently] I would never buy that this [intention] was conscious. So she wanted to maintain to herself that this was all conscious. I don't think it was conscious, because the slips that happened were often around things that would stir her up emotionally, that she couldn't tolerate.

The first dream that she had in the analysis was of a side view of the house with an iron gate which divided the front and the back lawns. In the backyard there were two boys and maybe three adults. A man came out of the house and started killing the boys in the backyard, beating them into the ground. When the patient acted shocked, the man said, "Why are you so ambiguous?" By which he meant that she was sending out double messages and really wanted this to happen. She felt terrified and felt there to be a faceless, nonparticipatory, judgmental person behind her in the dream, which she didn't have much trouble associating to the analysis.

GEDO: Maybe we should stop before we get overwhelmed. Perhaps somebody would like to comment about undertaking such an analysis.

COMMENT: The only comment I have is that it reminds me very much of my new case: there is all this material and there's no mention of mother.

PRESENTER: That's true.

COMMENT: I find that remarkable in a girl. Everything is supposedly directed toward the sexual influence of the father.

PRESENTER: There was some mention of her mother. But her mother was definitely [presented as] the judgmental, critical person.

GEDO: Maybe other people want to comment. This is a very attractive lady and she's accomplished, and she comes for help because something must be wrong [because] she's going to fall into an affair that she doesn't think she should [have]. Why is the treatment of choice psychoanalysis?

COMMENT: Because [the presenter] needs a control case! [laughter]

GEDO: She came to the clinic. Why did the clinic accept her? Do we need patients? Do we just accept them because we need warm bodies? What's the putative diagnosis? Quite a mass of information in the areas you have summarized for us. What's wrong with this person? I gather my puzzlement is not echoed in any of you.

COMMENT: Don't you think the fact that we're not speaking up is equivalent to your puzzlement? I can't get a toehold in this clinical material. I don't know what to do with it.

GEDO: Well, we'll hear more. I mean, presumably the clinic committee thought she needed analysis. What did they tell you when they sent you the record? Why is this lady to be considered for a third control?

PRESENTER: Well, actually, when she came to the clinic she was—she was very distraught and really anxious, and the person who saw her didn't know whether she would be reasonable for an analysis, because she was so upset at the time. In retrospect, the time that she applied to the clinic was the anniversary of her father's death, and by the time she came to me, three weeks later, she wasn't as anxious; she was more depressed. She described herself as having been quite depressed.

COMMENT: She was allowed to come back after she calmed down?

PRESENTER: I don't think she was given that message. I think that the interviewer didn't say one way or the other, but referred her to me with the comment, "I think that this woman might be analyzable, but you have to see."

GEDO: And when she came to you, what was the status between her and her husband?

PRESENTER: They were separated. They were proceeding with a divorce; it was in process.

GEDO: So why was it such a big deal for her to find another man? I mean, why did she feel that this was so unacceptable?

PRESENTER: Well, to have an affair, you mean?

GEDO: Yes.

PRESENTER: I would say that [it was] because she was still married. I'm not sure actually whether the almost-affair was before or after they had separated. I think it was before they actually separated.

COMMENT: But even so, isn't your point that it wasn't so much the issue of having an affair but the quality of the feeling that she experienced on the brink of having it? That is, she was feeling herself enmeshed in something that she was becoming increasingly aware of even prior to the analysis as having some kind of real devastating effect on her ability to relate.

PRESENTER: When you say "enmeshed," you mean the psychological difficulties, the emotional difficulties, of being involved with a man, when the whole issue is with her father? Yes.

COMMENT: Yes, yes.

PRESENTER: Yes, she was aware of that, yes.

COMMENT: Isn't the difficulty that she presents so much material that the analyst can't hear the material? Kind of like a deaf person who gets overwhelmed with stimuli just withdraws and . . .

PRESENTER: Do you think there's that much material in this?

COMMENT: My response was that I was unable to associate to anything you said. I couldn't grab onto anything long enough to get associations so that I could come up with a formulation. The material about the brother is interesting, and it's undoubtedly important to this lady's life, yet I can't hook into anything else. Her father's death, of course, had to be traumatic, and yet I found it hard to hook into anything else. And so my feeling was that I was presented with a lot of material that should have stimulated a formulation, and I couldn't come up with one. I just wonder whether or not she keeps people at a distance in this way. I mean, it's a distancing maneuver. That's why I use the analogy of the deaf person who wants very much to do things with other people and talk with other people and be involved with other people, but can't because [he's] cluttered by stimuli.

PRESENTER: Right.

GEDO: You're implying, I think, that while she is flooding you with information she's keeping a secret. There are a hundred rooms [in the dream house] but what's really going on is in [a] room that's locked away. Where Anne Frank lives, hmmm? And you don't hear anything about that prison. Well, of course, you can say, as I have told myself for many years now, "If people are not going to go crazy on me, I'll try." You can have that policy in choosing patients for analytic work. I think probably that's the policy most people, in fact, pursue, although they don't say so. In which case, sure, why not? An intelligent, mysterious lady, who's bound to be very interesting as one goes along. What's to lose? Of course, in training, credit is to lose.

PRESENTER: But, in a way, it was more straightforward than that. That's how I was hearing it. I heard her say, "I'm having difficulty with men. I can see that I'm having difficulty with men. I have a difficult relationship with a man . . ."—she was also dating somebody at that point—"I had trouble with my husband; it relates to my father. Since he died I have unresolved feelings about my father because we had a very difficult relationship [when I was] a child." That seems straightforward to me.

GEDO: Yes, that's a straightforward enough story. I mean, 30 years ago two-thirds of the people who applied to the institute clinic related that story; that was the classical reason for entering analysis. First of all, we don't hear that many stories of this kind any more. And, second, of course, it's not literally true that she has trouble with "men"; she has trouble with everybody. Women are judgmental figures who are going to let her have it, and she gets involved in a fist fight with somebody who takes her laundry out of . . .

COMMENT: [interrupting] With a woman.

GEDO: Yes, a woman. Does she have any friends in Chicago? Tell us about that part.

PRESENTER: She has a number of close girlfriends with whom she spends lots of time and in whom she can confide and [who] she felt were not judgmental. There were [no] difficulties in [those] relationships, but she always did feel that a relationship with a man was very different from a relationship with a woman and that she wanted a relationship with a man. The sense of protection she was looking for could not come from a woman.

GEDO: Well, that's a comment about her mother in some sense, isn't it? Is her mother of the same ethnic background as her father?

PRESENTER: No, she's not. Her father was Hispanic and her mother was not. She was of European [birth], but here for some time. The women in the family . . . she perceives the women as being relegated to a lonely existence. Her maternal grandmother was widowed when the mother was two years old and never remarried and had supported [her] child; she led a lonely existence without a man. The mother hadn't indicated that she would be interested in other men although she was [widowed] three years prior to this. [The patient] feels that women will ultimately be alone and isolated, without support.

GEDO: You mentioned that she would frequently hold over material—be it dreams, events, or whatever—to future sessions. When she presented the material, did she just present [primary] material or did she work it through and present a finished analysis, like coming up with her own interpretations of the dream? Were you part of that process?

PRESENTER: Oh, yeah. I felt I was. Despite [the fact that] for the first months of analysis, for the first year of analysis, there was tremendous volatility, she was very, very intent on what I was saying and in responding to that and how it would make her feel, and quite responsive, too. I'll tell you what I ended up doing. I think this was during the first month, and it was with some resistance on my part. [pause] Generally, in the events that she would report to me when they were outside of the analysis, she would feel extremely victimized and abused. When she would provoke these people to rages, she would get to a point where she would feel there is no circumstance on earth which could merit this kind of response. Nothing I could have done, she would say, nothing I could have done could possibly justify this kind of response.

COMMENT: Response on the other person's part?

PRESENTER: On anybody's part, the way they have mistreated her. So in that position she would feel a certain kind of relief—that she was no longer responsible because she knew that nothing she could have done [should] have provoked it, and the whole issue was her feeling, [her] overwhelming feeling of having brought on all the mistreatment in her life. So, she would begin to insist that I confirm this, that there was nothing that she had done which could have provoked this response. What she had done that provoked the response was pretty clear; she would make demands on these men that they anticipate what she was feeling. This has a narcissistic quality to it: she would insist that they know what she was feeling, because she was terrified of showing how she was feeling. Only if they could recognize it did she feel comfortable that it wasn't going to devastate them. So she would insist that they anticipate it, and when they didn't she would feel so injured and hurt and misunder- stood that she would withdraw. There were a number of men; she doesn't have difficulty finding them. Most of them would end up feeling really confused, but the one that she was [most] involved with would end up feeling enraged. He was in analysis and had learned in the course of his analysis that his mother had used withdrawal as a punishment to manipulate him, so [the patient's] withdrawal was especially potent for him and the two of them would get really angry. He accused her of not knowing anything about her rage, and that would make her furious. She'd say, "You want to see rage?!" and she would throw something, you know, across the room. [laughs] So . . .

GEDO: So what did you do? She demanded that you validate her paranoia.[a]

PRESENTER: Yeah, no, at first I would try [to] make a neutral comment, a neutral, supportive comment.

GEDO: Well, she didn't let you get away with that.

PRESENTER: [No, she didn't!] She would push and I would start feeling more and more uncomfortable, as if I [were] going to have to give up my version of reality in order somehow or other to support her, and I really resisted it. I really resisted it.

COMMENT: What did she try to get you to say?

PRESENTER: That she was completely right and an innocent victim, and abused. And I had difficulty doing it. Well, finally . . .

COMMENT: But isn't it likely that she just enjoyed it?

PRESENTER: What did she enjoy?

COMMENT: The whole routine.

PRESENTER: No, I don't think she enjoyed it . . .

COMMENT: But wouldn't the problem in treatment be, in terms of the interaction with the men, that she was gratified by it, and what kept it going was that she was persistently gratified by these arguments and [that's why she] was setting it up . . .

PRESENTER: There was some gratification. Keeping up the battles was the only way she had been able to maintain contact with her father and avoid being involved with her mother, whom she really perceived as some malevolent person. So, yes, there was some gratification from that standpoint. But I don't think that it was the primary thing that was going on at the time.

COMMENT: Well, I guess the question is, what's going on in terms of what she's trying to do with you at that point.

PRESENTER: Well, that's why I thought about my two-and-a-half-year-old son. I think that in some way she needed me to acknowledge the authenticity of what she was feeling, my being able to give up what I believed *for* her at that moment became extremely important. When I finally was able to do it, she had a wonderful dream which had to do with "victim-witness awards." This was a dream that was critical of me. Victim-witness awards actually do exist in the [criminal justice system]. These awards were given out only to men, and the fact was that she needed *me* to witness her victimization. When I could do it, it was amazing! When I learned that I could actually acknowledge that she had been abused and stifle the need to say, "You brought it on yourself," when I could do that, all of a sudden she would look at all the ways in which she brought it on herself. She was very responsive to it.

GEDO: Well, perhaps, in telling us that, you clarify that she's trying to master something in her dealings with her mother. The mother has said, in this concrete and stupid way: "You're responsible for everything that happens to you." Now [the patient] knows perfectly well that she's responsible for some of what happens to her, but she needs to hear that she's not omnipotent. And that she's not totally responsible and that others are not totally without blame.[b]

COMMENT: I don't know if you have more information on it, but the thoughts that I've been having as you've been discussing this last issue is why the family left for South America, why they set off when she was six. What are both parents' notions about responsibility? About how to justify things?

PRESENTER: Well, they took her with them.

COMMENT: Oh, I understand that. But it was a tremendous undertaking—what were the motivations?

PRESENTER: Well, I don't know. I don't know. That's probably a good point. As it came up later on, in South America, [she, unlike] her brothers, went to a Spanish-speaking school [although] she knew no Spanish at the time. People were very friendly and loving toward her, [but] she couldn't speak and she felt tremendously isolated. She [tried to] tell her mother about her feelings at the time, and she felt her mother didn't understand. Her brothers went to an American school.

COMMENT: It fits in with the analogy of deafness—because she was deaf for a period of years. I mean she's not deaf in [the sense] that she can't hear sound, but she can't make sense of the sound when she's being spoken to.

COMMENT: You raised an interesting technical problem, because it seemed like the technique that worked best for you was to suspend your reality testing and enter into her delusional system . . .

COMMENT: Why is that suspending her reality testing? It seems to me that this is an essential aspect of reality that she's picking up, it's the clinical reality.[c]

COMMENT: Well, [it was] her *psychic* reality, but the [consensual] reality was that this woman was self-sabotaging.

COMMENT: What other reality is there but the psychic reality, in this case or any other one? Why is there some other kind of judgment that has to be made? If [the analyst] makes some other kind of judgment about what's "really" happening, it seems to me [that] gets her into trouble.

COMMENT: Well, the patient told her what was actually happening.

COMMENT: On one level. But her sense of [the significance of] this was that she needed her mother to understand [her experience], that her mother could never understand [it].

COMMENT: I understand how it worked, but in order to [understand the analyst] had to empathize with a delusional system.

PRESENTER: No, not really, I just had to shift modes of functioning because she was operating as a child[d] and I was operating as an adult. It was very hard for me to give that up and be more of a mother to her, I guess.

GEDO: Well, but if she had been your child and she were 31 months instead of 31 years of age, that's not how you would have done it. You wouldn't have entered into the question of whether she'd been victimized at all. You would start with how to do it better. That's an alternative [therapeutic approach available for her]; in a traditional [framework] one wouldn't start this person in analysis. One would enter into a psychotherapy with her in which one teaches her how to do it better. Of course, I have written quite a bit on the fact that we can afford to do that even if we think we're doing an analysis, that with a person like this that's how one [best] starts an analysis. I suspect that [by doing that] you would have avoided the difficulty [you encountered with this case]. You found it very difficult that you couldn't establish rapport with her; that really feels like the ground is giving way beneath our feet. It is a terrific burden on our sense of professionalism if we can't get to first base in establishing our good will, or good reputation. It probably would have been much easier if you had said that one wasn't in a position to judge who was victim and who was victimizer and to what degree. "Of course it's terribly important to you, but how can I know? I wasn't there. All I know is that *you* have to learn how to avoid being victimized."

PRESENTER: I don't know. I think she would have heard that as "she was responsible."

COMMENT: I entirely agree [with Dr. Gedo]. I would question the terms of your statement, of having to "suspend reality." She had entered into a transference paradigm with you, perhaps somewhat prematurely, before you were ready to see it; and in order to interpret, eventually, what the transference was, you had to allow that. But at the end of an analysis, or when transference is well established, the patient has to suspend "reality" enough to allow you to be the transference object. [This patient] entered into it very early on, without giving you enough clues to realize what was going on. As soon as you realized what was going on, it became possible to make an interpretation within the transference.

PRESENTER: Except that her transference [constituted] her [whole] life in that regard. I mean, she did that with all sorts of people, and she did with me the same thing that she was doing elsewhere.

GEDO: I would have had tremendous discomfort with doing what you decided to do. My concern would be one of being involved in a folie à deux with her. She knows that she's being provocative in these relationships; [therefore] I would prefer to battle it out on that ground and try to find out why she's [enacting] this whole provocative business now with me as the analyst [so that it gets] in the way of whatever it is that's really bothering her underneath.

COMMENT: By the way, does [this] happen at work, or does it only happen in unstructured settings? I mean, she's a professional—does the same thing happen where she has clear rules, or does it only happen in unstructured social settings?

PRESENTER: Where the possibility of intimacy exists. It doesn't happen at work. She is very good . . .

COMMENT: That's why I think it's being set up by the transference paradigm, an unstructured setting.

PRESENTER: It happens with men though.

COMMENT: But it's an unstructured setting, and she's lying on the couch. She has no boundaries in which to operate, no clear rules, and she is reenacting with you the same thing that's happening socially. It doesn't happen when she has structure.

GEHRIE: [to Gedo] It seems to me in regard to your comment that battling it out with her on the level that you propose is kind of like asking a seduced child to perceive and explain the effects of its own seduction. You know, it's precisely because they can't do that that they do something else with it; that is, they enact and they need to have a situation in which it is possible for them to experience themselves as not having been omnipotent in that act. So that's what's going on here, not that she can somehow perceive through the right sense of conviction that she's being unreasonable.

PRESENTER: She told me that her mother's style of helping her deal with her father's rages, which were so upsetting, was to say, "You know you have to understand your father. When he was a child his mother did such and such. You have to understand." And so she would never say, "God, it's really hard," or, you know, "You poor thing," or "Your father's out of whack," or something like that. She would always say, "You have to understand him, where he's coming from."

GEDO: We are discussing a technical problem. It depends on who *you* are, which of the manifold approaches to such a technical problem is going to be effective. I don't doubt that everyone who has spoken is quite right in singling out that technical approach which she or he would find most congenial for him- or herself. I would like to come back to the one I proposed because it did not gain a weighty enough hearing. You say that it would fall on her ears as an echo of her mother. Maybe the first time; not the second time, because I would then change it accordingly. You know, you have to handle these things depending on how they work. I don't think that it's impossible to say to her, "Let's worry about what causes this later. Let's right now figure out what to do when it starts so it doesn't degenerate into throwing crockery at each other." Now, to be sure, that's not an interpretation. That's why I called such activities going "beyond interpretation" in the title of my 1979 book. It's an intervention based on the assumption that she is beyond the power of [explanations alone]. We have a terribly condensed report of a year of work, more or less. How long did it take you to get to the point where you established this workable situation?

Presenter: Six months.

Gedo: Six months. All right. She is so volatile at the beginning that the lexical meaning of words is probably not [entirely] available to her. She is enacting everything, as Dr. Gehrie correctly stated, so that the most effective technical response is to enter the enactment: to respond in the same language she is using, and that is the language of the 2½ year old. That's what [the presenter] tells us before she even [describes] the patient. This is the problem of how to deal with people at the level of organization of a 2½ year old. Words are superfluous a lot of the time, and certainly they are never [sufficient] when people are stuck in that mode. You have to *do* something for the person, and the crux of the matter is not *what* you do, whether you fight or you say, "I'm with you." The point is to get it across that you accept the responsibility of being of some concrete assistance, because [left to herself] the person can't do it. Left to her own devices, she dangles in the wind.

Presenter: I can just say that the next phase was her experiencing the analysis as terribly important for her—terribly scary too—but terribly important in that she could express the feelings with me; she could talk about her experience, her emotions, with me. [As a result, she] didn't have to take them to the men. [Thus there] was some real function that I was providing for her. I don't know if that's what you were talking about, but that's part of it.

GEDO: Well, yes, I was talking about providing one of the many functions that are not operating as they should be. I don't know how many one has to provide before one gets a response like that, but when one has demonstrated that, at least in an emergency, one has propped up these failing functions, then a tremendous lessening of tension and anxiety takes place, and the regression is reversed and the person comes up to his or her . . . I was going to say, "best level of functioning." That's not necessarily true, but [at least to] some level available much of the time. She's not a 2½ year old anymore; she's suddenly somebody who can deal with things in words alone.

COMMENT: I'd like to ask about that. If the form of the engagement, concretely, is "throwing the crockery," is confronting her with [her responsibility for] her provocation [going to] bring her out of the regressed mode, [or will] the whole cycle have to be repeated again?

GEDO: Well, it depends on how you throw crockery.

COMMENT: I guess that's true.

GEDO: If you throw crockery the way her father threw crockery— if you engage with her the way the father and the mother engaged, at least until father's heart attack—she won't be able to stand that, and she'll get out of treatment. But, my goodness, you can make a game out of throwing crockery because, as one of you correctly noted, even she has made something of a game out of fighting. She has that capacity, and you can engage in something of a confrontation with her that's infinitely more benign than any of the confrontations she has ever had.

COMMENT: I think that's right. It reminds me of the thing I've been confronting with patients [who were] seduced as children: you're going to start your effort to be helpful to her, and she's going to say, "That's not what's important. Your saying that shows that you don't support me," and she will then reengage you with that same issue.

GEDO: Well, she will try to reengage me with that same issue, and I will respond in exactly the way I responded to [the participant who dismissed] what I said: I will make a joke out of it.

COMMENT: It depends on where you are, too, in the analysis, wouldn't you say? I mean, [during] the first few months with a patient like this there's a level of artistry required that perhaps many of us may not have.

GEDO: I don't [know] whether I have the level of artistry that this woman [requires]. You see, that's what we haven't heard: what was [the presenter's] feeling about this woman when they started? We can go on to that. Good-looking young women are very hard to deal with for a man of my age. I don't know whether I [could] take this person. But if you feel easy about dealing with a person (not the illness, the *person*), then the artistry will come, provided you [also] feel free in your head of theoretical constraints, provided that you know that the task is to establish a bond with this person on some mutually acceptable level. If it's throwing crockery, it's throwing crockery, provided you don't break the cups.

COMMENT: The reason I raised [this is that] this lady is going to be looking for our seductive attempts . . .

GEDO: That's why a lady like this is much more difficult for a man of my age than it is for another young woman.

COMMENT: When you're talking about the technique that you're proposing, it gets back to the issue [of] the analyst establishing himself as a new object versus a transference object. It seems that at that point in the treatment [you are] establishing yourself as new, different, with a whole different agenda in terms of what sort of information you can provide to this person that will be helpful to her in dealing with her immediate situation. When the person then attempts to reengage you [in her usual transaction], it's not a transference.

GEDO: Yes, although you put it a bit too starkly, because if it were really correct that [what one provides] is an entirely novel experience for the patient, the patient wouldn't be in an analyst's office in the first place, since this person learns very well indeed. She has made quite a career of learning and doing well, so that she can accept instruction and presumably she's gotten along quite well with instructors who have something to offer her. I assume that they sent her to the Spanish school not because they wanted to give her a hard time, but because she was thought to be a good enough learner so she could pick up this foreign language.

PRESENTER: I don't know whether it was because she was singled out because of her abilities.

COMMENT: At that age she could have learned extremely easily.

PRESENTER: Well, I think she did do it. She did, she did her schooling in Spanish. Actually there must be something I don't know because when you bring that up I obviously don't have an answer to that.

GEDO: Well, even if that [is not a good example], it's not entirely true that in being truly helpful one is utterly, utterly new, utterly unprecedented. That, too, is a transference, but I would want to get out of the ready-made [defensive] negative mother transference. Of course, whether she would have such a transference to me is another question. She has such a transference to you. With me she might start out with something else. She might start with my being the perfect protector that she's always wanted. Who knows? I'm talking now as though it were [the presenter] trying a different approach, [one in which the analyst] succeeded in being a governess (this is a family that couldn't afford governesses, but you know what I mean)—the governess she never had—who, instead of dumping the entire burden of everything on an unprepared child, does what a proper caretaker will do for a child who doesn't know how. It's "new" in terms of psychoanalytic theories because it's not the pathogenic mother transference, but it's not really totally novel [for the patient].

COMMENT: But what [the analyst] did was to step outside the negative mother transference, by taking the position of seeing her as the victim rather than seeing her as . . .

GEDO: Right. That's exactly what worked, which is why I'm so confident in proposing my view. Now, whether I would have come up with it, who knows? I mean, if you have to *think* about what you're going to do, you're lost. Then it's too late, it's too late! Analysis is like fencing—you know, one false move and you're dead. I think it has to come totally spontaneously, or it's no good. I mean, [in a seminar] we're Monday-morning-quarterbacking, and it's easy.

COMMENT: But didn't she actually enter into the positive maternal transference? That of a parent who is listening to her children reporting a problem as if some other person [had been] at fault. It happens all the time. Quite commonly, parents enter into collusion with their children; the children report x, y, or z happened, and it's always the other kid's fault or it's the teacher's fault, or it's the school's fault; that is not all that uncommon.

GEDO: Entirely possible, but we have no evidence that her mother acted that way. I think that we would be on surer ground if we said that it's an exceedingly difficult maneuver, emotionally difficult for the analyst. I mean, we heard from [the presenter] that she resisted it for six months because it felt to her like she was being driven crazy. It is quite manifestly a reversal of the childhood situation. It stood the situation in which the patient was driven crazy on its head, so that in fact [the analyst] accepts the child's role in the transference. What you say may also be true, but I think what I am saying is *bound* to be true. It's a reversal of the mother transference; the patient is now the abusive mother and [the analyst] is the abused child. And, of course, that's the problem with which the patient comes in: "Who is the abuser, and who is the abused?" Now, that's why I proposed that the best solution is to say, "That's a stupid question. My dear, the trouble with you is, you ask stupid questions," I would say lovingly to her. "Why don't we ask an intelligent question?"

COMMENT: It's the "lovingly" that would come across, more than the content of the remark?

GEDO: Well, I would hope that both would come across, you see. If either one failed to come across, then in the next session you have to correct for that. You have to get across to the person that she is trapped in asking the wrong question, and she's been trapped in asking the wrong question for 30 years. It's the mother's question that she has swallowed as the relevant category of inquiry, and that's what she has to get past. "You and your mother both asked the wrong questions. The right question is not whose fault it was; the right question is how to avoid breaking the crockery." Of course, if you get there in six weeks instead of six months, that's a great triumph, a *great* triumph. Six months is pretty good. It's *very* good! But [in making these suggestions to the presenter] I'm demonstrating in action what should be done for such a patient: "Concentrate on how to do even better." As soon as you've accomplished that, you enter a new universe of discourse. All of a sudden, words are enough. That's what she told you, that words are now enough. "We don't have to show and tell, we can just tell."

PRESENTER: Yes. I'm wondering what it means when she experiences me in a positive way. Because she felt that her mother couldn't tolerate her autonomy. That's her statement: that her mother can't stand her independence and wants to control her. But she came in one session and said, "Hello, Mom. I'm home." Well, what does that mean? I was a good mother in that "Hello, Mom. I'm home," as opposed to this malevolent mother that she . . .

GEDO: Well, is that in accord with what one of you proposed? Was there also a good mother, and was it her mother who was the good mother, or was it someone else?

PRESENTER: Oh! Well, after that initial period, there was a shift in the transference.

COMMENT: Could we stay with this for a little bit before going on to the shift in the transference? The approach that you used . . . it seems to me that the model for it is the self-psychological model: things calmed down because you established a selfobject transference. Or, to put it in a different set of terms, you've been willing to accept a position that is at variance with something that you previously regarded as necessary for the retention of *your* autonomy. So you've now slipped into a little niche where she insists somebody has to tell her that she didn't do this thing wrong. Right?

PRESENTER: Right.

COMMENT: Just checking it out.

COMMENT: I have another question too about the technique. You're in a session with her and she is regaling you with how this jerk abused her in some way [although] she provoked him beyond anybody's limits. Suppose you were to say something like, "You know, I get the feeling that you want me to sympathize with your position as the victim. . . .

PRESENTER: [interrupting] Oh, she would just go . . .

COMMENT: [laughter] . . . "because that's something that your mother never did for you when you were victimized at home."

PRESENTER: Oh, well, your point is a good one. I think, though, that she would react just as I did to the "you want me." She couldn't bear that she wanted anything from me other than absolute [affirmation]. One time her boyfriend, who was an old big-time reporter, was giving her some advice about one of her assignments, and she was outraged. She felt depreciated, devalued, and undermined and sabotaged and [claimed] he was trying to control her, and all these things. And I mildly said that it sounded as if he was trying to give her some decent advice. She just went crazy!

GEDO: Well, when did you begin to understand that?

PRESENTER: What?

GEDO: That the mother dumped all responsibility on her. It's very hard to make such an interpretation until you know. You don't know in the beginning, right? You could ask it as a question, if you are super clever, *super* clever; that's really hitting the target from two miles away.

PRESENTER: The reason I brought this up [is that] I eventually said, "I guess that my using the word 'advice' is too ambiguous for you to qualify as being supportive." She then said, "Well, you're not supposed to be supportive. I don't want you to be supportive."

GEDO: Well, it's very complicated, because she can't stand [support] either. This is the true paradox of an internal problem: what is tolerable is as thin as a razor's edge.

COMMENT: Well, I was trying to find a technical way to get out of entering into [a parameter], a way to interpret what she's trying to enact with you without engaging in the enactment.

GEDO: Well, if the description of the first six months is to be relied on, there is no way of interpreting. She will not accept an interpretation. I just read a case report that starts this way: a young male therapist with a man just a few years younger. So it's a parallel situation, which starts in exactly the same way. For three years all that happened was that they fought about what is the duty of the therapist in responding to the endless paranoid nonsense. In that case he didn't verbally agree; he just gritted his teeth and waited it out. He also didn't disagree. But they could discuss nothing else, nothing else was to be said, no interpretations were possible.

I think here, too, no interpretations are possible. She will not tolerate anything other than an agreement with the paranoia. Now, that's an identification with the parents' ways. She had no voice as a child. She wasn't permitted to protest, or at least she didn't feel that it would be permitted for her to protest. We have this awful story that her brother gets her to cooperate with him in what they both really regard as a delinquent act, and she can't say no. So there's automatic obedience, although she feels devastated by the guilt of having become a delinquent and she can't turn to anybody for assistance. I think that's the evidence that protest [was actually] impossible and this [grievance] is not fictive.

Forgive me, I have to pull rank and say that, on the basis of experience, I don't think it pays to look for what kind of transference that is, in terms of what object relationship is being repeated. [What needs to be stressed is that] it's a *reversal*: the whole illness is a reversal; it's an attempt to master massive traumatization, by all sorts of people in all sorts of ways, [but by means of] turning the passive into the active. [The analyst] accepted the role of the victim because she is a certain type of analyst. But such a choice is unacceptable to most of the rest of us. There's no one right thing. It's wonderful to be able to accept the role of the victim without falling into a folie à deux—I mean that's a real *trick*! Mostly, when analysts accept such a role, they do fall into a counteridentification. Judith Kantrowitz reports about the outcome of such strategies: a very soft strategy, when employed by the wrong people, led to the undermining of the patient's reality testing. That was the outcome of the analysis.

COMMENT: The patient probably felt better.

GEDO: Yeah, yeah, the analysis was considered successful, but the patient's functioning had been impaired. It's very difficult not to fall into such traps, and insofar as you're able to avoid that, that's a special asset of your personality. I don't think that there are too many people who are likely to be able to go down that road. I certainly know I can't. Chances are, left to my own devices and ignorant of everything you have told us, just starting out, I would drive this patient out of treatment by being much too hard-line. I remember driving one person out of treatment after four weeks, with a great sense of relief that the man left and an absolute conviction that he was a paranoid psychopath. Chances are he wasn't a paranoid psychopath, but he was inflicting something on me [to which] I'm allergic. What I am proposing is a compromise way, but I can only do it when I'm not on the firing line, and that's easy!

PRESENTER: I feel that I really admired her, through all of this; I *admired* her. Even when she was really attacking someone, I kind of admired that. The patient is fascinated by murderers and people who commit violent crimes, pedophiles, that sort of thing. She really tries to understand what makes these people tick; she tries to predict violence and tries to understand whether there was anything that would indicate that a person would behave in this fashion. I admire how she's dealt with her problems . . .

COMMENT: She wants to get in the mind of the victimizers?

GEDO: Well, this certainly suggests that already as a small child she had to make judgments, moment to moment judgments, about the states of mind of actual victimizers.

COMMENT: I thought your point about the identification with the parents in that regard is really critical for the subsequent technical question that arises. If [we] consider the power and the underlying significance of that identification in her integration, then to engage her on the level you posited as one possibility of confrontation—[symbolically] throwing the crockery—how would that occur in a case like this? Especially at the outset, when any misstep is going to lead to the breakdown of the treatment . . .

GEDO: Right! I've made such missteps and have lost patients as a consequence. Occasionally, though, it is possible to find the right tone.

COMMENT: Why the conviction that if there are missteps, this woman is not going to be treated? She's into throwing crockery. I don't understand the idea that this woman's going to leave treatment so quickly, based on missteps.

GEDO: Oh, not necessarily this person. She tolerated it okay, but there was all this struggle and raging that then left you back at square one with her. There had to be some other means of engaging her around this critical issue. [In these circumstances] some other person might leave.

COMMENT: I have a question. What was the older brother who was involved in this? What happened to him?

PRESENTER: What happened to him?

COMMENT: How did he turn out?

PRESENTER: He has married but has a difficult marriage that tolerates a tremendous degree of separation. He lived in a different city from his wife for a long period of time, and when he's with my patient his behavior is inappropriate, literally.

GEDO: Sexually inappropriate?

PRESENTER: Literally. He will, he will often—well, he'll still touch her inappropriately. He will go to the bathroom and leave the door open when she's in an adjacent room. He really does need—he really seems to have some problems.

COMMENT: Serious problems.

PRESENTER: Yeah, some serious problems. She was recounting a conversation that he had with her mother. Her mother was saying something about [the fact] that she wanted to work for the next five years and then be able to take off a month a year to spend at the seashore, and then she said, "But, you know, who knows how long I'll live," or something like that. And the brother said, "You can't die before me." Her mother's response was to brush this off, but my patient saw it as being really odd that he would say something like this. She felt that the mother's inability to see that as odd exactly [paralleled] the way in which the mother had been unable to support her and always supported her brother. She felt that her mother supported her brother in the fights that the father and the brother would have; the mother would console the brother, but [the patient] was outcast and witnessed it all and would be left to her own devices.

GEDO: What was her father's occupation?

PRESENTER: When he was in Latin America it was some sort of teaching/missionary position. Then they came back here because he was offered a tenured position at a university.

GEDO: So he was an educated person.

PRESENTER: He was an educator. He lost that job when she was a teenager, and a terrible year followed because he was out of a job and was very unhappy about it and took a lot of it out on the family. He eventually got a job in a public school as a counselor, a school counselor, until he died.

GEDO: Was he American-born? Or was he an immigrant?

PRESENTER: No, he was American-born.

GEDO: Do you know what sort of specific background they had?

PRESENTER: No.

GEDO: Find out, find out.

PRESENTER: Why?

GEDO: Well, you know, in Castile they call South Americans "Indians." It's a different world. Cultural factors may be very important.

PRESENTER: I think they are very important to her. As a matter of fact, one time when I brought up cultural issues as being possibly significant in her life, especially [since she had] lived in two cultures, she missed a session following that. She [also] responded with great relief. She found it very meaningful to her, and then she missed the next session. It was not uncommon for her to do this when there had been meaningful material. But when she came back, she felt like I was ridiculing her.

GEDO: Well, good. So it's not Madrid, that's for sure! Colombia, or the slums of Caracas? And she's telling you that one of the things in Anne Frank's room is some kind of terrible ethnic prejudice. Perhaps the mother against the father. What nationality is [the mother]?

COMMENT: Then it strikes me that the father was a failure in this country. He made very little money, and before they moved to South America the family lived in lower class conditions. Whatever success he had in South America [did not last], and then he took quite a depreciated position subsequently. Not a very successful man here.

PRESENTER: Well, I think she really struggles to idealize him. She can only protect his image by seeing him as having consciously tried to teach her and [having] conscientiously tried to teach her a lesson about life: that he was a good man trying to teach her that emotions should not be expressed. That's how she sees him as protecting her, by helping her not to be emotional. On the other hand, when she feels that he had no control over himself and that he in fact damaged himself, she feels quite lost. In the last years, he may [have been] addicted—certainly using barbiturates and amphetamines to regulate his sleeping and waking. He didn't have a lot of internal controls from what I could tell.

GEDO: Well, are we ready to hear about the next phase?

PRESENTER: [For] the next six months she had a very hard time with my making any kind of statement about her presentation that she wasn't scared of. She had to be in control. So I would disrupt her periodically; I don't think it was avoidable. As she became more reliant on the analysis, she would deny it, of course. When I told her about my [upcoming] summer vacation, she immediately scheduled a vacation with her mother, [even though] she'd been complaining about her mother all the time—how distant she felt, and so forth and so on. I commented on the fact that she was compromising herself more in an already shortened analytic schedule.

She felt like I had taken away all her means of coping; this happened repeatedly. One time she was telling me about a weekend—it had been a long weekend—and she came in talking about how she had spent the weekend and how she had been pretty much alone. [She said] that that wasn't the greatest thing, but that she had been reading, and this was what her mother has taught her: how to read when you're alone. I said, just reflecting back, [that] she was saying that she had been able to cope with the long weekend in this particular way; and although it meant being more on her own, and it wasn't the most satisfying way to deal with it, it was what she had to do. She was furious with me because she felt like I was taking it away from her. She felt that I was depreciating what she had had to do in order to get through the time and that I was taking away reading specifically, and minimizing that.

Anyway, she was able to say that what really frightened her about my bringing these things out before she was ready was that she was afraid of reaching a [breaking] point. She was afraid, and all her dreams were about nuclear reactions and terrible explosions; she would be running around trying to erect a barricade around the core so that it wouldn't injure all the people around her. And there was something about the intensifying transference that produced those images. She felt terribly endangered for herself and felt the world was endangered by it.

GEDO: See, that's another reason (and one we haven't yet mentioned) for her inability to tolerate hearing about her contribution to the difficulties. In her mind, if she has any responsibility at all, she is destroying the world.

PRESENTER: Yes, that's exactly right. Before my vacation, there were a couple of dreams that I thought presaged what was to come further down the road. She had broken off with the boyfriend, and she was traumatized by it, really scared, really frightened; and for the first time she called me. I should say, that's the *only* time that she's ever called me. And then [this impasse] was resolved by two dreams. In the first one, she and another woman were going to plan the second woman's murder. The woman wanted to die, and the patient was going to participate. The murder was going to be therapeutic. At the same time, [a man was also] present. The room in which this other woman was going to die was left in chaos, and somehow or other she is knocked out and the woman is knocked out, and the man is also knocked out. When the patient wakes up, she goes into the room where the other woman is and at the woman's request puts a knife between her shoulder blades. The woman starts to convulse, but she is happy she's dying. Blood comes out of her nose and she dies, and the patient is horrified. There's a TV monitor, and she has to make sure that she's erased all the tapes. The second dream was . . .

GEDO: Well, how did you feel when you heard that?

PRESENTER: I felt like she thought that I was inviting a mercy killing, that she felt that I was saying, you know, "Oh, come on. Rely on me," and that she was going to destroy me by her volatility and whatever. That's what I thought.

GEDO: That's the *meaning*, right. But you must have had some reaction beyond this cognitive achievement.

COMMENT: A twitching between the shoulder blades.

COMMENT: I thought you were the accomplice; you were both going to kill the bad mother in her.

GEDO: It works every which way; that's true too. Golly! You have a tiger by the tail here, yet obviously it's gone a long way—for two years. So you're justified in having taken her on. But you haven't yet told us what gave you the courage to proceed.

GEHRIE: Admiration: the admiration was the antidote to the rage, to the victimization, to the murder in this woman's soul in the secret attic room. There was something that appealed to [the analyst].

PRESENTER: But the other thing that I have written to myself periodically is why analysis means so much to her. I mean it is so important to her that she gain as much conscious control about everything as she can that her desire to understand herself, even the most negative things, it really motivates her, I think.

GEDO: Well, okay, I think we are now beginning to spell out the assets that you smelled when this woman first came to see you. You gave us an image of some kind of glossy, modern young woman. For me, that's not enough. Many of them are quite crazy, and some of [this patient's] material makes her sound like she hovers on the brink of decompensation. Although, hopefully, it's only borrowed. But, of course, it makes a big difference whether she borrowed it at nine months or at 27 months or at age 16. And it may still turn out in the end that there is an irreducible core of craziness in her.[e]

PRESENTER: You want to hear the second dream?

GEDO: Sure.

COMMENT: You thought the first one was good, huh?

PRESENTER: She climbs out of a small window at the top of a tall building in order to clean off another window. She didn't want to disturb the cobwebs there, and then, after the cleaning, she tried to get back into the building but the window was no longer there. The entire structure turned to a jellolike consistency, and she awakened as she was falling, sliding off. That's an encouraging dream, don't you think? [laughter]

COMMENT: What thoughts did she have?

PRESENTER: What were her association?

COMMENT: Yeah. Or do you want to hear mine?

PRESENTER: Well, maybe part of the reason I could tolerate these moments easily, in retrospect, was because of my ignorance, in a way. Because I heard the dream as being her anxiety about what she was going to find when she tried to look deeper, [past] the provocations. Once she gets involved, she is scared about something in herself.

COMMENT: It sounds very much like what she describes is entering her brother's bunk—and a pit of anxiety—and then there's no way out. She's now in a situation from which, at least as she experienced it, there was no way out. She couldn't stop, and she couldn't tell her parents, and she couldn't control herself.

GEDO: That's clearly true on one level. But it doesn't explain to us why these forbidden games are so dreadfully serious. Why *is* it so dreadfully serious? [After all], children's sexual games are ubiquitous. Why was . . .

PRESENTER: She says that. She says that too, that those were sexual games that children play.

GEDO: Well, "Forbidden Games" was the title of a wonderful movie I remember; the rest of you are too young. It was a French movie made right after the second World War about children who were fleeing [and whose] parents were killed in an air raid. And they wander into a cemetery and start playing sexual games. Very poignant and beautiful. [This patient seems to feel that in this sexual game she did something irremediably damaging] to her brother, that she is radioactive, and she thinks that the radiation got him, that he's become crazy.

PRESENTER: Right.

GEDO: And she has not escaped unscathed. You know, [this game was] not at the level of a bit of innocent obscenity. I mean, this is a matter of life and death.

COMMENT: It seems like this dream would begin to give you the opportunity to answer the question that [Dr. Gedo] is asking. Why was it experienced as it was and [why did it] continue to be thought of in those terms.

GEDO: Why does she have the Anne Frank dream? You know, why is she about to be exterminated?

COMMENT: Well, they definitely lived with death? Didn't they? The father was . . . the father had a heart attack, and they go off . . .

GEHRIE: Or the feelings of having absolutely no contact with the mother and the utter abandonment on that level.

COMMENT: What did *she* say about the dream? The second dream?

PRESENTER: I think we agreed, more or less, that it had to do with her fear of losing her parents.

COMMENT: This was right before your vacation?

PRESENTER: No, the dream that she had right before my vacation was actually different. It was that she was to sit, tied to a chair of some sort, and there was a cockroach that came into the dream and was very threatening. She wasn't sure whether it came from the seat where she was sitting or from somewhere else. I thought the cockroach was some aspect of her that was going to emerge and that she was frightened [of]. Also, just being tied there, being forced to have [something awful] come out: she feels that way often [about being in analysis]. She often says to me that I want her to discuss these emotionally distressing things. You know, she always displaces [the responsibility for the necessities of the analytic procedure onto me].

GEDO: Well, Anne Frank and the cockroach, huh? She deserves to be exterminated because she's subhuman. And what makes her subhuman? Well, there are whole series of explanations that can be extracted from her history, but I would think that something of the kind that Dr. Gehrie is postulating will ultimately come into focus; that she felt she was treated like an insect when she was very young.

PRESENTER: Yes, I think that's right, but my focus has been more or less that what she seems to be afraid of is showing that she has an emotional response to anything that has occurred. That's paradoxical, because she responds so emotionally about everything, in a way, but what she's afraid of is that her emotional response will kill off someone. I mean, that the intensity is too great.

GEDO: Let me summarize. I'll put it all together on the basis of what we have heard thus far. She has a dream in which her brothers are being executed—so the great emotion is not love but infinite hatred, radioactive hatred, right? And why does she want her brothers executed? Well, we weren't there, but presumably there wasn't enough to go around; three children in 36 months. So she is the insect monster, as in Kafka's "Metamorphosis."

PRESENTER: All right. Yeah, right, and those feelings cannot be understood and therefore have to be squelched. That's why I've had such a different response to [all this]; I haven't felt like it's been unworkable . . .

COMMENT: Well, you've also said that you're working with it at home; you've compared her to your two-and-a-half-year-old son. In some sense, you're used to working with [this kind of thing], and you don't see it in the same way other people do. I didn't mean that pejoratively or to call your son [pathological].

Second Session

GEDO: As I recall what we discussed last time, we heard about a very difficult patient who was taken on for analysis because [candidates] need patients, and there was no absolute contraindication. But she very soon proved to be exceedingly difficult, and during the first period of the treatment, the difficulty consisted in the fact that she immediately entered into a complex enactment that sounded like the repetition on the patient's part of her mother's behavior in [the patient's]childhood and her intent to force the analyst into the position of her helpless childhood self, to have to submit to a regime of tyranny by assenting to observing it. And then we engaged in a discussion in which most people felt that they had to stick to the frame set by the patient and either jolly her along by saying "Okay, okay," or stop her in her tracks by saying, "This is crazy, I'm not willing to go along with such crazy stuff."

What I tried to say last time was that there is a third way, and that is to step outside of the frame of the enactment, to focus on noninterpretive interventions, exactly because you can't directly say, "I'm stepping outside of the frame of the enactment" in the first three months of an analysis with somebody who doesn't know about enactments. But an enactment of your own is what is required,[f] in which everything you say and do refuses to stand still for this absurd view of life, that of the slave and the slavemaster, [in which] the most you can even dream of doing is exchanging the role of slave for that of slavemaster. And one way I proposed for being able to do that is to say, "Look at the mistake you are making in viewing life in these terms. This is a very important finding. Touchdown! Touchdown! Time out! Time out! Let's celebrate that we have scored a touchdown. We understand something crucially important about you, and that is that you see life in these narrow terms. This can only mean that you were raised in a crazy way, that you need an after-education to get out of the framework of that crazy world. You have to learn how to view life differently and stop asking the fruitless question, 'whose fault is it?' "

Obviously, that's not what this analyst did. She apparently was able not to be driven crazy by [being] compelled to assent to something that she thought was false. I wouldn't recommend that as an everyday procedure. I think most of us cannot do that without getting unconsciously flooded with fury against the patient, with dire consequences either for the patient or for ourselves, or for both.

PRESENTER: But why should that be difficult to do? It *was* difficult to do in some ways, but it was only difficult until I thought that I had some understanding of what it was that I was doing. Once I felt that I understood what it was and why I was doing it, it was no longer so difficult.

GEDO: Well, it always depends on one's own childhood experience. I'm not going to ask you to tell everybody here why that was easy for you. I can tell you all why it would be impossible for me to do that.[g] I'm a born revolutionary. And when I hear a falsehood, I have great difficulty in refraining from yelling out, "That is untrue!" And if I have to stay quiet in such circumstances, I am sure that my blood pressure goes up 50 points.

GEHRIE: But, John, doesn't this address the point you've made in many different ways: that the nature of technique is dependent on the capacities and features of the analyst as well as of the patient? Therefore, the assessment of [the appropriateness of] that technique for a particular case has to take these features that you're describing now well into account: so that, if she could do this in this way, then it might not have been wrong in the same way that it might have been for you or me, let's say, who might have had to restrain this other set of internal responses.

GEDO: Oh, if it works, how could it be wrong? Since it worked, it was right. You know, we should give [the presenter] the Congressional Medal of Honor, but we shouldn't require everyone in our army to expose himself to such fire.

COMMENT: We don't know whether it worked with regard to the outcome of the analysis. It seems to me that the [presenter's] position is essentially that of the self psychologist, who would regard the failure to do what [the presenter] did as a countertrans-

ference, an inability to tolerate the patient's narcissistic needs, but
. . .

GEDO: I don't think that every self psychologist will accept that
assessment. I think that within self psychology there are strong
differences of opinion about this issue. I think certain people,
perhaps Ernest Wolf or Ornstein, would agree with how you just
put it. I'm quite sure Michael Basch does not.

COMMENT: Oh, I agree. Neither would Goldberg. Neither would
several other people, but I do think there's a view in self psychology
that you have to do whatever it takes and that anything other than
that is an empathic break, an error, which then would have to be
repaired if possible. But that's not a uniform theory.

GEDO: I don't think that the issue we are discussing is one that can
simply be broken down into self psychologists versus others, ego
psychologists versus others. I think in both camps there are people
who are able to do it this way and people who can't, and I think
people tend to say that the right way to do it is the way they're able
to do it.

GEHRIE: I think this is one of Gedo's major contributions. It comes
across to me as an assessment of technique [but] not just in terms of
the abstract qualities or features of the pathology and therefore
what model had to be applied or what intervention had to be
applied; [Gedo takes] into account the resources of the analyst,
[which] changes everything. When you read Gedo's cases in his
books, [you realize] we can't all do [what he describes], and yet I've
never felt, while reading those cases, that we're being told that this
is how you have to approach it. He's expanding a range of possibilities for us, telling us, in essence (as I read it anyway), that there are
aspects of us which we can use, which we have perhaps felt, for one
reason or another, that we had to refrain from using. That's going to
come out of each of us in a different way.

GEDO: Well, I should hope so. If you refer to what I have actually
published, I have never said one word about how to do it. I have said
this is what I *did*, at least [this is my impression, in retrospect, of
what occurred].

GEHRIE: It's seductive to read any clinical presentation as a set of
instructions on how to do things, yours included.

GEDO: [interrupting] Oh, mine are the most seductive. I work very
hard at seducing people through rhetorical tricks.

COMMENT: I agree that you have [never] suggested that it had to be done a certain way. You said this is how you'd do it, and this is what's been helpful, and these are the implications, which is different from saying, "Now we have this new model, this new technique for approaching the problem."

GEDO: Let's go back to the challenge [about the long-term effects of this technique], though. It's perfectly true that in terms of the final analytic result we don't know whether anything that was done early has "worked." [We cannot predict] what the consequences [of the analyst's interventions will be]. It ain't over until the fat lady sings, and this isn't over. You know, you may find out five years down the line that that was a fatal mistake, but we can't discuss that with the information now available—all we can talk about is what has already occurred. What K.R. Eissler recommended in his influential paper of 1953 is still the ideal: that if one does extraordinary things of this sort, one hopes to be able to discuss sometime during the course of an analysis why one had to do that, and what it meant that one had to do that. So five years down the line it may come to that. If it doesn't it's an imperfect analysis in terms of traditional analytic ideas; although when [the presenter] tells us that they got past this terrible struggle and that new transference material emerged, it's very tempting to conclude that that's the best one can do.

COMMENT: I wouldn't conclude it. To me the problem with this sort of thing is that we've got this patient who, if you don't go along with what she insists on as a version of reality, is all upset and furious. So now you go along with it, and now she's no longer upset and furious, and things can move along smoothly as long as you go along with it, but it still leaves the issue there.[h]

GEDO: [Did the patient see] that in the transference she was repeating the struggle with her mother?

PRESENTER: I want to say that it hasn't been a linear process: it's been up and down, and all I was trying to say last time was that that was the major [thrust] of the first six to nine months and it hasn't stopped altogether. One of the crises came up around the issue of fees. The way she pays for her analysis is that 50% of the $100 per session fee has been paid by her insurance and then she has a reduced fee of $15.00 per session—so that at that point the clinic was receiving $65.00 per session. Then she was going through a divorce and was in tremendous financial straits because of some of her own mismanagement; [she had] ignored a student loan that came due, and she really didn't have money. I agreed at that time that $160.00

a month would be acceptable to me, which put us in a difficulty. When she would miss a session, she wasn't really responsible in the same way that other people are responsible (since she just paid a monthly fee). So I considered *that* [as an example of] my "stretching" for her. So I've been fairly flexible for her. Her schedule was also a little bit difficult, and I was flexible with her about that. The other thing that happened was that she had scheduled a couple of vacations or trips during the course of this analysis, and again I hadn't interpreted it.

Well, so finally the transferences evolved; [I understood] that she's very afraid of a negative maternal transference and in some sense the men in her life have served to protect her from involvement with me in the analysis. So if she has been alone, without a man, she's become much more frightened of the analysis. During one of these episodes, when the man in her life was going to be out of town for a long period of time, she scheduled a vacation. [About] that, I mildly said to her that we would have to work out something about billing the insurance because insurance companies required that she be physically present in order for me to bill them. And she went through her usual rage with me and accused me of all sorts of things, but I had been through enough of these instances, so I could [remind] her how flexible I had been and how she was misrepresenting the facts. I was able to keep the focus on the fact that I wasn't a bad person, and we focused on her fear, what she was afraid of.

What came out of it is that she's terribly afraid of being obligated to me. She's been afraid to acknowledge [that] I've done anything for her, because when she feels obligated to me she begins to feel sucked into some kind of relationship in which she feels that I will restructure her according to my own needs. Only by denying the reality of what I've done for her can she maintain herself as separate and not feel as if she's pulled into such a relationship. The experience that she feels in those [instances] is one of floating, being outside of her body, transparent, ghostlike, that she has no substance.

GEDO: [Instances] when she feels you have invaded her?

PRESENTER: Yes. Her associations are [about] how she feels with her mother, how she feels that she [herself] doesn't exist and that that's what she's terrified of. So gradually what she's been doing has been increasingly to acknowledge the importance of the analysis to her, and also her fear.

GEHRIE: May I interrupt for a second? Because she's been able increasingly to acknowledge the significance of the analysis, and that [treatment] has not been experienced by her as an invasion, there's something crucial going on here [in addition to a] negative maternal transference reenactment. [And this has developed without requiring] confrontation on [the analyst's] part.

COMMENT: I'm not sure I agree. There's another way of looking at it. There's no evidence at the moment that [the presenter] is not describing an ego defect that is going to be unresolvable.

GEDO: She *is* describing an ego defect.

COMMENT: I am not certain it is resolvable. [They] are potentially on the way to a psychotic transference; [it seems] that the only way this lady can be maintained in analysis is to agree with her, because the rage . . .

PRESENTER: I'm not agreeing any more . . .

COMMENT: . . . the rage at some point is so great that it becomes a psychotic transference. She can acknowledge the importance [of analysis], she can acknowledge its meaning, she can possibly acknowledge the profound dependency, but can she give it up?

GEDO: But why are you so conditional in your statements? Has this not been a psychotic transference?

COMMENT: Well, I think it is.

GEDO: It has been from the first.

COMMENT: Yes.

GEDO: Okay, so it's not that there's a danger of driving this analysis into too deep a regression, because it started in as deep a regression as is conceivable within an analytic context. If it gets any deeper than that, it's the hospital, right?

COMMENT: What is the mark-off point of how poor reality testing has to be in the transference before it becomes psychotic? It seems [to me] any neurotic transference has some defects in reality testing, or else it wouldn't be neurotic.

GEDO: Oh, I don't agree with that! If you say that, you've never seen a *neurotic* patient in analysis. Of course, they are rare, exceedingly rare!

COMMENT: Other than ourselves, of course.

GEDO: All right. Other than ourselves, of course. Okay, let's talk about me. I have never had such a problem, even in the deepest regression that I experienced in my analysis.

COMMENT: Every transference is a distortion of the analyst, is it not?

GEDO: But a neurotic patient always knows he's distorting. Every [such] statement I ever made [in my analysis] was preceded with, "Oh, my God, I'm so embarrassed; what a crazy idea I've just had! This is preposterous! Why am I feeling this way?" That is what my analysis felt like, from the beginning to the end. As Little Hans says, "my craziness." Absolutely no interference with reality testing. This analysis is another ball game—a neurotic patient is not like that. [A neurotic] starts out being his customary realistic self, and he is gradually sucked in; it's a terribly frightening experience. You're terribly uneasy [as you are] being sucked into a regression, where you begin to feel that you're reacting in the most peculiar ways to [the situation]—but you know what the *reality* is. It's your affects that are inappropriate.

COMMENT: Yeah, and her patient can't distinguish.

COMMENT: To me, what [the presenter] did here is that somehow she was able to get the patient calmed down long enough for her to look at the fact that [the analyst] really was not such an awful person.

PRESENTER: Right.

COMMENT: I have no problem with that technique. The question I have is, does her ability to do this at this point represent an alteration? Is this different from the way things were before, and, if so, how? How were things before?

PRESENTER: Why is she able to listen to me now?

COMMENT: Well, you say that she's able to listen to you because she knows from experience that you're basically a good guy.

PRESENTER: Yeah. The history of our relationship—I keep reminding her of that.

COMMENT: But previously you weren't able to draw on that.

PRESENTER: Not at all.

GEDO: Well, let's go back to the point challenging the ultimate result of these interventions, because we haven't exhausted that. I think it's crucially important. Is this going to be an analysis, or is the patient's craziness going to be covered over with whipped cream? Well, of course, that remains to be seen. Incidentally, if the best we can do is to cover a craziness over with soothing syrup, that's all right too. I mean, that's not a disgraceful result.[i]

COMMENT: The American Psychoanalytic might not like it.

GEDO: That is not true. Let us not malign our colleagues from other cities. If you say that this was a patient with a psychotic core who developed a psychotic transference and you dealt with it in such and such a way and the patient could not overcome the defect in reality testing and you compromised on such and such a nonanalytic solution, they're not going to give you one iota of trouble. They'll give you trouble if you bullshit and say, "I analyzed the patient." They don't like that.

PRESENTER: [to Gedo] Well, I think that if *you* had been analyzing her, maybe that little corner of her that could observe [the situation might] have been tapped earlier than I was able to [reach it].

GEDO: [interrupting] You're not going far enough in making that distinction. Go back to Dr. Gehrie's point. If I were analyzing her, she would not be so panicked about being drawn into some kind of satellite role with a bad mother. Not merely because I am a man in my seventh decade, although that helps too, but because, even without knowing everything you have now told us about the patient, from the first—from the moment this woman walked into my office—I would unconsciously respond by conducting myself in a manner that is as unmaternal, and as subtly different from the ambience of her childhood, as possible. I would be working unconsciously, but double time, at staying out of the ditch. A ditch of sewage.

PRESENTER: Yes, her dream, washing her hair in the toilet.

GEDO: Right. Well, I would conduct myself in a manner that would make her feel she's in a palace. I saw somebody this morning before I came here who had a childhood in a slum, a real slum. You wouldn't know it; a rather distinguished professional person. And he brings in a dream of standing on the sidelines at a great ball [among] women in very fancy gowns. His mother appears across the ballroom in the kind of clothes that she always wore, very simple, not in fashion, not appropriate for the occasion. Then there is a figure like Marilyn Monroe with her skirts swirling in the famous-infamous "Seven Year Itch" scene, and he can't make out, is this some kind of hootchy-kootchy dancer, or is this the way people behave in the palace? Now this is after about a year of work in which neither the paternal nor the maternal transference has been in the forefront. I have been seen as the person he always longed for to pull him out of the ditch, so I have provided the ballroom. This is only the beginning; we've only been working together about a year. The dangers are there, on one hand, of my being too much, of my really turning into Marilyn Monroe and, [on the other hand, of] being too little, like the mother. The mother was the better parent; the father was crazy. One has a very, very narrow ledge to work on, and one has to establish some basis of working together within this very, very narrow framework.

In this case I haven't had to stretch anything. I have been able to provide the kind of external referent that he can hold on to, not like the parents' external referent, simply in terms of my office setting. I have a few pictures on the wall; I have a rug on the floor. It's the kind of setting that this man probably never saw until he was 40 years old.

I think that's what has happened [in the case we have been discussing] in this first period of treatment. [The analyst] established such a ledge, but not through the easy method of having a screen in her office depicting Freud and the Rat Man and the Wolf Man (as I have), but by bending herself out of shape in a way that for most of us would be impossible or terribly costly.

COMMENT: It seems that, in another way, you would be bending yourself out of shape by assiduously avoiding a maternal transference.[j]

GEDO: Oh, that's not hard.

COMMENT: Well, it may not be hard, but it seems like . . .

GEDO: I am bending myself out of shape when I am so carefully "neutral" that the maternal transference *can* develop. That's what we do all the time. That's called an analytic attitude, and that's what makes our hair fall out and puts the plaque in our coronary arteries. This work is crushing because you can never be yourself.

COMMENT: It's not the way you put it before. [You said] that you were assiduously avoiding acting in a maternal way, because you can be yourself and still have a nurturing side.

GEDO: It's still crushing, you see. I'm still not me, but I'm not the carefully neutral not-me that the textbooks claim we have to be. Of course, if you have to *think* about how to behave, that's hopeless, hopeless. You know, we don't have the kind of buttons which would permit us to program ourselves that way. It's an unconscious response to the person's need. But, of course, when I'm being *not-mother*, I am typecast. That's relatively easy.

COMMENT: At some point, though, don't you want to become mother to help this woman?

GEDO: Well, I could give you a conventional answer and say I don't want anything in particular. Presumably we don't want to tilt the table to promote one transference or another. I think that if things go relatively well, it's important that she reexperience her difficulties with her mother, but whether we liked it or not, that's what she *started* with. And now [one of you] rightly says that at times her rage at the mother was probably more volcanic than we have yet been told about. Whether you want to let the transference blossom to that degree, I don't know, because there are risks, obviously. If one wants to let it blossom as much as is possible, one sees how far one can go in frustrating such a patient. [The presenter is] telling us that she's beginning to do this very, very, very carefully. Just a little bit more at a time.

PRESENTER: I'd like to [talk about] what she finds so valuable about the analysis right now, despite the fact that she's terrified. The part she finds valuable is that she has always felt that the intensity, the volcanic nature, of her emotional response has destroyed every relationship she's had. It destroys her feeling about herself because it just devastates her self-esteem when she responds [in that way] emotionally. The pattern that she sees is that she will react with this intensity and that whatever she's reacting *to* is completely lost because all that people can see is her emotional intensity. So the analysis has come to be a place for her where she reacts, and [as a result] she doesn't destroy relationships on the outside, so that for the first time in her life she feels she can love a man. It was one of her initial complaints that she couldn't love a man because she feels pulled into this vortex of volcanic reactions.

GEDO: That's perfectly clear. She is very grateful for a transference cure, and, believe me, nothing is more helpful for the progress of an analysis than a quick transference cure. If all of the patient's troubles get focused in your office, fall on your knees and thank a merciful Lord for bringing that about, because then the treatment's going to go. If that doesn't happen, it's much more difficult. Much, much more difficult. I mean nothing succeeds like prosperity, and the outward gains, the adaptive gains of a transference cure, are invaluable, to enable the person to say, "All right! all that is all right now. Now I can look inward and work on my insides." That's progress. So, sure! She's going to be crazy with you, and she's going to be sane with as many people on the outside as that permits.

COMMENT: A couple of things about the story that you told and also this: the first has to do with the issue of the analyst as a new object rather than as a transference object, and your effort with such patients to carve out a position for yourself as someone new. It seems to me that with this case we're not talking about a transference; we're talking about something that's not a neurotic transference. It's a different phenomenon. In such cases the analyst needs to [define] himself as the new, different individual [to help] the patient to develop the reality testing, to understand that this is a different situation.

GEDO: That's correct. This is not to be confused with those theories of treatment which advocate a new relationship as an automatic curative agent.

COMMENT: Right.

GEDO: In my view, if you are not [regarded as] one of the equivocal transference figures of early childhood [transactions with whom] created the psychopathology, at least not at first, at least not most of the time, then you can provide the patient with something new. Not that you are the mother, not that you are the father, not that you are the people that the patient never had; but you're a trustworthy therapist, and the patient can accept what you have to offer, which is not parenting, but treatment.

COMMENT: Yeah, I like calling that the trustworthy therapist—a kind of collaborator that they've never had before.

GEDO: Exactly. Now, of course, they have always wanted such collaboration on some level, however dimly, however confusedly. The person I was speaking about with the ballroom dream sought such collaborators in books. That was the one contact during his childhood with the greater world—religion, particularly. So the books in my office are enormously important to this person; that's what we have in common. And he looks at the titles of the books, and it's very important that they should be the right titles. If they are the right titles, then I'm the kind of person, a living person, that he always wanted to make contact with as a child. So, yes, it's new, but it's not arbitrary.

COMMENT: You're describing something that's new, collaboration, something that's positive in terms of a working together to solve a problem in a positive relationship, which is eminently sensible. I tend to use the word "collaboration" a lot, so I certainly agree with it. The downside risk of collaborating is whether you are able to tolerate [great intensities of anger] to the point where it becomes dangerous. If the patient gets into a contest—"I want to see how you really tolerate my anger. I am such an angry person inside, such a rageful person inside, I'm not sure you can tolerate it, and I keep having to make *sure* that you can tolerate it, because otherwise the dependency is broken, or the involvement is broken"—that's where you get into a considerable downside risk.

GEDO: Well, that depends on how you deal with the rage. If you have become collaborators, the incidents of rage diminish.

COMMENT: That's true, if you have a successful collaboration.

GEDO: Yes. And dealing with the problem generally gets postponed to a later stage of the analysis, and by that time you may have had a chance to help the person to repair some of the defects. So there is better control over affective expression, more of a capacity to minimize enactment and maximize verbalization. There are a million downside risks if one undertakes to analyze people this impaired. There are *only* downside risks, no matter what you do.

I have no idea how I would respond to this lady, since we only get a second-hand account of it and there's no substitute for the living presence of the individual. Since I can't stretch myself in the direction that [the presenter] was able to take, I do tend to take the path that was mentioned: I tend to engage in shouting contests with such people, hopefully on purpose and under control, although the boundary is very thin. You may be under control when you start shouting, and by the end you may be in a profound sweat—a little bit of a John Rosen technique. Is John Rosen still a familiar name to you all? [He said,] "I can shout as loud as you and if it comes to being volcanic, I can hold my own with you." That kind of strategy. And sometimes that works, and sometimes the people I have tried it with have become panicked and left.[k]

COMMENT: Would you say that it works as long as there's this alliance you describe, as long as there's this collaboration?

COMMENT: Almost anything like that can work. It's when there isn't a true collaboration and when you're participating in combat that you have trouble and the thing just falls apart. Even the attempt to explain it is going to be experienced by such a person as an attack.

Gedo: Right. How many of you have been following Harold Searles over the years? Well, he collected his papers on so-called border-lines under hard covers recently. Because of the downside risks you are talking about, he is maximally careful when he begins; and because he has become convinced that you reach these downside risks with almost everyone, he is maximally careful with absolutely everyone. Now he stretches himself in a direction that I think would be intolerable for most of us—[he remains] essentially inactive for long [periods] of time, months and months, stretching into years. It becomes a very interesting circular process: his passivity is a powerful regression-inducing stimulus for the analysis. This very soft technique of his also makes it certain that if there is any chance of a psychotic transference occurring, it will occur. He says in the book that he now has analyzed 30-odd colleagues. I think he means psychoanalysts.

Comment: Does he mean "odd"?

Gedo: And the psychotic transference emerged in all of them. I think that if you can weather those storms the results are very important.

Comment: I wish you would say a little more about the issue of the existence of this core capacity for psychotic transference and its relationship to trauma and actual neurosis. I think that this is something that's not generally understood or much spoken about these days.

Gedo: Of course, I was hoping that having the cases presented would demonstrate the ubiquity of these problems. It may be that we've heard a selected sample of cases precisely because people hoped to hear my views on these problems, and that's why we haven't heard a single case where this wasn't a central issue. I certainly haven't supervised a single case since I became supervisor in this Institute where this didn't turn out to be a central issue. I won't say *the* central issue, [but one] of the central issues.

The case that [one seminar participant] and I are working on is just hair-raising in this regard. His patient defrauded the Institute of a rather large sum of money (and I mean *fraud!*) and when [the analyst] brought this to [the patient's] attention and insisted that it wasn't enough to talk about it, that something had to be *done*, not only was there rage—you see, rage is negotiable!—there was total uncooperativeness. It wasn't [merely] at the level of affect; it was a hard-line refusal to stay within the law: essentially a challenge— "Call the police. Sue me. Throw me out of treatment." We're still hanging in there.

COMMENT: Well, the patient is throwing himself out of treatment.

GEDO: No, he's coming. He hasn't missed a session.

COMMENT: But I mean, if he maintains, "I'm going to defraud my analyst and get better," how are you going to do that?

GEDO: How can he do that? The fact of the matter is that he is a virtuoso of doing that. He has done it for 30-odd years with great success. It turns out that the patient practically uses Freud's words in the paper on "The Exceptions." He's an exception. He is Richard III. He can murder the rightful kings and he can do anything, he can do *anything*. And for the very same reason [as Richard III]; because life "fucked him over." Are these different analytic patients than the analytic patients of 30, or 60, or 90 years ago? People keep rehashing old arguments. I'm on the side that says no, they're not different analytic patients. We use a different analytic technique, and the wheel of fortune comes up this way now.

GEHRIE: In the early 70s I did a long-term follow-up project on analyses. I did a series of analytic interviews with patients who had been analyzed in the period around 1950, so they were 25-year follow-ups. I was interested at the time in understanding what was left of the analysis, what the patients felt had been accomplished, and whether or not what the analyst said about the patient throughout the process and the termination would resemble what I found in the series of interviews. I did a series of six to eight free-associative interviews with these former patients, and I had the nearly complete analytic record for each one of those patients. In each of those cases, one of the outstanding features was that the analyst felt that at a certain point in the treatment things had to be limited or else the process was going to get to a level that was considered "too sticky, or too difficult, or not appropriate to the analysis," or something. There were active efforts to control the regression, or however they phrased this at that time. [Then] the analysis proceeded on a level which allowed the diagnosis to be maintained that these were neurotic patients (with one or another kind of easily recognizable disorder). [They] were successfully handled on that level, and, with one exception, the patients were grateful for the treatment, felt that it had really improved their lives. But, clearly, these other aspects had been avoided.

COMMENT: That there was a collusion between them to avoid certain more primitive parts . . .

COMMENT: It was not considered to be part of the analytic process.

GEDO: Before 1950, it probably was not collusion. You are forgetting how much progress has been made in this discipline in the last 40 years. In 1950 Wilhelm Reich's book was still relatively recent. When was *Character Analysis* translated into English? I think 1946. Most analysts absorbed the relevant conceptual notions through reading Anna Freud's *The Ego and the Mechanisms of Defense*. Well, when was that published in English?

COMMENT: I think it was [1946].

GEDO: Something like that. Well, the war came and those years we can essentially skip over. And so 1945 is not much different from 1930. So these cases Mark was looking at were analyzed with the conceptual schema that followed *The Ego and the Id* and *The Problem of Anxiety*, where the problem of character is absolutely not addressed.

COMMENT: What is not addressed?

GEDO: The problem of character. The idea that *character* could be analyzed was an achievement of the late 1920s. Until then, Freud said an analytic patient must be of "good" character, by which he meant not merely of good moral character, but without ego defects. The last 30 years have seen the [emergence of the kind of] collusion [someone referred to]. [By then] there was no justification for holding on to those antiquated notions from the time I went through training. Character [had to be] considered [by then]. When I was a candidate there was a course called "Special Problems" [dealing with these matters], and it took a while to acknowledge that they're not so special. But by that time it was in the public domain that character is destiny, and you can't do an analysis if you don't deal with character. Otherwise the barrel is bottomless. As fast as you take away the symptoms, new ones are going to be produced.

Steven Firestein's book on *Termination in Psychoanalysis* was a study rather similar to Mark Gehrie's, done with patients treated by the very best students that Firestein knew when they went through the Institute together, the supervised cases of his good friends, whom he respected—eight cases. [In those instances] the collusion [was present and was blameworthy]. All that was done after 1955, and the patients were sick, sick, sick, and a technique was imposed on them that was a sacred ritual, and if the patient didn't come out at the other end [in a satisfactory state], the patient was blamed. The outcomes are just shocking, shocking.

COMMENT: This reminds me of the paper that Kantrowitz wrote a couple of years ago on changes in reality testing during the course of psychoanalysis. In terms of psychological testing diagnoses, a fair number of the patients had major problems with reality testing and had diagnoses of borderline personality disorders. I don't remember how bad they were, the percentages, but they had all been diagnosed in the clinic as having neurotic character structures. In the course of the analysis there was an improvement in reality testing in the population as a whole, although reality testing wasn't addressed [explicitly]. It reminded me of *Beyond Interpretation* and your comment that these were issues that people have probably been addressing all along in the course of psychoanalyses.

GEDO: [As a young author I had] to be polite.

COMMENT: But [these problems] were getting addressed in some form or other; there were improvements in reality testing in the population and in all the patients except for a couple who had traumas in the year after the analysis. I mean, those issues— somehow they're dealt with.

GEDO: Well, "somehow they're dealt with" by good clinicians, but they don't talk about that aspect of their work in public because that seems so nonanalytic to them. That's the collusion, or the hypocrisy. They may do the right thing but hypocritically not confess that they have done it. Or they may refuse to do the right thing and just insist unrealistically that the only thing that counts is the neurotic aspect of the personality. Some years ago there were still people who justified this view on the basis of a developmental theory. I haven't heard that [idea] very much of late: that each developmental phase recapitulates all earlier phases, so that if you in fact dealt adequately with the oedipal crisis, by virtue of doing that you have automatically also dealt with all previous issues.

In my judgment that's an indefensible view of development. It's simply not true that every issue is recapitulated at each developmental phase. That overlooks the ubiquity and importance of what the Kleinians call splitting and the fact that large portions of the personality may be arrested and never participate in the Oedipus complex. Whatever you may think of Kohut's work in general and his report of the case of Mr. Z, I think this is the point he was trying to illustrate, that in the first analysis he had totally overlooked a large segment of the patient's personality that was split off.

COMMENT: One more question about this. A lot of what we're talking about today has to do with what you said you call "ego building measures" in psychotherapy. Since the free associative method is designed to move in the direction of associations which help to elicit unconscious mental contents, why is it necessary, or even useful, in dealing with a patient like this, who, the first time she lies down on the couch, Bang!—there's no issue of what's unconscious, [everything is] conscious and *right there* . . . Why is the method of choice psychoanalysis, rather than some sort of sitting up psychotherapy without use of the basic rule?

COMMENT: For that [kind of pathology] you don't need a person lying on the couch free associating; you need the frequency of visits.

GEDO: Well, of course, such a person may lie on the couch but [be unable to] free associate. You may instruct the patient to say whatever comes to mind, but that's not the way it's going to go. Or such a patient may sit up or start walking about the room, or whatever. I don't think there are too many people anymore who think that lying on the couch or the capacity to put everything into words are crucial issues, although people still prefer to operate in that framework, or to hold that up to a patient as the ideal framework, "If we can't use it today, maybe tomorrow." I don't know whether that answers your concern?

COMMENT: [I am] curious [to know] why in some instances like that you wouldn't advocate initial psychotherapy and then struggling with conversion to analysis . . .

GEDO: You've already answered your own question by using the word "struggle." It's much easier [this way]; then, of course, it comes down to the definition of analysis versus psychotherapy. I've talked about these matters hither and yon for many years. Nobody quarrels with what I recommend for these patients; people want to quarrel about what it's called. I don't have an objection to inventing a name for this different from the name for the treatment of neurotic patients through the free-association method. But I think it's infinitely more difficult than doing psychotherapy. It's also infinitely more difficult than doing psychoanalysis with a neurotic patient. When Roy Schafer came here about six or seven years ago, he presented a treatment of this kind and was very apologetic. He said, "I hesitate to call this a psychoanalysis." I told him he ought to call it "superanalysis."

I am advocating complexity and nonreduction, not underestimating the difficulties and taking into account how much our own personal contribution tips the balance—the issue that Dr. Gehrie brought up. On that account, some people want to say that [mine] is not a psychoanalytic method; I can only throw up my hands and laugh at them. I liked much better [what one reviewer wrote about my proposals]. He said that psychoanalysis has reached the point where every serious contributor has become a school of one.

Well, shall we hear about the next period? I'm curious about where this case went from there.

PRESENTER: When she talked about the confusion and the rages that she felt, in the context of talking about her father and the childhood sexual abuse, [I thought] she either had to protect the image of her father for herself as being a protector, not acknowledging the ways in which he had failed her, or she had slipped into a state in which she felt really disconnected. That's what I was seeing periodically, the way in which she would feel disconnected from her body, numb, and depersonalized, [with a] sense of "sliding through time." At least [at certain] moments she began to become really anxious about her ability to deal with reality issues in her life. In one of these instances, she maintained the idea that her father was protecting her by teaching her to be without emotion; she saw it as a conscious choice on her father's part, to do well by her and teach her this lesson of life. When she began to think that he wasn't in control of this and that this was some way which reflected his limitation, she became really panicky with me.

GEDO: It's fascinating.

PRESENTER: And then briefly she developed what I interpreted as a pregnancy fantasy. The way I understood it, it reflected what had gone on in her childhood, a sort of enactment [in reaction to] the loss of the image of her father as an idealized object. [In this context] she got involved with her brother; the sexual play was a way of trying to restore "the self." And she did it again with the pregnancy fantasy, the fantasy in the course of the analysis. The alternative is to get involved in a maternal relationship where she feels so . . .

GEDO: It's a pseudocyesis you're talking about?

PRESENTER: Yeah, well, yeah.

GEDO: She continued to fantasy that she was pregnant over some weeks?

PRESENTER: No, no, no, it was very brief, only a matter of days.

GEDO: Then she had no symptoms of pseudocyesis?

PRESENTER: No, I don't think it was that, no. She was beginning to wonder if she might be pregnant; she thought she might be pregnant. She does have a symptom, though. It came at the beginning of the analysis and occurred two times during the course of the analysis. It's always [in the context of] breaking up with a man, either her divorce or breaking up with men. [The symptom is] vaginal bleeding, not when it is expected in the menstrual cycle. Her gynecologist has told her that it was stress related, plus she gets a urinary tract infection at those times.

GEDO: Well, don't go so fast. You're not adding material that needs to change our view of her case, but the details are fascinating and I think can be used to illustrate [some ideas already discussed] about the structure of the case. What we are hearing is that her usual adaptation is at the level of a *gross* illusion, a gross illusion. Not quite at the level of a neurotic conflict, but it's not defective reality testing alone; although it helps to have defective reality testing, otherwise how can you live with such an illusion? She has a need for the illusion as a defense. And if you puncture the illusion, instead of reversing her regression and getting the neurotic content, which is [what] the theory of technique of 30 years ago would have predicted, instead of that you get a catastrophic *regression*.

In terms of the hierarchical model that Goldberg and I drew up, at her best she's in mode III, and if you try to nudge her to progress, instead of that she collapses into mode II—into at least the edge of mode II. Of course, she then gets up off the couch vigorously and goes to observe abused children in a competent way, right? Or a reasonably competent way. So these regressions are temporary. We are not talking about diagnosis; it would be utterly preposterous to diagnose her as "borderline" because she becomes depersonalized when you undermine her necessary adaptation by saying, "Your father was lousy." [He was] lousy in every respect but one, and that is that his very presence and whatever he tried to teach her, however ludicrous that seems to us, kept her away from the mother, right? I mean, that's what she's telling us.

PRESENTER: She had three dreams after that. [In the first] she was having a dinner, it was like a Thanksgiving dinner, but with her *beautiful* grandmother, the grandmother she had beautified. She was very beautiful. Her hair was loose and flowing, and she was terribly graceful—the actual disfigurement this grandmother has was completely removed. It was a "wonderful dream." [In the next] dream, someone's breasts had been removed, someone who was very vague. The third dream was [about] a dark-haired woman teaching herself things. She was in a hospital and having a baby and there was to be some sort of a trial of surgery; this woman was very stern. When the patient attempted to try out what she had learned from the woman, the woman disappeared. The baby was delivered and wrapped in opaque white plastic. Suddenly nurses appeared with cleaning carts and with cheery manner said, "Oh-oh, baby's dead!" The cord was wrapped around the baby's neck, and the patient in the dream thinks, "Well, if the cord is ripped, I'm supposed to die too." I saw all of it as her progressive fears of the involvement with the mother and being left without a lifeline.

GEDO: Well, one can jump to conclusions about manifest content, but it certainly sounds like, on one level, she sees you as the collaborator from whom she can learn something. I assume the dark-haired woman refers to you.

PRESENTER: That's right. I think last time I stopped at the cockroach dream, and I don't know that this could be terribly new material, but what started happening in the analysis was that she started going to sleep and, you know, for months she would . . .

GEDO: Slept on the couch.

PRESENTER: And sometimes it would be for a long time, sometimes as long as 20 minutes. I consider that a very long time. Sometimes it was brief, but it was . . .

GEDO: You need an earthquake machine.

PRESENTER: I mean, I was always trying to figure out whether I should wake her up or let her sleep, or what I was supposed to do. I more or less decided that she was so terrified that her sleeping was her [only recourse]—at least she was *there*. She no longer sleeps, once again, she no longer sleeps.

COMMENT: Afterwards, what was her understanding of the meaning of the sleeping?

PRESENTER: Well, first she tried to tell me that it was only because she was so fatigued in her life and she was working nights. And later she was able to say that she was really frightened, just very frightened.

GEDO: It was not a comfortable sleep. Sometimes late in an analysis one can see these phenomena when words become meaningless because you have reached a preverbal level and you're very comfortable with each other. That's wonderful, wonderful, when in the sessions of sweet silence "one summons up remembrance of things past," and so forth. But this is very different.

PRESENTER: I think once or twice she actually did say that she'd had a wonderful dream in the course of being asleep. I remember one dream of these cute little balls, balls bouncing around her. I don't know if you can call this a real dream or what, but anyway, this was pleasant for her.

GEDO: So it's a little bit like the paratroopers' stunt, to sleep when they were dropped behind the German lines. Quite similar to the phenomenon I tried to describe in a case I presented in my 1988 book: a man with neurasthenia. His fingers go blue, and so on, in a massive withdrawal reaction.

COMMENT: I have a patient in analysis now who does that, and as we've worked with it for quite a long period of time, it has become clear that he developed the capacity as a child to appear to be there with his mother, give the appearance of presence in a *pro forma* way, and yet underneath no one was home. He was asleep, out of it, a million miles away, dreaming about something. And that took a long time to reconstruct. When that happens [on the couch], his response to me on awakening will be the same words that he remembers he used to say to his mother, "Oh, I'm here."

GEDO: It's very interesting that the dreams, the pleasant dreams, are so entirely abstract. No cast of characters . . .

COMMENT: This same patient has dreams, if you want to call them that, just like that. You know, I'll ask him what he was thinking of while he was asleep. "I was thinking of this perfectly smooth egg. Smooth on the outside, against a black background."

GEDO: A claustrum.

COMMENT: Yeah.

GEDO: In which one can be safe and "the world is not too much with us."

COMMENT: Right.

PRESENTER: I'll now describe the other side of what happens too. When she's feeling better with me and she's feeling the safety that analysis provides her, she [thinks] she could fall in love with somebody for the first time. She's been involved with a man. [When] she resolved some difficult circumstances concerning her divorce, she spent the night with this man and then came in to the session in a very embarrassed and hesitant way [and told me that] she'd had the most wonderful orgasm that she'd ever had in her entire life. The rest of the session was not particularly remarkable, but the next day when she came in she was just bent out of shape once again. Of course, her assumption was that all I was interested in was orgasm and that I was not thrilled with her and that the analysis was over since we'd reached this understanding . . .

COMMENT: Reached genitality.

PRESENTER: Yes. And she was sure that I would be critical or disapproving of her for having had this wonderful experience. She does experience this terrific confusion when it comes to expressing her own feelings and sexuality, and that relates to the childhood incidents in some way. She gets very sure that she is a very bad person for having any kind of sexual feelings and that I will see her that way. Every time she feels comfortable in the analysis, this material starts coming out again about sexual feelings. Some of that is homosexual feelings she has begun to have about me—not me [explicitly] but [dreaming that] two women are kind of exploring each other in a real physical, sexual way; like two animals writhing on the floor with each other. That's one component of the sexual. The other one is heterosexual, but again it's abuse; she ends up being abused and [feeling that she was] too sexual in some ways. Does that make any sense to you?

GEDO: Well, on a speculative level one could make sense of it, but I don't know that that would be particularly useful. It'll take you years to disentangle all that. I mean, [one of you said] the patient thinks that she has reached the genital level—probably. And if she does think that, she's almost certainly mistaken. You can almost count on it, that what is so profoundly gratifying in these sexual encounters is some [type of] perverse control. Because of the level of regression I would predict that it's at the level of a fetish, which is why it *seems* heterosexual. Of course, you mustn't take that as a statement of eternal verities, but it would be very surprising if this weren't something very regressed and therefore very shameful.

PRESENTER: Right, okay, right. Yeah, and she feels very humiliated much of the time.

GEDO: [Heterosexuality represents a] flight into health.

PRESENTER: Well, at least to another level, a slightly higher level.

COMMENT: Something with which to organize.

PRESENTER: Yeah, right. Whatever this maternal stuff is which became so overwhelming to her that . . .

GEDO: At the level of secondary revision in a dream, an acceptable surface narrative is constructed out of components that come from very deep levels of regression. You don't necessarily have to spin this out, unless somebody wants to raise some other question about it. Shall we stop?

Commentary (Gehrie)

The analyst, a female candidate for whom this patient was the third supervised case, began with a reference to her own experience in child-rearing, the dynamics of managing her own two-and-a-half-year-old. Describing the struggle that arose with her child, the analyst ended the vignette by noting, "Once I addressed the proper level of organization, things went quite smoothly with him." This vignette sets the stage for a central question of technique that emerges in this case.

The analyst described the patient's relationship with her father, a relationship characterized by an oscillation between controlled coolness on one hand and "wild" emotionality on the other. The patient related her current anxiety to the history of exchanges with her father, in which she felt that he had demanded that she too develop the capacity to manage emotionality through "air-tight arguments." In addition, the patient felt that the father had "withheld himself from her"; in particular, she cited the circumstances of his death "while on vacation with mother" as an example of "the way in which she felt distanced from him." Attributing his withdrawal to her emerging sexuality, the patient noted that "his focus was always on a career and independence, and that how she looked was not important." The patient also described herself as feeling "devastated" by his death.

This history seems directly related to the difficulties the patient was having with her husband, with whom she also experienced "extended unavailability" evoked by his job situation.

"The business required his working at night and then working in the daytime to do paper work. So he was really both 'not there' and exhausted when he was at home. After her father died, she felt she couldn't tolerate this. She had had a brief affair when she was in journalism school." Her application for treatment at the Institute Clinic was preceded by her distress at nearly starting another affair.

The patient was the second of five children. Her parents moved to Peru when she was seven years old as part of their involvement with a Catholic missionary organization. They lived there until she was 13. The father and her older brother had a strong but hostile relationship, to which the patient attributed one of her father's heart attacks as well as the brother's subsequent difficulties. It was also with this older brother that the patient was exposed to early sexual involvement: she masturbated him from the time she was six until she was thirteen, after which "she has always had a man around to protect her." She said that, out of "guilt," she never told her parents about this.

We know little at this point about the patient's mother, other than that the patient felt that "mother had always stood between her and her father . . . that mother had hogged the relationship with father to herself." The mother is a social worker who works with some psychiatrists.

At the outset of the analysis, the patient experienced herself as fearful of her own overwhelming intensity. The analyst characterized the patient as "extraordinarily provocative everywhere she went . . . provoking [men] into rages with her," and then being "cool, calm and rational"—a clear allusion to her identification with her father and to how she felt he had managed her. The analyst, appearing to agree with the patient's assessment of herself as too intense, characterizes the patient's behavior in the laundry-room incident as "stimulating the other person to punch her." The patient is said to be upset that "the police could only react to her emotions, rather than to the way in which she had been injured." In this vein, the first dream of the analysis evokes from the patient associations of terror and feelings that there was "a faceless, nonparticipatory, judgmental person in the dream, which she didn't have much trouble associating to the analysis." It is at this point in the seminar that Gedo raises the question of undertaking an analysis with such a patient; yet he approves trying it out if there does not appear to be a risk of overt psychosis. The analyst argues that she saw no such risk, but only "a problem with men." Gedo replies that beyond this "classical reason" for seeking help, this patient "has trouble with everybody."

As the analyst begins to describe the unfolding process of the analysis, there soon emerges a critical point: that when the patient reported her experiences of "victimization" outside the analysis, she would insist that the analyst confirm that, indeed, her view of the experience was [objectively] true, that "there was nothing that she [the patient] had done which could have provoked this [hostile, retaliatory] response"—this despite the fact that the analyst saw the genesis of these incidents in the patient's unrealistic insistence that others "know what she was feeling." The analyst's understanding of this dynamic at that moment in the treatment is that the patient was "terrified" of "showing how she was feeling" and needed others to "anticipate" it. In other words, the analyst's view at this point was summarized by Gedo's comment that "she demanded that you validate her paranoia." The analyst reports struggling with this aspect of the interaction, at first by trying to make "neutral" comments (which would not be accepted by the patient) and finding herself "feeling more and more uncomfortable, as if I were going to have to give up my version of reality . . . I really resisted it."

The analyst felt pressured to accept the patient's sense of her own experience "that she [the patient] was completely right and an innocent victim, and abused." For the analyst, this was tantamount to participating in the patient's "paranoia"—an intolerable position. This predicament is not untypical of the experience of analysts who accept into treatment patients with narcissistic disorders who are already regressed, and whose lives are characterized by ongoing traumatic repetitions.[1] In this case, the circumstances that in childhood led to trauma were being reenacted in the analysis, and the analyst was struggling to establish a perspective on the process that would not disturb her own equilibrium. This analyst's solution was a product of her own personal flexibility, as well as of her understanding of the nature of the patient's need: that what was being enacted was the struggle for control over a sense of reality; that the patient—like a developing child—needed an acknowledgment of the reality of her own inner experience and not (at this moment) an externally imposed judgment about it. As the analyst remarks, "That's why I thought about my two-and-a-half-year-old son. I think that in some way she needed me to acknowledge the authenticity of what she was feeling, my being able to give up what I believed *for* her at that moment became extremely important. When I finally was able to do it, she had a wonderful dream which had to do with 'victim-witness' awards. This was a dream that was critical of me. Victim-witness awards were given out only to men, and the fact was that she needed *me* to witness her victimization. When I could do it, it was amazing! When I learned that I could actually acknowledge that she had been abused and stifle the need to say, 'You brought it on yourself,' when I could do that, all of a sudden she would look at all the ways in which she brought it on herself. She was very responsive to it."

Gedo agrees that among this patient's difficulties is an early identification with certain attitudes of her mother and that "she needs to hear that she's not omnipotent. . . . it seemed like the technique that worked for you [the analyst, to interfere with this identification] was to suspend your reality testing and enter into her delusional system." A seminar member asks, "Why is that suspending her reality testing? It seems to me that this is an essential aspect of reality that she is picking up . . . it's the clinical reality . . . the psychic reality." These views frame the debate that is at the heart of choice of technique in this case.

The assessment of reality is a fundamental orientation that broadly influences the understanding of both the nature of the pathology and the approach to treatment. Gedo raises a critical point: that the analyst's approach required more than simply treating this patient as if the patient were like a child; that the structure of this patient's grasp of reality was not homologous to that of a child. There is, however, the danger that, as with a child, a technical insistence on the patient's grasp of reality as faulty—"paranoid"—may have the effect of forcing the patient constantly to repeat the traumatic enactment that characterized her early pathogenic relationship with mother.[m]

The analyst stresses that in order to gain access to the operative dimension with this patient, she [the analyst] "had to shift modes of functioning because she's operating as a child and I was operating as an adult." Gedo, however, does not agree that the analyst's intervention was appropriate to a child's level of organization; he points out that "had she been your child and was 31 months instead of 31 years of age, that's not how you would have done it. You would start with how to do it better." Gedo's approach reflects his view that the adult's distorted reality, which must in essence be cleared away, is best replaced through a "technology of instruction" (see Gedo, 1988) that supplies critical missing skills. "One would enter into a psychotherapy [with such a patient] in which one teaches her how to do it better . . . with a person like this that's [also] how one starts an analysis."

The underlying technical debate in this case—and in many such instances—focuses on three broad issues. First is the question of the nature of the underlying pathology (deficit)—that is, whether or not the patient's psychic reality is so profoundly enmeshed with early negative identifications as to make nearly impossible access by empathic means. This diagnosis views the interactive dimension with the analyst as a kind of sealed enactment in which every angle of access to early experience is blocked by the overwhelmingness of the repetition at every juncture.

The approach dictated by such an assessment is the second major point: under these sorts of conditions—where the organization of the early deficit is understood as presymbolic (and possibly preverbal) in nature and where the chronic repetition in the treatment is a product of an archaic transference state—Gedo's prescription is to address this underlying level with tools that the conditions seem to require. If, on the other hand, the pathology in question is regressive from failures in a later phase or from a more integrated position, then the issue of the analyst's (empathic) failures is of necessity closer to the center of the stage. Given Gedo's sense of this particular patient's underlying disturbance, he is concerned about a folie à deux resulting from the analyst's attempt to engage her through an empathic approach. He remarks, "I would prefer to battle it out . . . and try to find out why she's [enacting] this whole provocative business now with me as the analyst, [so that it gets] in the way of whatever it is that's really bothering her underneath."[n]

The analyst, by contrast, has become convinced that this patient is *unable* to perceive the underlying nature of the trauma as a consequence of the analyst's attempt to uphold her own sense of reality. The analyst feels that she must address what amounts to the patient's experience in order that the patient may reorganize around a selfobject transference that might, at some later point, make it possible for her to "see" the nature of her own "distortion"; an experiential foundation must be constructed as the basis for the evolution of cognitive capacity (and improvement in reality testing). The analyst is concerned that to do otherwise risks repeating the trauma in the negative mother transference, but Gedo replies that he would adjust the nature of his comments to take that into account. In other words, Gedo remains confident that some aspect of the patient's capacity to process reality remains available to the properly framed call for reflection. The analyst seems less convinced of this and senses the necessity of accepting the experience of the patient as primary as a step toward establishing an (internal) environment that might promote the ability to reflect (see Gehrie, in press).[o]

Gedo introduces the third major point that follows from these considerations: that "it depends on who *you* are, which of the manifold approaches to such a technical problem is going to be effective." He describes the type of interactions he proposes as "based on the assumption that she [the patient] is beyond the power of [explanations alone]." Clearly, he means that these kinds of interventions are meant to provide an environment to which the patient can meaningfully relate. Such an orientation might also describe the reasoning behind the interventions actually made by the analyst in this case, although from a different functional/dynamic perspective. Both Gedo and the presenting analyst agree, tacitly, that the analyst must *do* something for this patient, who appears unable to take certain essential developmental steps on her own behalf. Gedo stresses this point:

"Words are superfluous a lot of the time, and certainly they are never [sufficient] when people are stuck in that mode. You have to *do* something for the person, and the crux of the matter is not *what* you do, whether you fight or you say, 'I'm with you.' The point is to get it across that you accept the responsibility of being of some concrete assistance, because [left to herself] the person can't do it. Left to her own devices, she dangles in the wind."

This is the essential theoretical and technical point that is at issue in this case, regardless of the fact that three entirely different means of engagement are described. There is fundamental agreement that the patient's failure to process reality adequately must be approached in the analytic environment and that the choice of technique will depend largely on the personality organization of the analyst. This variable is decisive in determining which form of approach is most comfortably (and therefore most effectively) taken. This functional availability of the analyst as an integral part of the patient's psychic repertory becomes the critical curative agent in the early phase of the analysis of a patient with disturbances in the processing of reality or similar deficits in psychological skills.

The choice of technique, however, must also be an accurate reflection of the analyst's understanding of the nature of the pathology. As Gedo (1988) has noted, "it is not always easy to make a secure distinction between iatrogenic regression in the service of the therapeutic task and those that betoken a collapse of essential compensatory structures" (p. 46). The patient must be prepared to accept the "confrontation" that the analyst's personality may make inevitable. Gedo notes, in reference to the patient's "provocations," that "you can make a game out of throwing crockery because . . . even she has made something of a game out of fighting. She has that capacity, and you can engage in something of a confrontation with her that's infinitely more benign than any of the confrontations she has ever had."

Once this baseline of emotional contact has been established—which requires an empathic grasp of the patient's available modes of relatedness—then the repertory of possibilities is vastly expanded and offers the patient the missing critical element: something (experientially) new and processable such that a bridge between inner and outer experience may be established and then used in the service of analysis.

On the issue of "artistry" in this mode of intervention, Gedo remarks that the appropriate form of engagement with the patient is more likely to emerge when the analyst feels "free . . . of theoretical constraints, provided that you know that the task is to establish a bond with this person on some mutually acceptable level. If it's throwing crockery, it's throwing crockery, provided you don't break the cups."

There is, of course, likely to be enormous variation in the ability and willingness of analysts to establish such a "bond." Gedo's central emphasis, however, is that the assistance that is offered be provided at the appropriate level. The danger he cites is of mistaking the level of pathology (usually assuming a developmentally more advanced level for one that is more archaic) and offering a short-cut that, in the long run, may not open access to the critical issues. For the case presented here, Gedo stresses that it must somehow be communicated to this patient that "she is trapped in asking the wrong question" and that this communication can be accomplished only when some distance is created from the otherwise overwhelming negative mother transference. The analyst in this case accomplished this by "accepting" the patient's experience as a means toward this end; Gedo's approach would have been more reliant on the immediate reality-processing capacity of the patient and more directed toward the change of venue that he felt was required. With either approach, once the transition is effected, "you enter a new universe of discourse. All of a sudden words are enough."

The actual "artistic" management of the transition to a new level of functioning is "very complicated. . . . this is the true paradox of an internal problem: what is tolerable is as thin as a razor's edge." There is agreement in the seminar that at the outset "there is no way of interpreting" these issues to such a patient as the one presented here; "she will not accept an interpretation." Gedo characterizes this difficulty as rooted in the patient's "paranoia . . . an identification with the parents' ways." For the child, however, this identification was almost certainly an unavoidable mode of survival, given the features of the early environment; to describe it as "paranoid" is to make a judgment about the adult's inability to process reality. Such a view must not be allowed to interfere with the analyst's ability to explore as broad a set of possibilities for interventions as possible. Gedo stresses that "the whole illness is a reversal; it's an attempt to master massive traumatization, by all sorts of people in all sorts of ways, [but by means of] turning the passive into active. [The analyst] accepted the role of the victim because she is a certain type of analyst."

It does not necessarily follow that for the analyst compliantly to enter into the patient's experience would be tantamount to a folie à deux. The analyst need not become the victim simply because the patient's experience is accepted as (psychic) reality as part of technique. This posture does carry risks of "counteridentification," but there are also risks involved in maintaining too great a distance from such phenomena, such as the possibility of forcing compliance with an externally imposed system of assessments and inadvertently re-creating the pathogenic environment. Gedo acknowledges that for the case presented here, "chances are, left to my own devices and ignorant of everything you [the presenter] have told us, just starting out, I would drive this patient out of treatment by being much too hard-line."

The analyst in this case was able to take the risk that she did in part by finding an underlying appeal: "I feel that I really admired her, through all of this. . . . I admire how she's dealt with her problems." In addition, the analyst was also able to tolerate the patient's need for illusion because she recognized its functional significance for herself personally as the provider of a context for development.

The analyst goes on to describe the developing process in the analysis and emphasizes her slowly emerging ability to understand the dynamics in the intensifying transference. The patient was extremely worried about the powerful, destructive potential for her anger and that "in her mind, if she has any responsibility [for her own difficulties] at all, she is destroying the world." This anxiety was so great as to interfere significantly with her ability to "tolerate hearing about her contributions to her difficulties" and was further reflected in violent, murderous dreams.

In the face of all this, however, the analyst is able to maintain her view that the patient's "desire to understand herself, even the most negative things . . . really motivates her." The analyst also feels able to "look past the provocations" and is not as put off by the malignant aspects of the dream material (or by the patient's latent intensity, hostility, and fragility), as are the members of the seminar because, as was noted near the end of the first session, "You've compared her to your two-and-a-half-year-old son . . . you're used to working with [this kind of thing], and you don't see it in the same way other people do."

Gedo begins the second session by reviewing three modes of approach to a case such as this one. The first type requires that the patient's "paranoid distortions" be directly confronted in order to avoid the "reversal" described in the previous meeting, in which the analyst becomes "forced into the position of [the patient's] helpless childhood self." In the second type of approach, employed by the presenting analyst, the analyst goes along with the patient's experience of her own reality but runs the risk of becoming embroiled in the enactment in which the patient's "crazy world" may come to dominate the analysis. Gedo underscores the point that "most of us cannot do that without getting unconsciously flooded with fury against the patient." In a third approach, Gedo suggests "stepping outside the frame of enactment." If the patient, especially at the outset, is unable to observe the enactment even with the analyst's help, then "an enactment of your own is what is required, in which everything you say and do refuses to stand still for this absurd view of life . . ." This approach appears to require that the patient be able to engage the analyst in this new territory; to create a new stage or forum for the engagement of the transference that would simultaneously give credence to the patient's experience while also not fully permitting it to dominate the interaction:

> If I were analyzing her . . . from the first, from the moment this woman walked into my office, I would unconsciously respond by conducting myself in a manner that is as unmaternal . . . as possible. I would be working

unconsciously, but double time, at staying out of the ditch. . . . I would conduct myself in a manner that would make her feel she's in a palace.

If it is to succeed, the last approach probably should also contain within it elements of the second. While Gedo stresses that it is important to "stay out of the ditch," the purpose of the new enactment seems to be to provide a platform from which the patient can participate—just as does the second approach, the one utilized by the analyst in this case. To some extent the patient's subjective reality must be involved in this new construction and eventually form the basis of progressive analytic work. The debate seems to rest more on an issue of relative emphasis: although the analyst in this case was characterologically able to immerse herself in the patient's reality (certainly an "enactment" in itself) without fear of losing herself or of becoming "flooded with rage," it is likely that this might not always be the case. Alternative means of engagement that permit changes in the relative weighting of the different experiential components are essential to such a technique. In this spirit, Gedo comments on the presenting analyst's technique: "Oh, if it works, how could it be wrong? Since it worked, it was right. You know, we should give [the presenter] the Congressional Medal of Honor, but we shouldn't require everyone in our army to expose himself to such fire."

One of the most compelling aspects of the presenting analyst's technique in this case was its evolution. As she noted, "it hasn't been a linear process: it's been up and down . . . and it hasn't stopped altogether . . . I've been fairly flexible for her." In other words, the analyst kept making adjustments to her technique, giving the patient gradually increasing contact to other realities, so that eventually the transference enactment could begin to be interpreted. It is a tricky and delicate process, however, requiring constant attentiveness to her own as well as to the patient's self-experience, and containing the omnipresent potential for the analyst or the patient to feel overwhelmed in the negative mother transference:

> I was able to keep the focus on the fact that I wasn't a bad person, and we focused on her fear, what she was afraid of.
>
> What came out of it is that she's terribly afraid of being obligated to me. She's been afraid to acknowledge [that] I've done anything for her, because when she feels obligated to me she begins to feel sucked into some kind of relationship in which she feels that I will restructure her according to my own needs. Only by denying the reality of what I've done for her can she maintain herself as separate and not feel as if she's pulled into such a relationship. The experience that she feels in those instances is one of floating, being outside of her body, transparent, ghostlike, that she has no substance. . . . Her associations are [about] how she feels with her mother. . . . and that's what she's terrified of. So gradually what she's been doing

has been increasingly to acknowledge the importance of the analysis to her, and also her fear.

Gedo acknowledges that when a patient such as this, in contrast to neurotic patients, begins an analysis, the regression "is [already] as deep as is conceivable within an analytic context." This is why alteration of technique becomes an overriding issue and why an analysis becomes "another ball game" under such conditions. In addition, the precise point at which an analysis is deemed to be possible (or impossible) is intimately connected to the analyst's experience of the patient's regression; this accounts for the magnitude of the role of the analyst's personality in the process. If indeed there is to be an analytic outcome from such an effort, and not "craziness covered over with whipped cream," then not only must theory and diagnostic considerations take such conditions into account, but technique must be adjusted for the nature of the analyst's characterological and transference responses. For Gedo, the form of technique for this patient might have been different.

> One way I proposed [for stepping out of the enactment with this patient] is to say, 'Look at the mistake you are making in viewing life in these terms. . . . Touchdown! Touchdown! Time out! Time out! Let's celebrate that we have scored a touchdown. We understand something crucially important about you, and that is that you see life in these narrow terms. This can only mean that you were raised in a crazy way, that you need an after-education to get out of the framework of that crazy world.

This approach amounts to as much of a corrective emotional experience (in the broad sense) as does the one utilized by the presenting analyst. Both attempt to "establish some basis of working together." Gedo goes on to elaborate on the experience of the analyst as central to choice of technique; he stresses that technique is not likely to succeed unless it takes into account certain essential aspects of the analyst's character and capacities. For Gedo, the presenting analyst's technique in this case would feel "impossible or terribly costly. . . . I am bending myself out of shape when I am so carefully 'neutral' that the maternal transference *can* develop. That's what we do all the time. That's called an analytic attitude, and that's what makes our hair fall out and puts the plaque in our coronary arteries. This work is crushing because you can never be yourself."

Finally, there is a discussion of the role of transference in the evolution of the analytic process. Gedo remarks that as the locus of the patient's difficulties becomes focused on the analytic relationship, "fall on your knees and thank a merciful Lord for bringing that about, because then the treatment's going to go. If that doesn't happen, it's much more difficult." This view is not, he stresses, "to be confused with those theories of treatment which advocate a new relationship as an automatic curative agent," but rather that the "something new" to be provided is in the context of the reality of psychological treatment, and not the replacement of failed early parenting. Here "transference cure" may be seen as a step in the evolution of an analysis, and not as an endpoint. This perspective is founded on the idea that a patient, by whatever means are available, must come to grasp the nature of the transference longings and that "the adaptive gains of a transference cure are invaluable, to enable the person to say, 'all right, all that is all right now. Now I can look inward and work on my insides.' " Gedo sees the viability of an analysis under these conditions as in large part reflective of a successful "collaboration" in which critical aspects of early developmental difficulties are "postponed to later stages of the analysis," when there are improved opportunities for the management of affects as well as for verbal expression.

Final Remarks (Gedo)

a. Pathognomonic signs of regression to archaic mentation

The patient was demanding affirmation of a paranoid position (to echo Melanie Klein, 1935), one in which the experience of having become a victim is divorced from her own responsibility for inviting the treatment she objects to. Insofar as this attitude is not amenable to alteration by considering the social context of the transaction as a whole, the person in question has constructed a delusion—in other words, in an analytic setting, a psychotic transference has supervened. It is entirely possible for such a paranoid state to be confined to the analytic sessions, but in the case under discussion it was at this juncture not at all certain that this was so. The thinly veiled murderous wishes revealed in the traumatic initial dream of the analysis seem to have been usually dealt with through projection in her recurrent dream of being a persecuted Anne Frank. The laundry room incident also suggests a loss of rational control over the paranoid ideation. In the seminar, I used the psychiatric designation "paranoia" to dramatize the fact that this attempt at analysis started with a catastrophic regression into a mode of functioning that cannot always be handled by verbal means alone.

b. The establishment of an analytic alliance

The analyst's effort to equate the patient's insistence on pulling her into a delusional system with a normally developing two-and-a-half-year-old's need to be in autonomous control of his behavior was surely inexact; the actual similarity consisted in her own manner of overcoming both dilemmas, that is, by yielding control to the other person. In the analysis, this surrender (which the analyst did not experience as if she had in turn been victimized) was followed by an about-face on the part of the patient: she abruptly shifted from a paranoid position to a realistic, nondelusional one. This change demonstrated that the actual problem did not consist of a deficit in testing reality (as Hamlet put it, when the wind was southerly, she knew a hawk from a handsaw!)—rather, the patient was engaged in bullying the analyst into accepting her views, however arbitrary these were. Thus, the analyst's conjecture that her patient needed acknowledgment of the authenticity of her feelings was certainly in error: the analysand knew perfectly well that the feelings in question were, in fact, *inauthentic.*

Nonetheless, the analyst's compliance with the patient's irrational demand succeeded in reversing the regression into a delusional state; as Gehrie implies in his Commentary, the shift from a dispute over control of the transaction into a mode of emotional harmony (by actually sacrificing the assertion that the analyst had been right all along) established a bond that made analytic work possible. Greenson (1965) and Zetzel (1965) called such a state an "alliance"; Winnicott (1954) and Modell (1976) wrote about it as a "holding environment"; Gehrie, emulating Kohut (1977) calls it a "selfobject transference." The potential pitfalls of this particular parameter are discussed in Note h.

In the seminar, I chose to support the Presenter's choice against expectable criticism from other participants by stressing the immediate therapeutic yield of her tactic: the revelation that this patient tends to slide into paranoia because her destructive impulses terrify her as a result of her conviction that they are omnipotent.

c. Psychic reality versus subjectivity

In this argument between seminar participants, neither party was on the mark. By yielding to the patient, the analyst had *not* suspended her reality testing (but only misrepresented the conclusions it suggested), nor was she "picking up . . . clinical reality." Actually, she did not understand the meaning of the patient's behavior, but she correctly concluded that to get past the impasse she needed to change her own. Utterly unaware that the patient was engaged in enacting the childhood role of a tyrannical parent and was forcing the analyst into the compliant position the analysand had had to adopt in the past, she chose to do so in the direction suggested by her experience as the mother of a negativistic two-and-a-half-year-old. In

Kleinian terms, the analyst had failed, during the six months of struggle that preceded her surrender, to detect the operation of projective identification (see Klein, 1952), nor did she realize that this was the "clinical reality" when she succeeded in side-stepping the problem through her compliance.

Rather than having identified the patient's psychic reality, the analyst merely endorsed the analysand's momentary subjective preference. From a psychoanalytic perspective, "psychic reality" involves an area much broader than that of subjectivity; much of psychic reality may be unconscious or (as in this clinical instance) disavowed.

d. Parental roles versus analytic roles

In asserting that a psychotic transference amounts to regression into a state characteristic of a young child, the Presenter greatly oversimplified a complex situation. She was correct only insofar as it behooves an analyst (as it does any parent in analogous circumstances) to come up with a workable solution when a treatment degenerates into a power struggle. But the patient did not turn into a child when her overt behavior lapsed into paranoia, as her subsequent understanding of her responsibility for lending herself to situations in which she would feel victimized demonstrated. Only a portion of her personality was affected by the paranoid position; another portion, split off and presumably disavowed during the transference crisis, maintained good reality testing.

In the seminar, I attempted to make this point indirectly, giving the analyst credit for having maintained an analytic position, rather than having inappropriately lapsed into parenting a patient in the midst of an archaic transference. I also tried to indicate that, if this patient had been in psychotherapy (rather than analysis), one might very well have tried to help her in a direct manner by instructing her in how to avoid being victimized. (I probably should have added that it is helpful to state that one does not believe anyone should be assaulted even if that person has been "asking for it.")

One can attempt to do the same thing in an analytic context as well, as I then tried to indicate. Perhaps with some justification, the Presenter objected to the particular form that I chose to encode the necessary message. However, it should not be too difficult to find a way to put this that the analysand would find helpful—after all, it is almost self-evident that if people are as dangerous and cruel as this patient feared, one has to learn how to protect oneself from them; one need, then, pay less attention to the issue of who is to be designated as the villain of the piece. This kind of instruction will often overcome an apraxia; in those cases, the analyst's role comes close to that of an educator—or a parent. However, in cases of severe character disorder, such as the one under discussion, the progress made in this manner generally heightens some other difficulty: the cessation of masochistic behavior may bring on great dysphoria, for example. These new developments then require careful therapeutic handling.

e. The question of a psychotic core

Although the term is not entirely precise, I believe it is useful to refer to hidden potentialities for psychotic behavior (particularly thinking) that is, those that emerge only at times of special regression (as will generally happen in the course of psychoanalytic treatment) as a "psychotic core." In accord with an epigenetic, hierarchical conception of mental functions, the emergence of such a nucleus of disorder is explained on the basis of such a state having characterized the person's behavior at some time in the past and having been covered over by later, more adaptive developments; the potentially pathological condition presumably remains unaltered because it has been split off and disavowed (or repressed).

In my clinical experience, two major etiologies account for the persistence of a psychotic core: either the person suffered in childhood a state of disorganization that, when it returns in adulthood, has to be classified as a "psychosis," or the behaviors in question were acquired in the course of more or less expectable development as inevitable identifications with impaired caretakers. As I mentioned in the seminar, it makes a great deal of difference whether such an identification took place at the earliest stages of development or somewhat later: if it occurred early enough, its results may constitute the very foundations of the self-organization—a "primary identity" (Lichtenstein, 1964) that cannot be abandoned without a catastrophic sense of inner collapse. As I have previously reported (Gedo, 1981a, chap. 3; 1984, chap. 7; 1991, chap. 10), conditions of this kind are often irremediable—at least in my hands—and define one of the current limits of analyzability.

f. The analyst's use of enactments

Although analysts are perforce limited to behaviors whereby they communicate messages to analysands, these predominantly verbally encoded signals may or may not function as interpretations. One of the ways in which a communication may constitute an enactment is through a refusal to respond in the manner expectable in the framework of the other person's understanding of the situation. To cite only the simplest of examples, when someone refuses to answer a direct question but says, instead, "Tell me what next occurs to you," this intervention is an act whereby a potential conversation is aborted and a process of free associating is encouraged in its place. In an analytic setting, such an enactment amounts to resort to professional authority, often a more effective tool than the alternatives of silence or compromise by reasoning with patients about the appropriate roles of the participants.

The three options I have just outlined are analogous to the three tactics the analyst might have used to deal with the technical quandary presented by the patient under discussion: resisting irrational demands, compromising with them, or changing the framework of the dialogue. Incidentally, we might note that in demanding concurrence with her absurd claim, this analysand was also trying to change the basic framework necessary for a psychoanalysis, that of allowing a more or less impartial observer to state his or her authentic understanding of the data. Clearly, one of the ways in which the analyst might have switched the dialogue into more productive channels would have been to say that she never felt qualified to judge what is or is not justified in situations of interpersonal conflict, but that she was *certain* that the patient's pressing need to gain the analyst's agreement with her point of view was a highly significant finding about her personality. This might have led promptly to the conclusion I next discussed in the seminar, that the patient had been raised in an irrational world of slaves and slavemasters.

g. The analyst's personality and psychoanalytic technique

Before the second session of this seminar, the Presenter shared with me the information that she had experience in dealing with irrationality not only as the mother of young children but also as a successful psychiatrist within a hospital setting and, as a private person, in various other contexts. I was reluctant to have a discussion about the sources of the Presenter's unusual flexibility; this is why I focused on my own relative inflexibility about compromising with unreason. In saying I am a "born revolutionary," I was summarizing my lengthy struggle to oppose my mother's propensity to defend herself through the use of projection, in the manner demonstrated in the case we were considering.

The Presenter behaved with her patient as Galileo did when he confronted the Inquisition: it will be recalled that he agreed to their demands in public and asserted his dissent privately. For me, such behavior reopens old wounds in a way I find costlier than is warranted, in view of the availability of alternative procedures.

h. The danger of compromising with irrationality

The comment by one of the participants pointing out that the patient's rage about any disagreement with her unreasonable assertions was merely avoided by the analyst's choice to comply with her demand for concurrence was certainly cogent. However, postponing a showdown about an issue that seems intractable when it first arises is often the prudent thing to do and need not jeopardize subsequent work on that problem or any other, provided that the avoidance is neither disavowed nor misinterpreted as mastery of the difficulty.

To get some clue about whether or not the analyst's technical approach had succeeded in promoting the process of analysis, I inquired about the possibility that the transaction might have led to insight about the enactment's having constituted a repetition, in reverse, of a childhood struggle with the mother. Unfortunately, this question was side-tracked. Judging by the account of subsequent events in the analysis, however, it seems that until this seminar clarification of the mother transference had not taken place.

In the seminar, I chose not to raise the issue that I do not believe an analyst has the right knowingly to utter a falsehood in the course of doing the work, however convenient such a "little white lie" may be in terms of some other therapeutic *desideratum*. First of all, the entire thrust of psychoanalysis-as-treatment must be that truth is the highest of values—a position that cannot be maintained unless it applies to the analyst as rigorously as it does to the analysand. Even more important, however, is the fact that our patients are not fools and generally will detect our falsehoods sooner or later. What would this young analyst have done if her capitulation to the patient's tyranny had been followed by furious accusations of being dishonest just to avoid a bit of unpleasantness?

i. The therapeutic effects of corrective experience

In chapter 3, I stressed the unlikelihood of effecting changes in personality by means of corrective emotional experience. Here, it is suitable to mention the other side of the coin, namely, that benign experiences in treatment (what self psychologists prefer to call the provision of an empathic ambience [Wolf, 1976]) may temporarily soothe even those patients who are chronically dysphoric. If one succeeds in dealing with many or most intercurrent upsets in this manner (by covering the problem with the whipped cream of decency and understanding), it is entirely feasible to maintain in a relatively stable equilibrium a wide range of patients who are not analyzable. From an adaptational viewpoint, prolonged intervals of relief from emotional disruption may make possible significant external improvements of lasting value—such achievements, for example, as qualification for more gratifying work.

In other words, a treatment that fails as an analysis may turn out to be very helpful indeed as a supportive psychotherapy. I discussed this issue more extensively in my 1991 book (see chap. 10).

j. Countertransference and the analytic attitude

It is worth giving added emphasis to the point that the degree to which an analyst conforms to a role assigned to him or her in the transference is largely determined by unconscious forces generally labeled as "counter-transference." At the same time, traditional technical precepts have acted as a spur to behave consciously so ambiguously as to make transference developments as easy as possible. Of course, it is not possible literally not to be oneself in the analytic situation, nor is it conceivable to fail to respond on an unconscious level to transference expectations. The question is always about the direction in which such countertransference responses may tilt the analytic process.

In the seminar, I ventured the claim that in cases where a serious, traumatic disillusionment with the primary caretaker is a major issue, I tend to respond automatically in a manner that counteracts the analysand's transference expectation that I shall be equally disappointing. Of course, the lavish manner in which I have furnished my office (inspired, incidentally, by a visit to Freud's house in Hampstead some 25 years ago) is a permanent reminder to my analysands that they may hope for something better than their past disappointments. Obviously, material possessions will not by themselves convey this message to everyone: some of my analysands were raised in palazzi, not slums. For some patients, the message is carried in one's manner of speaking, for others in one's scrupulousness in matters of time and money—and so forth.

k. Battling it out with the volcanic patient

At this juncture in the seminar, the discussion focused on that group of patients with whom the option of altering the framework of discourse when they make irrational demands proves not to work. In circumstances of that kind, the lexical meaning of words tends to get lost; communication takes place primarily in terms of the affects, especially as they are conveyed by the paraverbal aspects of speech (see Gedo, in press-c). Hence, it may become necessary to speak with strong emphasis or even in an angry manner. In my experience, if one chooses the form of one's interventions on a rational basis, the vast majority of patients in analysis accept such communications without problems. The rare exceptions occurred in cases that were going badly in a number of ways, so that it is by no means certain that any specific intervention on my part was in fact the primary cause of the rupture. In this sense, the *caveat* I articulated in the seminar was somewhat misleading; it would have been more accurate to say that in certain transference crises, even the desperate remedies sometimes effective in other emergencies fail to salvage a failing treatment.

l. Archaic transferences and narcissistic disorders

Gehrie correctly points out that patients who enter analysis in a state of deep regression (and who, in my terms, are therefore bound to develop transferences of an archaic variety, referable to modes I through III in the hierarchical model) often keep reenacting traumatic situations that characterized their childhood and make irrational demands on the analyst in the process. More conjecturally, Gehrie diagnoses patients who behave in this way as victims of "narcissistic disorders." Insofar as this designation refers to persons who develop the archaic transferences Kohut (1971) sometimes called "narcissistic"—idealizing transference, mirror transference, and twinship transference were the varieties Kohut listed—Gehrie's statement is not inaccurate, but it is overly restrictive.

As I have discussed in detail elsewhere (see esp. Gedo, 1988), archaic syndromes transcend the boundaries of the field Kohut explored. Without filling in all the details here, the point may be substantiated by citing the work of Searles (1986), who described a set of archaic transferences he calls "borderline psychotic." In my judgment, the patient discussed in this seminar more closely approximates the clinical picture of the syndromes described by Searles than she does Kohut's "narcissistic personality disorders." During the period when he used that term (which he later abandoned in favor of the concept of "selfobject transferences"), Kohut tended to diagnose patients who had regressed into a psychotic transference as compensated psychotics; he advised against offering analysis to such patients.

m. The danger of reality confrontation

Gehrie attempts to balance the criticisms voiced in the seminar about the Presenter's compromise with the patient's irrationality (and the attendant risk of sweeping an important aspect of her pathology under the rug) by pointing out that the traditional technique of insisting on confronting the lack of validity of a paranoid attitude also carries certain dangers. He is certainly right that continuous reiteration of such diametrically opposed views of "reality" would merely serve to repeat the traumatic childhood circumstances in which truth was disregarded in the quest for power and control. As I have already indicated, I would try to minimize this risk by focusing on the fact that it is the analysand who is making efforts to brainwash the analyst—the latter had not tried to impose her views on the patient. A clarification of this kind might have made it possible to attempt a reconstruction of the relevant transactions in childhood and to arrive at a transference interpretation.

To repeat, the main point is not that the patient's grasp of reality is faulty, but that she is unable to accept that she and her analyst may have a difference of opinion. Ultimately, that difference concerns the issue of when and where the patient was victimized without sharing responsibility for that outcome: the analysand insists that this is the case in adult life, while the analyst should affirm that such a circumstance is conceivable only in early childhood.

n. Did the analyst use an empathic approach by compromising?

Gehrie contrasts the recommendation to focus on the patient's motives for her provocative demands on the analyst with the actual solution used in this treatment, that of surface compliance with those demands, which he characterizes as "an empathic approach." It is true that the Presenter rationalized her choice by reference to a successful piece of empathic parenting, but that does not prove that her work with the patient was based on valid empathic understanding. As I have already stated (Note b), I believe that her reasoning about this matter was faulty; she acted in a manner that got her past the impasse, but she did so without understanding the significance of the patient's behavior—or that of her own actions.

It seems to me that in calling the analyst's intuitive change of tack "an empathic approach," Gehrie comes uncomfortably close to equating empathy with an acceptance of the priority of the other's subjective preference. An approach based on valid empathy would have called for a statement to the effect that the patient was confused, that she was disavowing her crushing sense of guilt about her potential destructiveness, or that she was trying to externalize her conscience and pleading for absolution that could come only from within. . . . Moreover, it is highly unlikely that the Presenter was operating within the self-psychological framework Gehrie attributes to her (allegedly giving her patient a chance to "reorganize around a selfobject transference")—at no point during the seminar did she indicate that she used such concepts.

o. Was the patient beyond the call of rational discourse?

Gehrie seems to endorse the Presenter's sense that the course of action she had chosen was a *necessity*—that no workable alternative was available. This is a question that could only be answered empirically; because no other option was tried, we have no evidence one way or the other. In contrast, I am confident that the voice of reason can always gain a hearing; in close to four decades of analytic experience with more than 60 patients, I have never failed to find a way to make contact with the "reality ego"—not even in those cases in which I was ultimately unable to get an analytic result.

It seems to me that this possibility must have been available in the case under discussion in view of the fact that, as soon as the analyst gave in to her verbally, the patient became essentially reasonable about the very matters about which she had been spouting paranoid nonsense. It is even conceivable that she never *meant* these preposterous statements in the first place: regressed patients are often unable to make clear that they do not regard their associations as valid representations of their convictions.

Follow-up Notes by the Analyst—Summer 1992

As predicted, this has been a stormy analysis. Yet we are now considering termination, and, for the most part, the patient is able to use words instead of actions to communicate her experience without feeling despair about the sense of isolation she used to experience. Initially, when she had moments of being truly introspective, so that I could respond to her with interpretations, she felt that we were engaged in mutual masturbation, akin to the sexual play with her brother, which she could not tolerate. Thus, those moments had to be rapidly disrupted through provocation, and we spent much time trying to understand why she experienced being an analytic patient as so lonely.

Since what we focused on in the seminar was the change in my attitude regarding what I believed to be the necessity for me to accept her version of reality, I thought I might say something about how my attitude has changed. When her insistence that I validate her reality concerned the behavior of others, it was difficult enough; but this issue intensified as we dealt with her responses to me in the transference. She was enraged with me for even suggesting that she had any emotional response to me.

(And, of course, because there could be no emotional interaction between us, the analysis seemed like an intellectual exercise, useful only to provide her a place to vent emotions about those she was truly involved with, yet doing nothing to alter the defect in herself.) My attempts to link her experience with responses to transference phenomena were met with denial, withdrawal (emotional and physical), scathing depreciation of me, or all of those. As I was able to elucidate that what had precipitated these episodes were my attempts to emphathize with her distress, she let me know that that was exactly what she had to avoid; she feared that such empathy would precipitate the nuclear response that, once begun, had a life of its own and could not be contained. She likened these experiences to a "grand mal seizure," in response to which any bystander can only hope to help the person not to break any bones, but about which one can do nothing. Thus my empathic comments were experienced as if I were malevolently prodding her with red hot pokers to push her into one of these states. (This was elucidated in the context of the negative paternal transference from which she escaped through an identification with her mother.) I learned that, once she shifted into these states, I could interrupt them with an affective response that she would experience as something like a "slap in the face," after which she would be aware that I existed as a separate individual. In her words, she felt I would not allow her to treat me badly, nor to leave me emotionally, and I would not abandon her by merely allowing the seizure to run its course. The seizures were different in quality from her usual depreciating attacks.

Another motive for her attacks was to cover up what she felt was a profound deficit in her ability to understand other people's motivations. (This contributed to her interest in studying the motivations of criminals.) She was unable to learn from me about these matters because she experienced my observations as depreciating attacks on her, and each exchange was disrupted by her rage that I could think so little of her. Ultimately, we discovered that acknowledging my affective response (in the service of trying to understand my motivations) would lead to a loss of boundaries such that she experienced me as out of control and herself as evil and destructive. Her identification with a mother who denied the validity of affective responses helped ward off this experience of annihilation and destruction. When I have been able to point out to her that it is her denial of any association between her state of mind and what occurred in the analysis that drove me—and would drive anyone—to distraction, she has been able to grasp why she always had the subjective sense of there being a vacuum that separated her from others. To acknowledge that she felt hurt in response to something I did or said was equivalent to ending the analysis, and denying it was the only way she knew of to preserve the relationship. In my opinion, these insights have enabled her to contemplate termination, and, in contemplating termination, we have been discussing the strategies I used in the early part of the analysis.

One of the difficulties this woman encountered in life was understanding the motivations of others. That is why she had to study them so hard. In the course of the analysis, contemporaneously with her becoming able to maintain her boundaries, she has developed (recovered is probably more accurate) the capacity to empathize. She can understand, accept, and empathize with another person's emotional response to her and is thus better able to understand motivations in a much more personal way. Related to this achievement is her growing ability to introspect and use her introspection as a guide to action. These changes are, in my opinion, monumental in scope, but not immediately apparent because she has always been able to give lip service to understanding others, but could not really understand without losing her boundaries. It is achievements in this area that have allowed her to form a solid relationship with a man from whom she does not demand omniscience and who is very available to her. By her own description, she can feel a range of affects that no longer threaten her or the relationship. Since she is able to sustain emotional contact, she seldom needs to provoke angry interactions; and the rages and physical battles prevalent at the beginning of the analysis have ceased. She is no longer so brittle that narcissistic injuries threaten her equilibrium, nor is she paranoid. Thus she can now feel supported in her work by people who admire her abilities.

6

The Integration of Theory and Technique

No doubt our readers have been struck by the *Chicago* flavor of the seminars we conducted at the Chicago Institute. Although the case presentations seemed relatively free of ideology, the discussions failed to give equal time to any of the traditional viewpoints within psychoanalysis—in fact, if they were to be represented at all, much of the time it was John Gedo who had to play devil's advocate. For the most part, of course, he gave voice to his own point of view—one that is far from traditional!—and, insofar as this viewpoint was challenged at all, most frequently by Mark Gehrie but some of the time by one or another candidate, the dialectic took place vis-à-vis the tenets of "self psychology." In the late 1980s, ego psychology had little influence in Chicago, and Kleinian or Lacanian viewpoints have never gained a following there.

This tilt toward nontraditional ideas was accentuated by the declared goal of the seminar to address the technical difficulties encountered in practice. As the preceding chapters show, this program encouraged participants to select for presentation analyses in which therapeutic regression sooner or later proceeded to very primitive levels of organization—some of the time to the emergence of a "psychotic transference." In the Presenter's view, a regression to archaic mentation even characterized certain analysands (discussed in chap. 1) about whom the consensus of the seminar was in disagreement with the Presenter. In accord with ego-psychological theory, the four patients presented *in extenso* suffered from ego defects serious enough to call analyzability into grave question. In Chicago, such patients were not taken into analysis by most practitioners until Kohut's writings of the late 1960s gave analysts sanction to relax their selection criteria.

Of course, many of us did know that the followers of Melanie Klein were engaged in bold experiments to analyze just about anyone interested in what we have to offer. Moreover, some of their clinical reports (e.g., Herbert Rosenfeld's posthumous collection of 1987) demonstrated impressive therapeutic achievements even with overtly psychotic patients. As Gedo (1986, chap. 6) recently acknowledged, Klein was the first to assert that analytic success depends on overcoming the patient's pregenital fixations; she always stressed the need to allow negative transferences to echo the strains of earliest childhood, and she reported that the infantile neurosis serves to bind more primitive anxieties, even those of a hidden psychosis. It is regrettable, then, that no Kleinian voice was heard in the seminar—as instructors we did not feel that her ideas, despite their cogency largely unfamiliar to the participants, could be introduced without losing the requisite focus on following the clinical material.

Now that it is fitting to consider broader issues on the basis of that clinical material as a whole, it may be useful to note that Klein developed her technical approach (as did most of the contributors whose work *was* mentioned in the seminar) from a *theoretical* position. In her case, this theoretical system was an extension of the libido theory as enunciated by Freud and Abraham (Klein, 1952). From these propositions, she derived a set of interpretive permutations that she viewed as expressions of human universals; hence her clinical procedure consisted in promptly confronting analysands with the putative unconscious meanings of their associations (Klein, 1945, see esp. pp. 408-410). As can readily be seen from her book-length *Narrative of a Child Analysis*, Klein (1961) was confident that articulating id interpretations in the face of resistance diminishes the patient's anxiety and ultimately leads to the introjection of the "good object" the analyst should be (pp. 427, 457).

If to nonbelievers Klein's interpretations seem highly arbitrary and implausible, these skeptics are left with the challenge of explaining the apparent therapeutic effectiveness of her "dubious" assertions. Insofar as Kleinian interpretations lack validity, they nonetheless constitute a visionary portrayal of the analysand's inner world as a landscape populated by monsters.[1] The analyst's calm acceptance of these "worst case scenarios" clearly has a soothing effect on the patient and must greatly assist in transforming treatment into a holding environment. In other words, a

---

[1]Many, perhaps most, patients are likely to take these startling communications metaphorically. Understood in such terms, they constitute an offer of an entirely novel, private language the analysand is invited to share with the analyst. Such a translation would have a powerfully calming effect on the afflicted.

Kleinian approach might very well have been effective with the therapeutic crises described by several Presenters: there is nothing like a
startling id interpretation to focus a patient's attention on the therapeutic
transaction and put on the back burner concerns about who is to blame in
a laundry-room quarrel!

Of course, for a candidate analyzed in Chicago to adopt a Kleinian
interpretive schema would constitute a more radical surrender of convictions than did a temporary concurrence with the analysand's distortion of
reality. In the early 1980s, a recent graduate of the Chicago Institute was
bound to be most concerned about the possibility that he might be guilty
of an "empathic break," failing properly to grasp the nature and meaning
of the patient's subjective experience, leading to retraumatization and
distortion of the underlying process. Whereas the analyst of the woman
who "forgot her" worried that he might be doing something bad to his
patient by not accepting uncritically the totality of her view of him, he did
not seem concerned to interpret "projective identification," her effort to
make him accept that view, as a Kleinian would have done. However,
neither did he choose to interpret that break in empathy which concerned him, and to follow the technical course suggested by self psychology theory. Self psychologists believe that such events in empathy are
expectable and that analyzing their consequences constitutes an essential aspect of the working-through process. This particular analyst took a
substantially more radical position.

We are trying to say that analysts everywhere are bound to be paro-
chial and need not apologize for their assimilation into a specific analytic
community. (For an assessment of what it means to be an *American*
psychoanalyst, see Gedo, 1991, chap. 12). It is very likely that every
psychoanalytic ideology that has retained adherents over a considerable
period of time has done so because it is serviceable in a wide range of
clinical contingencies—especially in the hands of talented and experienced practitioners. No doubt this is just as true of Kleinian analysts as it
is of those trained in Chicago; in the British analytic milieu, it was
perfectly natural that Klein was able to attract many talented followers.

What we mean when we talk of an analyst's talent and experience is
that he or she has been able to adapt the tradition in which his or her
apprenticeship took place and has developed a supple personal approach
to analytic technique superior to whatever is expectable from the theory
that underlies it. Take, for instance, the therapeutic prescriptions of
Herbert Rosenfeld for dealing with the kinds of analysands presented in
our seminar. (Rosenfeld did not outline these in a single place—we have
culled them from his 1987 collection of papers.) Above all, he cautioned
that an analyst must not "accept" a patient's projections (as several of the
Presenters were trapped into doing); rather, projections should be "con-

tained" by apprehending their meaning as primitive communications and translating these into consensual language. Rosenfeld terms such activities "doing the thinking" for both participants in the treatment.

To create a "containing environment," according to Rosenfeld, analysts must be able to participate in transactions with patients in an emotional manner—to show themselves to be experiencing but *sane* actors taking part in the analysands' inner life. It then becomes the therapeutic task to integrate and organize the various uncoordinated islands of the patient's mental life (a process Gedo and Goldberg, 1973, proposed to call "unification"). Rosenfeld stressed that, at levels of profound regression, much of the essential communication in analysis takes place through nonverbal channels. Although he was keenly aware of the dangers of humiliating vulnerable patients, Rosenfeld also pointed out that many "narcissists" are "thick-skinned" and well able to tolerate confrontations about their hostility and destructiveness.

Rosenfeld frequently returned to the point that the *manner* of therapeutic interventions is just as important as is their lexical content. He reported that regressed patients, who may not possess adequate skills in using the secondary process, tend best to grasp messages that are lively and dramatic—albeit they may become panicked if the drama is overdone. If the analyst is able to find the right words for communication, these will enhance the holding function of the analytic situation. Ultimately, of course, the analyst's task includes encoding the *entire* analytic transaction in words. Hence, interventions must avoid both vagueness and repetitiveness; they must also take into account the tendency of regressed patients to concretize. It is ever the *analyst's* responsibility to avoid breakdowns in communication.

Rosenfeld averred that, to be effective with regressed conditions, analysts must be in touch with their own regressive propensities—the "psychotic core." Because, like infants, regressed patients are able to apprehend another person's emotional state, analysts must be able to face their own depths and recognize errors. We must not deny our wish to be helpful, nor can we afford to have therapeutic ambitions to satisfy *our* narcissistic needs: we must find the middle of the road between intrusiveness and unempathic detachment. In the midst of these manifold aspects of effective analytic activity, it is up to us to deal with patients' disorders of thought, the lack of integration in their mental life, and their self-destructiveness.

These recommendations, the fruits of decades of Kleinian practice, are completely lacking in any sectarian flavor—they are, in fact, strikingly congruent with the Chicago consensus dominant in the seminar. Thus the analyst's vigorous, if nontraditional, efforts to neutralize his patient's self-destructiveness, presented in chapter 3, would have met with Rosenfeld's explicit approval. On the other side, the common inability of candidates to understand that any wish to conclude the analysis hastily constitutes a counteridentification with the analysand's resistance to change exemplifies the pitfall that Rosenfeld singled out as the most significant iatrogenic cause of treatment impasse.

To our knowledge, Rosenfeld was never able to take the next step in promoting scientific progress, that of confronting the discrepancy between his successful technical innovations and the theory from which the technique accepted in his school was derived. (Had he done so, he would have ceased being merely Kleinian; had he persuaded his colleagues that theoretical revision was imperative, he would have healed the breach between Kleinians and the rest of us.) Whenever changes in analytic technique yield superior results and novel observational data, improvements in clinical theory should follow. These alterations should, in turn, lead to modifications in the special theory of technique—in other words, they may give birth to a new clinical tradition (see Gedo and Pollock, 1967).

Although we have chosen to illustrate this cycle by using the example of an innovator from the Kleinian school, it would be just as easy to do so using the Chicago scene and self psychology or the strongholds of ego psychology in North America; perhaps even the French Lacanians might demonstrate the same progression. To be sure, various traditions are likely at any particular time to be at different phases in this cyclical process, so that one or another may seem more (or less) congealed in its procedures—or, to put this more tactfully, more or less "theory driven."

In the seminar, many participants expressed the opinion that the use of a "classical" interpretive technique, with strong reluctance to modify it through Eissler's "parameters," characterizes the tradition of ego psychology. When such procedures are tried with analysands prone to regress profoundly, despite expectably poor therapeutic outcomes (as reported by Firestein, 1978, Schlessinger and Robbins, 1983, and Kantrowitz, 1987), it is tempting to conclude that scientific theory and praxis have yielded to dogma and ritual. Of course, ego psychology is a mature paradigm, born almost 70 years ago, so it is hardly surprising if many of its adherents use it too rigidly. Many others doubtless do so with sufficient flexibility to match Rosenfeld in his virtuosity with difficult patients (see Stone, 1954, 1965).

More surprising was the tendency of some seminar participants incorrectly to apply the concepts of self psychology, enunciated only 10 or 12 years previously, as if it were a rigid schema that dictates an unvarying policy of trying to *become* an idealizable "selfobject" for all patients. In the seminar we heard instances of collusion between candidate and patient to disavow illegitimate pressure brought to bear on the latter to abandon a lifelong value system.[2] One might suspect that the bizarre termination of the analysis presented in chapter 4 was accepted as satisfactory by all concerned on the basis of the same kind of misunderstanding: that the onset of an idealizing transference (based on secret fantasies after the Thanksgiving phone contact) having established narcissistic equilibrium, the spontaneous relinquishment of this idealizing attitude (after the revelations of an obituary) was theoretically supposed to lead automatically to "transmuting internalization" (Kohut, 1977). Except that all that glitters is not gold. . . . Adherents of self psychology who are able to use that tradition as creatively as Rosenfeld or Stone employ theirs are aware that working-through remains as critical and essential a dimension of the analytic process as ever.

In recent years the kind of convergence of praxis we have just postulated has been made explicit in works that echo the ecumenical spirit of Gedo and Goldberg's *Models of the Mind* (1973), for instance Modell's (1990) *Other Times, Other Realities* and Pine's (1990) *Drive, Ego, Object, Self*. These authors reject making a partisan choice among the clinical schools competing for our allegiance; rather, they insist that each tradition offers some valid concepts but is by itself excessively reductionistic. If it is granted that psychoanalysis makes available several valid frames of reference for dealing with clinical contingencies, it becomes urgently necessary to develop theoretical guidelines that will yield reliable rules of transition among the possible alternatives for intervention. These new theories would necessarily have to employ novel premises, for the existing clinical *theories* of the competing schools (ego psychology, self psychology, object relations theory) are irreconcilable with each other; the convergence we have noted does not extend to the conceptual realm.[3]

To turn to a somewhat different vantage point about these matters, we find it remarkable that some of the most intractable impasses presented to the seminar occurred in cases that came closest to the personality structure Eissler (1953) considered to be analyzable without parameters. It is possible that this apparent paradox is merely a function of the fact that, even though most of the presenters were analytic beginners, they

---

[2]This collusion amounted to a push in the direction of idealizing the analyst, because facing these facts squarely would have caused the patient to conclude either that psychoanalysis is merely indoctrination into a new religion or that the analyst was illegitimately traducing the procedure.

[3]Gedo and Goldberg (1973) did not offer such a novel theory; the supraordinate model they constructed made do with those aspects of existing theories that were not incompatible with each other. Gedo's theoretical work from 1979 onwards (see esp. Gedo, 1979, 1981b, 1988, 1991) has attempted to develop a new framework of this kind. The technical consequences of this theoretical schema are articulated in his contributions to the present volume.

were all experienced and successful psychotherapists, competent to deal with psychological emergencies of all kinds. In other words, perhaps it is to be expected that it is the elucidation of unconscious intrapsychic conflicts that presents inexperienced analysts with their greatest challenge; this may have become truer than ever now that relatively few persons seek analysis for problems that are focused on issues in that realm.

It is equally plausible, however, to assume that our paradoxical finding cannot be explained on the basis of the analysts' prior professional experience. It is entirely possible that neurotic conflicts are inherently more difficult to elucidate than are derivatives of more archaic vicissitudes—perhaps it is especially problematic to gain insight into matters that are warded off by means of repression proper. When repressed impulses and wishes and their countermotives are uniformly verbally encoded, it is very difficult for the analyst to discern them accurately by means of empathy; for, in such aspects of the inner world, individual differences are much more cogent than is our common humanity. Occasionally, not only did the supervisors of these analyses fail to teach the candidates the proper basic technique for a routine psychoanalysis; even more damaging was their failure to encourage the candidates to assist the analysands to master the task of self inquiry (Gardner, 1983), for ultimately it is the patient's introspective efforts that have to uncover unconscious mental contents.

To put this in still another way, analysts who start out with the assumption that they are dealing with an archaic problem, as certain presenters did, are guilty of the same dogmatic rigidity displayed by analysts who insist on "classical" technique when confronted by primitively organized patients. Such a priori assumptions (or, if you will, unwarranted diagnoses) lead candidates to be prematurely active instead of promoting the process of free association. For example, many analysts intervene on the side of sexual "freedom" without investigating what in childhood made sexuality unacceptable to their patients. This is the way of suggestion, the method psychoanalysis has had such a long struggle to abandon, despite Freud's lucid understanding that patients had good reason to resist such infringements of their autonomy.

Freud learned from Charcot that it is good to have theories but that one should never forget that they do not prevent anything from existing: *La théorie, c'est bon, mais ça n'empêche pas d'exister*. In preaching against analytic procedures that are excessively theory bound, we have been spelling out the meaning of this aphorism. The issue, however, may also be viewed from the opposite vantage point: without knowledge (encoded in scientific theories), one cannot practice artfully. *Ars sine scientia nihil est*. We have to redress the balance by discussing the disastrous consequences of procedures uninformed by coherent theory. It is perfectly possible for analysts (especially beginners) to alternate wildly between rigid adherence to theories that do not necessarily apply to the clinical material and the abandonment of all theoretical guidelines in favor of procedures reduced to a series of rules of thumb.

Take, for instance, the analysis presented in chapter 4. Through much of its duration, this treatment followed the classical technique dictated by the theory of the transference neuroses—at least until the analyst's decisive change of technique in allowing the patient to contact her in a family setting at Thanksgiving. The same theoretical position, however, should have impelled her to scrutinize closely the analysand's rageful outburst when she was told that missing analytic sessions was "not optimal" from a prognostic viewpoint—but no such inquiry was carried out. The failure to investigate this explosion of irrational hatred—indeed, as far as the analysand knew, even to note it!—cannot be explained on the basis of any of the competing clinical theories of psychoanalysis. The analytic procedure that was followed amounted to blind faith in the power of the psychoanalytic situation itself to influence favorably any contingency that may arise in the course of treatment, without any specific effort on the part of the analyst to manage the problem. Such an attitude reduces psychoanalysis to the status of an act of magic.

Resort to ritualized procedures without any theoretical rationale could lead only to the outcome that eventually supervened: the return of the disavowed irrational behavior, on a massive scale. If those who argued for the cogency of self-psychological assumptions and techniques in dealing with this analysand were on the right track, the resort to classical premises and procedures through much of the treatment did not make sense and the "empathic" approach of accepting the need for emergency contacts by telephone should not have been abandoned. In sum, the numerous inconsistent changes of tack from one technical schema to another are best accounted for by the candidate's lack of commitment to any rational framework. Not that we would fault a beginner for lacking firm convictions about psychoanalytic controversies; it is the responsibility of the supervisor to give guidance in this regard and to see to it that a consistent policy is followed—and understood—by the student.

Contrast the course of the foregoing treatment with the analysis conducted by the junior faculty member shortly after graduating from the Institute (chapter 3). This transaction also confronted the analyst with critical difficulties not long after it began and for many years thereafter; he responded at every juncture by intervening to the maximum extent possible to preserve the patient's health and welfare through his direct helpfulness. Although this relatively inexperienced analyst was too modest to claim that his interventions preserved an "analytic" framework, his primary commitment was therapeutic (rather than being concerned with technical "purity"). He attended the seminar because of his interest in Gedo's views on the theory of technique, according to which (as he well knew!) interventions of the kind he had used are permissible in an analytic context whenever they are therapeutically indicated. Judging by his confidence in his technique at the time of the follow-up (faculty) seminar, as he gained analytic experience this person solidified his commitment to this theoretical position.

Another analysis conducted in a manner divorced from any theory of technique (not available as a transcript) was characterized by the candidate's omniscient style. This dogmatism made the analyst sound like the adherent of whichever school of thought is most closely associated with the content of the "interpretations" being misused. Not only did this student oscillate between her own self-psychological conjectures and the classical ones favored by her supervisor, without paying the requisite attention to the analysand's responses showing that the interpretations made no sense to the latter; even worse, she never allowed the necessary insights to emerge as a result of the analysand's own efforts to pursue the associative method. In this sense, her interpretations were less solidly grounded than those of Melanie Klein at her most arbitrary; moreover, what she told her patient was too mundane to inspire faith, and the candidate herself was lacking in Kleinian charisma. No wonder the treatment degenerated into mutual efforts to assure each other that it was following an expectable course . . .

We have devoted much thought to the question whether the four cases discussed extensively in this volume constitute a representative sample of the clinical problems encountered in psychoanalytic practice.[4] Judging by cases we have heard discussed in many settings, both in North America and in Europe, we believe that a proportion of one case centered on a transference neurosis to four in which archaic transferences predominate reflects the actualities of contemporary psychoanalysis (see Gedo, 1977). We therefore regret our inability to present an impasse in a case of transference neurosis. It is particularly noteworthy that among the four analysands whose problems involved mostly the primitive psyche, only one (the ballet dancer presented in chap. 4) seems clearly to have suffered

---

[4]We assume that the consensus reached in the seminar about the nature of the personality organization in each case was a valid response to the material selected for presentation. Whether the presenters actually chose reliable data sufficient to draw valid conclusions about their patients is another matter, but one not relevant to the present discussion.

from what Kohut (1971) initially called a "narcissistic personality disturbance," although the patient in chapter 5 might also have been seen in this light, given the nature of her response to the analyst's shift in technique. However, caution must be advised in such evaluations, given the risks inherent in the assessment of the nature of underlying pathology; clearer evidence about whether the most primitive levels have been adequately addressed had to await further developments in the analysis. (The analyst's recent follow-up report suggests that the crux of this patient's pathology lay in the preverbal realm.) The other two patients were profoundly involved with matters of life and death: Gedo's analysand and the one presented by the junior faculty member (chaps. 2 and 3) were close to suicide.

We make the foregoing distinction on the basis of the report that the dancer spontaneously developed an idealizing transference and, when adventitious events abruptly undermined this idealization, she reacted with unbounded rage (see Kohut, 1972) and regression to an unrealistic stance of self-reliance. These are pathognomonic signs of problems in the realm of self-esteem regulation—the realm of illusions Gedo and Goldberg (1973) labeled mode III in their hierarchy. In contrast, the analysands in chapters 2 and 3 were conspicuously incapable of recognizing their analysts' good qualities or performance. Nor was their attitude in analysis characteristic of any of the other "narcissistic" transferences listed by Kohut (1971), either the "twinship," wherein the analyst is experienced as an alter ego, or a "mirror transference," in which the person seeks affirmation or a psychic merger.

In these cases, an adequate social façade (in the nature of what Winnicott, 1954, termed a "false self") was covering a split-off nucleus of the self that was arrested in an archaic mode of organization. Such a lack of self-cohesion is characteristic of mode II in the Gedo and Goldberg schema. These syndromes are therefore even more primitive in their genesis than are the narcissistic problems on which Kohut focused his clinical work. In psychiatric terms, persons exhibiting such symptoms tend to be labeled "borderline patients"; from a psychoanalytic perspective (see Gedo, 1988), these are personalities in need of unification into a cohesive hierarchy of motivations—an effort that requires the measures "beyond interpretation" described in the sessions of the seminar devoted to such cases.

The current challenge for the theory of psychoanalytic technique is to codify the measures appropriate to deal with the ego defects inevitably found in patients whose development was in some measure arrested. These therapeutic tasks are very difficult to carry out because such patients are seldom able to learn in an optimal manner, for they tend to have dealt with their handicaps through denial, aversive withdrawal, symbiotic adaptive maneuvers that are largely disavowed, and similar measures that add up to a severe disorder of character when they reach adulthood.

As yet we lack consensus about the most effective ways to approach such problems. We trust that the discussions in this volume have at least demonstrated that there is no warrant for any psychoanalytic dogmatism about these challenging questions of technique.

References

Alexander, F. & French, T. (1946), *Psychoanalytic Therapy*. New York: Ronald Press.

Balint, M. (1968), *The Basic Fault*. London: Tavistock.

Bucci, W. (1992), The development of emotional meaning in free association: A multiple code theory. In: *Hierarchical Conceptions in Psychoanalysis*, ed. A. Wilson & J. Gedo. New York: Guilford.

Eissler, K. (1953), The effect of the structure of the ego on psycho-analytic technique. *J. Amer. Psychoanal. Assn.*, 1:104–143.

Erle, J. & Goldberg, D. (1984), Observations on assessment of analyzability by experienced analysts. *J. Amer. Psychoanal. Assn.*, 32:715–738.

Fenichel, O. (1941), *Problems of Psychoanalytic Technique*. New York: Psychoanalytic Quart.

Ferenczi, S. (1908–1933), *Final Contributions to the Problems and Methods of Psychoanalysis*. New York: Basic Books, 1955.

_____ & Rank, O. (1924), *The Development of Psychoanalysis*. New York: Nervous and Mental Dis.

Firestein, S. (1978), *Termination in Psychoanalysis*. New York: IUP.

Freud, A. (1936), *The Ego and the Mechanisms of Defense*. New York: IUP, 1946.

Freud, S. (1900), *The Interpretation of Dreams. Standard Edition*, 4 & 5. London: Hogarth Press, 1953.

_____ (1905), Fragment of an analysis of a case of hysteria. *Standard Edition*, 7:7–123. London: Hogarth Press, 1953.

_____ (1910), "Wild" psycho-analysis. *Standard Edition*, 11:219–30. London: Hogarth Press, 1957.

_____ (1911–15), Papers on technique. *Standard Edition*, 12:85–171. London: Hogarth Press, 1958.

_____ (1923), The ego and the id. *Standard Edition*, 19:12–59. London: Hogarth Press, 1961.

_____ (1926), Inhibitions, symptoms, and anxiety. *Standard Edition*, 20:87–172. London: Hogarth Press, 1959.

Friedman, L. (1988), *The Anatomy of Psychotherapy*. Hillsdale, NJ: The Analytic Press.

Gardner, R. (1983), *Self Inquiry*. Hillsdale, NJ: The Analytic Press, 1987.

Gedo, J. (1967), The wise baby reconsidered. In: *Freud: The Fusion of Science and Humanism*, ed. J. Gedo & G. Pollock. *Psychological Issues*, Monogr. 34/35. New York: IUP, 1976, pp. 357–378.

_____ (1975), Forms of idealization in the analytic transference. *J. Amer. Psychoanal. Assn.*, 23:485–505.

_____ (1977), Notes on the psychoanalytic management of archaic transferences. *J. Amer. Psychoanal. Assn.*, 25:787–803.

_____ (1979), *Beyond Interpretation*. New York: IUP.

_____ (1980), Reflections on some current controversies in psychoanalysis. *J. Amer. Psychoanal. Assn.*, 28:363–383.

_____ (1981a), *Advances in Clinical Psychoanalysis*. New York: IUP.

_____ (1981b), Measure for measure: A response. *Psychoanal. Inq.*, 1:289–316.

_____ (1983), *Portraits of the Artist*. Hillsdale, NJ: The Analytic Press, 1989.

_____ (1984), *Psychoanalysis and Its Discontents*. New York: Guilford.

_____ (1986), *Conceptual Issues in Psychoanalysis*. Hillsdale, NJ: The Analytic Press.

_____ (1988), *The Mind in Disorder*. Hillsdale, NJ: The Analytic Press.

_____ (1989), Self psychology: A post-Kohutian view. In: *Self Psychology: Comparisons and Contrasts*, ed. D. Detrick & S. Detrick. Hillsdale, NJ: The Analytic Press, pp. 415–420.

_____ (1991), *The Biology of Clinical Encounters*. Hillsdale, NJ: The Analytic Press.

_____ (in press-a), Ferenczi as the orthodox vizier. *Psychoanal. Inq.*

_____ (in press-b), Academicism, romanticism, and science in the psychoanalytic enterprise. *Psychoanal. Inq.*

_____ (in press-c), Analytic interventions: The question of form. In: *Festschrift for Martin Bergmann*, ed. A. Richards & A. Richards.

_____ & Goldberg, A. (1973), *Models of the Mind*. Chicago: University of Chicago Press.

_____ & Pollock, G. (1967), The question of research in psychoanalytic technique. In: *Psychoanalytic Techniques*, ed. B. Wolman. New York: Basic Books, pp. 560–582.

Gehrie, M. (in press), Psychoanalytic technique and the development of the capacity to reflect. *J. Amer. Psychoanal. Assn.*

Gill, M. (1983), *The Analysis of Transference, Vol. 1. Psychological Issues*, Monogr. 53. New York: IUP.

Goldberg, A., ed. (1978), *The Psychology of the Self: A Casebook*. New York: IUP.

Greenson, R. (1965), The working alliance and the transference. In: *Explorations in Psychoanalysis*. New York: IUP, 1978, pp. 199–224.

Jung, C. (1963), *Memories, Dreams, Reflections*. New York: Vintage.

Kantrowitz, J. (l986), The role of the patient-analyst "match" in the outcome of psychoanalysis. *Annual of Psychoanalysis*, 14:273–297. New York: IUP.

_____ (1987), Suitability for psychoanalysis. *Yearbook Psychoanal. Psychother.*, 2:403–415. New York: Guilford.

_____ Katz, A. & Paolitto, F. (1990), Follow-up of psychoanalysis five to ten years after termination: I. Stability of change. *J. Amer. Psychoanal. Assn.*, 38:471–496.

Klein, M. (1935), A contribution to the psychogenesis of manic-depressive states. *Writings*, 1:262–289. New York: Free Press, 1984.

_____ (1945), The Oedipus complex in the light of early anxieties. *Writings*, 1:370–419. New York: Free Press, 1984.

_____ (1952), Some theoretical conclusions regarding the emotional life of the infant. *Writings*, 3:61–93. New York: Free Press, 1984.

_____ (1961), *Narrative of a Child Analysis. Writings*, 4. New York: Free Press, 1984.

Kohut, H. (1968), The psychoanalytic treatment of narcissistic personality disorders: Outline of a systematic approach. In: *The Search for the Self*, ed. P. Ornstein. New York: IUP, 1978, pp. 477–509.

_____ (1971), *The Analysis of the Self*. New York: International Universities Press.

_____ (1972), Thoughts on narcissism and narcissistic rage. In: *The Search for the Self*, ed. P. Ornstein. New York: IUP, 1978, pp. 615–658.

_____ (1977), *The Restoration of the Self*. New York: IUP.

_____ (1979), The two analyses of Mr. Z. *Internat. J. Psycho-Anal.*, 60:3–18.

_____ (1984), *How Does Analysis Cure?* ed. A. Goldberg & P. Stepansky, Chicago: University of Chicago Press.

Lichtenstein, H. (1964), The role of narcissism in the emergence and maintenance of primary identity. *Internat. J. Psycho-Anal.*, 45:49–56.

Little, M. (1985), Winnicott working in areas where psychotic anxieties predominate: A personal record. *Free Associations*, 3:9–42.

Modell, A. (1965), On having the right to a life: An aspect of the superego's development. *Internat. J. Psycho-Anal.*, 46:323–331.

_____ (1976), "The holding environment" and the therapeutic action of psychoanalysis. *J. Amer. Psychoanal. Assn.*, 24:285–308.

_____ (1990), *Other Times, Other Realities*. Cambridge, MA: Harvard University Press.

_____ (1992), The private life and private space. *The Annual of Psychoanalysis*. 20:1–14. Hillsdale, NJ: The Analytic Press.

Pine, F. (1990), *Drive, Ego, Object, Self*. New York: Basic Books.

Reich, W. (1933), *Character Analysis*. New York: Orgone Institute Press, 1948.

Rieff, P. (1966), *The Triumph of the Therapeutic*. New York: Harper & Row.

Rosenfeld, H. (1987), *Impasse and Interpretation*. London: Tavistock.

Schlessinger, N. & Robbins, F. (1983), *A Developmental View of the Psychoanalytic Process*. New York: IUP.

Schwaber, E. (1981), Empathy: A mode of analytic listening. *Psychoanal. Inq.*, 1:357–392.

_____ (1983), Psychoanalytic listening and psychic reality. *Internat. Review Psycho-Anal.*, 10:379-392.

Searles, H. (1986), *My Work with Borderline Patients*. Northvale, NJ: Aronson.

Stone, L. (1954), The widening scope of indications for psychoanalysis. *J. Amer. Psychoanal. Assn.*, 2:567–594.

——— (1965), *The Psychoanalytic Situation*. New York: IUP.

Winnicott, D. (1954), Metapsychological and clinical aspects of regression in the psycho-analytical set-up. In: *Collected Papers*. London: Tavistock, 1958, pp. 278–294.

Wolf, E. (1976), Ambience and abstinence. *The Annual of Psychoanalysis*. 4:101–115. New York: IUP.

Zetzel, E. (1965), The theory of therapy in relation to a developmental model of the psychic apparatus. *Internat. J. Psycho-Anal.*, 46:39–52.

Index

Robbins, F., 296, 305
Role(s)
  creation of, 45
  reversal of, 216
Role playing, 77–78
Rosen, J., 259
Rosenfeld, H., 293, 294, 295, 296, 305

S

Sadism, 20, 49, 55
  Don Juanism and, 66
Sadistic perversion, 3, 46, 64
Sadomasochism, 46
Same issue, reengagement of analyst in, 234
Schizophrenia, 20
Schlessinger, N., 296, 305
Schwaber, E., 42, 211, 305
Screen memory, 2
Sculpture versus painting metaphor, 110
Searles, H., 44, 45, 260, 287, 306
Secrecy, related to transitional experience, 205
Secret(s), 226
  analysis as, 197
"Secret sharer," 149, 206
Self
  affective, 37
  concept of, 213
  false, 87, 213, 301
  helpless childhood, 248, 277
  restoration of, 100, 265
  true, 32
Self-abuse, 111
Self-accusations, 104
Self-cohesion, 33
  lack of, 301
Self-destruction, 81
Self development, 201
  idealization and, 213–214
Self-esteem, 64
  boosting of, 60
  regulation, problems in, 301
Self-expression, 48
Self-inquiry, 298
  introspective, 136
Self-integration, maintaining of, 50
Self-organization, 60
Self-presentation, primitive transference longings in, 121
Self psychology, 41–42, 249–250, 292, 296, 297

adherents of, 297
disruption of selfobject transference in, 42–43
ego building in, 42
interpretation in, 42
parental functions in, 42
use of transference in, 99–100
Self-restraint, 33
Self-restrictions, 73
  consequences of, safeguarding patient from, 132
Self-sabotaging, 230
Self-soothing, 50
  inability in, 189
Self-sufficiency, 193
Self-understanding, verbally encoded messages for, inability in usage, 137
Selfobject, 41, 110
  finding of, 46
  good, 103
  idealizable, 296
  Kohut's view, 53
Selfobject failure, 127
Selfobject function, Kohut's view, 101
Selfobject transference, *See* Transference, selfobject
Separation guilt, 59, 132, 209, 212
  influence of, 214
Sessions, *See* Analytic sessions
Sexual relationship, in massive developmental arrest, 89
Sexuality, 5, 8
  concerns about, 157
Shapiro, L., 163, 164n
Short-term therapies, multiple attempts at, 157–158
Shouting contests, 259
Sibling
  malice against, 39
  murdering of, dreams of, 43
Skills, essential, deficiencies in, 137, *see also* Apraxias
Sleeping, during analytic session, 267–268
Social relations, satisfactory network of, 55
Somnolence, 56
Soothing, *See also* Self-soothing
  need for, 56
Special problems, 166, 262
Speech, paraverbal aspects of, 135
Splitting, 263, 264
Stalemate
  cases reaching, 3–4

Unresolved issues, reliving of, 8
Untoward event, significance of, failure in
    dealing with, 208

V

Value system, 183
Verbal statements, transformation of en-
    actments into, 108
Verbally encoded messages, 137
Victimization, 231
  analysand's responsibility for, confirma-
    tion of, 229, 271–272, 277
Virtue, patient's conception of, 8
Vocabulary, 190

W

Wild analysis, 3
Winnicott, D., 87, 215, 281, 301, 306
Wishes, repressed, 298
Wolf, E., 285, 306
Wolf Man, 165
Wordless actions, communication through,
    85
World, infantile view of, 204

Z

Zetzel, E., 281, 306